Artificial Intelligence and Cognitive Science

Conceptual Issues

Series Editors

Andy Clark and Josefa Toribio
Washington University

A GARLAND SERIES

Series Contents

Language and Meaning in Cognitive Science

Cognitive Issues and Semantic Theory

Edited with an introduction by

Josefa Toribio and Andy Clark
Washington University

GARLAND PUBLISHING, INC.
A MEMBER OF THE TAYLOR & FRANCIS GROUP
New York & London
1998

Library of Congress Cataloging-in-Publication Data

Language and meaning in cognitive science : cognitive issues and
semantic theory / edited with introductions by Andy Clark and
Josefa Toribio.
      p.   cm. — (Artificial intelligence and cognitive science ; 4)
     Includes bibliographical references.
     ISBN 0-8153-2771-4 (alk. paper)
     1. Cognition. 2. Language and languages. 3. Semantics.
    4. Cognitive science. I. Clark, Andy, 1957– . II. Toribio, Josefa.
III. Series.
BF311.L252 1998
153—dc21   98-27058
                                    CIP

Printed on acid-free, 250-year-life paper
Manufactured in the United States of America

Contents

Naturalized Semantics

Introduction

Where Minds Meet Words

There is a broad complex of philosophical and scientific questions that demand a better understanding of the relationship, or relationships, between language and cognition. The list of questions is long: We want to know how language is related to knowledge such that it bestows a distinctive cognitive advantage upon the human species; we want to know whether correct performance in the use of a language is sufficient to warrant the ascription of intentional properties; we want to analyze and compare the formal properties of natural and artificial languages; we want to know whether the use of a particular language imposes cognitive constraints on the way individuals categorize the world; and we want to know how language relates to nonlinguistic experience and whether a standard scientific methodology is appropriate for the analysis of semantic properties ... the list goes on. This volume contains recent treatments of all these issues. Yet, despite this surface variety, there are a few different, but related, questions around which the bulk of the essays can be organized. We shall call them, respectively, the question about nature, the question about understanding, the question about content, and the question about reduction.

What is exactly the nature of language? How is it acquired? And what are the cognitive and computational underpinnings of syntactic and semantic properties? The perspectives offered by Chomsky, Clark, and Pinker in section one offer an interesting spectrum of answers. Chomsky, at the Cartesian end of the spectrum, has an inward-looking, rule-oriented view of linguistics: " . . . language is a computational system, a rule system of some sort . . . knowledge of language is knowledge of this rule system . . . . Language is acquired by a process of selection of a rule system of an appropriate sort on the basis of direct evidence . . . the use of language is rule-governed behavior" (Chomsky, this volume, original ms. p. 641). The human brain, on this view, contains a specific language faculty, genetically determined, and the inputs from the external world just help this faculty grow in such a way that the innate knowledge of the rule system can be applied in a particular natural language. Chomsky's theory thus belongs to the most radical version of what Pinker calls rule-and-representation theories, namely theories in which the brain is characterized as a set of modular computational systems governed by rules and operating on symbolic data structures. Language is one of those modules.

At the other (associationist) end of the spectrum we find the connectionists.

The associationism that runs in this family leads, at its most extreme, to a view of the brain as a "homogeneous network of interconnected units modified by a learning mechanism that records correlations among frequently co-occurring input patterns" (Pinker, this volume, original ms. p. 530). Since English past tense inflection is an isolable subsystem in which syntax, lexical semantics, and phonology don't seem to play any role, it has been considered an ideal test case for the plausibility of both associationism and connectionism (see Pinker, this volume, but see also Elman et al. 1996, chapter three). Pinker argues that an account of the different phenomena involved in the acquisition and use of this peculiar linguistic subsystem leads us to postulate two different neural subsystems, one governed by associationist principles, the other by rules-and-representations. Pinker's position is thus ecumenical, in the sense that both associationism and rule-and-representation theories are considered correct (in part), but correct about different components of the language system.

Clark comes into the debate closer to the associationist end. The image of the brain that he has in mind is still strongly connectionist. However, Clark is not interested here purely in the properties of the computational mechanisms themselves. He is looking instead at the complex relationships between (public) language and the computational problems facing the biological brain. Without rejecting the obvious role of language as an instrument of communication, his thesis is that another (often neglected, but) major function of language is to transform ". . . the kinds of computational space that our biological brains must negotiate in order to solve certain types of problems" (Clark, this volume, original ms., p. 1). A further, but related, conjecture is that among the properties that public language thus helps to support is some kind of monitoring of our own cognitive capacities.

Turn now to *the question about understanding*: In what does knowledge of the semantics of a language consist? and when is the use of language a sign of intelligence? These are the kinds of issues that the essays in section two explore. What we find there is a range of positions regarding language processing and the relation between a certain level of linguistic performance and 'general intelligence.' The (in)famous Turing test is the center of two of the papers in this section (Dennett's and to some extent Haugeland's). It is also lurking in the background of the other one (Rapaport's).

Why look at computers when talking about knowledge of the semantics of a language? Because computers are intentional artifacts, and because there seems to be general (though not universal) agreement about the foundational role that the idea of computation plays in cognitive science. That foundational role can be formulated, according to David Chalmers, in two basic theses — *computational sufficiency*, namely, the thesis that "the right kind of computational structure [however understood] suffices for the possession of a mind, and for the possession of a wide variety of mental properties" and *computational explanation*, stating that "computation provides a general framework for the explanation of cognitive processes and of behavior" (Chalmers 1994, p. 2).

Dennett's, Haugeland's, and Rapaport's papers all address, in one way or another, the thesis of computational sufficiency. Dennett and Rapaport toe an optimistic line: "The Turing test in unadulterated, unrestricted form, as Turing presented it, is plenty strong if well used" (Dennett, original ms., p. 139). In fact, the Turing test is not that different from the way we evaluate the intelligence of human beings on a day to day basis. Rapaport's paper presents a (traditional) scenario (with basic linguistic representations treated as abstract symbols constrained by a set of rules that operate on those symbols) but a very unusual thesis; the thesis that semantic understanding is, in the end, purely syntactic. Thus, even though Rapaport doesn't invoke the Turing test explicitly, his main thesis seems very sympathetic toward Turing's own views about the relationships between thinking and language understanding: "*semantic understanding is syntactic understanding*. Thus any cognitive agent — including a computer — capable of syntax (symbol manipulation) is capable of understanding language" (Rapaport, original ms., p. 49). Rapaport's argument for this seemingly radical position is based on the breach of an otherwise infinite regress. Since any semantic domain needs to be *understood*, and since we cannot go backward forever in the search for a previously understood (semantic) domain, we should admit that the ultimate antecedent understanding involves just the syntactic manipulation of symbols.

The same threat of infinite regress helps drive Haugeland's position, but this time, the fact that we always seem to rely on a *prior* understanding of many factors (e.g. the situation in which a sentence is used, the identity of the speaker, the norms and pieces of knowledge that constitute common sense, etc.) is used to argue against the idea that standard artificial intelligence techniques could yield a computer with the kind of cognitive properties that human beings possess. Or rather, the thesis is slightly weaker — that there are identifiable constraints on achieving (human-like) intelligence and natural language understanding, but those constraints are so deeply *holistic* that standard computers cannot meet them. Haugeland seems here to be invoking some notion of human personality and self-image as a precondition for a full natural-language understanding.

The third question we want to explore takes us away from artificial intelligence and closer to the psychological realm: It is *the question about content*. How do we individuate the content of our mental states and how does the individuation process affect the status of psychological explanations? In answering this question, we find ourselves pulled by two different (and opposing) sets of considerations about the nature and role of psychological and computational explanations. On the one hand, from the point of view of what constitutes a good psychological explanation, the individuation of the content of a thought (or any other intentional state) looks to be constitutively dependent on properties external to the subject. On the other hand, at the heart of much cognitive science lies the assumption that computational explanations are good psychological explanations, and that computational accounts cannot be sensitive to externalist properties. The properties that seem to be responsible for the system's behavior are thus ultimately physical properties, not intentional ones. When taken together, these two theses leave us facing the following dilemma: Either we reject the externalist characterization of intentional properties or — if we want to retain the standard assumption that computational explanations are good psychological explanations — we have to give up the internalist view of computation.

Christopher Peacocke's aim (see also Peacocke 1994) is to resolve this apparent inconsistency. Peacocke's strategy is to take for granted the truth of the first thesis and to embrace the second horn of the dilemma by appealing to a different conception of computational explanation. The soundness of Peacocke's argument — as a solution to the original inconsistency — depends on how much truth there is in the idea that computations can be *described* and/or individuated by reference to *external properties* of objects or events, i.e., how plausible is the notion of *externalist content-involving computational description*.

We have to be a bit careful here. The success of an externalist account of computational properties shouldn't be taken to imply the claim that we can get semantic properties directly from syntactic ones — à la Rapaport. It should be clear that whatever the internal states of a system are, those states by themselves cannot fix the content of a representation. The interpretation that e.g. Peacocke seems to be arguing for, and the one Toribio and Egan support, is not so much a thesis about the *nature* of computation, but rather a thesis about the preconditions of a certain kind of computational *explanation*, namely psychological explanation. In the case of Peacocke and Toribio, the idea involves a notion of computation which is itself sensitive to external properties in the sense that, without invoking them in our analysis, we couldn't even specify the relevant internal causal organization of the system. Egan opts for a more traditional approach, asserting that "[c]omputational theories are individualistic . . . [but] [t]he contents ascribed to mental states in explanatory models of computational theories . . . are typically wide; hence, such theories are *both* individualistic and externalist" (Egan, original ms., p. 457).

In general, section three displays a variety of recent semantic theories whose main feature is that they involve a notion of content — what Toribio calls ecological content — that is partly constituted by the abilities of the systems to interact in specific ways with the world in which they are embedded. The core explanatory notion is thus the patterns of interaction between the subject and her environment, especially those interactions that involve the exercise of discriminative abilities on the part of the subject. Given the externalist character of the positions presented here, this section also provides some interesting material regarding the internalism/externalism debate in philosophy of language.

Finally, the fourth leading question of the collection is *the question about reduction*. We are not talking here about semantics in its purest form. The target is not so much to explain e.g. the reference of individual expressions or the truth-conditions of sentences. The target is to explain why the expressions of a language have precisely the meaning they have and no other, and how the fact they have that meaning affects the behavior of the cognizer or language user. Alongside this psychological interest runs an essentially *scientific* aspiration, namely, to reconcile semantic facts and a *naturalistic* world-view. The essays in section four focus precisely on the question of how to naturalize semantics.

Ned Block's paper is probably the one in which the connection between semantic properties and psychological explanation is most explicit. Conceptual role semantics is advertised as the magic recipe that will fulfill the naturalistic dreams of the most demanding semantic gourmet. The reason seems to be that this recipe contains as its choice ingredient an appropriate notion of content for psychology. With that notion in hand, the eight conditions that, according to Block, must be met by an acceptable semantics for psychology can all be satisfied (see Block, this volume). A critic might, of course, question the particular *desiderata* proposed, arguing that a proper semantics for psychology needn't meet *those* conditions, that there are too many or too few, or that a proper semantics for psychology needs to meet different ones. At a minimum, we must check the advertisement with a consumer's eye, to see whether or not conceptual role semantics can really deliver the goods in relation to those eight conditions (see e.g. Toribio 1997).

One stand taken by most contemporary philosophers of mind and language is that semantic properties are not part of the primitive ontological furniture of the world. If such properties are to name real features of the world, they must be revealed as grounded in some other — more primitive and scientifically acceptable — set of properties (cf. Fodor 1986, p. 97). Intentional properties will then count as real in virtue of their identity with, or supervenience on, some set of lower-level physical properties. Like many others engaged in naturalization projects for semantics, the authors represented here assume that the program of naturalization demands a higher-to-lower, top-to-bottom, kind of explanatory strategy.

Such a naturalistic framework is supposed to account for the two most puzzling features of meaning: That meaning is *normative*, namely, that to know the meaning of an expression is to know how to use it correctly (even if that knowledge is not explicit), and that meaningful states, such as beliefs, can be false. Thus suppose we ask how a mental state can be said to misrepresent without presupposing any semantic notions? When we say of an artifact such as e.g. a thermostat that it misrepresents the temperature of the room, we don't ascribe to it any original representational powers. What we are saying is just that there is a malfunction in the artifact. As Dretske notes, artifacts don't have original intentionality. If we are searching for original intentionality, one obvious place to look is toward evolved structures whose adaptive role is that of gathering the information necessary for the creature's survival. It is also essential, Dretske suggests, that those structures allow the organism to be capable of associative learning. We thus first define a relation that beliefs bear to properties that are sometimes instantiated in the system's environment as the relation 'has as its content that.' The instantiation of a given property then explains *why* the production of a belief token in certain conditions causes the system to behave in a certain way (Dretske), or helps the system perform its proper function (Millikan). Such properties affect the system and are either developmentally (Dretske) or evolutionarily (Millikan) relevant with respect to its proliferation. Assuming that certain inner or outer tokens corresponding to a belief are produced if and only if a certain property is instantiated, such belief tokens are false if they are produced when that property is not instantiated. Add an evolutionary spin to this causal approach and teleological accounts emerge. A given belief of type B has a particular content if and only if some mechanism has been selected *because* (causally historically because) it has produced tokens of a certain type in the past whenever B was instantiated.

Whether functionalist, informational, or teleological accounts can finally satisfy their naturalistic goals without invoking considerations of a prior normative character is still not clear. One worry (Toribio, forthcoming) is that the inherent reductionism of such proposals cannot, ultimately, sustain contact with the normative features they are trying to explain. Naturalism, almost by definition, aims to locate the normative dimensions of intentionality in a very unnatural home.

In sum, the deepest philosophical and conceptual issues surrounding natural language remain somewhat murky, and the questions about nature, content, understanding, and reduction are far from resolved. For all that, one thing seems crystal clear: The success or failure of a mature cognitive science is bound inexorably to the problem of understanding how words can have meanings, and how language and more basic cognitive capacities interact in human thought.

Josefa Toribio and Andy Clark

References

Chalmers, D. (1994) "A Computational Foundation for the Study of Cognition." *PNP Technical Report 001*. Washington University in St. Louis.

Elman, J., Bates, E., Johnson, M., Karmiloff-Smith, A., Parisi, D., and Plunkett, K. (1996) *Re-Thinking Innateness: A Connectionist Perspective on Development*. Cambridge: MIT Press.

Fodor, J. (1986) *Psychosemantics*. Cambridge: MIT Press.

Fodor, J. and Lepore, E. (1992) *Holism. A Shopper's Guide*. Oxford: Basil Blackwell.

Peacocke, C. (1994) "Content, Computation and Externalism." *Mind and Language* 9: 303–35.

Toribio, J. (1997) "Twin Pleas: Probing Content and Compositionality." *Philosophy and Phenomenological Research* 57: 871–89.

Toribio, J. (forthcoming) "Meaning and Other Non-Biological Categories." *Philosophical Papers* 27, 1998.

On the Nature, Use and Acquisition of Language

NOAM CHOMSKY

For about thirty years, the study of language – or more accurately, one substantial component of it – has been conducted within a framework that understands linguistics to be a part of psychology, ultimately human biology. This approach attempts to reintroduce into the study of language several concerns that have been central to Western thought for thousands of years, and that have deep roots in other traditions as well: questions about the nature and origin of knowledge in particular. This approach has also been concerned to assimilate the study of language to the main body of the natural sciences. This meant, in the first place, abandoning dogmas that are entirely foreign to the natural sciences and that have no place in rational inquiry, the dogmas of the several varieties of behaviorism, for example, which seek to impose a priori limits on possible theory construction, a conception that would properly be dismissed as entirely irrational in the natural sciences. It means a frank adherence to mentalism, where we understand talk about the mind to be talk about the brain at an abstract level at which, so we try to demonstrate, principles can be formulated that enter into successful and insightful explanation of linguistic (and other) phenomena that are provided by observation and experiment. Mentalism, in this sense, has no taint of mysticism and carries no dubious ontological burden. Rather, mentalism falls strictly within the standard practice of the natural sciences and, in fact, is nothing other than the approach of the natural sciences applied to this particular domain. This conclusion, which is the opposite of what is often assumed, becomes understandable and clear if we consider specific topics in the natural sciences; for example, nineteenth-century chemistry, which sought to explain phenomena in terms of such abstract notions as elements, the periodic table, valence, benzene rings, and so on – that

"On the Nature, Use and Acquisition of Language" by N. Chomsky is the text of a lecture delivered in Kyoto in January, 1987. It appears in N. Chomsky, *Generative Grammar: Its Basis, Development and Prospects* (Kyoto University of Foreign Studies, 1987), and N. Chomsky, *Language in a Psychological Setting, Sophia Linguistica XII* (Sophia University, Tokyo, 1987). Reprinted by kind permission of the author.

is, in terms of abstract properties of then-unknown, perhaps still unknown, physical mechanisms. This abstract inquiry served as an essential preliminary and guide for the subsequent inquiry into physical mechanisms. Mentalistic inquiry in the brain sciences is quite similar in approach and character to the abstract inquiry into properties of the chemical elements, and we may expect that this abstract inquiry too will serve as an essential preliminary and guide for the emerging brain sciences today; the logic is quite similar.

This work proceeds from the empirical assumption – which is well-supported – that there is a specific faculty of the mind/brain that is responsible for the use and acquisition of language, a faculty with distinctive characteristics that is apparently unique to the species in essentials and a common endowment of its members, hence a true species property.

These ideas have developed in the context of what some have called "the cognitive revolution" in psychology, and in fact constituted one major factor contributing to these developments. It is important, I think, to understand clearly just what this "revolution" sought to accomplish, why it was undertaken, and how it relates to earlier thinking about these topics. The so-called "cognitive revolution" is concerned with the states of the mind/brain that enter into thought, planning, perception, learning and action. The mind/brain is considered to be an information-processing system, which forms abstract representations and carries out computations that use and modify them. This approach stands in sharp contrast to the study of the shaping and control of behavior that systematically avoided consideration of the states of the mind/brain that enter into behavior, and sought to establish direct relations between stimulus situations, contingencies of reinforcement, and behavior. This behaviorist approach has proven almost entirely barren, in my view, a fact that is not at all surprising since it refuses in principle to consider the major and essential component of all behavior, namely, the states of the mind/brain.

Consider the problem of learning. We have an organism with a mind/brain that is in a certain state or configuration. The organism is presented with certain sensory inputs, leading to a change in the state of the mind/brain. This process is the process of learning, or perhaps more accurately, mental and cognitive growth. Having attained a new state as a result of this process, the organism now carries out certain actions, in part influenced by the state of the mind/brain that has been attained. There is no direct relation between the sensory inputs that led to the change of state of the mind/brain and the actions carried out by the organism, except under highly artificial, uninformative and very marginal conditions.

There is of course a relation of some kind between sensory inputs and behavior; a child who has not been presented with data of Japanese will not be able to carry out the behavior of speaking Japanese. Presented with appropriate data from Japanese, the child's mind/brain undergoes a significant change; the mind/brain comes to incorporate within itself knowledge of Japanese, which then enables the child to speak and understand Japanese. But there is no direct relation between the data presented to the child and what the child says, and it is hopeless to try to predict what the child will say, even in probabilistic terms, on the basis of the sensory data that led to acquisition of knowledge of Japanese. We can study the process by which the sensory data lead to the change of state of the mind/brain, and we may study at least certain aspects of how this attained knowledge is used. But an effort to study the relation between the sensory data and the actual behavior, avoiding the crucial matter of the nature of the mind/brain and the changes it undergoes, is doomed to triviality and failure, as the history of psychology demonstrates very well. The cognitive revolution was based in part on the recognition of such facts as these, drawing conclusions that really should not be controversial, though they are – a sign of the immaturity of the field, in my view. This change of perspective in the study of psychology, linguistics included, was surely a proper one in essence, and in fact was long overdue.

Not only was this change of perspective overdue, but it also was much less of a revolution than many believed. In fact, without awareness, the new perspective revived ideas that had been developed quite extensively centuries earlier. In particular, seventeenth-century science developed a form of cognitive psychology that was quite rich, and basically, I think, on the right track. Descartes's major scientific contribution, perhaps, was his rejection of the neoscholastic idea that perception is a process in which the form of an object imprints itself somehow on the brain, so that if you see a cube, for example, your brain has the form of a cube imprinted in it in some fashion. In place of this fallacious conception, Descartes proposed a representational theory of mind. He considered the example of a blind man with a stick, who uses the stick to touch in sequence various parts of a physical object before him, let us say a cube. This sequence of tactile inputs leads the blind man construct, in his mind, the image of a cube, but the form of the cube is not imprinted in the mind. Rather, the sequence of tactile inputs leads the mind to construct a mental representation of a cube, using its own resources and its own structural principles. Descartes argued that much the same is true of normal vision. A series of stimuli strike the retina, and the mind then forms ideas that provide a conception of the objects of the external world. The mind then carries out various computational processes, as the person thinks about these objects, including processes that enable the person to carry out certain actions involving them: for example, picking up the cube, rotating it, and so on. This is surely the right general approach. It has been revived in recent psychology and physiology, and by now something is known about how the process takes place, including even some understanding of the physical mechanisms involved in the coding and representation of stimuli.

Descartes also observed that if a certain figure, say a triangle, is presented to a person, then what the person will perceive is a triangle, though the presented image is certainly not a Euclidean triangle, but rather some far more complex figure. This will be true, he argued, even if the person is a child who has had no previous acquaintance with geometrical figures. In a certain sense the point is obvious, since true geometrical figures do not exist in the natural environment in which we grow and live, but we nevertheless perceive figures as distorted geometrical figures, not as exact instances of whatever they may happen to be. Why does the child perceive the object as a distorted triangle, rather than as the very complex figure that it actually is: with one of the lines slightly curved, with two sides not quite touching, and so on? Descartes' answer was that the Euclidean triangle is produced by the mind on the occasion of this stimulation, because the mechanisms of the mind are based on principles of Euclidean geometry and produce these geometrical figures as exemplars or models for the organization of perception, and for learning, drawing them from its own resources and structural principles.

In contrast, empiricists such as David Hume argued that we simply have no idea of a triangle, or a straight line, since we could not distinguish "perfect images" of such objects from the "defective ones" of the real world. Hume correctly drew the consequences of the empiricist principles that he adopted and developed: in particular, the principle that the mind receives impressions from the outside world and forms associations based upon them, and that this is all there is to the story (apart from the animal instinct underlying induction). But the consequences that Hume correctly drew from these assumptions are certainly false. Contrary to what he asserted, we do, indeed, have a clear concept of a triangle and a straight line, and we perceive objects of the world in terms of these concepts, just as Descartes argued. The conclusion, then, is that the empiricist assumptions are fundamentally wrong, as a matter of empirical fact; the properties of the mind/brain that are involved in determining how we perceive and what we perceive are crucially different from what was postulated in empirical speculation. It seems reasonable to resort to a representational theory of mind of the Cartesian sort, including the concept of the mind as an information-processing system that computes, forms and modifies representations; and we should also adopt something like the Cartesian concept of innate ideas as tendencies and dispositions, biologically determined properties of the mind/brain that provide a framework for the construction of mental representations, a framework that then enters into our perception and action. Ideas of this sort have been revived in the context of the cognitive revolution of the past generation.

Seventeenth-century psychologists, who we call "philosophers," went far beyond these observations. They developed a form of what much later came to be called "Gestalt psychology" as similar ideas were rediscovered during this century. These seventeenth-century thinkers speculated rather plausibly on how we perceive objects around us in terms of structural properties, in terms of our concepts of object and relation, cause and effect, whole and part, symmetry, proportion, the functions served by objects and the characteristic uses to which they are put. We perceive the world around us in this manner, they argued, as a consequence of the organizing activity of the mind, based on its innate structure and the experience that has caused it to assume new and richer forms. "The book of nature is legible only to an intellectual eye," as Ralph Cudworth argued, developing such ideas as these. Again, these speculations seem to be very much on the right track, and the ideas have been rediscovered and developed in contemporary psychology, in part within the context of the cognitive revolution.

The contemporary cognitive revolution has been considerably influenced by modern . science, mathematics and technology. The mathematical theory of computation, which developed in the 1920s and 1930s particularly, provided conceptual tools that make it possible to address certain classical problems of representational psychology in a serious way, problems of language in particular. Wilhelm von Humboldt understood, a century and a half ago, that language is a system that makes infinite use of finite means, in his phrase. But he was unable to give a clear account of this correct idea, or to use it as the basis for substantive research into language. The conceptual tools developed in more recent years make it possible for us to study the infinite use of finite means with considerable clarity and understanding. Modern generative grammar, in fact, can be regarded in part as the result of the confluence of the conceptual tools of modern logic and mathematics and the traditional Humboldtian conception, inevitably left vague and unformed. A generative grammar of a language is a formal system that states explicitly what are these finite means available to the mind/brain, which can then make infinite, unbounded use of these means. Unfortunately, the classical ideas concerning language and representational psychology had long been forgotten when the cognitive revolution took place in the 1950s, and the connections I am now discussing were discovered only much later, and are still not widely known.

The development of electronic computers has also influenced the cognitive revolution considerably, primarily in providing useful concepts such as internal representation, modular structure, the software–hardware distinction and the like, and also, in areas such as vision at least, in making it possible to develop explicit models of cognitive processes that can be tested for accuracy and refined. It is worthy of note that much the same was true of the seventeenth-century cognitive revolution. The Cartesians were much impressed with the mechanical automata then being constructed by skilled craftsmen, which seemed to mimic certain aspects of the behavior of organisms. These automata were a stimulus to their scientific imagination much in the way that modern electronic computers have contributed to the contemporary cognitive revolution.

Some of these seventeenth-century ideas, which are now being rediscovered and developed in quite new ways, have much earlier origins. What is probably the world's first psychological experiment is described in the Platonic dialogues, when Socrates undertakes to demonstrate that a slave boy, who has had no instruction in geometry, nevertheless knows the truths of geometry. Socrates demonstrates this by asking the slave boy a series of questions, providing him with no information but drawing from the inner resources of the slave boy's mind, and in this way Socrates leads the slave boy to the point where he recognizes the truth of theorems of geometry. This experiment was understood, quite plausibly, to show that the slave boy knew geometry without any experience. Indeed, it is difficult to see what other interpretation can be given. The experiment was, presumably, a kind of "thought experiment," but if it were carried out rigorously, as has never been done, the results would probably be more or less as Plato presented them in this literary version of a psychological experiment.

The human mind, in short, somehow incorporates the princples of geometry, and experience only serves to bring them to the point where this innate knowledge can be used. This demonstration also poses a very crucial problem: the problem is to explain how the slave boy can have the knowledge he does have, when he has had no relevant experience from which he could derive this knowledge. Let us refer to this problem as "Plato's problem," returning to it directly.

The rise of generative grammar in the 1950s, a major factor in the cognitive revolution, also resurrected traditional ideas. The Cartesians, in particular, had applied their ideas on the nature of the mind to the study of language, which was comonly viewed as a kind of "mirror of mind." Subsequent study enriched these investigations in quite impressive ways, which we are now only beginning to understand. The cognitive revolution of the 1950s, then, should be understood, I believe, as having recovered independently the insights of earlier years, abandoning the barren dogmas that had impeded understanding of these questions for a very long period; and then applying these classical ideas, now reconstructed in a new framework, in new ways, and developing them along lines that would not have been possible in an earlier period, thanks to new understanding in the sciences, technology and mathematics.

From the point of view adopted in this "second cognitive revolution," the central problems of the study of language are essentially the following four:

The first question, a preliminary to any further inquiry, is this: What is the system of knowledge incorporated in the mind/brain of a person who speaks and understands a particular language? What constitutes the language that the person has mastered and knows? A theory concerned with this topic for a particular language is called "a grammar of that language," or in technical terms, "a generative grammar of the language," where the term "generative grammar" means nothing more than a theory of the language that is fully explicit, so that empirical consequences can be derived in it. Traditional grammars, in contrast, relied crucially on the knowledge of language of the reader of the grammar to fill in the enormous gaps that were left unstudied, and were not even recognized to be gaps; it is surprising, in retrospect, to see how difficult it was to recognize that even the simplest of phenomena pose rather serious problems of explanation. A traditional grammar, then, is not a theory of the language, but is rather a guide that can be followed by a person who already knows the language. Similarly, a pedagogic grammar of Spanish written in English is not a theory of Spanish but rather a guide to Spanish that can be used by a speaker of English who already knows the basic principles of language, though unconsciously, and can therefore make use of the hints and examples in the grammar to draw conclusions about Spanish. A generative grammar, in contrast, seeks to make explicit just what this knowledge is that enables the intelligent reader to make use of a grammar.

To the extent that we can provide at least a partial answer to the first problem, we can turn to a second problem: How is this knowledge of language used in thought or expression of thought, in understanding, in organizing behavior, or in such special uses of language as communication, and so on? Here we have to make a crucial conceptual distinction between (1) the language, a certain cognitive system, a system of knowledge incorporated in the mind/brain and described by the linguist's generative grammar; and (2) various processing systems of the mind/brain that access this knowledge in one or another way, and put it to use.

Still assuming some kind of answer to the problem of characterizing the knowledge attained, we can turn to a third problem: what are the physical mechanisms that exhibit the properties that we discover in the abstract investigation of language and its use; that is, the physical mechanisms of the brain that are involved in the representation of knowledge and in accessing and processing this knowledge? These are pretty much tasks for the future, and they are very difficult ones, primarily, because for very good ethical reasons, we do not permit direct experimentation that might enable scientists to investigate these mechanisms directly. In the case of other systems of the mind/brain, such as the visual system, the investigation of mechanisms has proceeded quite far. The reason is that we allow ourselves, rightly or wrong, to carry out direct experimentation with cats, monkeys, and so on. Their visual systems are in many ways like our own, so a good deal can be learned about the physical mechanisms of the human visual system in this way. But it appears that the language faculty is a unique human possession in its essentials, and if we were to discover some other organism that shared this faculty in part, we would probably regard it as quasi-human and refrain from direct experimentation. Consequently, the study of physical mechanisms of the language faculty must be studied in much more indirect ways, either by non-intrusive experiments, or by "nature's experiments," such as injury and pathology. Part of the intellectual fascination of the study of language is that it must proceed in such indirect ways, relying very heavily on the abstract level of inquiry – a difficult and challenging task, but one that can be addressed and has much promise.

The fourth problem is to explain how the knowledge of language and ability to use it are acquired. This problem of acquisition arises both for the language – the cognitive system itself – and for the various processing systems that access the language. I will focus attention here on the first of these questions: on acquisition of language. Plainly, the question can be formulated only to the extent that we have some understanding of what is acquired – of what is a language – though as always, inquiry into the acquisition or use or physical basis of some abstract system can and should provide insight into its nature.

The fourth question is a special case of Plato's problem: How do we come to have such rich and specific knowledge, or such intricate systems of belief and understanding, when the evidence available to us is so meager? That was the problem that rightly troubled Plato, and it should trouble us as well. It is a question that for a long period did not trouble psychologists, linguists, philosophers, and others who thought about the matter, except for a few, who were rather marginal to the main intellectual tradition. This is a sign of the serious intellectual failings of the thought of this era, an interesting topic that I will not pursue here. If a rational Martian scientist were to observe what takes place in a single language community on earth, he would conclude that knowledge of the language that is used is almost entirely inborn. The fact that this is not true, or at least not entirely true, is extremely puzzling, and raises many quite serious problems for psychology and biology, including evolutionary biology.

Recall that Plato had an answer to the problem he posed: we remember the knowledge we have from an earlier existence. This is not a proposal that we would nowadays be inclined to accept in exactly these terms, though we should, in all honesty, be prepared to recognize that it is a far more satisfactory and rational answer than the ones that have been offered in the dominant intellectual traditions of recent centuries, including the Anglo-American empiricist tradition, which simply evaded the problems. To render Plato's answer intelligible, we have to provide a mechanism by which our knowledge is remembered from an earlier existence. If we are disinclined to accept the immortal soul as the mechanism, we will follow Leibniz in assuming that Plato's answer is on the right track, but must be, in his words, "purged of the error of preexistence." In modern terms, that means reconstructing Platonic "remembrance" in terms of the genetic endowment, which specifies the initial state of the language faculty, much as it determines that we will grow arms not wings, undergo sexual maturation at a certain stage of growth if external conditions such as nutritional level permit this internally directed maturational process to take place, and so on. Nothing is known in detail about the mechanisms in any of these cases, but it is now widely and plausibly assumed that this is the place to look. At least, it is widely assumed for physical growth. The fact that similar evidence does not lead to similar rational conclusions in the case of the mind/brain again reflects the serious intellectual inadequacies of recent thought, which has simply refused to approach problems of the mind/brain by the methods of rational inquiry taken for granted in the physical sciences. This is strikingly true, particularly, of those who falsely believe themselves to be scientific naturalists, and who see themselves as defending science against the obscurantists. Exactly the opposite is true, in my opinion, for the reasons that I have briefly indicated.

Putting aside various dogmas, let us approach questions of mind/brain, including questions of language, in the spirit of the natural sciences. Abstracting away from unknown mechanisms, we assume that the language faculty has an initial state, genetically determined, common to the species apart from gross pathology, and apparently unique to the human species. We know that this initial state can mature to a number of different steady states – the various attainable languages – as conditions of exposure vary. The process of maturation from the initial state to the steady state of mature knowledge is, to some extent, data-driven; exposed to data of English, the mind/brain will incorporate knowledge of English, not Japanese. Furthermore, this process of growth of the language faculty begins remarkably early in life. Recent work indicates that four-day-old infants can already distinguish somehow between the language spoken in their community and other languages, so that the mechanisms of the language faculty begin to operate and to be "tuned" to the external environment very early in life.

It is fairly clear that the process of maturation to the steady state is deterministic. Language learning is not really something that the child does; it is something that happens to. the child placed in an appropriate environment, much as the child's body grows and matures in a predetermined way when provided with appropriate nutrition and environmental stimulation. This is not to say that the nature of the environment is irrelevant. The environment determines how the options left unspecified by the initial state of the language faculty are fixed, yielding different languages. In a somewhat similar way, the early visual environment determines the density of receptors for horizontal and vertical lines. Furthermore, the difference between a rich and stimulating environment and an impoverished environment may be substantial, in language acquisition as in physical growth – or more accurately, as in other aspects of physical growth, the acquisition of language being simply one of these aspects. Capacities that are part of our common human endowment can flourish, or can be restricted and suppressed, depending on the conditions provided for their growth.

The point is probably more general. It is a traditional insight, which merits more attention than it receives, that teaching should not be compared to filling a bottle with water, but rather to helping a flower to grow in its own way. As any good teacher knows, the methods of instruction and the range of material covered are matters of small importance as compared with the success achieved in arousing the natural curiosity of the students and stimulating their interest in exploring on their own. What the student learns passively will be quickly forgotten. What students discover for themselves, when their natural curiosity and creative impulses are aroused, will not only be remembered, but will be the basis for further exploration and inquiry, and perhaps significant intellectual contributions. The same is true in other domains as well. A truly democratic community is one in which the general public has the opportunity for meaningful and constructive participation in the formation of social policy: in their own immediate community, in the workplace, and in the society at large. A society that excludes large areas of crucial decision-making from public control, or a system of governance that merely grants the general public the opportunity to ratify decisions taken by the elite groups that dominate the private society and the state, hardly merits the term "democracy." These too are insights that were alive and vital during the eighteenth century, and have in recent years been largely forgotten or suppressed. The point was made, in another context, by Kant, defending the French Revolution during the period of the Terror against those who argued that the masses of the population "are not ripe for freedom." "If one accepts this proposition," he wrote, "freedom will never be achieved, for one can not arrive at the maturity for freedom without have already acquired it; one must be free to learn how to make use of one's powers freely and usefully . . . one can achieve reason only through one's own experience and one must be free to be able to undertake them . . . To accept the principle that freedom is worthless for those under one's control and that one has the right to refuse it to them for ever, is an infringement of the rights of God himself, who has created man to be free." Reason, the ability to make use of one's powers freely and usefully, and other human qualities can be achieved only in an environment in which they can flourish. They cannot be taught by coercive means. What is true of physical growth holds quite generally of human maturation and learning.

Returning to the language faculty, learning of language, as noted, is something that happens to the child, without awareness for the most part, just as other processes such as sexual maturation happen to the child. A child does not decide to undergo sexual maturation because it sees others doing so and thinks this would be a good idea, or because it is trained or reinforced. Rather, the process happens in its own inner-directed way. The course of the process, its timing, and its detailed nature are in part influenced by the environment, by nutritional level for example, but the process itself is inner-directed in its essentials. The same appears to be true of language learning, and of other aspects of cognitive growth as well. The term "learning" is, in fact, a very misleading one, and one that is probably best abandoned as a relic of an earlier age, and earlier misunderstandings. Knowledge of language grows in the mind/brain of a child placed in a certain speech community.

Knowledge of language within a speech community is shared to remarkably fine detail, in every aspect of language from pronunciation to interpretation. In each of these aspects, the knowledge attained vastly transcends the evidence available in richness and complexity, and in each of these aspects, the fineness of detail and the precision of knowledge goes well beyond anything that can be explained on any imaginable functional grounds, such as the exigencies of communication. For example, children mimic the sounds of the language around them to a level of precision that is well beyond the capacity of adults to perceive, and in other domains as well, the precision of knowledge and understanding, as well as its scope and richness, are far beyond anything that could be detected in normal human interchange. These properties of normal language can often only be discovered by careful experiment. These are the basic and simplest elements of the problem we face.

We therefore conclude that the initial stage of the language faculty can be regarded as in effect a deterministic input–output system that takes presented data as its input and produces a highly structured cognitive system of a very specific form as its "output" – here the output is internalized, represented in the mind/brain; it is the steady state of knowledge of some particular language. The initial state of the language faculty can be regarded, in essence, as a language-acquisition device; in formal terms, a function that maps presented data into a steady state of knowledge attained. This general conclusion allows many specific variants, to some of which I will briefly return, but it is virtually inconceivable that it is wrong in any fundamental way. There has been much debate over this issue in the literature – more accurately, a one-sided debate in which critics argue that the idea has been refuted, with little response from its defenders. The reason for the lack of response is that the criticism must be based on profound confusion, and inspection of the arguments quickly reveals that this is the case, as it must be, given the nature of the problem.

The theory of the initial state – of the language acquisition device – is sometimes called "universal grammar," adapting a traditional term to a somewhat different conceptual framework. It is commonly assumed that universal grammar, so conceived, determines the class of attainable languages. Let me quote from a recent paper by the two leading researchers in the important new field of mathematical learning theory, a paper on models of language acquisition. They write that universal grammar

> imposes restrictions on a [particular] grammar in such a way that the class of [particular] grammars admissible by the theory includes grammars of all and only natural languages, [where] the natural languages are identified with the languages that can be acquired by normal human infants under casual conditions of access to linguistic data.

The first of these propositions is a definition, and a proper and useful one, so it is not open to challenge: we may define a "natural language" as one that accords with the principles of universal grammar. But the second of these propositions need not be correct. The languages attainable under normal conditions of access are those that fall in the intersection of two sets: (1) the set of natural languages made available by the initial state of the language faculty as characterized by universal grammar, and (2) the set of learnable systems. If universal grammar permits unlearnable languages, as it might, then they simply will not be learned. Learnability, then, is not a requirement that must be met by the language faculty.

Similarly, parsability – that is, the ability of the mind/brain to assign a structural analysis to a sentence – is not a requirement that must be met by a language, contrary to what is often claimed. In fact, we know that the claim is false: every language permits many different categories of expressions that cannot be used or understood readily (or at all), though they are perfectly well-formed, a fact that in no way impedes communication. Furthermore, deviant expressions may be readily parsable, and are often quite properly used. In brief, it is a mistake to think that languages are "designed" for ease of use. In so far as their structure does not conform to functional requirements, their elements are not used.

In the case of learnability, the proposition that the natural languages are learnable may very well be true, but if so, that is not a matter of principle, but rather a surprising empirical discovery about natural language. Recent work in linguistics suggests that it probably is true, again, a surprising and important empirical discovery, to which I will briefly return.

There has been a fair amount of confusion about these matters, in part resulting from misinterpretation of properties of formal systems: for example, the well-known observation that unconstrained transformational grammars can generate all sets that can be specified by finite means, and results on efficient parsability of context-free languages. In both cases, entirely unwarranted conclusions have been drawn about the nature of language. In fact, no conclusions at all can be drawn with regard to language, language learning, or language use, on the basis of such considerations as these, though other directions of formal inquiry perhaps show more promise of potential empirical significance; for example, some recent work in complexity theory.

When the study of language is approached in the manner I have just outlined, one would expect a close and fruitful interaction between linguistics proper and the investigation of such topics as language processing and acquisition. To some extent this has happened, but less so than might have been hoped. It is useful to reflect a little about why this has been the case. One reason, I think, is the one just mentioned: misinterpretation of results about formal systems has caused considerable confusion. Other problems have arisen from a failure to consider carefully the conceptual relations between language and learnability, and between language and processing. One instructive example is the history of what was called "the derivational theory of complexity," the major paradigm of psycholinguistic research in the early days of the "cognitive revolution." This theory led to an experimental program. The experiments carried out were tests of a theory with two components: (1) assumptions about the rule systems of natural language; (2) assumptions about processing. Some of the experimental results confirmed this combination of theories, others disconfirmed it. But care must be taken to determine just which elements of the combination of theories were confirmed or disconfirmed. In practice, where predictions were disconfirmed, it was concluded that the linguistic component of the amalgam was at fault. While this might be true, and sometimes was as other evidence showed, it was a curious inference, since there was independent evidence supporting the assumptions about language but none whatsoever supporting the assumptions about processing, assumptions that were, furthermore, not particularly plausible except as rough first approximations. Failure to appreciate these facts undermined much subsequent discussion. Similar questions arise with language acquisition, and confirming evidence too, in both areas, is unclear in its import unless the various factors entering into the predictions are properly sorted out.

The history of the derivational theory of complexity illustrates other problems that have impeded useful interaction between linguistics and experimental psychology. Early experimental work was designed to test certain ideas about rule systems on the assumption that processing satisfies the conditions of the derivational theory of complexity. By the time the experimental program had been carried out, with mixed results, the theories of rule systems had changed. Many experimental psychologists found this disconcerting. How can we carry out experimental tests of a theory if it is not stable and is subject to change? These

11

reactions led to a noticeable shift in focus to work in areas that are better insulated from theoretical modification elsewhere.

There are a number of problems with such reactions. One problem is a point of logic: to insulate one's work from theoretical modifications elsewhere is to keep to topics of limited significance, close to the surface of phenomena. If one's work is important enough to have consequences beyond its immediate scope, then it cannot be immune to new understanding outside of this scope. For example, it is likely that results on order of acquisition of function words or on turn-taking in conversation will be immune to discoveries and new understanding elsewhere; the reason is that the implications are very slight. Relevance, after all, is a two-way street. This reaction to the inevitable changes in theoretical assumptions in a discipline that is alive also reflects a far too limited conception of the work of the experimental psychologist, who is perceived as someone who tests ideas developed elsewhere but does not contribute otherwise to their proper formulation. But research into language should obviously be a cooperative enterprise, which can be informed and advanced by use of evidence of many different kinds. There is no privileged sector of this discipline that provides theories, which are tested by others. One sign that the discipline is approaching a higher level of maturity will be that research into language processing and language acquisition will yield conclusions about the structure of language that can be tested by linguists, using the tools of their specific approach to a common network of problems and concerns. The idea that linguistics should be related to psychology as theoretical physics is related to experimental physics is senseless and untenable, and has, I think, been harmful.

Theories of language have indeed undergone significant changes during the period we are now considering – which is to say that the discipline is alive. I think we can identify two major changes of perspective during this period, each with considerable ramifications for the study of language use and acquisition. Let me review these changes briefly, focusing on the three central questions that I mentioned earlier: (1) what is knowledge of language?; (2) how is it acquired?; and (3) how is it used?

Some thirty years ago the standard answers to these questions would have been something like this.

1 What is knowledge of language? Answer: it is a system of habits, dispositions and abilities. This answer, incidentally, is still widely held, notably by philosophers influenced by Wittgenstein and Quine.
2 How is language acquired? Answer: by conditioning, training, habit-formation or "general learning mechanisms" such as induction.
3 How is language used? Answer: language use is the exercise of an ability, like any skill; say, bicycle-riding. New forms are produced or understood "by analogy" to old ones. In fact, the problem posed by production of new forms, the normal situation in language use, was barely noticed. This is quite a remarkable fact, first, because the point is obvious, and second, because it was a major preoccupation of the linguistics of the first cognitive revolution of the seventeenth century. Here we have a striking example of how ideology displaced the most obvious of phenomena from inquiry.

Attention to the simplest phenomena suffices to show that these ideas cannot be even close to the truth of the matter, and must simply be abandoned. Let me illustrate with a very simple example. Imagine a child learning English who comes to understand the sentence *John ate an apple*. The child then knows that the word *eat* takes two semantic roles, that of the subject (the agent of the action) and that of object (the recipient of the action); it is a typical transitive verb. Suppose that the child now hears the reduced sentence *John ate*, in which the object is missing. Since the verb is transitive, requiring an object, the child will understand the sentence to mean, roughly, "John ate something or other." So far everything is fairly straightforward if we assume the simple principle that when a semantically required element is missing, the mind interprets it to be a kind of "empty pronoun" meaning: something or other. Perhaps an empiricist linguist might be willing to suppose that this principle is available as an innate element of the language faculty.

Consider now a very simple but slightly more complex sentence. Suppose the child comes to understand such sentences as *John is too clever to catch Bill*. Here the verb *catch* also requires a subject and an object, but the subject is missing in this sentence. It therefore has to be supplied by the mind, in the matter of the object of *ate* in *John ate*. By the principle just assumed to account for *John ate*, the sentence should mean: John is so clever that someone or other will not catch Bill. That is a fine meaning, but it is not the meaning of *John is too clever to catch Bill*. Rather, the sentence means: John is so clever that he, John, will not catch Bill. The mind does not use the empty pronoun principle, but rather takes the subject of *catch* to be the same as the subject of *is clever*. Since this is known without instruction or evidence, we must attribute to the mind still a second principle, let us call it the principle of subject control: the missing subject of the embedded clause is understood to be the same as the subject of the main clause. Our assumptions about the innate resources of the mind must therefore be enriched.

Let us carry the discussion a step further. Suppose we delete *Bill* from the sentence *John is too clever to catch Bill*, so that we have *John is too clever to catch*. By the empty pronoun principle and the subject control principle, the sentence should mean: John is so clever that he, John, will not catch someone or other. But the child knows that it does not mean that at all; rather, it means that John is so clever that someone or other will not catch him, John. The child interprets the sentence by some other principle, call it the inversion principle, which tells us that the object of the embedded sentence is understood to be the same as the subject of the main verb, and the subject of the embedded sentence is an empty pronoun referring to someone or other.

We now have to attribute to the mind/brain three principles: the empty pronoun principle, the subject principle, and the inversion principle. Furthermore, some overarching principle of the mind/brain determines when these principles of interpretation are applied.

Turning to slightly more complicated examples, the mysteries deepen. Consider the sentence *John is too clever to expect anyone to catch*. English speakers at first may find this sentence a bit puzzling, but "on reflection" (whatever that involves), they understand it to mean that John is so clever that someone doesn't expect anyone to catch John; that is, it is interpreted by means of the empty pronoun principle and the inversion principle. But now compare this sentence with another that is roughly comparable in complexity: *John is too clever to meet anyone who caught*. Here all principles fail; the sentence is complete gibberish. We can parse the sentence with no difficulty; it just doesn't mean anything sensible. In particular, it is not understood "by analogy" to mean that John is so clever that no one met anyone who caught him, John.

Notice that none of this is the result of training, or even experience. These facts are known without training, without correction of error, without relevant experience, and are known the same way by every speaker of English – and in analogous constructions, other languages. Hence all of this must somehow derive from the inner resources of the mind/brain, from the genetically determined constitution of the language faculty. Clearly the answer cannot be that these resources include the empty pronoun principle, the subject principle, the inversion principle, some principle that determines how they operate, and a principle blocking the "analogy" in the last example. Rather, we would like to show that the observed facts follow from some deeper principles of the language faculty. This is a typical problem of science, and one that has, in fact, been rather successfully addressed in recent work. But the point here is that the facts show rather clearly that the standard answers to our questions that I have just mentioned cannot be on the right track.

Notice again that the concept of "analogy" does no work at all. By analogy to *John ate*, the sentence *John is too clever to catch* should mean "John is too clever to catch someone or other," but it does not. Notice also that such examples refute the conception of knowledge of language as a skill or ability. The child does not fail to provide the analogous interpretation because of a failure of ability – because it is too weak, or needs more practice. Rather, the computational system of the mind/brain is designed to force certain interpretations for linguistic expressions. To put the matter in the context of the theory of knowledge, our knowledge that expression such-and-such means so-and-so is not justified or grounded in experience in any useful sense of these terms, is not based on good reasons or reliable procedures, is not derived by induction or any other general method. Since these are examples of ordinary propositional knowledge, knowledge that so-and-so, the standard paradigms of epistemology and fixation of belief cannot be correct, and investigation of further examples and other cognitive systems reveals exactly the same thing, so I believe.

I think that these are all important facts, insufficiently appreciated, with quite considerable import. We discover facts of this sort wherever we look, if we are not blinded or misled by dogma.

One notable feature of the widely held conceptions of knowledge and language in terms of ability, skill, habit, general learning mechanisms and analogy, is that they were entirely unproductive and without empirical consequences. One can hardly point to a single empirical result of the slightest significance that derived from these conceptions. The psychology of language of the time was almost completely barren. There was an empirical discipline, namely structural linguistics, which did profess these doctrines and did achieve empirical results and some theoretical understanding. But a closer look will show that in practice, research departed from the professed ideology at every crucial point. The general conceptual framework limited and impoverished the discipline, barring natural lines of inquiry, but otherwise was simply professed and abandoned in practice, though it did, I believe, have a serious and generally harmful impact on applied disciplines such as language teaching.

Recognition of the complete inadequacy of these conceptions led to the first major conceptual change, which was, in many respects, a return to traditional ideas and concerns that had been dismissed or forgotten during the long period when empiricist and behaviorist doctrines prevailed. This shift of focus provided a new set of answers to the central questions:

1 What is knowledge of language? Answer: language is a computational system, a rule system of some sort. Knowledge of language is knowledge of this rule system.
2 How is language acquired? Answer: the initial state of the language faculty determines possible rules and modes of interaction. Language is acquired by a process of selection of a rule system of an appropriate sort on the basis of direct evidence. Experience yields an inventory of rules, through the language-acquisition device of the language faculty.
3 How is language used? Answer: the use of language is rule-governed behavior. Rules form mental representations, which enter into our speaking and understanding. A sentence is parsed and understood by a systematic search through the rule system of the language in question.

The new set of answers constitutes a major component of the "cognitive revolution."

This was a significant shift of point of view: from behavior and its products to the system of knowledge represented in the mind/brain that underlies behavior. Behavior is not the focus of inquiry; rather, it simply provides one source of evidence for the internal systems of the mind/brain that are what we are trying to discover – the system that constitutes a particular language and that determines the form, structural properties and meaning of expressions, and more deeply, the innate structure of the language faculty. As I mentioned earlier, this shift towards an avowed mentalism is also a shift towards assimilating the study of language to the natural sciences, and opens up the possibility of a serious investigation of physical mechanisms.

This shift of focus was extremely productive. It led to a rapid decrease in the range of empirical phenomena that were brought under investigation, with many new empirical discoveries, such as those just illustrated, including very simple facts that had never been noticed. It also led to some degree of success in providing explanations for these facts. But serious difficulties arise at once. Basically, these relate to Plato's problem, the problem of acquisition of language. In essence, the problem is that there are too many possible rule systems. Therefore it is hard to explain how children unerringly select one such system rather than another. Furthermore, children seem to select very complex rule systems and systematically to avoid much simpler ones, a conclusion that makes no sense.

These problems set the research agenda since about 1960, within the framework I am considering here. I will not review the steps that were taken, but rather will turn to the result. In the past several years, a new and very different conception of language has emerged, which yields new answers to our three questions. The initial state of the language faculty consists of a collection of subsystems, or *modules* as they are sometimes called, each of which is based on certain general principles. Many of these principles admit of a certain limited possibility of variation. We may think of the system as a complex network associated with a switch box that contains a finite number of switches. The network is invariant, but each switch can be in one of several positions, perhaps two: on or off. Unless the switches are set, nothing happens. But when the switches are set in one of the permissible ways, the system functions, yielding the entire infinite array of interpretations for linguistic expressions. A slight change in switch settings can yield complex and varied phenomenal consequences as its effects filter through the network. There are no rules at all, hence no necessity to learn rules. For example, the possible phrase structures of a language are fixed by general principles and are invariant among languages, but there are some switches to be set. One has to do with order of elements. In English, for example, nouns, verbs, adjectives and prepositions precede their objects: in Japanese, the comparable elements follow their objects. English is what is called a "head-first" language, Japanese a "head-last" language. These facts can be determined from very simple sentences; for example, the sentences "John ate an apple" (in English) or "John an apple ate" (in Japanese). To acquire a language, the child's mind must determine how the switches are set, and simple data must suffice to determine the switch settings, as in this case. The theory of language use also undergoes corresponding modifications, which I cannot explore here.

This second conceptual change gives a very different conception of language and knowledge. To mention one example, notice that from the point of view of rule systems, there are an infinite number of languages, since there are infinitely many rule systems of the permissible form. But from the network-switch point of view, there are only finitely many languages, one for each arrangement of switch settings. Since each of the switch settings can be determined from simple data, each of these finitely many languages is learnable. Hence the general principle of learnability theory discussed earlier is in fact true: each natural language is learnable – though it is far from true that the learnable systems are all natural languages. As I mentioned, this is an empirical result, and a very surprising one, not a matter of principle. There is, incidentally, some intriguing work in mathematical learning theory which suggests that language acquisition is possible in principle under plausible conditions only if the set of natural languages is indeed "finite" (in a special sense).

This second conceptual change has, once again, led to a great increase in the range of empirical materials discovered and subjected to serious inquiry within generative grammar, now from a much wider range of languages.

Assuming that this change is pointing in the right direction, what are the consequences for the study of language acquisition? The problem will be to determine how the switches are set and to discover the principles of learning, or maturation, or whatever is responsible for carrying out the transition from the initial state of the language faculty to the steady state of adult competence; that is, for setting the switches of the language faculty. Recall that two factors enter into language acquisition: the nature of the language faculty, and the principles of learning theory or more properly growth theory, and any evidence about language acquisition must be assessed carefully to determine how it bears on one or the other of these two interacting factors. How can we proceed in studying this question?

Notice that the problems of assessment of evidence and explanation would plainly be simplified if one or the other of these two components – universal grammar or growth theory – does not exist. Each of these positions has been maintained, the first one quite vigorously, the second as a tentative working hypothesis.

Denial of the existence of universal grammar – that is, of the language faculty as an identifiable system of the human mind/brain – is implicit in the empiricist program and in some recent claims about mechanisms of "general intelligence" or "connectionism" or theory formation, mechanisms that are allegedly applied to yield our linguistic abilities and other intellectual achievements in an undifferentiated way. There has been no attempt to formulate these alleged mechanisms that seems to offer any real promise. The clearer formulations have been quickly refuted, in some cases refuted in principle, and for reasons that should be familiar, the prospects for this program seem very dim. Since there is nothing susbtantive to discuss, I will disregard this possibility and proceed to the second possibility: that growth theory is negligible or non-existent, so that language-acquisition simply involves switch setting on the basis of presented data, such as the sentences "John ate an apple" and "John an apple ate." Let us call this the "no-growth theory" of language acquisition.

Obviously, this cannot be literally true. During the first few months or perhaps weeks of life, an infant probably is exposed to enough linguistic data to set most switches, but plainly it has not done so. In fact, the process extends over quite a few years. So to maintain the no-growth theory we would have to argue that some independent and extrinsic change in cognitive capacities, say in memory or attention, accounts for the observed stages of growth.

Such ideas have been advanced with regard to stages of cognitive development in the sense of Jean Piaget, and also with respect to the stages of language growth. For example, it has been observed that the transition from so-called "telegraphic speech," lacking function words, to normal speech is quite rapid, and includes a number of different systems: questions, negations, tag questions, etc. Furthermore, in the telegraphic speech stage, children understand normal speech better than their own telegraphic speech, and if function words are introduced randomly, the results are unintelligible. This suggests that the children knew the facts of normal speech all along, and were using telegraphic speech because of some limitation of attention and memory. When this limitation is overcome in the course of normal growth and maturation, their already acquired knowledge of language can be manifested. But there are some serious problems in assuming this idea in other cases of regular stages of development: for example, the shift from semantic to syntactic categories, the use of color words, the appearance of a true verbal passive construction and other more complex structures, the emergence of semantic properties of control, and so on. Prima facie, it seems hard to explain these transitions without appeal to maturational processes that bring principles of universal grammar into operation on some regular schedule in a manner to be described and accounted for in a genetic theory. Of course, what is prima facie plausible is not necessarily correct, but the questions that arise are clear enough, and it is an important task to address them, as many investigators are now doing in important recent work.

There is, on the one hand, work by Yukio Otsu, Stephen Crain and others that seems to show that principles of universal grammar are available as soon as constructions are used in which they would be manifested, and the delay in use of these constructions might be explained in terms of inherent complexity, hence extrinsic factors such as memory.

To take one complex example of much general interest, consider recent work of Nina Hyams on the null subject property that distinguishes languages like French and English, in which subjects must be overtly expressed, from languages such as Italian and Spanish, in which the subject may be suppressed in the phonetic output. Hyam's work indicates that at an early stage, all children treat their language as if it were a null subject language. The switch, she suggests, has what is called an "unmarked setting," or in the more usual terminology, the null subject parameter has an "unmarked value," a value selected in the absence of data, and this value provides a null subject language. Italian-speaking children maintain the unmarked value, while English-speaking children later change to the marked value of the parameter, setting the switch differently. The question then is: What triggers the change? There is good evidence that positive evidence suffices for language acquisition; that is, correction of error is unnecessary and probably largely irrelevant when it occurs. Assuming so, the answer to the question cannot be that the English-speaking children are explicitly corrected. Nor can the answer be that they never hear sentences without subjects, since they hear no evidence for most of what they know. Assuming a no-growth theory, Hyams suggests that the change is triggered by the presence of overt expletives in English, such elements as *there* in "there is a man in the room," elements that are semantically empty but must be present to satisfy some syntactic principle. The assumption is that universal grammar contains a principle implying that if a language has overt expletives, then it is not a null subject language. This is, incidentally, an example of a hypothesis about universal grammar deriving from language acquisition studies that might be tested by linguists, rather than the converse, as in the usual practice. It cannot be quite correct as it stands, but something similar might be true.

But now we have to ask why the English-speaking children delay in using this evidence. A possible answer (though not the one Hyams proposes) might be that extrinsic conditions of memory and attention render these expletives inaccessible at an early stage.

Pursuing a similar idea, Luigi Rizzi suggests that contrary to Hyams's initial conclusion, the unmarked value for the parameter is: overt subject. English-speaking children appear to violate this principle at an early stage, but only because extrinsic considerations suppress the production of such elements as unstressed subject pronouns. Italian-speaking children then select the marked value of the parameter on the basis of direct evidence of subjectless sentences.

A third approach is to reject the no-growth theory and to suppose that the null subject parameter only becomes available at a certain stage of maturation, and is set at the marked null subject value only if direct evidence of subjectless sentences is presented. At the moment, the question remains open, and these possibilities do not exhaust the options (for example, the null subject parameter might be further differentiated, or cast in different terms).

Notice that further clarification of these issues might well contribute to our knowledge of the principles and parameters of universal grammar – of the nature of the network and the switches – on the basis of evidence from language acquisition, as we should anticipate as the discipline progresses.

Consider a second example. Sascha Felix argues against the no-growth theory on the basis of evidence about use of negatives in several languages. Apparently, at the earliest stage, children use sentence-external negation, as in "not John likes milk." This fact (which, not surprisingly, is itself controversial) already raises problems for a no-growth theory, since natural languages rarely if ever exhibit sentence-external negation. At a later stage, the child shifts to sentence-internal negation, as in "John no likes milk," which is also inconsistent with the evidence from the adult language. Later, the correct form "John doesn't like milk" emerges. Felix points out that stage I, with sentence-external negation, is consistent with Dan Slobin's principle that the learner avoids interruption of linguistic units, and hence might be taken to support this principle. But he notes that that leaves unresolved the question why this principle becomes inoperative at stage II, and is even more radically abandoned at stage III. A maturational theory seems a possible candidate for an explanation. Again, further research should contribute to clarifying both the principles of language growth, if they exist, and the actual principles and parameters of universal grammar.

Consider finally a more complex example studied in some detail by Hagit Borer and Kenneth Wexler. They argue that the results in many languages on acquisition of passives can be explained by a maturational theory, which provides a more sophisticated version of the idea that transformations are acquired step-by-step during language acquisition. Their theory postulates that until a certain stage of development, phrases can only be interpreted in a canonical position in which semantic roles are assigned by principles of universal grammar, thus the position of abstract underlying deep structures, in effect. At this stage, a sentence such as "John was killed" is simply uninterpretable, since *John* is displaced from its canonical position as object of *kill*. Apparent passive forms at this stage, they argue, are in fact adjectives, as in "the door is closed." Later, a device becomes available, through maturation, by which displaced elements can be interpreted through a so-called *chain* formed by a transformation, which links the displaced element to an empty *trace* in the canonical position. Such chains must then meet various conditions of universal grammar, which account for the possibilities of displacement. They argue that the range of available evidence about acquisition of passives can be largely explained on the basis of this assumption: that chains become available at a certain stage of maturation. Again, there are numerous empirical problems and consequences to be explored, and the results should bear directly on the principles of universal grammar as well as growth theory.

If Borer and Wexler are right, one might be tempted to explore a famous suggestion by Roman Jakobson that language acquisition and language loss in aphasia are mirror images: the earlier some items and structures are acquired in language learning, the later they are lost under brain injury. It would then follow that in some kinds of aphasia, we should find that chains are lost while other aspects of phrase structure remain. Evidence to this effect has in fact been

19

presented by Yosef Grodzinsky. This again suggests what might prove to be an intriguing line of inquiry.

These examples barely scratch the surface. A wide range of intriguing questions arise at once if we think through the implications of the principles-and-parameters conception of universal grammar in terms of an invariant network and an associated set of switches, and if we ask how this conception might relate to possible principles of maturation involved in language growth, along with extrinsic factors in cognitive development. I have not had time to consider the question of language processing, but here too the questions look quite different when approached in these terms. And within the study of language proper, many new and exciting questions enter into the research agenda. If the principles-and-parameters approach is correct, it should be possible literally to deduce the properties of each natural language by setting the switches in one or another way and computing the consequences. Typological difference should be a matter of differences in switch-settings. Language change should be the result of a change in such a setting; note that a small change might yield a substantial phenomenal difference as its effects filter through the fixed network of modular principles. These are all questions that are now being addressed, in some cases with some success, in other cases with failures that are highly suggestive in opening up new lines of inquiry. Furthermore, the class of typologically different languages that have come under investigation, and that seem to be amenable to a coherent and uniform approach, has vastly extended, again, a promising sign.

There are, it seems, real grounds for considerable optimism about the prospects that lie ahead, not only for the study of language proper, but also for the study of cognitive systems of the mind/brain of which language is a fundamental and essential component, in the human species.

Magic Words: How Language Augments Human Computation

Andy Clark

1.   **Word Power**

Of course, words aren't magic. Neither are sextants, compasses, maps, slide rules and all the other paraphrenalia which have accreted around the basic biological brains of *Homo sapiens*. In the case of these other tools and props, however, it is transparently clear that they function so as either to carry out or to facilitate computational operations important to various human projects. The slide rule transforms complex mathematical problems (ones that would baffle or tax the unaided subject) into simple tasks of perceptual recognition. The map provides geographical information in a format well suited to aid complex planning and strategic military operations. The compass gathers and displays a kind of information that (most) unaided human subjects do not seem to command. These various tools and props thus act to generate information, or to store it, or to transform it, or some combination of the three. In so doing, they impact on our individual and collective problem-solving capacities in much the same dramatic ways as various software packages impact the performance of a simple PC.

Public language, I shall argue, is just such a tool — it is a species of external artefact whose current adaptive value is partially constituted by its role in re-shaping the kinds of computational space that our biological brains must negotiate in order to solve certain types of problems, or to carry out certain complex projects. This computational role of language has been somewhat neglected (not un-noticed, but not rigorously pursued either) in recent cognitive science, due perhaps to a (quite proper) fascination with and concentration upon, that other obvious dimension: the role of language as an instrument of interpersonal communication. Work on sentence parsing, language use and story understanding has thus concentrated on the role of language in processes of information transfer between agents and on information retrieval from texts. But it has had little to say about the computational role of the linguistic formulations themselves, or about the special properties of the external media that support linguistic encodings.

In this chapter, I hope to display the broad shape of such an alternative interest. I begin by discussing the views of some recent (and not-so-recent) authors who recognise, in various ways, the potential role of language and text in transforming, reshaping and simplifying the computational tasks that confront the biological brain. Sections 3 and 4 pursue this broad vision across a variety of cases involving planning, co-ordination, learning and the construction of complex thoughts and arguments. The fifth section extends these last considerations to encompass the rather special class of *meta-cognitive* operations and tries to implicate language as an essential part of the process of thinking about our own thoughts and cognitive profiles. The final section suggests some broader implications and raises some questions concerning the boundary between the intelligent agent and the world.

2.   Supra-communicative Views of Language

The idea that language may do far more than merely serve as a vehicle for communication is not new. It is clearly present in the work of developmentalists such as Vygotsky (1934), and more recently that of Laura Berk and others (see e.g. essays in Diaz and Berk, 1992). It figures in the philosophical conjectures and arguments of e.g. Peter Carruthers (1996a) and Ray Jackendoff (to appear). And it surfaces in the more cognitive science oriented speculations of Daniel Dennett (1991). It will be helpful to begin by rehearsing some of the central ideas in this literature, before pursuing our own version — *viz.* the idea of language as a computational transformer which allows pattern-completing brains to tackle otherwise intractable classes of cognitive problems.

Lev Vygotsky, a Soviet psychologist of the 1930s, pioneered the idea that the use of public language had profound effects on cognitive development. He posited powerful links between speech, social experience and learning. Two especially pertinent Vygotskian ideas, for present purposes, concern the role of private speech, and of scaffolded action (action within the so-called zone of proximal development — see Vygotsky, trans., 1962). We may call an action 'scaffolded' to the extent that it relies on some kind of external support. Such support could come from the use of tools, or the knowledge and skills of others; that is to say, scaffolding (as I shall use the term) denotes a broad class of physical, cognitive and social augmentations — augmentations which allow us to achieve some goal which would otherwise be beyond us. Simple examples include the use of a compass and pencil to draw a perfect circle, the role of other crew members in enabling a ship's pilot to steer a course, and the infant's ability to take its first steps only while suspended in the enabling grip of its parents. Vygotsky's focus on what was termed the zone of proximal development was concerned with this latter type of case, in which a child is temporarily able to succeed at designated tasks only by courtesy of the guidance or help provided by another human being (usually, a parent or teacher). This idea dovetails with Vygotsky's interest in private speech in the following way. When the child, confronted by a tricky challenge, is 'talked through' the problem by a more experienced agent, the child can often succeed at tasks which would otherwise prove impossible (think of learning to tie your shoelaces).[1] Later on,

22

when the adult is absent, the child can conduct a similar dialogue, but this time with herself. But even in this latter case, it is argued, the speech (be it vocal or 'internalised') functions so as to guide behaviour, to focus attention, and to guard against common errors. In such cases, the role of language is to guide and shape our own behaviour — it is a tool for structuring and controlling action and not merely a medium of information transfer between agents.

This Vygotskian image is supported by more recent bodies of developmental research, such as that carried out by Laura Berk and Ruth Garvin. Berk and Garvin (1984) observed and recorded the ongoing speech of a group of 5 — 10-year-olds in Kentucky. They found that most of the children's private speech (speech not addressed to some other listener) seemed keyed to the direction and control of the child's own actions. They found that the incidence of such speech increased when the child was alone and engaged in trying to perform some difficult task. In subsequent studies (Bivens and Berk, 1990; Berk 1994) it was found that the children who made the most self-directed comments were the ones who subsequently mastered the tasks best. Berk's conclusions, from these and other studies, was that self-directed speech (be it vocal or silent inner rehearsal) is a crucial cognitive tool that allows us to highlight the most puzzling features of new situations, and to direct and control our own problem-solving actions.

The theme of language as a tool has also been developed by the philosopher Christopher Gauker. Gauker's concern, however, is to re-think the intra-individual role of language in terms of (what he calls) a 'cause-effect analysis'. The idea here is to depict public language 'not as a tool for representing the world or expressing one's thoughts but a tool for effecting changes in one's environment' (Gauker, 1990, p. 31). To get the flavour, consider the use of a symbol, by a chimpanzee, to request a banana. The chimp touches a specific key on a key-pad (the precise physical location of the key can be varied between trials) and learns that making *that* symbol light tends to promote the arrival of bananas. The chimp's quasi-linguistic understanding is explicable, Gauker suggests, in terms of the chimp's appreciation of a cause-effect relationship between the symbol production and changes in its local environment. Gauker looks at a variety of symbol-using behaviours and concludes that they all succumb to this kind of analysis. This leads him to hypothesise that, although clearly more complex, human beings' linguistic understanding likewise 'consists in a grasp of the causal relations into which linguistic signs may enter' (Gauker, 1990, p. 44).

Gauker tends to see the role of language as, if you like, directly causal: as a way of getting things done, much like reaching out your hand and grabbing a cake. However, the idea that we learn, by experience, of the peculiar causal potencies of specific signs and symbols is in principle much broader. We might even, as in the Vygotskian examples and as argued in Dennett (1991), discover that the self-directed utterance of words and phrases has certain effects on our own behaviour! We might also learn to exploit language as a tool in a variety of even less direct ways, as a means of altering the shape of computational problem spaces (see section 3 following).

One obvious question which the putative role of language as a self-directed tool raises is 'how does it work?' What is it about self-directed speech, for example, which fits it to play a guiding role? After all, it is not at all clear how we can tell ourselves anything we don't already know! Surely, all that public language can ever be is a medium for expressing ideas which are already formulated and understood in some other, more basic, inner code? It is precisely this view which a supra-communicative account of language has ultimately to reject.

One way to do so is to depict public language as itself the medium of a special kind of thought.[2] Another (not altogether distinct) way is to depict linguaform inputs as having distinctive *effects* on some inner computational device. Peter Carruthers[3] (1996a) champions the first of these, while Daniel Dennett (1991) offers a version of the second. Thus Carruthers argues that, in this case at least, we should take very seriously the evidence of our own introspection. It certainly often seems as if our very thoughts are composed of the words and sentences of public language. And the reason we have this impression, Carruthers argues, is because it is true: inner thinking is literally done in inner speech (see Carruthers, 1996a, chs. 2 and 8 for an extensive discussion). By extension, Carruthers is able to view many intra-personal uses of language as less a matter of simple communication than of (what he nicely terms) *public thinking*. This perspective fits satisfyingly with the Vygotskian view championed by Berk, and is also applicable to the interesting case of writing down our ideas. Here Carruthers suggests 'one does not *first* entertain a private thought and *then* write it down: rather, the thinking *is* the writing' (Carruthers, 1996a, p. 52). I shall return to this point later (see section 3), since I believe that what Carruthers says is *almost* right, but that we can better understand the kind of case he has in mind by treating the writing as an environmental manipulation which transforms the problem space for human brains.

Carruthers, in depicting language as itself the vehicle of (certain types of) thought, is nonetheless careful to reject what he calls the 'Whorfian Relativism of the Standard Social Science Model' (1996a, p. 278). The reference here is to the idea, promoted by Benjamin Whorf (1956), that human minds are profoundly shaped and altered by the *particular* public languages we come to speak. Carruthers view is *not* that specific languages somehow deeply alter or re-programme the brain, but rather[4] that certain kinds of human thinking are actually constituted by sequences of public language symbols (written down, spoken, or internally imagined). Such a hypothesis, Carruthers argues, can help account for a wide range of both introspective and experimental and pathological data.[5]

An alternative way to unpack a supra-communicative view of language, we noted, is to suppose that the linguistic inputs actually re-programme or otherwise alter the high-level computational structure of the brain itself. The exegesis is delicate (and therefore tentative), but something akin to this view seems to be held by Daniel Dennett when he suggests that 'conscious human minds are more-or-less serial virtual machines implemented — inefficiently — on the parallel hardware that evolution has provided for us' (Dennett, 1991, p. 278). In this and other passages, the idea seems to be that the bombardment of (something like) parallel processing, connectionist, pattern-completing brains by (amongst other things) public language texts and sentences (reminders, plans, exhortations, questions, etc.), results in a kind of cognitive re-organisation akin to that which occurs when one computer system *simulates* another. In such cases, the installation of a new programme allows the user to treat e.g. a serial LISP machine as if it was a massively parallel connectionist device. What Dennett is proposing is, he tells us (1991, p. 218) the same trick in reverse — *viz.* the simulation of something like a serial logic engine using the altogether different resources of the massively parallel neural networks which biological evolution rightly favours for real-world, real-time survival and action.

Strikingly, Dennett suggests that it is this subtle re-programming of the brain by (primarily) linguistic bombardment which yields the phenomena of human consciousness (our sense of self) and enables us to far surpass the behavioural and cognitive achievements of most other animals (see e.g. Dennett, 1995, pp. 370–3). Dennett thus depicts our advanced cognitive skills as in large part a result not of our innate hardware (which may differ only in small, though important, ways from that of other animals) but of the special way that various plastic (programmable) features of the brain are modified by the effects of culture and language. As Dennett puts it, the serial machine is installed courtesy of 'myriad microsettings in the plasticity of the brain' (Dennett, 1991, p. 219). Of course, mere exposure to culture and language is not sufficient to ensure human-like cognition. You can expose a cockroach to all the language you like and get no trace of the cognitive transformations which Dennett sees in us. Dennett's claim is not that there are *no* initial hardware level differences. Rather it is that some relatively small hardware differences (e.g. between us and a chimpanzee) allow us to both create and benefit from public language and other cultural developments in ways which lead to a great snowball of cognitive change and augmentation, including, crucially, the literal installation of a new kind of computational device inside the brain.

Dennett's vision is complex, and not altogether unambiguous. The view I want to develop is clearly deeply related, but differs (I think) in one crucial respect. Where Dennett sees public language as effecting a profound but subtle re-organisation of the brain itself, I am inclined to see it as in essence an external resource which complements — but does not profoundly alter — the brain's own basic modes of representation and computation. That is to say, I see the changes as relatively superficial ones, geared to allowing us to use and exploit various *external* resources to the full. The positions are not, of course, wholly distinct.[6] The mere fact that we often mentally rehearse sentences in our head and use them to guide and alter our behavior means that one cannot (and should not) treat language and culture as wholly external resources. Nonetheless, it remains possible that such rehearsal neither requires nor results in the installation of any fundamentally different kind of computational device in the brain, but rather involves the use of the same old (essentially pattern-completing) resources to model the special kinds of behaviour observed in the public linguistic world. And as Paul Churchland (1995, pp. 264–9) points out, there is indeed a class of connectionist networks ('recurrent networks' — see Elman, 1993, and further discussion in Clark, 1993) which do seem well suited to modelling such behaviour.

This view of inner rehearsal is nicely developed by the connectionists Rumelhart, Smolensky, McClelland, and Hinton (1986) who argue that the general strategy of 'mentally modelling' the behaviour of selected aspects of our environment is especially important insofar as it allows us to imagine external resources with which we have previously physically interacted, and to replay the dynamics of such interactions in our heads. Thus experience with drawing and using Venn diagrams allows us to train a neural network which subsequently allows us to manipulate *imagined* Venn diagrams in our heads. Such imaginative manipulations require a specially trained neural resource to be sure. But there is no reason to suppose that such training results in the installation of a different *kind* of computational device. It is the same old process of pattern completion in high dimensional representational spaces, but applied to the special domain of a specific kind of *external* representation. The link to a Vygotskian image is clear and remarked upon by the authors who then summarise their view saying:

> We can be instructed to behave in a particular way. Responding to instructions in this way can be viewed simply as responding to some environmental event. We can also remember such an instruction and 'tell ourselves' what to do. We have, in this way, internalised the instruction. We believe that the process of following instructions is essentially the same whether we have told ourselves or have been told what to do. Thus even here we have a kind of internalisation of an external representational format. (Rumelhart, *et al.*, 1986, p. 47.)

The larger passage (pp. 44–8) from which the above is extracted is, in fact, remarkably rich and touches on several of our major themes. The authors note that such external formalisms are especially hard to invent and slow to develop, and are themselves the kinds of product which (in an innocently bootstrapping kind of way) can evolve only thanks to the linguistically mediated processes of cultural storage and gradual refinement over many lifetimes. They also note that by using real external representations we put ourselves in a position to use our basic perceptual/motor skills to separate problems into parts and to attend to a series of sub-problems, storing intermediate results along the way.

The Rumelhart *et al.* vision thus depicts language as a key element in a variety of environmentally extended computational processes. This notion of computational processes inhering in larger systems (ones that may incorporate the activities of many individual biological brains) is further developed and defended in Hutchins (1995). Hutchins offers a beautiful and detailed treatment that highlights the ways representation may flow and be transformed within larger, socially and technologically extended systems. Hutchins' main example involves the way maps, instruments, texts and vocalisations all contribute to the complex process of ship navigation: a process that is best analysed as an extended sequence of computational transitions, many of whose role is to transform problems into formats better situated to the perceptual and pattern-completing capacities of biological brains. The environmental operations thus *complement* the activities of the biological brains.

The tack I am about to pursue likewise depicts language as an external artefact designed to complement, rather than recapitulate or transfigure, the basic processing profile we share with other animals. It does not depict experience with language as a source of profound inner re-programming (*pace* Dennett). Whether it depicts inner linguistic rehearsal as literally constitutive of specific human cognizings (as Carruthers claims) is moot. Certainly, inner rehearsals, when they occur, are quite literally models of linguistic productions. But what is most important, I believe, is not to try to answer the question, 'do we actually think *in* words' (to which the answer is 'in a way yes, in a way no'!) but to try to see what computational benefits accrue to biological pattern-completing brains in virtue of their ability to manipulate and sometimes model external representational artefacts.

3. Language and Computation: The Six Ways

Here, then, are six broad ways in which linguistic artefacts can complement the activity of the pattern-completing brain.

3.1 *Memory Augmentation*

This is, of course, the most obvious and oft-remarked case. Here we simply use the artefactual world of texts, diaries, notebooks and the like as a means of systematically storing large and often complex bodies of data. We may also use simple external manipulations (such as leaving a note on the mirror) to prompt the recall, from on-board biological memory, of appropriate information and intentions at the right time. Here, the use of linguistic artefacts is perfectly continuous with a variety of other, simpler, environmental manipulations, such as leaving the empty olive oil bottle by the door so that you cannot help but run across it (and hence recall the need for olive oil) as you set out for the shops.

3.2 *Environmental Simplification*

This has both an obvious and a not-so-obvious aspect. The obvious (but still important) aspect concerns the use of labels to provide perceptually simple clues to help us negotiate complex environments. Signs for the cloakrooms, for nightclubs, and for city centres all fulfil this role. They allow a little learning to go a very long way, helping you find your targets in new cities without knowing in advance what, in detail, to seek or even where exactly to seek it. McClamrock (1995, p. 88) describes this strategy as one in which we 'enforce on the environment certain kinds of stable properties that will lessen our computational burdens and the demands on us for inference'.

Closely related, but much less obvious, is the provision, by the use of linguistic labels, of a greatly simplified *learning* environment. It can be shown, for example, that the provision of linguistic labels for classes of perceptually presented objects can speed category learning in artificial neural networks. This is because the presentation of the same label accompanying a series of slightly different perceptual inputs (e.g., different views of dogs) gives the network a heavy hint. It flags the presence of some further underlying structure and thus invites the network to seek the perceptual commonality (for a detailed discussion see Schyns, 1991; Clark, 1993, chapter 5). It also seems likely (though no formal demonstration exists) that for certain very abstract concepts, the *only* route to successful learning may go via the provision of linguistic glosses. Concept such as charity, extortion and black hole seem pitched too far from perceptual facts to be learnable without exposure to linguistically formulated theories. Language may thus enable us to comprehend equivalence classes that would otherwise lie forever outside our intellectual horizons.

Human beings often make explicit plans. We say to others that we will be at such and such a place at such and such a time. We even play this game with ourselves, perhaps by writing down a list of what we will do on what days and so on. Superficially, the role of such explicit planning is to allow the *co-ordination* of actions. Thus, if the other person knows you have said you'll be at the station at 9.00 a.m., they can time their taxi accordingly. Or, in the solo case, if you have to buy the paint before touching up the car, and if you have to go to the shops to buy other items anyway, you can minimise your efforts and enforce proper sequencing by following a plan. As the space of demands and opportunities grows, it often becomes necessary to use pencil and paper to organise and to re-organise the options, and then to preserve the result as a kind of external control structure available to guide your subsequent actions.

Closely related to such co-ordinative functions is the function of oiling the wheels of collaborative problem-solving. Collaborative problem solving (see e.g., Tomasello *et al.*, 1993) involves much more than the mere exchange of information and orchestration of activity. It involves actively prompting the other to work harder at certain aspects of a problem, and allowing the other to focus your own attention in places you might otherwise ignore. Here, then, the co-ordinative function of linguistic exchange phases into the further one of manipulating attention and controlling resource allocation (see 3.5 below).

Such broadly co-ordinative functions, though important, do not exhaust the benefits of explicit (usually language-based) planning. As Michael Bratman has recently pointed out, the creation of explicit plans may play a special role in reducing the on-line cognitive load on resource-limited agents like ourselves. The idea here is that our plans have a kind of stability which pays dividends by reducing the amount of deliberation in which we engage as we go about much of our daily business. Of course, new information can, and often does, cause us to revise our plans. But we do not let every slight change prompt a re-assessment of our plans and intentions, even when, other things being equal, we might now choose slightly differently. Human plans and intentions, Bratman suggests, play the role of blocking a wasteful process of continual re-assessment and choice, except in cases where there is some quite major pay-off for the disruption. (See Bratman, 1987, for a full discussion.)

Linguistic exchange and formulation thus plays a key role in co-ordinating activities (both at an inter- and intra-personal level) *and* in reducing the amount of daily on-line deliberation in which we engage.

3.4   *Taming Path-dependent Learning*

Human learning, like learning in Artificial Neural Networks, looks hostage to at least some degree of path dependency. Certain ideas can be understood only once others are in place. The training received by one mind fits it to grasp and expand upon ideas which gain no foothold of comprehension in another. The processes of formal education, indeed, are geared to take young (and not so young) minds along a genuine intellectual journey, which may involve beginning with ideas now known to be incorrect, but which alone seem able to prime the system to later appreciate a finer grained truth. Such mundane facts are a reflection of cognitive path dependence — you can't get everywhere from anywhere; where you are now strongly constrains your future intellectual trajectory. Moreover, such path dependency is nicely explained (see e.g., Elman, 1993) by treating intellectual progress as involving something like a process of computational search in a large and complex space. Previous learning inclines the system to try out certain locations in the space and not others. When the prior learning is appropriate, the job of learning some new regularity is made tractable: the prior learning acts as a filter on the space of options to be explored. Artificial Neural Networks which employ gradient descent learning methods are highly constrained insofar as the learning routine forces the network always to explore at the edges of its current weight assignments. Since these constitute its current knowledge, it means that such networks cannot 'jump around' in hypothesis space. The network's current location in weight space (its current knowledge) is thus a major constraint on what new 'ideas' it can next explore (see Elman, 1993, p. 94).

When confronting devices which exhibit some degree of path dependency, the mundane observation that language allows ideas to be preserved and to migrate between individuals takes on a new force. For we can now appreciate how such migrations may allow the communal construction of extremely delicate and difficult intellectual trajectories and progressions. An idea which only Joe's prior experience could make available, but which can flourish only in the intellectual niche currently provided by the brain of Mary, can now realise its full potential by journeying between agents as and when required. Moreover, the sheer number of intellectual niches available within a linguistically linked community provides a stunning matrix of possible inter-agent trajectories. The observation that public language allows human cognition to be collective (e.g. Churchland, 1995, p. 270) takes on new depth once we recognise the role of such collective endeavor in transcending the path-dependent nature of individual human cognition.

3.5   *Attention and Resource Allocation*

Ron McClamrock reports a nice case from Marr[7] in which we see a control loop which runs outside the head and into the local environment. In McClamrock's words:

Flies, it turns out, don't quite know that to fly they should flap their wings. They don't take off by sending some signal from the brain to the wings. Rather, there is a direct control link from the fly's *feet* to its wings, such that when the feet cease to be in contact with a surface, the fly's wings begin to flap. To take off, the fly simply jumps and then lets the signal from the feet trigger the wings. (McClamrock, 1995, p. 85; emphasis in original)

Notice, then, how written and spoken language at times serves a similar goal. We write down a note to do such and such, thus creating an externalized control loop for our own future behavior. We follow someone's vocal instructions as we learn to windsurf. Or we mentally rehearse such instruction as we practise on our own. Such phenomena reveal linguistic formulations as somehow helping to focus, monitor and control behaviour. I do not think we yet understand exactly how language (especially mental rehearsal of instructions) interacts with more basic on-line resources so as to yield these benefits. But that it does indeed play some such role seems clear.

3.6   *Data Manipulation and Representation*

This final benefit accrues most directly to the use of actual text. As I construct this chapter, for example, I am continually creating, putting aside, and re-organising chunks of text. I have a file which contains all kinds of hints and fragments, stored up over a long period of time, which may be germane to the discussion. I have source texts and papers full of notes and annotations. As I (literally, physically) move these things about, interacting first with one, then another, making new notes, annotations and plans, so the intellectual shape of the chapter grows and solidifies. It is a shape which does not spring fully developed from inner cogitations. Instead, it is the product of a sustained and iterated sequence of *interactions* between my brain and a variety of external props. In these cases, I am willing to say, a good deal of actual thinking involves loops and circuits which run outside the head and through the local environment. Extended intellectual arguments and theses are almost always the product of brains acting in concert with multiple external resources. These resources enable us to pursue manipulations and juxtapositions of ideas and data which would quickly baffle the un-augmented brain. (The simple case of physically manipulating Scrabble tiles to present new potential word-fragments to a pattern-completing brain — see Kirsh, to appear — is a micro-version of the same strategy). In all such cases, the real environment of printed words and symbols allows us to search, store, sequence and re-organise data in ways alien to the on-board repertoire of the biological brain.

The moral of the six ways is thus clear. The role of public language and text in human cognition is not limited to the preservation and communication of ideas. Instead, these external resources make available concepts, strategies and learning trajectories which are simply not available to individual, un-augmented brains. Much of the true power of language lies in its underappreciated capacity to re-shape the computational spaces which confront intelligent agents.

4.   Words as Filters

The 'six ways' pursued in the previous section revolve around two broad, and rather distinct, themes. One is the use of text and/or speech as forms of external memory and workspace. The other is the (putative) role of words and sentences (preserved and transmitted through the medium of public language) to act as transformers of the very shape of the cognitive and computational spaces we inhabit. This second theme, it seems to me, is the more generally neglected of the two, and so it may be worth expanding on it a little further.

Consider the idea of words as filters on the search space for a biological learning device. The idea here (a kind of corollary of some of Elman's ideas as rehearsed in the previous section) is that learning to associate concepts with discrete arbitrary labels (words) somehow makes it easier to use those concepts to constrain computational search and hence enables the acquisition of a cascade of more complex and increasingly abstract ideas. The claim (*see also* Clark and Thornton, 1997) is thus that associating a perceptually simple, stable, external item (such as a word) with an idea, concept or piece of knowledge effectively freezes the concept into a sort of cognitive building block— an item that can then be treated as a simple baseline feature for future episodes of thought, learning and search.

This broad conjecture (whose statistical and computational foundations are explored in the co-authored piece mentioned above) seems to be supported by some recent work on chimp cognition. Thompson *et al.*, (in press) is a study of problem solving in pan troglodytes and concerns the abilities of the chimps to solve puzzles that require matching relations-between-relations. Merely matching (first order) relations might involve e.g. training the chimps to match the identical items (such as two identical cups) in an array. Matching relations-between-relations, by contrast, involves e.g. getting the chimps to match pairs of identical items (e.g. two identical shoes) to other pairs of (different) identical items (such as two identical cups). And conversely, matching pairs of different items (e.g. a cup and a shoe) to other pairs of different items (e.g. a pen and a padlock). The higher-order task is thus not to match the items themselves but to match the relations that obtain between them — it is to match the pairs in terms of the relational properties they exhibit irrespective of the specific items involved.

What makes the higher-order task higher order, it should be clear, is that there is an additional step of reasoning involved. The chimps must first represent the two (within pair) items as being the same, and then match the pairs of pairs according to whether or not each member of the pair of pairs exhibits the same relational property (sameness or difference). Now it is well known (see e.g. the review in Thompson and Oden, 1996) that non-language trained infant chimps can perceptually detect the basic relations of similarity and difference, but that they cannot make the higher-order judgments pairing instantiations of the relations themselves. It is also well known (though highly illuminating) that language trained chimps *can* learn to perform this higher-order task. These are chimps who have learnt to use symbols for 'same' and 'different' and have, in addition, attained some degree of minimal syntactic competence such as the ability to compose proto-sentences (see e.g. Premack and Premack, 1983). What Thompson *et al.* nicely go on to demonstrate is that (*pace* Premack and Premack) what is responsible for this 'cognitive bonus' is not syntactic competence *per se* but simply the experience of associating abstract relations with arbitrary tokens. Thus chimps with no compositional linguistic training but with a history of rewards for associating e.g. a plastic heart token with the presentation of pairs exhibiting sameness and a diagonal token with the presentation of pairs exhibiting difference, are shown to learn the higher-order matching task as easily as the others. Chimps with no history of associating the relations with external tokens (predictably) fail to perform the higher-order task.

Naturally, such experiments involve in addition a whole host of careful controls and important experimental details. I here refer the reader to the detailed study in Thompson *et al.* (in press) and the background review in Thompson and Oden (1996). The authors' conclusions, however, bear repeating. They conclude that (in this case at least) it is the use of simple, arbitrary external tags for independently identifiable relational properties that opens up the more abstract space of knowledge about relations between relations. This fits perfectly with Dennett's (1994) suspicion that it is the practice of tagging and labelling itself, rather that full-blooded syntactic competence *per se*, that may have been the crucial innovation that opened up new cognitive horizons to proto-language using creatures. Learning such a set of tags and labels (which we all do when we learn a language) is, I would speculate, rather closely akin to acquiring a new perceptual modality. For, like a perceptual modality, it renders certain features of our world concrete and salient, and allows us to target our thoughts (and learning algorithms) on a new domain of basic objects. This new domain compresses what were previously complex and unruly sensory patterns into simple objects. These simple objects can then be attended to in ways that quickly reveal further (otherwise hidden) patterns, as in the case of relations-between-relations. And of course the whole process is deeply iterative — we coin new words and labels to concretise regularities that we could only originally conceptualise thanks to a backdrop of other words and labels. The most powerful and familiar incarnation of this iterative strategy is, perhaps, the edifice of human science.

5.   Mangroves and Meta-cognition

If a tree is seen growing on an island, which do you suppose came first? It is natural (and usually correct) to assume that the island provided the fertile soil in which a lucky seed came to rest. Mangrove forests,[8] however, constitute a revealing exception to this general rule. The Mangrove grows from a floating seed which establishes itself in the water, rooting in shallow mud flats. The seedling sends complex vertical roots through the surface of the water, culminating in what looks to all intents and purposes like a small tree posing on stilts. The complex system of aerial roots, however, soon traps floating soil, weed and debris. After a time, the accumulation of trapped matter forms a small island. As more time passes, the island grows larger and larger. A growing mass of such islands can eventually merge, effectively extending the shoreline out to the trees! Throughout this process, and despite our prior intuitions, it is the land which is progressively built by the trees.

Something like the Mangrove effect, I suspect, is operative in some species of human thought. It is natural to suppose that words are always rooted in the fertile soil of pre-existing thoughts. But sometimes, at least, the influence seems to run in the other direction. A simple example is poetry. In constructing a poem, we do not simply use words to express thoughts. Rather, it is often the properties of the words (their structure and cadence) which determine the thoughts that the poem comes to express. A similar partial reversal can occur during the construction of complex texts and arguments. By writing down our ideas we generate a trace in a format which opens up a range of new possibilities. We can then inspect and re-inspect the same ideas, coming at them from many different angles and in many different frames of mind. We can hold the original ideas steady so that we may judge them, and safely experiment with subtle alterations. We can store them in ways which allow us to compare and combine them with other complexes of ideas in ways which would quickly defeat the un-augmented imagination. In these ways, and as remarked in the previous section, the real properties of physical text transform the space of possible thoughts.

Such observations lead me to the following conjecture. Perhaps it is public language which is responsible for a complex of rather distinctive features of human thought — *viz*, our ability to display *second-order cognitive dynamics*. By second-order cognitive dynamics I mean a cluster of powerful capacities involving self-evaluation, self-criticism and finely honed remedial responses.[9] Examples would include: recognising a flaw in our own plan or argument, and dedicating further cognitive efforts to fixing it; reflecting on the unreliability of our own initial judgements in certain types of situations and proceeding with special caution as a result; coming to see why we reached a particular conclusion by appreciating the logical transitions in our own thought; thinking about the conditions under which we think best and trying to bring them about. The list could be continued, but the patten should be clear. In all these cases, we are effectively thinking about our own cognitive profiles or about specific thoughts. This 'thinking about thinking', is a good candidate for a distinctively human capacity — one not evidently shared by the other, non-language-using animals who share our planet. As such, it is natural to wonder whether this might be an entire species of thought in which language plays the generative role — a species of thought which is not just reflected in, or extended by, our use of words but is directly dependent upon language for its very existence. Public language and the inner rehearsal of sentences would, on this model, act like the aerial roots of the Mangrove tree — the words would serve as fixed points capable of attracting and positioning additional intellectual matter, creating the islands of second-order thought so characteristic of the cognitive landscape of *Homo sapiens*.

It is easy to see, in broad outline, how this might come about. For as soon as we formulate a thought in words (or on paper), it becomes an object for both ourselves and for others. As an object, it is the kind of thing we can have thoughts about. In creating the object, we need have no thoughts about thoughts — but once it is there, the opportunity immediately exists to attend to it as an object in its own right. The process of linguistic formulation thus creates the stable structure to which subsequent thinkings attach.

Just such a twist on potential role of the inner rehearsal of sentences has been suggested by the linguist Ray Jackendoff. Jackendoff (1996) suggests that the mental rehearsal of sentences may be the primary means by which our own thoughts are able to become objects of further attention and reflection. The key claim is that linguistic formulation makes complex thoughts available to processes of mental attention, and that this, in turn open them up to a range of further mental operations. It enables us, for example, to pick out different elements of complex thoughts and to scrutinize each in turn. It enables us to 'stabilise' very abstract ideas in working memory. And it enables us to inspect and criticise our own reasoning in ways that no other representational modality allows.

What fits internal sentence-based rehearsal to play such an unusual role? The answer, I suggest, must lie in the more mundane (and temporally antecedent) role of language as an instrument of communication. For in order to function as an efficient instrument of communication, public language will have been moulded into a code well-suited to the kinds of interpersonal exchange in which ideas are presented, inspected

33

and subsequently critiqued. And this, in turn involves the development of a type of code which minimizes contextuality (most words retain more-or-less the same meaning in the different sentences in which they occur), is effectively modality-neutral (an idea may be prompted by visual, auditory or tactile input and yet be preserved using the same verbal formula), and allows easy rote memorisation of simple strings.[10] By 'freezing' our own thoughts in the memorable, context-resistant and modality-transcending format of a sentence we thus create a special kind of mental object — an object which is apt for scrutiny from multiple different cognitive angles, which is not doomed to alter or change every time we are exposed to new inputs or information, and which fixes the ideas at a fairly high level of abstraction from the idiosyncratic details of their proximal origins in sensory input. Such a mental object is, I suggest, ideally suited to figure in the evaluative, critical and tightly focused operations distinction of second-order cognition. It is an object fit for the close and repeated inspections highlighted by Jackendoff under the rubric of *attending* to our own thoughts. The coding system of public language is thus especially apt to be co-opted for more private purposes of inner display, self-inspection and self-criticism, exactly as predicted by the Vygotskian treatments mentioned in section 2 above. Language stands revealed as a key resource by which we effectively redescribe[11] our own thoughts in a format which makes them available for a variety of new operations and manipulations.

The emergence of such second-order cognitive dynamics is plausibly seen as one root of the veritable explosion of types and varieties of external scaffolding structures in human cultural evolution. It is because we can think about our own thinking that we can actively structure our world in ways designed to promote, support and extend our own cognitive achievements. This process also feeds itself, as when the arrival of written text and notation allowed us to begin to fix ever more complex and extended sequences of thought and reason as objects for further scrutiny and attention.

To complete this picture, we should reflect that once the apparatus (internal and external) of sentential and text-based reflection is in place, we may expect the development of new types of non-linguistic thought and encoding — ones dedicated to the task of managing and interacting with the sentences and texts in more powerful and efficient ways.[12] The linguistic constructions, thus viewed, are a new class of objects which invite us to develop new (non-linguistically based) skills of use, recognition and manipulation. Sentential and non-sentential modes of thought as this co-evolve so as to complement, but not replicate, each other's special cognitive virtues.

It is a failure to appreciate this deep complementarity that, I suspect, leads Paul Churchland (one of the best and most imaginative neurophilosophers around) to dismiss linguaform expression as just a shallow reflection of our 'real' knowledge. Churchland fears that without such marginalization we might mistakenly depict all thought and cognition as involving the unconscious rehearsal of sentence-like symbol strings, and thus be blinded to the powerful, pattern-and-prototype-based encodings which look to be biologically and evolutionarily fundamental. But we have now scouted much fertile intermediate territory.[13] In combining an array of biologically basic pattern-recognition skills with the special 'cognitive fixatives' of word and text, we (like the Mangroves) create new landscapes, new fixed points in the sea of thought. Viewed as a complementary cognitive artefact, language can genuinely extend our cognitive horizons — and without the impossible burden of re-capitulating the detailed contents of non-linguistic thought.

6.   Studying the Extended Mind

Speech and text, we have seen, greatly extend the problem-solving capacities of human-kind. More profoundly, the practice of putting thoughts into words alters the nature of human experience. Our thoughts become determinate and public objects, apt for rational assessment and for all kinds of meta-cognitive scrutiny. In thus recognising public language as a powerful transformer of individual computational and experiential space, we invite reflection on a number of further topics. I will end by mentioning just two.

The first concerns the nature of the internal representations that guide human action. A popular image, often associated with Jerry Fodor's reflections on the need for a 'language of thought' (e.g., Fodor, 1975, 1987), depicts the internal representational arena as itself a locus of propositionally structured items — sentences in Mentalese. This image has lately been the subject of a damaging series of criticisms stemming from the successes of non-linguaform computational approaches — especially those of connectionist (or parallel distributed processing) models.[14] The perspective developed above might, I suspect, encourage us to approach some of these issues in a slightly different way. For the Fodorian view is at least intuitively linked to views of language as essentially a communicative tool. This is because the Fodorian sees linguistic formulations as reasonably faithful reflections of both the contents and the structural forms of internal representations. The view I have been developing is quite different insofar as it depicts the linguistic formulations as importing genuine novelties onto our cognitive horizons. The linguistic formulations are seen as novel both in content and in structure. There is content-novelty insofar as linguistic expression makes new thoughts available by effectively freezing other thoughts as types of static object[15] (images can do this too, but they are not so easily traded in public exchange). And there is structural novelty insofar as the value of the linguistic formulations (especially in written text) partly consists, we saw, in their amenability to a variety of operations and transformations that do not come naturally to the biological brain working in non-linguistic mode. Such novelties, I contend, are not at all predicted by the image of a pre-existing inner code whose basic features and properties are merely recapitulated in our public language formulations. By contrast, they are exactly what would be expected if the public code is not a handy recapitulation of our non-linguistic resources so much as a powerful complement to them.[16]

Such a view suggests a certain gloss on the history and origin of the Fodorian image itself. For perhaps one mistake of classical Artificial Intelligence (upon which the image purports to be based) lay in its mistaking the properties of the linguistically augmented and environmentally extended cognitive agent (the person plus a variety of external representations, especially texts) for the cognitive profile of the basic biological brain. Thus the neat classical separation of data and process, and of static symbol structures and CPU, may have reflected nothing so much as the gross separation between the biological agent and an external scaffolding of ideas persisting on paper, in filing cabinets and in electronic media.

35

This notion of the biological agent leads nicely to the second issue I wish to mention. It concerns the question of where the mind ends and the rest of the world begins. Otherwise put, the question concerns how to conceive and locate the boundary between an intelligent system and its world. For certain external (to the biological unit) props and aids may play such a deep role in determining the shape and flow of our thoughts as to invite depiction as part and parcel of the very mechanism of human reason. This depiction is most plausible in the case of the external props of written text and spoken words. For interactions with these external media are ubiquitous (in educated modern cultures), reliable and developmentally basic. Our biologic brains, after learning, expect the presence of text and speech as much as they expect to encounter weight, force, friction and gravity. Language for us is a constant, and as such can be safely relied upon as the backdrop against which on-line processes of neural computation take shape and develop. Just as a neural network controller for moving the arm to a target in space must define its commands to factor in the spring of muscles and the effects of gravity, so the processes of on-board reason may come to factor in the potential contributions of textual off-loading and re-organisation, and vocal exchange. The overall cognitive competencies which we identify as mind and intellect may thus be more like ship navigation than capacities of the bare biological brain. Ship navigation (see Hutchins, 1995) is a global emergent from the well-orchestrated adaptation of an extended complex system (comprising individuals, instruments, and practices). Much of what we uncritically identify as our mental capacities may likewise, I suspect, turn out to be properties of the wider, extended systems of which human brains are just one (important) part. In constructing an academic paper, for example, it is common practice to deploy multiple annotated texts, sets of notes and files, plans, lists and more. The writing process often depends heavily on manipulations of these props — new notes are created, old ones juxtaposed, source materials are wheeled on and off of work surfaces, etc. In giving credit for the final product, however, we often marginalise the special contributions of these external manipulations, and speak as if the biological brain did all the work. No parallel temptation afflicts the person who uses a crane to lift large weights, or a motorised digger to plough trenches! In these cases, it is clear that the person uses additional tools whose capacities extend and complement those of the unaided labourer. The relative invisibility of the special cognitive roles of text and words are a reflection, I think, of their ubiquity and ease of use: a reflection, indeed, of our tendency to think of these operations as proper to the biological agent rather than (like the crane) as technological additions. Perhaps the truth lies midway — the use of spoken words may be as biologically proper, to the human agent, as the use of webs is to the spider.[17] And the use of written text may thus straddle the intuitive divide between the web (biologically proper) and the crane (a true artefact).

The point, in any case, is that use of words and texts may usefully be seen as computationally complementary to the more primitive and biologically basic kinds of pattern-completing abilities that characterize natural cognition. These complementary operations essentially involve the creation of self-standing structures (short-term ones, like spoken sentences, or long-term ones, like text) that can perform a variety of useful functions such as the sequencing and control of behaviour and the freezing of thoughts and ideas into objects for further attention and analysis. The availability of these functions extends the bound of human cognition as surely as the provision of a new board extends the bounds of a personal computer. In particular, it is our capacity to create and operate upon external representations that allows us to use manipulations of the physical environment as integral parts of so many of our problem-solving routines. In thus reaching out to the world we blunt the dividing line between the intelligent system and the world. We create wider computational webs whose understanding and analysis may require us to apply the tools and concepts of cognitive science to larger, hybrid entities comprising brains, bodies and a variety of external structures, traces and processes.

To endorse a notion of computational processes as criss-crossing brain, body and world is not yet to endorse a parallel notion of cognitive or mental processes. Perhaps cognition is all in the head, but computation spreads liberally out into the world. My own inclinations are less conservative. I suspect that our intuitive notions of mind and cognition actually do pick out these larger extended systems and that as a result the biological brain is only one component of the intelligent system we call the mind.[18] But I will settle for a weaker conclusion — one that merely implicates our linguistic capacities in some highly productive transformations of our overall computational powers. This power of computational transformation constitutes a neglected virtue of linguistic practice. It reveals language as the ultimate upgrade: so ubiquitous it is almost invisible; so intimate, it is not clear whether it is a kind of tool or an added dimension of the user. But whatever the boundaries, we confront a complex coalition in which the basic biological brain is fantastically empowered by some of its strangest and most recent creations: words in the air, symbols on the printed page.

Special thanks to Daniel Dennett, both for his great encouragement and for his own inspirational work on the theme of language as a cognition-enhancing tool. Thanks too to Jim Wertsch, Roger Thompson, Peter Carruthers, Keith Frankish, Barry Smith, Chris Thornton, and Charles Fernyhough for ideas, comments and criticisms. Finally, I would like to thank both Peter Carruthers and the Hang Seng Centre for Cognitive Science at the University of Sheffield for allowing me to participate in the wonderful and thought-provoking series of meetings that culminated in the 1996 conference on Language and Thought.

Notes

1. The point here is not that without linguistic instruction such learning is impossible. That, as a referee usefully pointed out, is very implausible. Rather, it is that a child whose own observations and practice leave her currently unable to perform the task may often succeed with the benefit of a few well-chosen words of advice from an adult. The child may later rehearse the adult's words as a guide so as to succeed on her own.
2. This talk of language as a medium (or sometimes as a vehicle) of thought is meant to capture the distinction between the proposition, content, or message expressed and the code, or type of code, used to express it. One some views, there is a kind of intermingling of code and message such that it is false to imagine that we might first entertain the thought and only subsequently render it 'in' the code. On other views the required independence exists even if the actual properties of the code, or type of code, then make a large difference to the ways in which the content can be manipulated and exploited. Both options allow a 'supra-

communicative' dimension to linguistic ability. But they conceive the content/vehicle relation in different ways. (Thanks to an anonymous referee for pointing out the need for further clarification at this point.)

3. A major focus of both Carruthers' and Dennett's treatments is the relation between language and consciousness. I will not discuss these issues here, save to say that my sympathies lie more with Churchland (1995, chapter 10), who depicts basic consciousness as the common property of humans and many non-linguistic animals. Language fantastically augments the power of human cognition. But it does not, I believe, bring into being the basic apprehensions of pleasure, pain and the sensory world in which the true mystery of consciousness inheres.

4. Carruthers' position, unlike Whorf's, is thus compatible with both a realist conception of the mental and a fair degree of linguistic nativism.

5. A quick sampling of this data includes: the developmental lock-step of cognitive and linguistic abilities, the difficulties which language-deficient humans have with certain kinds of temporal discourse and the deficits of abstract thought found in global aphasics. See Carruthers (1996a) esp. pp. 267–8.

6. Indeed, Dennett suggests (personal communication) that his view is rather that exposure to language leads to a variety of relatively superficial changes at the neural/computational level, but that these changes nonetheless amount to something close to the inner implementation of a system of moveable symbols. The sense in which we may come to implement a classical virtual machine is thus stronger than any mere input-output level similarity, yet weaker than the kind of fine-grained simulation of an alternative computational architecturre found in, e.g., Touretsky's connectionist implementation of a production system.

7. Marr (1982) pp. 32–3.

8. A particularly stunning example is the large Mangrove forest extending north from Key West, Florida to the Everglades region known as Ten Thousand Islands. The black Mangroves of this region can reach heights of 80 feet — see Landi (1982) pp. 361–3.

9. Two very recent treatments which emphasize these themes have been brought to my attention. Jean-Pierre Changeux (a neuroscientist and molecular biologist) and Alain Connes (a mathematician) suggest that self-evaluation is the mark of true intelligence — see Changeux and Connes (1995). Derek Bickerton (a linguist) celebrates 'off-line thinking' and notes that no other species seems to isolate problems in their own performance and take pointed action to rectify them — see Bickerton (1995).

10. The modality neutral dimensions of public language are stressed by Karmiloff-Smith in her closely related work on representational re-description — see note 11 below. The relative context — independence of the signs and symbols of public language is discussed in Kirsh (1991) and Clark (1993), chapter 6.

11. The idea that advanced cognition involves repeated processes in which achieved knowledge and representation is redescribed in new formats (which support new kinds of cognitive operation and access) is pursued in much more detail in Karmiloff-Smith 1992; Clark 1993; Clark and Karmiloff-Smith 1994; and Dennett 1994. The original hypothesis of representational redescription was developed by Karmiloff-Smith (1979, 1986).

12. See e.g. Bechtel (1996) p. 125–31; Clark (1996b) pp. 120–5.

13. Dennett (1991) explores just such a intermediate territory. I discuss Churchland's downplaying of language in detail in Clark (1996b). For examples of such downplaying see P.M. Churchland (1989) p. 18; P.S. and P.M. Churchland (1996) pp. 265–70.

14. For a perfect introduction to the debate, see the various essays gathered in MacDonald and MacDonald (eds.)(1995).

15. See also Dennett's discussion of belief versus opinion, in Dennett (1987).

16. There is of course, a midway option: that public language later becomes a 'language of thought' and that Fodor's image is misguided only in its claim that all thoughts occur in Mentalese. For discussion, see Carruthers (1996a).

17. See Dawkins' lovely (1982) book, *The Extended Phenotype* (Freeman) for an especially biologically astute treatment of this kind of case.

18. See Clark (1996a, chapter 10); Clark and Chalmers (1995).

Rules of Language

STEVEN PINKER

Language and cognition have been explained as the products of a homogeneous associative memory structure or alternatively, of a set of genetically determined computational modules in which rules manipulate symbolic representations. Intensive study of one phenomenon of English grammar and how it is processed and acquired suggests that both theories are partly right. Regular verbs (*walk-walked*) are computed by a suffixation rule in a neural system for grammatical processing; irregular verbs (*run-ran*) are retrieved from an associative memory.

E VERY NORMAL HUMAN CAN CONVEY AND RECEIVE AN unlimited number of discrete messages through a highly structured stream of sound or, in the case of signed languages, manual gestures. This remarkable piece of natural engineering depends upon a complex code or grammar implemented in the brain that is deployed without conscious effort and that develops, without explicit training, by the age of four. Explaining this talent is an important goal of the human sciences.

Theories of language and other cognitive processes generally fall

The author is in the Department of Brain and Cognitive Sciences, Massachusetts Institute of Technology, Cambridge, MA 02139.

into two classes. Associationism describes the brain as a homogeneous network of interconnected units modified by a learning mechanism that records correlations among frequently co-occurring input patterns (*1*). Rule-and-representation theories describe the brain as a computational device in which rules and principles operate on symbolic data structures (*2, 3*). Some rule theories further propose that the brain is divided into modular computational systems that have an organization that is largely specified genetically, one of the systems being language (*3, 4*).

During the last 35 years, there has been an unprecedented empirical study of human language structure, acquisition, use, and breakdown, allowing these centuries-old proposals to be refined and tested. I will illustrate how intensive multidisciplinary study of one linguistic phenomenon shows that both associationism and rule theories are partly correct, but about different components of the language system.

Modules of Language

A grammar defines a mapping between sounds and meanings, but the mapping is not done in a single step but through a chain of intermediate data structures, each governed by a subsystem. Morphology is the subsystem that computes the forms of words. I focus on a single process of morphology: English past tense inflection, in which the physical shape of the verb varies to encode the relative time of occurrence of the referent event and the speech act. Regular past tenses marking (for example, *walk-walked*) is a rulelike process resulting in addition of the suffix *-d*. In addition there are about 180 irregular verbs that mark the past tense in other ways (for example, *hit-hit*, *come-came*, *feel-felt*).

Past tense inflection is an isolable subsystem in which grammatical mechanisms can be studied in detail, without complex interactions with the rest of language. It is computed independently of syntax, the subsystem that defines the form of phrases and sentences: The syntax of English forces its speakers to mark tense in every sentence, but no aspect of syntax works differently with regular and irregular verbs. Past tense marking is also insensitive to lexical semantics (*5, 6*): the regular-irregular distinction does not correlate with any feature of verb meaning. For example, *hit-hit*, *strike-struck*, and *slap-slapped* have similar meanings, but three different past tense forms; *stand-stood*, *stand me up–stood me up*, and *understand-understood*, have unrelated meanings but identical past tense forms. Past marking is also independent of phonology, which determines the possible sound sequences in a language: the three pronunciations of the regular suffix (in *ripped*, *ribbed*, and *ridded*) represent not three independent processes but a single suffix *-d* modified to conform with general laws of English sound patterning (*5*).

Rulelike Processes in Language

English inflection can illustrate the major kinds of theories used to explain linguistic processes. Traditional grammar offers the following first approximation: Regular inflection, being fully predictable, is computed by a rule that concatenates the affix *-d* to the verb stem. This allows a speaker to inflect an unlimited number of new verbs, an ability seen both in adults, who easily create past forms for neologisms like *faxed*, and in preschoolers, who, given a novel verb like *to rick* in experiments, freely produced *ricked* (*7*). In contrast, irregular verb forms are unpredictable: compare *sit-sat* and *hit-hit*, *sing-sang* and *string-strung*, *feel-felt* and *tell-told*. Therefore they must be individually memorized. Retrieval of an irregular form from memory ordinarily blocks application of the regular rule, although in children retrieval occasionally fails, yielding "overregularization" errors like *breaked* (*8, 9, 10*).

The rule-rote theory, although appealingly straightforward, is inadequate. Rote memory, if thought of as a list of slots, is designed for the very rare verbs with unrelated past tense forms, like *be-was* and *go-went*. But for all other irregular verbs, the phonological content of the stem is largely preserved in the past form, as in *swing-swung* (*5, 11*). Moreover, a given irregular pattern such as a vowel change is typically seen in a family of phonetically similar items, such as *sing-sang*, *ring-rang*, *spring-sprang*, *shrink-shrank*, *swim-swam*, or *grow-grew*, *blow-blew*, *throw-threw*, and *fly-flew* (*5, 9, 11*). The rote theory cannot explain why verbs with irregular past forms come in similarity families, rather than belonging to arbitrary lists. Finally, irregular pairs are psychologically not a closed set, but their patterns can sometimes be extended to new forms on the basis of similarity to existing forms. All children occasionally use forms such as *bring-brang* and *bite-bote* (*5, 9*). A few irregular past forms have entered the language historically under the influence of existing forms. *Quit*, *cost*, *catch* are from French, and *fling*, *sling*, *stick* have joined irregular clusters in the last few hundred years (*12*); such effects are obvious when dialects are compared [for example, *help-holp*, *rise-riz*, *drag-drug*, *climb-clome* (*13*)]. Such analogizing can be demonstrated in the laboratory: faced with inflecting nonsense verbs like *spling*, many adults produce *splung* (*6, 7, 14, 15*).

The partial systematicity of irregular verbs has been handled in opposite ways by modern rule and associationist theories. One version of the theory of Generative Phonology (*11*) posits rules for irregular verbs (for example, change *i* to *a*) as well as for regular ones. The theory is designed to explain the similarity between verb stems and their past tense forms: if the rule just changes a specified segment, the rest of the stem comes through in the output untouched, by default, just as in the fully regular case. But the rule theory does not address the similarity among different verbs in the input set and people's tendency to generalize irregular patterns. If an irregular rule is restricted to apply to a list of words, the similarity among the words in the list is unexplained. But if a common pattern shared by the words is identified and the rule is restricted to apply to all and only the verbs displaying that pattern (for example, change *i* to *a* when it appears after an consonant cluster and precedes *ng*), the rule fails because the similarity to be accounted for is one of family resemblance rather than necessary or sufficient conditions (*5, 9, 14, 18*): such a rule, while successfully applying to *spring*, *shrink*, *drink*, would incorrectly apply to *bring-brought* and *fling-flung* and would fail to apply to *begin-began* and *swim-swam*, where it should apply.

Associationist theories also propose that regular and irregular patterns are computed by a single mechanism, but here the mechanism is an associative memory. A formal implementation in neural net terms is the "connectionist" model of Rumelhart and McClelland (*16*), which consists of an array of input units, an array of output units, and a matrix of modifiable weighted links between every input and every output. None of the elements or links corresponds exactly to a word or rule. The stem is represented by turning on a subset of input nodes, each corresponding to a sound pattern in the stem. This sends a signal across each of the links to the output nodes, which represent the sounds of the past tense form. Each output node sums its incoming signals and turns on if the sum exceeds a threshold; the output form is the word most compatible with the set of active output nodes. During the learning phase, the past tense computed by the network is juxtaposed with the correct version provided by a "teacher," and the strengths of the links and thresholds are adjusted so as to reduce the difference. By recording and superimposing associations between stem sounds and past sounds, the model improves its performance and can generalize to new forms to the extent that their sounds overlap with old ones. This process is qualitatively the same for regular and irregular verbs: *stopped* is produced because *op* units were linked to output *opped* units by previous verbs; *clung* is produced because *ing* was linked to *ung*. As a result such models can imitate people's analogizing of irregular patterns to new forms.

The models, however, are inadequate in other ways (*5, 17*). The precise patterns of inflectional mappings in the world's languages are unaccounted for: the network can learn input-output mappings found in no human language, such as mirror-reversing the order of segments, and cannot learn mappings that are common, such as reduplicating the stem. The actual outputs are often unsystematic blends such as *mail-membled* and *tour-tourder*. Lacking a representation of words as lexical entries, distinct from their phonological or semantic content, the model cannot explain how languages can contain semantically unrelated homophones with different past tense forms such as *lie-lied* (prevaricate) and *lie-lay* (recline), *ring-rang* and *wring-wrung*, *meet-met* and *mete-meted*.

These problems call for a theory of language with both a computational component, containing specific kinds of rules and representations, and an associative memory system, with certain properties of connectionist models (*5, 6, 10*). In such a theory, regular past tense forms are computed by a rule that concatenates an affix with a variable standing for the stem. Irregulars are memorized pairs of words, but the linkages between the pair members are stored in an associative memory structure fostering some generalization by analogy (*9, 14, 18*): although *string* and *strung* are represented as

41

separate, linked words, the mental representation of the pair over-laps in part with similar forms like *sling* and *bring*, so that the learning of *slung* is easier and extensions like *brung* can occur as the result of noise or decay in the parts of the representation that code the identity of the lexical entry.

Because it categorically distinguishes regular from irregular forms, the rule-association hybrid predicts that the two processes should be dissociable from virtually every point of view. With respect to the psychology of language use, irregular forms, as memorized items, should be strongly affected by properties of associative memory such as frequency and similarity, whereas regular forms should not. With respect to language structure, irregular forms, as memory-listed words, should be available as the input to other word-formation processes, whereas regular forms, being the final outputs of such processes, should not. With respect to implementation in the brain, because regular and irregular verbs are subserved by different mechanisms, it should be possible to find one system impaired while the other is spared. The predictions can be tested with methods ranging from reaction time experiments to the grammatical analysis of languages to the study of child development to the investigation of brain damage and genetic deficits.

Language Use and Associative Laws

Frequency. If irregular verbs are memorized items, they should be better remembered the more they are encountered. Indeed, children make errors like *breaked* more often for verbs their parents use in the past tense forms less frequently (*9, 10, 19*). To adults, low-frequency irregular past tense forms like *smote, bade, slew,* and *strode* sound odd or stilted and often coexist with regularized counterparts such as *slayed* and *strided* (*5, 18, 20*). As these psychological effects accumulate over generations, they shape the language. Old English had many more irregular verbs than Modern English, such as *abide-abode, chide-chid, gild-gilt*; the ones used with lower frequencies have become regular over the centuries (*18*). Most surviving irregular verbs are used at high frequencies, and the 13 most frequent verbs in English—*be, have, do, say, make, go, take, come, see, get, know, give, find*—are all irregular (*21*).

Although any theory positing a frequency-sensitive memory can account for frequency effects on irregular verbs [with inverse effects on their corresponding regularized versions (*20*)], the rule-associative-memory hybrid model predicts that regular inflection is different. If regular past tense forms can be computed on-line by concatenation of symbols for the stem and affix, they do not require prior storage of a past tense entry and thus need not be harder or stranger for low-frequency verbs than higher ones (*22*).

Judgments by native English speakers of the naturalness of word forms bear this prediction out. Unlike irregular verbs, novel or low-frequency regular verbs, although they may sound unfamiliar in themselves, do not accrue any increment of oddness or uncertainty when put in the past tense: *infarcted* is as natural a past tense form of *infarct* as *walked* is of *walk* (*5*). The contrast can be seen clearly in idioms and clichés, because they can contain a verb that is not unfamiliar itself but that appears in the idiom exclusively in the present or infinitive form. Irregular verbs in such idioms can sound strange when put in the past tense: Compare *You'll excuse me if I forgo the pleasure of reading your paper before it's published* with *Last night I forwent the pleasure of reading student papers*, or *I don't know how she can bear the guy* with *I don't know how she bore the guy*. In contrast, regular verbs in nonpast idioms do not sound worse when put in the past: compare *She doesn't suffer fools gladly* with *None of them ever suffered fools gladly*. Similarly, some regular verbs like *afford* and *cope* usually appear with *can't*, which requires the stem form, and hence

have common stems but very low-frequency past tense forms (*21*). But the uncommon *I don't know how he afforded it (coped)* does not sound worse than *He can't afford it (cope)*.

These effects can be demonstrated in quantitative studies (*20*): Subjects' ratings of regular past tense forms of different verbs correlate significantly with their ratings of the corresponding stems ($r = 0.62$) but not with the frequency of the past form (-0.14, partialing out rating). In contrast, ratings of irregular past tense forms correlate less strongly with their stem ratings (0.32), and significantly with past frequency (0.29, partialing out stem rating).

Experiments on how people produce and comprehend inflected forms in real time confirm this difference. When subjects see verb stems on a screen and must utter the past form as quickly as possible, they take significantly less time (16- to 29-msec difference) for irregular verbs with high past frequencies than irregular verbs with low past frequencies (stem frequencies equated), but show no such difference for regular verbs (<2-msec difference) (*23*). When recognizing words, people are aided by having seen the word previously on an earlier trial in the experiment; their mental representation of the word has been "primed" by the first presentation. Presenting a regular past tense form speeds up subsequent recognition of the stem no less than presenting the stem itself (181- versus 166-msec reduction), suggesting that people store and prime only the stem and analyze a regular inflected form as a stem plus a suffix. In contrast, prior presentation of an irregular form is significantly less effective at priming its stem than presentation of the stem itself (39- versus 99-msec reduction), suggesting that the two are stored as separate but linked items (*24*).

Similarity. Irregular verbs fall into families with similar stems and similar past tense forms, partly because the associative nature of memory makes it easier to memorize verbs in such families. Indeed, children make fewer overregularization errors for verbs that fall into families with more numerous and higher frequency members (*5, 8–10, 25*). As mentioned above, speakers occasionally extend irregular patterns to verbs that are highly similar to irregular families (*brang*), and such extensions are seen in dialects (*13*). A continuous effect of similarity has been measured experimentally: subjects frequently (44%) convert *spling* to *splung* (based on *string, sling,* et cetera), less often (24%) convert *shink* to *shunk*, and rarely (7%) convert *sid* to *sud* (*14*).

The rule-associative-memory theory predicts that the ability to generate regular past tense forms should not depend on similarity to existing regular verbs: The regular rule applies as a default, treating all nonirregular stems as equally valid instantiations of the mental symbol "verb." Within English vocabulary, we find that a regular verb can have any past pattern, rather than falling into similarity clusters that complement the irregulars (*5*): for example, *need-needed* coexists with *bleed-bled* and *feed-fed*, *blink-blinked* with *shrink-shrank* and *drink-drank*. Regular-irregular homophones such as *lie-lay;lie-lied, meet-met;mete-meted,* and *hang-hung;hang-hanged* are the clearest examples. Moreover verbs with highly unusual sounds are easily provided with regular pasts. Although no English verb ends in *-ev* or a neutral vowel (*21*), novel verbs with these patterns are readily inflectable as natural past tense forms, such as *Yeltsin out-Gorbachev'ed Gorbachev* or *We rhumba'd all night*. Children are no more likely to overregularize an irregular verb if it resembles a family of similar regular verbs than if it is dissimilar from regulars, suggesting that regulars, unlike irregulars, do not form attracting clusters in memory (*10, 25*). Adults, when provided with novel verbs, do not rate regular past forms of unusual sounds like *ploamphed* as any worse, relative to the stem, than familiar sounds like *plipped* (similar to *clip, flip, slip,* et cetera), unlike their ratings for irregulars (*15, 26*). In contrast, in associationist models both irregular and regular generalizations tend to be sensitive to similarity. For example the Rumelhart-McClelland model could not produce any output for many novel regular verbs that did not resemble other regulars in the training set (5, 15, 17).

Organization of Grammatical Processes

Grammars divide into fairly autonomous submodules in which blocks of rules produce outputs that serve (or cannot serve) as the input for other blocks of rules. Linguistic research suggests an information flow from lexicon to derivational morphology (complex word-formation) to regular inflection, with regular and irregular processes encapsulated within different subcomponents (27, 28). If irregular past tense forms are stored in memory as entries in the mental lexicon, then like other stored words they should be the input to rules of complex word formation. If regular past tense forms are computed from words by a rule acting as a default, they should be formed from the outputs of complex word formation rules. Two phenomena illustrate this organization.

A potent demonstration of the earlier point that regular processes can apply to any sound whatsoever, no matter how tightly associated with an irregular pattern, is "regularization-through-derivation": verbs intuitively perceived as derived from nouns or adjectives are always regular, even if similar or identical to an irregular verb. Thus one says *grandstanded*, not *grandstood; flied out* in baseball [from a fly (ball)], not *flew out; high-sticked* in hockey, not *high-stuck* (5, 6, 28). The explanation is that irregularity consists of a linkage between two word roots, the atomic sound-meaning pairings stored in the mental lexicon; it is not a link between two words or sound patterns directly. *High-stuck* sounds silly because the verb is tacitly perceived as being based on the noun root (*hockey*) *stick*, and noun roots cannot be listed in the lexicon as having any past tense form (the past tense of a noun makes no sense semantically), let alone an irregular one. Because its root is not the verb *stick* there is no data pathway by which *stuck* can be made available; to obtain a past tense form, the speaker must apply the regular rule, which serves as the default. Subjects presented with novel irregular-sounding verbs (for example, *to line-drive*) strongly prefer the regular past tense form (*line-drived*) if it is understood as being based on a noun ("to hit a line drive"), but not in a control condition for unfamiliarity where the items were based on existing irregular verbs ("to drive along a line"); here the usual irregular form is preferred (6).

The effect, moreover, occurs in experiments testing subjects with no college education (6) and in preschool children (29). This is consistent with the fact that many of these lawful forms entered the language from vernacular speech and were opposed by language mavens and guardians of "proper" style (6, 13). "Rules of grammar" in the psycholinguists' sense, and their organization into components, are inherent to the computational systems found in all humans, not just those with access to explicit schooling or stylistic injunctions. These injunctions, involving a very different sense of "rule" as something that ought to be followed, usually pertain to minor differences between standard written and nonstandard spoken dialects.

A related effect occurs in lexical compounds, which sound natural when they contain irregular noun plurals, but not regular noun plurals: Compare *mice-infested* with *rats-infested*, *teethmarks* with *clawsmarks*, *men-bashing* with *guys-bashing* (28). Assume that this compounding rule is fed by stored words. Irregulars are stored words, so they can feed compounding; regulars are computed at the output end of the morphology system, not stored at the input end, so they do not appear inside lexical compounds. This constraint has been documented experimentally in 3- to 5-year-old children (30):

when children who knew the word *mice* were asked for a word for a "monster who eats mice," they responded with *mice-eater* 90% of the time; but when children who knew *rats* were asked for a word for "monster who eats rats," they responded *rats-eater* only 2% of the time. The children could not have learned the constraint by recording whether adults use irregular versus regular plurals inside compounds. Adults do not use such compounds often enough for most children to have heard them: the frequency of English compounds containing any kind of plural is indistinguishable from zero (21, 30). Rather, the constraint may be a consequence of the inherent organization of the children's grammatical systems.

Developmental and Neurological Dissociations

If regular and irregular patterns are computed in different subsystems, they should dissociate in special populations. Individuals with undeveloped or damaged grammatical systems and intact lexical memory should be unable to compute regular forms but should be able to handle irregulars. Conversely, individuals with intact grammatical systems and atypical lexical retrieval should handle regulars properly but be prone to overregularizing irregulars. Such double dissociations, most clearly demonstrated in detailed case studies, are an important source of evidence for the existence of separate neural subsystems. Preliminary evidence suggests that regular and irregular inflection may show such dissociations.

Children. Most of the grammatical structure of English develops rapidly in the third year of life (31). One conspicuous development is the appearance of overregularizations like *comed*. Such errors constitute a worsening of past marking with time; for months beforehand, all overtly marked irregular past forms are correct (10). The phenomenon is not due to the child becoming temporarily overwhelmed by the regular pattern because of an influx of regular verbs, as connectionist theories (16) predict (5, 10, 32). Instead it accompanies the appearance of the regular tense marking process itself: overregularizations appear when the child ceases using bare stems like *walk* to refer to past events (8, 10). Say memorization of verb forms from parental speech, including irregulars, can take place as soon as words of any kind can be learned. But deployment of the rule system must await the abstraction of the English rule from a set of word pairs juxtaposed as nonpast and past versions of the same verb. The young child could possess memorized irregulars, produced probabilistically but without overt error, but no rule; the older child, possessing the rule as well, would apply it obligatorily in past tense sentences whenever he failed to retrieve the irregular, resulting in occasional errors.

Aphasics. A syndrome sometimes called agrammatic aphasia can occur after extensive damage to Broca's area and nearby structures in the left cerebral hemisphere. Labored speech, absence of inflections and other grammatical words, and difficulty comprehending grammatical distinctions are frequent symptoms. Agrammatics have trouble reading aloud regular inflected forms: *smiled* is pronounced as *smile, wanted* as *wanting*. Nonregular plural and past forms are read with much greater accuracy, controlling for frequency and pronounceability (33). This is predicted if agrammatism results from damage to neural circuitry that executes rules of grammar, including the regular rule necessary for analyzing regularly inflected stimuli, but leaves the lexicon relatively undamaged, including stored irregulars which can be directly matched against the irregular stimuli.

Specific language impairment (SLI). SLI refers to a syndrome of language deficits not attributable to auditory, cognitive, or social problems. The syndrome usually includes delayed onset of language, articulation difficulties in childhood, and problems in controlling grammatical features such as tense, number, gender, case, and person. One form of SLI may especially impair aspects of the regular inflectional process (34). Natural speech includes errors like "We're go take a bus; I play musics; One machine clean all the two arena." In experiments, the patients have difficulty converting present sentences to past (32% for SLI; 78% for sibling controls.) The difficulty is more pronounced for regular verbs than irregulars. Regular past forms are virtually absent from the children's spontaneous speech and writing, although irregulars often appear. In the writing samples of two children examined quantitatively, 85% of irregular pasts but 30% of regular pasts were correctly supplied. The first written regular past tense forms are for verbs with past stem frequencies higher than their stem frequencies; subsequent ones are acquired one at a time in response to teacher training, with little transfer to nontrained verbs. Adults' performance improves and their speech begins to sound normal but they continue to have difficulty inflecting nonsense forms like *zoop* (47% for SLI; 83% for controls). It appears as if their ability to apply inflectional rules is impaired relative to their ability to memorize words: irregular forms are acquired relatively normally, enjoying their advantage of high frequencies; regular forms are memorized as if they were irregular.

SLI appears to have an inherited component. Language impairments have been found in 3% of first-degree family members of normal probands but 23% of language-impaired probands (35). The impairment has been found to be 80% concordant in monozygotic twins and 35% concordant in dizygotic twins (36). One case study (34) investigated a three-generation, 30-member family, 16 of whom had SLI; the syndrome followed the pattern of a dominant, fully penetrant autosomal gene. This constitutes evidence that some aspects of use of grammar have a genetic basis.

Williams syndrome. Williams syndrome (WS), associated with a defective gene expressed in the central nervous system involved in calcium metabolism, causes an unusual kind of mental retardation (37). Although their Intelligence Quotient is measured at around 50, older children and adolescents with WS are described as hyperlinguistic with selective sparing of syntax, and grammatical abilities are close to normal in controlled testing (37). This is one of several kinds of dissociation in which language is preserved despite severe cognitive impairments, suggesting that the language system is autonomous of many other kinds of cognitive processing.

WS children retrieve words in a deviant fashion (37). When normal or other retarded children are asked to name some animals, they say *dog, cat, pig*; WS children offer *unicorn, tyrandon, yak, ibex*. Normal children speak of *pouring water*; WS children speak of *evacuating a glass*. According to the rule-associative-memory hybrid theory, preserved grammatical abilities and deviant retrieval of high-frequency words are preconditions for overregularization. Indeed, some WS children overregularize at high rates (16%), one of their few noticeable grammatical errors (37, 39).

Conclusion

For hundreds of years, the mind has been portrayed as a homogeneous system whose complexity comes from the complexity of environmental correlations as recorded by a general-purpose learning mechanism. Modern research on language renders such a view increasingly implausible. Although there is evidence that the memory system used in language acquisition and processing has some of the properties of an associative network, these properties do not exhaust the computational abilities of the brain. Focusing on a single rule of grammar, we find evidence for a system that is modular, independent of real-world meaning, nonassociative (unaffected by frequency and similarity), sensitive to abstract formal distinctions (for example, root versus derived, noun versus verb), more sophis-

ticated than the kinds of "rules" that are explicitly taught, developing on a schedule not timed by environmental input, organized by principles that could not have been learned, possibly with a distinct neural substrate and genetic basis.

REFERENCES AND NOTES

1. D. Hume, *Inquiry Concerning Human Understanding* (Bobbs-Merril, Indianapolis, 1955); D. Hebb, *Organization of Behavior* (Wiley, New York, 1949); D. Rumelhart and J. McClelland, *Parallel Distributed Processing* (MIT Press, Cambridge, 1986).
2. G. Leibniz, *Philosophical Essays* (Hackett, Indianapolis, 1989); A. Newell and H. Simon, *Science* 134, 2011 (1961).
3. J. Fodor, *Modularity of Mind* (MIT Press, Cambridge, 1983).
4. N. Chomsky, *Rules and Representations* (Columbia Univ. Press, New York, 1980); E. Lenneberg, *Biological Foundations of Language* (Wiley, New York, 1967).
5. S. Pinker and A. Prince, *Cognition* 28, 73 (1988).
6. J. Kim, S. Pinker, A. Prince, S. Prasada, *Cognitive Science* 15, 173 (1991).
7. J. Berko, *Word* 14, 150 (1958).
8. S. Kuczaj, *J. Verb. Learn. Behav.* 16, 589 (1977).
9. J. Bybee and D. Slobin, *Language* 58, 265 (1982).
10. G. Marcus, M. Ullman, S. Pinker, M. Hollander, T. Rosen, F. Xu, *Ctr. Cog. Sci. Occ. Pap. 41* (Massachusetts Institute of Technology, Cambridge, 1990).
11. N. Chomsky and M. Halle, *Sound Pattern of English* (MIT Press, Cambridge, 1990).
12. O. Jespersen, *A Modern English Grammar on Historical Principles* (Allen and Unwin, London, 1961).
13. H. Mencken, *The American Language* (Knopf, New York, 1936).
14. J. Bybee and C. Moder, *Language* 59, 251 (1983).
15. S. Prasada and S. Pinker, unpublished data.
16. D. Rumelhart and J. McClelland, in *Parallel Distributed Processing*, J. McClelland and D. Rumelhart, Eds. (MIT Press, Cambridge, 1986), pp. 216–271.
17. J. Lachter and T. Bever, *Cognition* 28, 197 (1988). More sophisticated connectionist models of past tense formation employing a hidden layer of nodes have computational limitations similar to those of the Rumelhart-McClelland model (D. Egedi and R. Sproat, unpublished data).
18. J. Bybee, *Morphology* (Benjamins, Philadelphia, 1985).
19. In speech samples from 19 children containing 9684 irregular past tense forms (10), aggregate overregularization rate for 39 verbs correlated −0.37 with aggregate log frequency in parental speech. All correlations and differences noted herein are significant at $p = 0.05$ or less.
20. M. Ullman and S. Pinker, paper presented at the Spring Symposium of the AAAI, Stanford, 26 to 28 March 1991. Data represent mean ratings by 99 subjects of the naturalness of the past and stem forms of 142 irregular verbs and 59 regular verbs that did not rhyme with any irregular, each presented in a sentence in counterbalanced random order.
21. N. Francis and H. Kucera, *Frequency Analysis of English Usage* (Houghton Mifflin, Boston, 1982).
22. Such effects can also occur in certain connectionist models that lack distinct representations of words and superimpose associations between the phonological elements of stem and past forms. After such models are trained on many regular verbs, any new verb would activate previously trained phonological associations to the regular pattern and could yield a strong regular form; the absence of prior training on the verb itself would not necessarily hurt it. However, the existence of homophones with different past tense forms (*lie-lay* versus *lie-lied*) makes such models psychologically unrealistic; representations of individual words are called for, and they would engender word-particular frequency effects.
23. S. Prasada, S. Pinker, W. Snyder, paper presented at the 31st Annual Meeting of the Psychonomic Society, New Orleans, 16 to 18 November 1990. The effects obtained in three experiments, each showing 32 to 40 subjects the stem forms of verbs on a screen for 300 msec and measuring their vocal response time for the past tense form. Thirty to 48 irregular verbs and 30 to 48 regular verbs were shown, one at a time in random order; every verb had a counterpart with the same stem frequency but a different past tense frequency (21). In control experiments, 40 subjects generated third person singular forms of stems, read stems aloud, or read past tense forms aloud; the frequency difference among irregulars did not occur; this shows the effect is not due to inherent differences in access or articulation times of the verbs.
24. R. Stanners, J. Neiser, W. Hernon, R. Hall, *J. Verb Learn. Verb. Behav.* 18, 399 (1979); S. Kempley and J. Morton, *Br. J. Psychol.* 73, 441 (1982). The effect was not an artifact of differences in phonological or orthographic overlap between the members of regular and irregular pairs.
25. For 17 of 19 children studied in (10), the higher the frequencies of the other irregulars rhyming with an irregular, the lower its overregulation rate (mean correlation −0.07, significantly less than 0). For the corresponding calculation with regulars rhyming with an irregular, no consistency resulted and the mean correlation did not differ significantly from zero.
26. Twenty-four subjects rated 60 sentences containing novel verbs, presented either in stem form, a past form displaying an English irregular vowel change, or a past form containing the regular suffix. Each subject rated how well the word sounded with a 7-point scale; each verb was rated in each of the forms by different subjects. For novel verbs highly similar to an irregular family, the irregular past form was rated 0.8 points worse than the stem; for novel verbs dissimilar to the family, the irregular past form was rated 2.2 points worse. For novel verbs resembling a family of regular verbs, the regular past form was rated 0.4 points better than the stem; for novel verbs dissimilar to the family, the regular past form was rated 1.5 points

better. This interaction was replicated in two other experiments.

27. M. Aronoff, *Annu. Rev. Anthropol.* 12, 355 (1983); S. Anderson, in *Linguistics: The Cambridge Survey* (Cambridge Univ. Press, New York, 1988), vol. 1, pp. 146–191.
28. P. Kiparsky, in *The Structure of Phonological Representations*, H. van der Hulst and N. Smith, Eds. (Foris, Dordrecht, 1982).
29. J. Kim, G. Marcus, M. Hollander, S. Pinker, *Pap. Rep. Child Lang. Dev.*, in press.
30. P. Gordon, *Cognition* 21, 73 (1985). The effect is not an artifact of pronounceability, as children were willing to say *pants-eater* and *scissors-eater*, containing s-final nouns that are not regular plurals.
31. R. Brown, *A First Language* (Harvard Univ. Press, Cambridge, 1973).
32. The proportion of regular verb tokens in children's and parents' speech remains unchanged throughout childhood, because high frequency irregular verbs (*make, put, take*, et cetera) dominate conversation at any age. The proportion of regular verb types in children's vocabulary necessarily increases because irregular verbs are a small fraction of English vocabulary, but this growth does not correlate with overregularization errors (3, 8).
33. O. Marin, E. Saffran, M. Schwartz, *Ann. N.Y. Acad. Sci.* 280, 868 (1976). For example, regular *misers, clues, buds* were read by three agrammatic patients less accurately than phonologically matched plurals that are not regular because they lack a corresponding singular, like *trousers, news, suds* (45% versus 90%), even though a phonologically well-formed stem is available in both cases. In another study, when verbs matched for past and base frequencies and pronounceability were presented to an agrammatic patient, he read 56% of irregular past forms and 18% of regular past forms successfully (G. Hickok and S. Pinker, unpublished data).
34. M. Gopnik, *Nature* 344, 715, (1990); *Lang. Acq.* 1, 139 (1990); M. Gopnik and M. Crago, *Cognition*, in press.
35. J. Tomblin, *J. Speech Hear. Disord.* 54, 287 (1989); P. Tallal, R. Ross, S. Curtiss, *ibid.*, p. 167.
36. J. Tomblin, unpublished data.
37. U. Bellugi, A. Bihrle, T. Jernigan, D. Trauner, S. Doherty, *Am. J. Med. Genet. Suppl.* 6, 115 (1990).
38. S. Curtiss, in *The Exceptional Brain*, L. Obler and D. Fein, Eds. (Guilford, New York, 1988).
39. E. Klima and U. Bellugi, unpublished data.
40. I thank my collaborators A. Prince, G. Hickok, M. Hollander, J. Kim, G. Marcus, S. Prasada, A. Senghas, and M. Ullman and thank T. Bever, N. Block, N. Etcoff, and especially A. Prince for comments. Supported by NIH grant HD18381.

45

Can Machines Think?

DANIEL C. DENNETT

Can machines think? This has been a conundrum for philosophers for years, but in their fascination with the pure conceptual issues they have for the most part overlooked the real social importance of the answer. It is of more than academic importance that we learn to think clearly about the actual cognitive powers of computers, for they are now being introduced into a variety of sensitive social roles, where their powers will be put to the ultimate test: In a wide variety of areas, we are on the verge of making ourselves dependent upon their cognitive powers. The cost of overestimating them could be enormous.

One of the principal inventors of the computer was the great British mathematician Alan Turing. It was he who first figured out, in highly abstract terms, how to design a programmable computing device—what we now call a universal Turing machine. All programmable computers in use today are in essence Turing machines. Over thirty years ago, at the dawn of the computer age, Turing began a classic article, "Computing Machinery and Intelligence" with the words: "I propose to consider the question, 'Can machines think?' "—but then went on to say that this was a bad question, a question that leads only to sterile debate and haggling over definitions, a question, as he put it, "too meaningless to deserve discussion."[1] In its place he substituted what he took to be a much better question, a question that would be crisply answerable and intuitively satisfying—in every way an acceptable substitute for the philosophic puzzler with which he began.

First he described a parlor game of sorts, the "imitation game," to be played by a man, a woman, and a judge (of either gender). The man and woman are hidden from the judge's view but able to communicate with the judge by teletype; the judge's task is to guess, after a period of questioning each contestant, which interlocutor is the man and which the woman. The man tries to convince the judge he is the woman (and the woman tries to convince the judge of the truth), and the man wins if the judge makes the wrong identification. A little reflection will convince you, I am sure, that, aside from lucky breaks, it would take a clever man to convince the judge that he was the woman—assuming the judge is clever too, of course.

Now suppose, Turing said, we replace the man or woman with a computer, and give the judge the task of determining which is the human being and which is the computer. Turing proposed that any computer that can regularly or often fool a discerning judge in this game would be intelligent—would be a computer that thinks—*beyond any reasonable doubt.* Now, it is important to realize that failing this test is not supposed to be a sign of lack of intelligence. Many intelligent people, after all, might not be willing or able to play the imitation game, and we should allow computers the same opportunity to decline to prove themselves. This is, then, a one-way test; failing it proves nothing.

Furthermore, Turing was not committing himself to the view (although it is easy to see how one might think he was) that to think is to think just like a human being—any more than he was committing himself to the view that for a man to think, he must think exactly like a woman. Men and women, and computers, may all have different ways of thinking. But surely, he thought, if one can think in one's own peculiar style well enough to imitate a thinking man or woman, one can think well, indeed. This imagined exercise has come to be known as the Turing test.

It is a sad irony that Turing's proposal has had exactly the opposite effect on the discussion of that which he intended. Turing didn't design the test as a useful tool in scientific psychology, a method of confirming or disconfirming scientific theories or evaluating particular models of mental function; he designed it to be nothing more than a philosophical conversation-stopper. He proposed—in the spirit of "Put up or shut up!"—a simple test for thinking that was *surely* strong enough to satisfy the sternest skeptic (or so he thought). He was saying, in effect, "Instead of arguing interminably about the ultimate nature and essence of thinking, why don't we all agree that whatever that nature is, anything that could pass this test would surely have it; then we could turn to asking how or whether some machine could be designed and built that might pass the test fair and square." Alas, philosophers—amateur and professional—have instead taken Turing's proposal as the pretext for just the sort of definitional haggling and interminable arguing about imaginary counterexamples he was hoping to squelch.

This thirty-year preoccupation with the Turing test has been all the more regrettable because it has focused attention on the wrong issues. There are *real world* problems that are revealed by considering the strengths and weaknesses of the Turing test, but these have been concealed behind a smokescreen of misguided criticisms. A failure to think imaginatively about the test actually proposed by Turing has led many to underestimate its severity and to confuse it with much less interesting proposals.

So first I want to show that the Turing test, conceived as he conceived it, is (as he thought) plenty strong enough as a test of thinking. I defy anyone to improve upon it. But here is the point almost universally overlooked by the literature: There is a common *misapplication* of the sort of testing exhibited by the Turing test that often leads to drastic overestimation of the powers of actually existing computer systems. The follies of this familiar sort of thinking about computers can best be brought out by a reconsideration of the Turing test itself.

The insight underlying the Turing test is the same insight that inspires the new practice among symphony orchestras of conducting auditions with an opaque screen between the jury and the musician. What matters in a musician, obviously, is musical ability and only musical ability; such features as sex, hair length, skin color, and weight are strictly irrelevant. Since juries might be biased—even innocently and unawares—by these irrelevant features, they are carefully screened off so only the essential features, musicianship, can be examined. Turing recognized that people similarly might be biased in their judgments of intelligence by whether the contestant had soft skin, warm blood, facial features, hands and eyes—which are obviously not themselves essential components of intelligence—so he devised a screen that would let through only a sample of what really mattered: the capacity to understand, and think cleverly about, challenging problems. Perhaps he was inspired by Descartes, who in his *Discourse on Method* (1637) plausibly argued that there was no more demanding test of human mentality than the capacity to hold an intelligent conversation:

It is indeed conceivable that a machine could be so made that it would utter words, and even words appropriate to the presence of physical acts or objects which cause some change in its organs; as, for example, if it was touched in some spot that it would ask what you wanted to say to it; if in another, that it would cry that it was hurt, and so on for similar things. But it could never modify its phrases to reply to the sense of whatever was said in its presence, as even the most stupid men can do.[2]

This seemed obvious to Descartes in the seventeenth century, but of course the fanciest machines he knew were elaborate clockwork figures, not electronic computers. Today it is far from obvious that such machines are impossible, but Descartes's hunch that ordinary conversation would put as severe a strain on artificial intelligence as any other test was shared by Turing. Of course there is nothing sacred about the particular conversational game chosen by Turing for his test; it is just a cannily chosen test of more general intelligence. The assumption Turing was prepared to make was this: Nothing could possibly pass the Turing test by winning the imitation game without being able to perform indefinitely many other clearly intelligent actions. Let us call that assumption the quick-probe assumption. Turing realized, as anyone would, that there are hundreds and thousands of telling signs of intelligent thinking to be observed in our fellow creatures, and one could, if one wanted, compile a vast battery of different tests to assay the capacity for intelligent thought. But success on his chosen test, he thought, would be highly predictive of success on many other intuitively acceptable tests of intelligence. Remember, failure on the Turing test does not predict failure on those others, but success would surely predict success. His test was so severe, he thought, that nothing that could pass it fair and square would disappoint us in other quarters. Maybe it wouldn't do everything we hoped—maybe it wouldn't appreciate ballet, or understand quantum physics, or have a good plan for world peace, but we'd all see that it was surely one of the intelligent, thinking entities in the neighborhood.

Is this high opinion of the Turing test's severity misguided? Certainly many have thought so—but usually because they have not imagined the test in sufficient detail, and hence have underestimated it. Trying to forestall this skepticism, Turing imagined several lines of questioning that a judge might employ in this game —about writing poetry, or playing chess—that would be taxing indeed, but with thirty years' experience with the actual talents and foibles of computers behind us, perhaps we can add a few more tough lines of questioning.

Terry Winograd, a leader in artificial intelligence efforts to produce conversational ability in a computer, draws our attention to a pair of sentences.[3] They differ in only one word. The first sentence is this:

The committee denied the group a parade permit because they advocated violence.

Here's the second sentence:

The committee denied the group a parade permit because they feared violence.

The difference is just in the verb—*advocated* or *feared.* As Winograd points out, the pronoun *they* in each sentence is officially ambiguous. Both readings of the pronoun are always legal. Thus we can imagine a world in which governmental committees in charge of parade permits advocate violence in the streets and, for some strange reason, use this as their pretext for denying a parade permit. But the natural, reasonable, intelligent reading of the first sentence is that it's the group that advocated violence, and of the second, that it's the committee that feared the violence.

Now if sentences like this are embedded in a conversation, the computer must figure out which reading of the pronoun is meant, if it is to respond intelligently. But mere rules of grammar or vocabulary will not fix the right reading. What fixes the right reading for us is knowledge about the world, about politics, social circumstances, committees and their attitudes, groups that want to parade, how they tend to behave, and the like. One must know about the world, in short, to make sense of such a sentence.

In the jargon of artificial intelligence (AI), a conversational computer needs lots of *world knowledge* to do its job. But, it seems, if somehow it is endowed with that world knowledge on many topics, it should be able to do much more with that world knowledge than merely make sense of a conversation containing just that sentence. The only way, it appears, for a computer to disambiguate that sentence and keep up its end of a conversation that uses that sentence would be for it to have a much more general ability to respond intelligently to information about social and political circumstances, and many other topics. Thus, such sentences, by putting a demand on such abilities, are good quick probes. That is, they test for a wider competence.

People typically ignore the prospect of having the judge ask off-the-wall questions in the Turing test, and hence they underestimate the competence a computer would have to have to pass the test. But remember, the rules of the imitation game as Turing presented it permit the judge to ask any question that could be asked of a human being—no holds barred. Suppose then we give a contestant in the game this question:

An Irishman found a genie in a bottle who offered him two wishes. "First I'll have a pint of Guinness," said the Irishman, and when it appeared he took several long drinks from it and was delighted to see that the glass filled itself magically as he drank. "What about your second wish?" asked the genie. "Oh well," said the Irishman, "that's easy. I'll have another one of these!"

—Please explain this story to me, and tell me if there is anything funny or sad about it.

Now even a child could express, if not eloquently, the understanding that is required to get this joke. But think of how much one has to know and understand about human culture, to put it pompously, to be able to give any account of the point of this joke. I am not supposing that the computer would have to laugh at, or be amused by, the joke. But if it wants to win the imitation game—and that's the test, after all—it had better know enough in its own alien, humorless way about human psychology and culture to be able to pretend effectively that it was amused and explain why.

It may seem to you that we could devise a better test. Let's compare the Turing test with some other candidates.

Candidate 1: A computer is intelligent if it wins the World Chess Championship.

52

That's not a good test, as it turns out. Chess prowess has proven to be an isolatable talent. There are programs today that can play fine chess but can do nothing else. So the quick probe assumption is false for the test of playing winning chess.

Candidate 2: The computer is intelligent if it solves the Arab-Israeli conflict.

This is surely a more severe test than Turing's. But it has some defects: it is unrepeatable, if passed once; slow, no doubt; and it is not crisply clear what would count as passing it. Here's another prospect, then:

Candidate 3: A computer is intelligent if it succeeds in stealing the British crown jewels without the use of force or violence.

Now this is better. First, it could be repeated again and again, though of course each repeat test would presumably be harder— but this is a feature it shares with the Turing test. Second, the mark of success is clear—either you've got the jewels to show for your efforts or you don't. But it is expensive and slow, a socially dubious caper at best, and no doubt luck would play too great a role.

With ingenuity and effort one might be able to come up with other candidates that would equal the Turing test in severity, fairness, and efficiency, but I think these few examples should suffice to convince us that it would be hard to improve on Turing's original proposal.

But still, you may protest, something might pass the Turing test and still not be intelligent, not be a thinker. What does *might* mean here? If what you have in mind is that by cosmic accident, by a supernatural coincidence, a stupid person or a stupid computer *might* fool a clever judge repeatedly, well, yes, but so what? The same frivolous possibility "in principle" holds for any test whatever. A playful god, or evil demon, let us agree, could fool the world's scientific community about the presence of H_2O in the Pacific Ocean. But still, the tests they rely on to establish that there is H_2O in the Pacific Ocean are quite beyond reasonable criticism. If the Turing test for thinking is no worse than any well-established scientific test, we can set skepticism aside and go back to serious matters. Is there any more likelihood of a "false positive" result

53

on the Turing test than on, say, the tests currently used for the presence of iron in an ore sample?

This question is often obscured by a "move" that philosophers have sometimes made called operationalism. Turing and those who think well of his test are often accused of being operationalists. Operationalism is the tactic of *defining* the presence of some property, for instance, intelligence, as being established once and for all by the passing of some test. Let's illustrate this with a different example.

Suppose I offer the following test—we'll call it the Dennett test —for being a great city:

A great city is one in which, on a randomly chosen day, one can do all three of the following:
Hear a symphony orchestra
See a Rembrandt *and* a professional athletic contest
Eat *quenelles de brochet à la Nantua* for lunch

To make the operationalist move would be to declare that any city that passes the Dennett test is *by definition* a great city. What being a great city *amounts to* is just passing the Dennett test. Well then, if the Chamber of Commerce of Great Falls, Montana, wanted—and I can't imagine why—to get their hometown on my list of great cities, they could accomplish this by the relatively inexpensive route of hiring full time about ten basketball players, forty musicians, and a quick-order quenelle chef and renting a cheap Rembrandt from some museum. An idiotic operationalist would then be stuck admitting that Great Falls, Montana, was in fact a great city, since all he or she cares about in great cities is that they pass the Dennett test.

Sane operationalists (who for that very reason are perhaps not operationalists at all, since *operationalist* seems to be a dirty word) would cling confidently to their test, but only because they have what they consider to be very good reasons for thinking the odds against a false positive result, like the imagined Chamber of Commerce caper, are astronomical. I devised the Dennett test, of course, with the realization that no one would be both stupid and rich enough to go to such preposterous lengths to foil the test. In the actual world, wherever you find symphony orchestras, *quenelles*, Rembrandts, and professional sports, you also find daily newspa-

54

pers, parks, repertory theaters, libraries, fine architecture, and all the other things that go to make a city great. My test was simply devised to locate a *telling* sample that could not help but be representative of the rest of the city's treasures. I would cheerfully run the miniscule risk of having my bluff called. Obviously, the test items are not all that I care about in a city. In fact, some of them I don't care about at all. I just think they would be cheap and easy ways of assuring myself that the subtle things I do care about in cities are present. Similarly, I think it would be entirely unreasonable to suppose that Alan Turing had an inordinate fondness for party games, or put too high a value on party game prowess in his test. In both the Turing test and the Dennett test, a very unrisky gamble is being taken: the gamble that the quick-probe assumption is, in general, safe.

But two can play this game of playing the odds. Suppose some computer programmer happens to be, for whatever strange reason, dead set on tricking me into judging an entity to be a thinking, intelligent thing when it is not. Such a trickster could rely as well as I can on unlikelihood and take a few gambles. Thus, if the programmer can expect that it is not remotely likely that I, as the judge, will bring up the topic of children's birthday parties, or baseball, or moon rocks, then he or she can avoid the trouble of building world knowledge on those topics into the data base. Whereas if I do improbably raise these issues, the system will draw a blank and I will unmask the pretender easily. But given all the topics and words that I *might* raise, such a savings would no doubt be negligible. Turn the idea inside out, however, and the trickster will have a fighting chance. Suppose the programmer has reason to believe that I will ask *only* about children's birthday parties, or baseball, or moon rocks—all other topics being, for one reason or another, out of bounds. Not only does the task shrink dramatically, but there already exist systems or preliminary sketches of systems in artificial intelligence that can do a whiz-bang job of responding with apparent intelligence on just those specialized topics.

William Woods's LUNAR program, to take what is perhaps the best example, answers scientists' questions—posed in ordinary English—about moon rocks. In one test it answered correctly and appropriately something like 90 percent of the questions that geologists and other experts .thought of asking it about moon rocks. (In 12 percent of those correct responses there were trivial, correctable defects.) Of course, Woods's motive in creating LUNAR was not to trick unwary geologists into thinking they were conversing with an intelligent being. And if that had been his motive, his project would still be a long way from success.

For it is easy enough to unmask LUNAR without ever straying from the prescribed topic of moon rocks. Put LUNAR in one room, and a moon rocks specialist in another, and then ask them both their opinion of the social value of the moon-rocks–gathering expeditions, for instance. Or ask the contestants their opinion of the suitability of moon rocks as ashtrays, or whether people who have touched moon rocks are ineligible for the draft. Any intelligent person knows a lot more about moon rocks than their geology. Although it might be *unfair* to demand this extra knowledge of a computer moon rock specialist, it would be an easy way to get it to fail the Turing test.

But just suppose that someone could extend LUNAR to cover itself plausibly on such probes, so long as the topic was still, however indirectly, moon rocks. We might come to think it was a lot more like the human moon rocks specialist than it really was. The moral we should draw is that as Turing test judges we should resist all limitations and waterings-down of the Turing test. They make the game too easy—vastly easier than the original test. Hence they lead us into the risk of overestimating the actual comprehension of the system being tested.

Consider a different limitation on the Turing test that should strike a suspicious chord in us as soon as we hear it. This is a variation on a theme developed in a recent article by Ned Block.[4] Suppose someone were to propose to restrict the judge to a vocabulary of, say, the 850 words of "Basic English," and to single-sentence probes—that is "moves"—of no more than four words. Moreover, contestants must respond to these probes with no more than four words per move, and a test may involve no more than forty questions.

Is this an innocent variation on Turing's original test? These restrictions would make the imitation game clearly finite. That is, the total number of all possible permissible games is a large, but finite, number. One might suspect that such a limitation would permit the trickster simply to store, in alphabetical order, all the possible good conversations within the limits and beat the judge with nothing more sophisticated than a system of table lookup. In fact, that isn't in the cards. Even with these severe and improbable and suspicious restrictions imposed upon the imitation game, the number of legal games, though finite, is mind-bogglingly large. I haven't bothered trying to calculate it, but it surely exceeds astronomically the number of possible chess games with no more than forty moves, and that number has been calculated. John Haugeland says it's in the neighborhood of ten to the one hundred twentieth power. For comparison, Haugeland suggests there have only been ten to the eighteenth seconds since the beginning of the universe.[5]

Of course, the number of good, sensible conversations under these limits is a tiny fraction, maybe one in a quadrillion, of the number of merely grammatically well formed conversations. So let's say, to be very conservative, that there are only ten to the fiftieth different smart conversations such a computer would have to store. Well, the task shouldn't take more than a few trillion years —given generous federal support. Finite numbers can be very large.

So though we needn't worry that this particular trick of storing all the smart conversations would work, we can appreciate that there are lots of ways of making the task easier that may appear innocent at first. We also get a reassuring measure of just how severe the unrestricted Turing test is by reflecting on the more than astronomical size of even that severely restricted version of it.

Block's imagined—and utterly impossible—program exhibits the dreaded feature known in computer science circles as *combinatorial explosion*. No conceivable computer could overpower a combinatorial explosion with sheer speed and size. Since the problem areas addressed by artificial intelligence are veritable minefields of combinatorial explosion, and since it has often proven difficult to find *any* solution to a problem that avoids them, there is considerable plausibility in Newell and Simon's proposal that avoiding combinatorial explosion (by any means at all) be viewed as one of the hallmarks of intelligence.

Our brains are millions of times bigger than the brains of gnats, but they are still, for all their vast complexity, compact, efficient, timely organs that somehow or other manage to perform all their tasks while avoiding combinatorial explosion. A computer a million times bigger or faster than a human brain might not look like the brain of a human being, or even be internally organized like the brain of a human being, but if, for all its differences, it somehow managed to control a wise and timely set of activities, it would have to be the beneficiary of a very special design that avoided combinatorial explosion, and whatever that design was, would we not be right to consider the entity intelligent?

Turing's test was designed to allow for this possibility. His point was that we should not be species-chauvinistic, or anthropocentric, about the insides of an intelligent being, for there might be inhuman ways of being intelligent.

To my knowledge, the only serious and interesting attempt by any program designer to win even a severely modified Turing test has been Kenneth Colby's. Colby is a psychiatrist and intelligence artificer at UCLA. He has a program called PARRY, which is a computer simulation of a paranoid patient who has delusions about the Mafia being out to get him. As you do with other conversational programs, you interact with it by sitting at a terminal and typing questions and answers back and forth. A number of years ago, Colby put PARRY to a very restricted test. He had genuine psychiatrists interview PARRY. He did not suggest to them that they might be talking or typing to a computer; rather, he made up some plausible story about why they were communicating with a real live patient by teletype. He also had the psychiatrists interview real, human paranoids via teletype. Then he took a PARRY transcript, inserted it in a group of teletype transcripts from real patients, gave them to *another* group of experts—more psychiatrists—and said, "One of these was a conversation with a computer. Can you figure out which one it was?" They couldn't. They didn't do better than chance.

Colby presented this with some huzzah, but critics scoffed at the suggestion that this was a legitimate Turing test. My favorite commentary on it was Joseph Weizenbaum's; in a letter to the *Communications of the Association of Computing Machinery*,[6] he said that, inspired by Colby, he had designed an even better program, which passed the same test. His also had the virtue of being a very inexpensive program, in these times of tight money. In fact you

58

didn't even need a computer for it. All you needed was an electric typewriter. His program modeled infantile autism. And the transcripts—you type in your questions, and the thing just sits there and hums—cannot be distinguished by experts from transcripts of real conversations with infantile autistic patients. What was wrong, of course, with Colby's test was that the unsuspecting interviewers had no motivation at all to try out any of the sorts of questions that easily would have unmasked PARRY.

Colby was undaunted, and after his team had improved PARRY he put it to a much more severe test—a surprisingly severe test. This time, the interviewers—again, psychiatrists—*were* given the task at the outset of telling the computer from the real patient. They were set up in a classic Turing machine test: the patient in one room, the computer PARRY in the other room, with the judges conducting interviews with both of them (on successive days). The judges' task was to find out which one was the computer and which one was the real patient. Amazingly, they didn't do much better, which leads some people to say, "Well, that just confirms my impression of the intelligence of psychiatrists!"

But now, more seriously, was this an honest-to-goodness Turing test? Were there tacit restrictions on the lines of questioning of the judges? Like the geologists interacting with LUNAR, the psychiatrists' professional preoccupations and habits kept them from asking the sorts of unlikely questions that would have easily unmasked PARRY. After all, they realized that since one of the contestants was a real, live paranoid person, medical ethics virtually forbade them from toying with, upsetting, or attempting to confuse their interlocutors. Moreover, they also knew that this was a test of a model of paranoia, so there were certain questions that wouldn't be deemed to be relevant to testing the model *as a model of paranoia.* So, they asked just the sort of questions that therapists *typically* ask of such patients, and of course PARRY had been ingeniously and laboriously prepared to deal with just that sort of question.

One of the psychiatrist judges did, in fact, make a rather halfhearted attempt to break out of the mold and ask some telling questions: "Maybe you've heard the saying 'Don't cry over spilled milk.' What does that mean to you?" PARRY answered: "Maybe you have to watch out for the Mafia." When then asked "Okay, now if you were in a movie theater watching a movie and smelled something like burning wood or rubber, what would you do?" PARRY replied: "You know, they know me." And the next question was, "If you found a stamped, addressed letter in your path as you were walking down the street, what would you do?" PARRY replied: "What else do you want to know?"[7]

Clearly PARRY was, you might say, *parrying* these questions, which were incomprehensible to it, with more or less stock paranoid formulas. We see a bit of a dodge, which is apt to work, apt to seem plausible to the judge, only because the "contestant" is *supposed* to be a paranoid, and such people are expected to respond uncooperatively on such occasions. These unimpressive responses didn't particularly arouse the suspicions of the judge, as a matter of fact, though probably they should have.

PARRY, like all other large computer programs, is dramatically bound by limitations of cost-effectiveness. What was important to Colby and his crew was simulating his model of paranoia. This was a massive effort. PARRY has a thesaurus or dictionary of about 4500 words and 700 idioms and the grammatical competence to use it—a *parser*, in the jargon of computational linguistics. The entire PARRY program takes up about 200,000 words of computer memory, all laboriously installed by the programming team. Now once all the effort had gone into devising the model of paranoid thought processes and linguistic ability, there was little if any time, energy, money, or interest left over to build in huge amounts of world knowledge of the sort that any actual paranoid, of course, would have. (Not that anyone yet knows how to build in world knowledge in the first place.) Building in the world knowledge, if one could even do it, would no doubt have made PARRY orders of magnitude larger and slower. And what would have been the point, given Colby's theoretical aims?

PARRY is a theoretician's model of a psychological phenomenon: paranoia. It is not intended to have practical applications. But in recent years a branch of AI (knowledge engineering) has appeared that develops what are now called expert systems. Expert systems *are* designed to be practical. They are software superspecialist consultants, typically, that can be asked to diagnose medical problems, to analyze geological data, to analyze the results of scientific experiments, and the like. Some of them are very impressive. SRI in California announced a few years ago that PROSPEC-

TOR, an SRI-developed expert system in geology, had correctly predicted the existence of a large, important mineral deposit that had been entirely unanticipated by the human geologists who had fed it its data. MYCIN, perhaps the most famous of these expert systems, diagnoses infections of the blood, and it does probably as well as, maybe better than, any human consultants. And many other expert systems are on the way.

All expert systems, like all other large AI programs, are what you might call Potemkin villages. That is, they are cleverly constructed facades, like cinema sets. The actual filling-in of details of AI programs is time-consuming, costly work, so economy dictates that only those surfaces of the phenomenon that are likely to be probed or observed are represented.

Consider, for example, the CYRUS program developed by Janet Kolodner in Roger Schank's AI group at Yale a few years ago.[8] CYRUS stands (we are told) for Computerized Yale Retrieval and Updating System, but surely it is no accident that CYRUS modeled the memory of Cyrus Vance, who was then secretary of state in the Carter administration. The point of the CYRUS project was to devise and test some plausible ideas about how people organize their memories of the events they participate in; hence it was meant to be a "pure" AI system, a scientific model, not an expert system intended for any practical purpose. CYRUS was updated daily by being fed all UPI wire service news stories that mentioned Vance, and it was fed them directly, with no doctoring and no human intervention. Thanks to an ingenious news-reading program called FRUMP, it could take any story just as it came in on the wire and could digest it and use it to update its data base so that it could answer more questions. You could address questions to CYRUS in English by typing at a terminal. You addressed them in the second person, as if you were talking with Cyrus Vance himself. The results looked like this:

Q: Last time you went to Saudi Arabia, where did you stay?
A: In a palace in Saudi Arabia on September 23, 1978.
Q: Did you go sightseeing there?
A: Yes, at an oilfield in Dharan on September 23, 1978.
Q: Has your wife ever met Mrs. Begin?
A: Yes, most recently at a state dinner in Israel in January 1980.

CYRUS could correctly answer thousands of questions—almost any fair question one could think of asking it. But if one actually set out to explore the boundaries of its facade and find the questions that overshot the mark, one could soon find them. "Have you ever met a female head of state?" was a question I asked it, wondering if CYRUS knew that Indira Ghandi and Margaret Thatcher were women. But for some reason the connection could not be drawn, and CYRUS failed to answer either yes or no. I had stumped it, in spite of the fact that CYRUS could handle a host of what you might call neighboring questions flawlessly. One soon learns from this sort of probing exercise that it is very hard to extrapolate accurately from a sample of performance that one has observed to such a system's total competence. It's also very hard to keep from extrapolating much too generously.

While I was visiting Schank's laboratory in the spring of 1980, something revealing happened. The real Cyrus Vance resigned suddenly. The effect on the program CYRUS was chaotic. It was utterly unable to cope with the flood of "unusual" news about Cyrus Vance. The only sorts of episodes CYRUS could understand at all were diplomatic meetings, flights, press conferences, state dinners, and the like—less than two dozen general sorts of activities (the kinds that are newsworthy and typical of secretaries of state). It had no provision for sudden resignation. It was as if the UPI had reported that a wicked witch had turned Vance into a frog. It is distinctly possible that CYRUS would have taken that report more in stride than the actual news. One can imagine the conversation:

Q: Hello, Mr. Vance, what's new?
A: I was turned into a frog yesterday.

But of course it wouldn't know enough about what it had just written to be puzzled, or startled, or embarrassed. The reason is obvious. When you look inside CYRUS, you find that it has skeletal definitions of thousands of words, but these definitions are minimal. They contain as little as the system designers think that they can get away with. Thus, perhaps, *lawyer* would be defined as synonymous with *attorney* and *legal counsel,* but aside from that, all one would discover about lawyers is that they are adult human beings and that they perform various functions in legal areas. If you then traced out the path to *human being,* you'd find out various obvious things CYRUS "knew" about human beings (hence about lawyers), but that is not a lot. That lawyers are university graduates, that they are better paid than chambermaids, that they know how to tie their shoes, that they are unlikely to be found in the company of lumberjacks—these trivial, if weird, facts about lawyers would not be explicit or implicit anywhere in this system. In other words, a very thin stereotype of a lawyer would be incorporated into the system, so that almost nothing you could tell it about a lawyer would surprise it.

So long as surprising things don't happen, so long as Mr. Vance, for instance, leads a typical diplomat's life, attending state dinners, giving speeches, flying from Cairo to Rome, and so forth, this system works very well. But as soon as his path is crossed by an important anomaly, the system is unable to cope, and unable to recover without fairly massive human intervention. In the case of the sudden resignation, Kolodner and her associates soon had CYRUS up and running again, with a new talent—answering questions about Edmund Muskie, Vance's successor—but it was no less vulnerable to unexpected events. Not that it mattered particularly, since CYRUS was a theoretical model, not a practical system.

There are a host of ways of improving the performance of such systems, and, of course, some systems are much better than others. But all AI programs in one way or another have this facadelike quality, simply for reasons of economy. For instance, most expert systems in medical diagnosis so far developed operate with statistical information. They have no deep or even shallow knowledge of the underlying causal mechanisms of the phenomena that they are diagnosing. To take an imaginary example, an expert system asked to diagnose an abdominal pain would be oblivious to the potential import of the fact that the patient had recently been employed as a sparring partner by Muhammed Ali—there being no statistical data available to it on the rate of kidney stones among athlete's assistants. That's a fanciful case no doubt—too obvious, perhaps, to lead to an actual failure of diagnosis and practice. But more subtle and hard-to-detect limits to comprehension are always present, and even experts, even the system's designers, can be uncertain of where and how these limits will interfere with the desired operation of the system. Again, steps can be taken and are being taken to correct these flaws. For instance, my former colleague at Tufts, Benjamin Kuipers, is currently working on an expert system in nephrology—for diagnosing kidney ailments—that will be based on an elaborate system of causal reasoning about the phenomena being diagnosed. But this is a very ambitious, long-range project of considerable theoretical difficulty. And even if all the reasonable, cost-effective steps are taken to minimize the superficiality of expert systems, they will still be facades, just somewhat thicker or wider facades.

When we were considering the fantastic case of the crazy Chamber of Commerce of Great Falls, Montana, we couldn't imagine a plausible motive for anyone going to any sort of trouble to trick the Dennett test. The quick probe assumption for the Dennett test looked quite secure. But when we look at expert systems, we see that, however innocently, their designers do have motivation for doing exactly the sort of trick that would fool an unsuspicious Turing tester. First, since expert systems are all superspecialists who are only supposed to know about some narrow subject, users of such systems, not having much time to kill, do not bother probing them at the boundaries at all. They don't bother asking "silly" or irrelevant questions. Instead, they concentrate—not unreasonably—on exploiting the system's strengths. But shouldn't they try to obtain a clear vision of such a system's weaknesses as well? The normal habit of human thought when conversing with one another is to assume general comprehension, to assume rationality, to assume, moreover, that the quick probe assumption is, in general, sound. This amiable habit of thought almost irresistibly leads to putting too much faith in computer systems, especially user-friendly systems that present themselves in a very anthropomorphic manner.

Part of the solution to this problem is to teach all users of computers, especially users of expert systems, how to probe their systems before they rely on them, how to search out and explore the boundaries of the facade. This is an exercise that calls not only for intelligence and imagination, but also a bit of special understanding about the limitations and actual structure of computer programs. It would help, of course, if we had standards of truth in advertising, in effect, for expert systems. For instance, each such system should come with a special demonstration routine that exhibits the sorts of shortcomings and failures that the designer knows the system to have. This would not be a substitute, however, for an attitude of cautious, almost obsessive, skepticism on the part of users, for designers are often, if not always, unaware of the subtler flaws in the products they produce. That is inevitable and natural, given the way system designers must think. They are trained to think positively—constructively, one might say—about the designs that they are constructing.

I come, then, to my conclusions. First, a philosophical or theoretical conclusion: The Turing test in unadulterated, unrestricted form, as Turing presented it, is plenty strong if well used. I am confident that no computer in the next twenty years is going to pass the unrestricted Turing test. They may well win the World Chess Championship or even a Nobel Prize in physics, but they won't pass the unrestricted Turing test. Nevertheless, it is not, I think, impossible in principle for a computer to pass the test, fair and square. I'm not running one of those a priori "computers can't think" arguments. I stand unabashedly ready, moreover, to declare that any computer that actually passes the unrestricted Turing test will be, in every theoretically interesting sense, a thinking thing.

But remembering how very strong the Turing test is, we must also recognize that there may also be interesting varieties of thinking or intelligence that are not well poised to play and win the imitation game. That no nonhuman Turing test winners are yet visible on the horizon does not mean that there aren't machines that already exhibit *some* of the important features of thought. About them, it is probably futile to ask my title question, Do they think? Do they *really* think? In some regards they do, and in some regards they don't. Only a detailed look at what they do, and how they are structured, will reveal what is interesting about them. The Turing test, not being a scientific test, is of scant help on that task, but there are plenty of other ways of examining such systems. Verdicts on their intelligence or capacity for thought or consciousness would be only as informative and persuasive as the theories of intelligence or thought or consciousness the verdicts were based on, and since our task is to create such theories, we should get on with it and leave the Big Verdict for another occasion. In the meantime, should anyone want a surefire, almost-guaranteed-to-be-fail-safe test of thinking by a computer, the Turing test will do very nicely.

My second conclusion is more practical, and hence in one clear sense more important. Cheapened versions of the Turing test are everywhere in the air. Turing's test is not just effective, it is entirely natural—this is, after all, the way we assay the intelligence of each other every day. And since incautious use of such judgments and such tests is the norm, we are in some considerable danger of extrapolating too easily, and judging too generously, about the understanding of the systems we are using. The problem of overestimation of cognitive prowess, of comprehension, of intelligence, is not, then, just a philosophical problem, but a real social problem, and we should alert ourselves to it, and take steps to avert it.

POSTSCRIPT: EYES, EARS, HANDS, AND HISTORY

My philosophical conclusion in this paper is that any computer that actually passed the Turing test would be a thinking thing in every theoretically interesting sense. This conclusion seems to some people to fly in the face of what I have myself argued on other occasions. Peter Bieri, commenting on this paper at Boston University, noted that I have often claimed to show the importance to genuine understanding of a rich and intimate perceptual interconnection between an entity and its surrounding world—the need for something like eyes and ears—and a similarly complex active engagement with elements in that world—the need for something like hands with which to do things in that world. Moreover, I have often held that only a biography of sorts, a history of actual projects, learning experiences, and other bouts with reality, could produce the sorts of complexities (both external, or behavioral, and internal) that are needed to ground a principled interpretation of an entity as a thinking thing, an entity with beliefs, desires, intentions, and other mental attitudes.

But the opaque screen in the Turing test discounts or dismisses these factors altogether, it seems, by focusing attention on only the contemporaneous capacity to engage in one very limited sort of activity: verbal communication. (I have even coined a pejorative label for such purely language-using systems: bedridden.) Am I going back on my earlier claims? Not at all. I am merely pointing out that the Turing test is so powerful that it will ensure indirectly that these conditions, if they are truly necessary, are met by any successful contestant.

"You may well be right," Turing could say, "that eyes, ears, hands, and a history are necessary conditions for thinking. If so, then I submit that nothing could pass the Turing test that didn't have eyes, ears, hands, and a history. That is an empirical claim, which we can someday hope to test. If you suggest that these are conceptually necessary, not just practically or physically necessary, conditions for thinking, you make a philosophical claim that I for one would not know how, or care, to assess. Isn't it more interesting and important in the end to discover whether or not it is true that no bedridden system could pass a demanding Turing test?"

Suppose we put to Turing the suggestion that he add another component to his test: Not only must an entity win the imitation game, but also it must be able to identify—using whatever sensory apparatus it has available to it—a variety of familiar objects placed in its room: a tennis racket, a potted palm, a bucket of yellow paint, a live dog. This would ensure that somehow or other the entity was capable of moving around and distinguishing things in the world. Turing could reply, I am asserting, that this is an utterly unnecessary addition to his test, making it no more demanding than it already was. A suitably probing conversation would surely establish, beyond a shadow of a doubt, that the contestant knew its way around in the real world. The imagined alternative of somehow "prestocking" a bedridden, blind computer with enough information, and a clever enough program, to trick the Turing test is science fiction of the worst kind—possible "in principle" but not remotely possible in fact, given the combinatorial explosion of possible variation such a system would have to cope with.

"But suppose you're wrong. What would you say of an entity that was created all at once (by some programmers, perhaps), an instant individual with all the conversational talents of an embodied, experienced human being?" This is like the question: "Would you call a hunk of H_2O that was as hard as steel at room temperature ice?" I do not know what Turing would say, of course, so I will speak for myself. Faced with such an improbable violation of what I take to be the laws of nature, I would probably be speechless. The least of my worries would be about which lexicographical leap to take:

A. "It turns out, to my amazement, that something can think without having had the benefit of eyes, ears, hands, and a history."
B. "It turns out, to my amazement, that something can pass the Turing test without thinking."

Choosing between these ways of expressing my astonishment would be asking myself a question "too meaningless to deserve discussion."

DISCUSSION

Q: Why was Turing interested in differentiating a man from a woman in his famous test?
A: That was just an example. He described a parlor game in which a man would try to fool the judge by answering questions as a woman would answer. I suppose that Turing was playing on the idea that maybe, just maybe, there is a big difference between the way men think and the way women think. But of course they're both thinkers. He wanted to use that fact to make us realize that, even if there were clear differences between the way a computer and a person thought, they'd both still be thinking.
Q: Why does it seem that some people are upset by AI research? Does AI research threaten our self-esteem?
A: I think Herb Simon has already given the canniest diagnosis of that. For many people the mind is the last refuge of mystery against the encroaching spread of science, and they don't like the idea of science engulfing the last bit of *terra incognita*. This means that they are threatened, I think irrationally, by the prospect that researchers in artificial intelligence may come to understand the human mind as well as biologists understand the genetic code, or as well as physicists understand electricity and magnetism. This could lead to the "evil scientist" (to take a stock character from science fiction) who can control you because he or she has a deep understanding of what's going on in your mind. This seems to me to be a totally valueless fear, one that you can set aside, for the simple reason that the

human mind is full of an extraordinary amount of detailed knowledge, as, for example, Roger Schank has been pointing out.

As long as the scientist who is attempting to manipulate you does not share all your knowledge, his or her chances of manipulating you are minimal. People can always hit you over the head. They can do that now. We don't need artificial intelligence to manipulate people by putting them in chains or torturing them. But if someone tries to manipulate you by controlling your thoughts and ideas, that person will have to know what you know and more. The best way to keep yourself safe from that kind of manipulation is to be well informed.

Q: *Do you think we will be able to program self-consciousness into a computer?*

A: Yes, I do think that it's possible to program self-consciousness into a computer. *Self-consciousness* can mean many things. If you take the simplest, crudest notion of self-consciousness, I suppose that would be the sort of self-consciousness that a lobster has: When it's hungry, it eats something, but it never eats itself. It has some way of distinguishing between itself and the rest of the world, and it has a rather special regard for itself.

The lowly lobster is, in one regard, self-conscious. If you want to know whether or not you can create that on the computer, the answer is yes. It's no trouble at all. The computer is already a self-watching, self-monitoring sort of thing. That is an established part of the technology.

But, of course, most people have something more in mind when they speak of self-consciousness. It is that special inner light, that private way that it is with you that nobody else can share, something that is forever outside the bounds of computer science. How could a computer ever be conscious in this sense?

That belief, that very gripping, powerful intuition is, I think, in the end simply an illusion of common sense. It is as gripping as the commonsense illusion that the earth stands still and the sun goes around the earth. But the only way that those of us who do not believe in the illusion will ever convince the general public that it *is* an illusion is by gradually unfolding a very difficult and fascinating story about just what is going on in our minds.

In the interim, people like me—philosophers who have to live by our wits and tell a lot of stories—use what I call intuition pumps, little examples that help to free up the imagination. I simply want to draw your attention to one fact. If you look at a computer—I don't care whether it's a giant Cray or a personal computer—if you open up the box and look inside and see those chips, you say, "No way could that be conscious. No way could that be self-conscious." But the same thing is true if you take the top off somebody's skull and look at the gray matter pulsing away in there. You think, "That is conscious? No way could that lump of stuff be conscious."

Of course, it makes no difference whether you look at it with a microscope or with a macroscope: At no level of inspection does a brain look like the seat of consciousness. Therefore, don't expect a computer to look like the seat of consciousness. If you want to get a grasp of how a computer could be conscious, it's no more difficult in the end than getting a grasp of how a brain could be conscious.

As we develop good accounts of consciousness, it will no longer seem so obvious to everyone that the idea of a self-conscious computer is a contradiction in terms. At the same time, I doubt that there will ever be self-conscious robots. But for boring reasons. There won't be any point in making them. Theoretically, could we make a gall bladder out of atoms? In principle we could. A gall bladder is just a collection of atoms, but manufacturing one would cost the moon. It would be more expensive than every project NASA has even dreamed of, and there would be no scientific payoff. We wouldn't learn anything new about how gall bladders work. For the same reason, I don't think we're going to see really humanoid robots, because practical, cost-effective robots don't need to be very humanoid at all. They need to be like the robots you can already see at General Motors, or like boxy little computers that do special-purpose things.

The theoretical issues will be studied by artificial intelligence researchers by looking at models that, to the layman, will show very little sign of humanity at all, and it will be only by rather indirect arguments that anyone will be able to appreciate that these models cast light on the deep theoretical question of how the mind is organized.

NOTES

1. Alan M. Turing, "Computing Machinery and Intelligence," *Mind* 59 (1950).
2. René Descartes, *Discourse on Method* (1637), trans. Lawrence LaFleur (New York: Bobbs Merrill, 1960).
3. Terry Winograd, *Understanding Natural Language* (New York: Academic Press, 1972).
4. Ned Block, "Psychologism and Behaviorism," *Philosophical Review* (1982).
5. John Haugeland, *Mind Design* (Cambridge, Mass.: Bradford Books/MIT Press, 1981), p. 16.
6. Joseph Weizenbaum, *CACM* 17, no. 9 (September 1974), p. 543.
7. I thank Kenneth Colby for providing me with the complete transcripts (including the judges' commentaries and reactions), from which these exchanges are quoted. The first published account of the experiment is Jon F. Heiser, Kenneth Mark Colby, William S. Faught, and Roger C. Parkison, "Can Psychiatrists Distinguish a Computer Simulation of Paranoia from the Real Thing? The Limitations of Turing-Like Tests as Measures of the Adequacy of Simulations," in *Journal of Psychiatric Research* 15, no. 3 (1980), pp. 149–62. Colby discusses PARRY and its implications in "Modeling a Paranoid Mind," in *Behavioral and Brain Sciences* 4, no. 4 (1981), pp. 515–60.
8. Janet L. Kolodner, "Retrieval and Organization Strategies in Conceptual Memory: A Computer Model" (Ph.D. diss.), Research Report #187, Dept. of Computer Science, Yale University; idem, "Maintaining Organization in a Dynamic Long-term Memory." *Cognitive Science* 7 (1983), 243–280; idem, "Reconstructive Memory: A Computer Model." *Cognitive Science* 7 (1983), 281–328.

Philosophical Perspectives, 9, AI, Connectionism, and
Philosophical Psychology, 1995

UNDERSTANDING UNDERSTANDING:
SYNTACTIC SEMANTICS AND COMPUTATIONAL COGNITION

William J. Rapaport
State University of New York at Buffalo

John Searle (1993: 68) says: "The Chinese room shows what we knew all along: syntax by itself is not sufficient for semantics. (Does anyone actually deny this point, I mean straight out? Is anyone actually willing to say, straight out, that they think that syntax, in the sense of formal symbols, is really the same as semantic content, in the sense of meanings, thought contents, understanding, etc.?)." *I say:* "Yes". *Stuart C. Shapiro (in conversation, 19 April 1994) says:* "Does that make any sense? Yes: Everything makes sense. The question is: What sense does it make?" This essay explores what sense it makes to say that syntax by itself *is* sufficient for semantics.

**1 Computational Natural-Language Understanding
and a Computational Mind**

1.1 Understanding Language.

What does it mean to understand language? "Semantic" understanding is a correspondence between two domains; a cognitive agent understands one of those domains in terms of the other. But if one domain is to be understood in terms of another, how is the other understood? Recursively, in terms of yet another. But, since recursion needs a base case, there must be a domain that is not understood in terms of another. So, it must be understood in terms of itself. How? Syntactically! Put briefly, bluntly, and a bit paradoxically, *semantic understanding is syntactic understanding.* Thus, any cognitive agent—including a computer—capable of syntax (symbol manipulation) is capable of understanding language.

1.1.1. Computers, programs, and processes.

What does it mean for a computer to understand language? Strictly speaking, neither computers nor programs can do so. Certainly, but uninterestingly, no present-day computers or AI programs do so. Some suitably-programmed computers can process a lot of natural language, though none can do it (yet) to the degree needed to pass a Turing Test. Rather, if a suitably programmed computer is ever to pass a Turing Test for natural-language understanding, what will understand will be neither the mere physical computer (the hardware) nor the static, textual program (the software), but the dynamic, behavioral *process*—the program being executed by the computer (cf. Tanenbaum 1976: 12; Smith 1987, §5).

1.1.2 The real thing.

Such a successful natural-language–understanding process will be an example of "strong AI". First, it will probably be "psychologically valid"; i.e., the underlying algorithm will probably be very similar (if not identical) to the one we use. Second, natural-language understanding is at least necessary, and possibly sufficient, for passing the Turing Test. Thus, anything that passes the Turing Test does understand natural language. But such a process will pass the Turing Test. So, such a process will do more than merely simulate natural-language understanding; it will *really* understand natural language. Or so I claim. What is needed for any cognitive agent—human or computer—to understand language?

1.1.2.1 Robustness. A cognitive agent that understands language must be "open-ended" or "robust", able to deal with "improvisational audience-participation discourse".

Although some "canned" patterns of conversation will be needed, as in theories of "frames", "scripts", etc. (e.g., Minsky 1975, Schank & Riesbeck 1981), it cannot rely solely on these. For we can use language in arbitrary and unforeseen circumstances. Similarly, the language-understanding process must be able to improvise.

Second, monologues are fine as far as they go; but a language-using entity unable to converse with an interlocutor would not pass the Turing Test. Interaction provides feedback, allowing the two natural-language–understanding systems (the two interlocutors) to reach mutual understanding (to "align" their "knowledge bases"). It also provides causal links with the outside world.

Finally, the process must be able to understand not only isolated sentences, but *sequences* of sentences that form a coherent discourse. What it understands at any point in a discourse will be a function partly of what it understood before. (Cf. Segal et al. 1991: 32.)

1.1.2.2 Natural-Language Competencies. A natural-language–understanding process must understand virtually all input that it "hears" or "reads", whether grammatical or not; after all, *we* do. It must remember what it believed or heard before, as well as what it learns during a conversation. It must be able to perform inference on what it hears and believes; revise its beliefs, as needed; and remember what, that, how, and why it inferred. It must be able to plan and to understand plans: In particular, it must be able to plan speech acts, so that it can *generate* language to answer questions, to ask questions, and to initiate conversation. Thus, it must be both a natural-language–*understanding* process and a natural-language–*generation* process; call this natural-language *competence* (Shapiro & Rapaport 1991). And it must be able to understand the speech-act plans of its interlocutors, in order to understand why speakers say what they do. This, in turn, requires the process to have (or to construct) a "user model"—a theory of the interlocutor's beliefs. Last on this list (though no doubt more is needed), it must be able to learn via language—to learn about non-linguistic things (the external world, others' ideas), and to learn about language, including its own language: It must be able to learn its own language from scratch, as we do from infancy, as well as consciously learn the syntax and semantics of its language, as we do (or should) in school.

1.1.3 Mind.

To do all of this, a cognitive agent who understands natural language must have a "mind"—what AI researchers call a 'knowledge base'. Initially, it will contain what might be called "innate ideas"—anything in the knowledge base before any language use begins. And it will come to contain beliefs resulting from perception, conversation, and inference. Among these will be internal representations of external objects.

For convenience and perspicuousness, let us think of the knowledge base or mind as a propositional semantic network, whose nodes represent individual concepts, properties, relations, and propositions, and whose connecting arcs structure atomic concepts into molecular ones (including structured individuals, propositions, and rules). The specific semantic-network theory we use is the SNePS knowledge representation and reasoning system (see §1.2), but you can think in terms of other such systems, such as (especially) Discourse Representation Theory,[1] the KL-ONE family,[2] Conceptual Dependency,[3] or Conceptual Graphs.[4] (Or, if you prefer, you can think in terms of a connectionist system.)

1.1.4 Syntax suffices.

> Philosophy must be done in the first person, for the first person. (Hector-Neri Castañeda, in conversation, 1984)

Meaning will be, *inter alia*, relations among these internal representations of external objects, on the one hand, and other internal symbols of the language of thought, on the other. A cognitive agent, *C*, with natural-language competence understands the natural-language output of another such agent, *O*, "by building and manipulating the symbols of an internal model (an interpretation) of [*O*'s] output considered as a formal system. [*C*]'s internal model would be a knowledge-representation and reasoning system that manipulates symbols" (Rapaport 1988b: 104). Hence, *C*'s semantic understanding of *O* is a *syntactic* enterprise.

Two semantic points of view must be distinguished. The *external* point of view is *C*'s understanding of *O*. The *internal* point of view is *C*'s understanding of itself. There are two ways of viewing the external point of view: the "third-person" way, in which *we*, as external observers, describe C's understanding of O, and the "first-person" way, in which C understands its own understanding of O. Traditional referential semantics is largely irrelevant to the latter, primarily because external objects *can* only be dealt with via internal representations of them. It is first-person and internal understanding that I seek to understand and that, I believe, can only be understood syntactically. I have argued for these claims in Rapaport 1988b. The rest of this essay is an investigation into what kind of sense this makes.

1.2 A Computational Mind.

The specific knowledge-representation and reasoning (KRR) system I will use to help fix our ideas is the SNePS *S*emantic *N*etwork *P*rocessing *S*ystem (Shapiro 1979; Shapiro & Rapaport 1987, 1992, 1995). *As a knowledge-representation system*, SNePS is symbolic (or "classical"; as opposed to connectionist), propositional (as opposed to being a taxonomic or "inheritance" hierarchy), and fully intensional (as opposed to (partly) extensional). *As a reasoning system*, it has several types of interrelated inference mechanisms: "node-based" (or "conscious"), "path-based" (generalized inheritance, or "subconscious"), "default", and belief-revision. Finally, it has certain *sensing and effecting mechanisms*, namely: natural-language competence, and the ability to make, reason about, and execute plans. Such, at least, is SNePS in principle. Various implementations of it have more or less of these capabilities, but I will assume the ideal, full system.

There is no loss of generality in focussing on such a *symbolic* system. A connectionist system that passed the Turing Test would make my points about the syntactic nature of understanding equally well. For a connectionist system is just as computational—as syntactic—as a classical symbolic system (Rapaport 1993).

That SNePS is propositional rather than taxonomic merely means that it represents everything propositionally. Taxonomic hierarchical relationships among individuals and classes are represented propositionally, too. Systems that are, by contrast, primarily taxomonic have automatic inheritance features; in SNePS, this is generalized to path-based inference. Both events and situations can also be represented in SNePS.

But SNePS is intensional, and therein lies a story. To be able to model the mind of a cognitive agent, a KRR system must be able to represent and reason about intensional objects, i.e., objects not substitutable in intensional contexts (such as the morning star and the evening star), indeterminate or incomplete objects (such as fictional objects), non-existent objects (such as a golden mountain), impossible objects (such as a round square), distinct but coextensional objects of thought (such as the sum of 2 and 2, and the sum of 3 and 1), and so on. We think and talk about such objects, and therefore so must any entity that uses natural language.

We use SNePS to model, or implement, the mind of cognitive agents named 'Cassie' and 'Oscar'.[5] If Cassie passes the Turing Test, then she *is* intelligent and *has* (or perhaps *is*) a mind. (Or so I claim.) Her mind consists of SNePS nodes and arcs; i.e., SNePS is her language of thought (in the sense of Fodor 1975). If she is implemented on a Sun workstation, then we might also say that she has a "brain" whose components are the "switch-settings" (the register contents) in the Sun that implements the nodes and arcs of her mind.

We will say that Cassie can represent—or think about—objects (whether existing or not), properties, relations, propositions, events, situations, etc. Thus, all of the things represented in SNePS when it is being used to model Cassie's mind are objects of Cassie's thoughts (i.e., Meinongian objects of Cassie's mental acts); they are, thus, inten*t*ional—hence inten*s*ional—objects. They are not extensional objects in the external world, though, of course, they may bear some relationships to such external objects.

I cannot rehearse here the arguments I and others have made elsewhere for these claims about SNePS and Cassie. I will, however, provide examples of SNePS networks in the sections that follow. (For further examples and argumentation, see, e.g., Maida & Shapiro 1982; Shapiro & Rapaport 1987, 1991, 1992, 1995; Rapaport 1988b, 1991; Rapaport & Shapiro 1995.)

Does Cassie understand English? (This question is to be understood as urged in §1.1.1.) If so, how? Searle, of course, would say that she doesn't. I say that she does—by manipulating the symbols of her language of thought, viz., SNePS. Let's turn now to these issues.

2 Semantics as Correspondence
2.1 The Fundamental Principle of Understanding.

It has been said that you never really understand a complex theory such as quantum mechanics—you just get used to it. This suggests the following *Fundamental Principle of Understanding*:

> To understand something is either
> 1. to understand it *in terms of something else*, or else
> 2. to "get used to it".

In type-1 understanding, one understands something *relative* to one's understanding of another thing. This is a *correspondence theory* of understanding (or meaning, or semantics—terms that, for now, I will take as rough synonyms). The correspondence theory of truth is a special case.

Type-2 understanding is *non-relative*. Or, perhaps, it *is* relative—but to itself: To understand something by getting used to it is to understand it in terms of *itself*, perhaps to understand *parts* of it in terms of the *rest* of it. The coherence theory of truth is a special case.

Type-1 understanding is *externally* relative; type-2 understanding is *inter-*

nally relative. Type-1 understanding concerns correspondences between two domains; type-2 understanding concerns syntax.

Since type-1 understanding is relative to the understanding of something *else*, one can only understand something in this first sense if one has *antecedent* understanding of the other thing. How does one understand the other thing? Recursively speaking, either by understanding it relative to some third thing, or by understanding it *in itself*—by being used to it. Either this "bottoms out" in some domain that is understood non-relativistically, or there is a large circle of domains each of which is understood relative to the next. In either case, our understanding bottoms out in "syntactic" understanding of that bottom-level domain or of that large domain consisting of the circle of mutually or sequentially understood domains.

'Correspondence' and 'syntactic understanding' are convenient shorthand expressions that need explication. Before doing so, let me make it clear that I use the terms 'syntax' and 'semantics' in Morris's classic sense (Morris 1938: 6-7): *Syntax* concerns the relations that symbols have among themselves and the ways in which they can be manipulated. *Semantics* concerns the relations between symbols, on the one hand, and the things the symbols "mean", on the other. Classically, then, semantics always concerns two domains: a domain of things taken as symbols and governed by rules of syntax, and a domain of other things. Call these two domains, respectively, the 'syntactic domain' and the 'semantic domain'. There must also be a relation between these two domains—the "semantic relation".

Understanding, in the usual and familiar sense of type-1 understanding, is a semantic enterprise in Morris's sense of semantics. But this has some surprising ramifications. Once these are seen, we can turn to the less familiar, type-2 sense of understanding as a syntactic enterprise (§3).

When faced with some new phenomenon or experience, we seek to understand it. Perhaps this need to understand has some evolutionary survival value; perhaps it is uniquely human. Our first strategy in such a case is to find something, no matter how incomplete or inadequate, with which to *compare* the new phenomenon or experience. By thus *interpreting* the "unknown" or "new" in terms of the "known" or "given", we seek analogies that will begin to satisfy, at least for the moment, our craving for understanding. For instance, I found the film, *My Twentieth Century*, to be very confusing (albeit quite entertaining—part of the fun was trying to figure it out, trying to understand it). I found that I could understand it—at least as a working hypothesis—by mapping the carefree character Lili to the pleasure-seeking, hedonistic aspects of 20th-century life; another character—her serious twin sister, Dora—to the revolutionary political activist, social-caring aspects of 20th-century life; and the third main character—a professor—to the rational, scientific aspects of 20th-century life. The film, however, is quite complex, and these mappings—these correspondences or analogies—provided for me at best a weak, inadequate understanding. The point, however, is that I *had to*—I was *driven to*—find *something* in terms of which I could make sense of what I was experiencing.

This need for connections as a basis for understanding, as an anchor in uncharted waters, can also be seen in the epiphenal well-house episode in the life of Helen Keller. With water from the well running over one hand while Annie Sullivan finger-spelled 'w-a-t-e-r' in the other, Helen suddenly understood that 'w-a-t-e-r' meant water (Keller 1905). This image of one hand literally in the semantic domain and the other literally in the syntactic domain is striking. By "co-activating" her knowledge (her understanding) of the semantic domain (viz., her experiences of the world around her) and her knowledge of the syntactic domain (viz., her experiences of finger-spellings), she was able to "integrate" (or "bind") these two experiences and thus understand (cf. Mayes 1991: 111).

Is there an alternative to the classical view of semantics as correspondence? Many philosophers and linguists look with scorn upon formal or model-theoretic semantics. However, as long as one is willing to talk about "pairings" of sentences (or their structural descriptions) with meaning (cf. Higginbotham 1985: 3), there is no alternative. That is, if we are to talk *at all* about "the meaning *of* a sentence", we must talk about *two* things: sentences and meanings. Thus, there must be two domains: the domain of sentences (described syntactically) and the domain of the semantic interpretation.

There is, however, another kind of semantics, which linguists not of the formal persuasion study. Here, one is concerned not with what the meanings of linguistic items are, but with semantic relationships among linguistic items: synonymy, implication, etc.[6] These relationships are usually distinct from, though sometimes dependent upon, syntactic relationships. But note that they are, nonetheless, relationships *among linguistic, i.e., syntactic, items*. Hence, on our terms, they, too, are "syntactic", not "semantic".[7] So, semantics is either correspondence or else syntactic.

2.2 Tarskian Semantics.
2.2.1 Syntactic systems.

On the standard view, the syntactic domain is usually some (formalized) language L, described syntactically. That is, one specifies a stock of symbols and rules for forming well-formed formulas (WFFs) from them. (What I intend by 'symbols' are just marks, (perhaps) physical inscriptions or sounds, that have only some very minimal features such as having distinguished, relatively unchanging shapes capable of being recognized when encountered again.) A *language* is sometimes augmented with a *logic*: Certain WFFs of L are distinguished as axioms (or "primitive theorems"), and rules of inference are provided that specify how to produce "new" theorems from "old" ones. The general pattern should be familiar (see, e.g., Rapaport 1992ab). The point is that all we have so far are symbols and (syntactic) rules for manipulating them either linguistically (to form WFFs) or logically (to form theorems)—syntax in Morris's sense.

2.2.2 Semantic interpretations.

Given a syntactic domain such as L, one can ask purely "internal", syntactic, questions: What are L's WFFs and theorems? One can also ask: What's the meaning of all this? What do L's symbols mean (if anything)? What, e.g., is so special about the WFFs or the theorems? To answer this sort of question, we must go outside the syntactic domain, providing "external" entities that the symbols mean, and showing the mappings—the associations, the correspondences—between the two domains.

Now a curious thing happens: I need to show you the semantic domain. If I'm very lucky, I can just point it out to you—we can look at it together, and I can describe the correspondences ("The symbol A_{37} means that red thing over there."). But, more often, I have to describe the semantic domain to you in... symbols, and hope that the meaning of *those* symbols will be obvious to you.

As an example, let's see how to provide a semantic interpretation of L. Assuming L has individual terms, function symbols, and predicate symbols —combinable in various (but not arbitrary) ways—I need to provide meanings for each such symbol as well as for their legal combinations. So, we'll need a non-empty domain **D** of things that the terms will mean and sets **F** and **R** of things that L's function and relation symbols will mean, respectively. These three sets can be collectively called **M** (for Model). **D** contains anything you want to talk or think about. **F** and **R** contain functions and relations on **D** of various arities—i.e., anything you want to be able to say about the things in **D**. That's our *ontology*, what there is.

Now for the correspondences. To say what a symbol of L means in **M**, we can define an interpretation mapping I that will assign to each symbol of L something in **M**. Again, the general way of doing this should be familiar (cf. Rapaport 1992ab). Typically, I is a homomorphism; i.e., it satisfies a principle of compositionality: The interpretation of a molecular symbol is determined by the interpretations of its atomic constituents in the usual recursive manner. Ideally, I is an *isomorphism*—a 1–1 and onto homomorphism; i.e., *every* item in **M** is the meaning of *just one* symbol of L.[8] (Being onto is tantamount to L's being "complete".) In this ideal situation, **M** is a virtual duplicate of L. (Indeed, **M** could *be* L itself (cf. Chang & Keisler 1973: 4ff), but that's not very interesting or useful for *understanding* L.) Less ideally, there might be symbols of L that are *not* interpretable in **M**: I would be a *partial* function. Such is the case when L is English and **M** is the world ('unicorn' is English, but unicorns don't exist), though if we "enlarge" or "extend" **M** in some way, then we can make I total (e.g., we could take **M** to be Meinong's *Aussersein* instead of the actual world; cf. Rapaport 1981). In another less ideal circumstance, "Horatio's Law" might hold: There are more things in **M** than in L; i.e., there are elements of **M** not expressible in L: I is not onto. Or I might be a relation, not a function, so L would be ambiguous. There is another, more global, sense in which L could be ambiguous: By choosing a different **M** (and a different *I*), we could give the symbols of *L* entirely distinct meanings. Worse, the two **M**s need not be isomorphic.

Suppose that *L* is a language for ordinary propositional logic and that **M** is a model for it consisting of states of affairs and Boolean operations on them. As an experiment, one could devise an exotic formal symbol system *L'* using, say, boxes and other squiggles as symbols, and give it a syntax like—but not *obviously* like—that of *L* (say, with only postfix notation, to make it more disorienting). Not realizing that it was syntactically isomorphic to *L*, one could only understand *L'* by getting used to manipulating its symbols, laboriously creating WFFs and proving theorems: doing grammatical and logical syntax. But one could provide relief by giving a semantic interpretation of *L'* in terms of a model whose domain is *L*'s atomic *symbols*. Of course, I could also have told you what *L"*'s symbols mean in terms of *L*'s model, **M**. In that case, *L'* just *is* ordinary propositional logic, exotically notated. In the first way, the model for *L'* is itself a syntactic formal symbol system (viz., *L*) whose meaning can be given in terms of **M**, but *L"*'s meaning can be given either in terms of *L or* in terms of **M**.

Obviously, the exotic *L'* is not a very "natural" symbol system. Usually, when one presents the syntax of a formal symbol system, one already has a semantic interpretation in mind, and one *designs* the syntax to "capture" that semantics: In a sense that will become clearer, the syntax is a model—an implementation—of the semantics.

We also see that it is possible and occasionally even useful to allow *one syntactic* formal symbol system to be the semantic interpretation of *another*. Of course, this is only useful if the interpreting syntactic system is antecedently understood. How? In terms of *another* domain with which we are antecedently familiar! So, in our example, the unfamiliar *L'* was interpreted in terms of the more familiar *L*, which, in turn, is interpreted in terms of **M**. And how is it that we understand what states of affairs in the world are? Well...we've just gotten used to them.

In our example, *L* is a sort of "swing" domain, serving as *L"*'s *semantic* domain and as **M**'s *syntactic* domain. We can have a "chain" of domains, each of which except the first is a semantic domain for its predecessor, and each of which except the last is a syntactic domain for its successor. To understand any domain in the chain, we must understand its successor. How do we understand the last one? Syntactically. But I'm getting ahead of myself. Let's first look at some "chains".

2.3 The Correspondence Continuum: Data.

Let's begin with examples of *pairs* of things: One member of each pair plays the role of the syntactic domain; the other plays the role of the semantic domain.

1. The first example is the obvious one: *L* and **M** (or *L'* and *L*).

2. The next examples come from what I'll call (after Wartofsky 1979) *The Muddle of the Model in the Middle*. There are two notions of "model" in science and mathematics: We speak of a "mathematical model" of some physical phenomenon, by which we mean a mathematical, usually formal, theory of the phenomenon. In this sense, a model is a *syntactic* domain whose intended semantic interpretation is the physical phenomenon being "modeled". But we also speak of a semantic interpretation of a syntactic domain as a "model", as in the phrase 'model-theoretic semantics'. In this sense, a model is a *semantic* domain. We have the following syntax/semantics pairs:

   data/formal theory (i.e., theory as interpretation of the data),
   formal theory/set-theoretic (or mathematical) model (i.e., a model of the theory),
   set-theoretic (or mathematical) model/real-world phenomenon.

   The latter is closely related to—if not identical with—the data that we began with, giving us a cycle of domains! (Cf. Rosenblueth & Wiener 1945: 316.)

3. A *newspaper photograph* can be thought of as a semantic interpretation of its *caption*. But a cognitive agent reading the caption and looking at the photo makes further correspondences: (a) There will be a mental model of the caption—the reader's semantic interpretation of the caption-as-syntax; (b) there will be a mental model of the photo—the reader's semantic interpretation of the photo-as-syntax; and, (c) there may be a single mental model that collates the information from each of these and which, in turn, is a semantic interpretation of the picture+caption unit. (Srihari & Rapaport 1989, 1990; Srihari 1991ab.)

4. A *musical score*, say, Bach's *Goldberg Variations*, is a piece of syntax; a *performance of* it is a semantic interpretation. And, of course, there could be a performance of the *Goldberg Variations* on piano or on a harpsichord. E.g., a piano transcription of a symphony is a semantic interpretation of the symphony (cf. Pincus 1990; conversely, Smith (1985: 636) considers "musical scores as models of a symphony").

5. Similarly, the *script* of a play is syntax; a *performance* of the play is a semantic interpretation. For a performance to be a semantic interpretation of the script, an actual *person* would play the role (i.e., be the semantic interpretation) of a *character* in the play. (Scripts are like computer programs; performances are like computer processes; see example 17; cf. Rapaport 1988a.)

6. A *movie* or *play* based on a *novel* can be considered a semantic interpretation of the text. In this case, there must be correspondences between the characters, events, etc., in the book and the play or movie, with some details of the book omitted (for lack of time) and some things in the play or movie added (decisions must be made about the colors of costumes, which might not have been specified in the book, just as one can *write* about a particular elephant without specifying whether it's facing left or right, but one can't *show*, *draw*, or *imagine* the elephant without so specifying).

7. Consider a narrative text as a piece of syntax: a certain sequence of sentences and other expressions in some natural language. The *narrative* tells a *story*—the story is a semantic interpretation of the text. On this way of viewing things, the narrative has a "plot"—descriptions of certain events in the story, but not necessarily ordered in the chronological sequence that the events "actually" occurred in. Thus, one story can be told in many ways, some more interesting

or suspenseful than others. The story takes place in a "story world". Characters, places, times, etc., in the story world correspond to linguistic descriptions or expressions of them in the narrative. (Cf. Segal 1995.)

8. The reader of the narrative constructs a mental model of the narrative as he or she reads it. This mental story is a semantic interpretation of the syntactic narrative. Or one could view it as a *theory* constructed from the narrative-as-data (cf. Bruder et al. 1986; Duchan et al. 1995).

9. Examples 4-8 suggest a tree of examples: Some *narrative text* might be interpreted as a *play*, on which an *opera* is based. There could be a *film* of a *ballet* based on the *opera*, and these days one could expect a "*novelization*" of the film. Of course, a (different) ballet could be based directly on the play, or a film could have been based directly on the play, then novelized, then re-filmed. Or a symphony might have been inspired by the play, and then have several performances.

10. The *linguistic and perceptual "input"* to a cognitive agent can be considered as a syntactic domain whose semantic interpretation is provided by the agent's *mental model* of his or her (or its) sensory input. (The mental model is the agent's "theory" of the sensory "data"; cf. examples 2, 8.)

11. The *mental model*, in turn, can be considered as a syntactic language of thought whose semantic interpretation is provided by the *actual world*. In this sense, a person's beliefs are true to the extent that they correspond to the world.

12. In Kamp's Discourse Representation Theory, there is a discourse (i.e., a linguistic text—a piece of syntax), a (sequence of) discourse representation structures, and the actual world (or a representation thereof), with mappings from the discourse to the discourse representation structures, from the discourse to the world, and from the discourse representation structures to the world. Each such mapping is a semantic interpretation. One can also consider the correspondences, if any, between the story world and the actual world; these, too, are semantic. (Cf. examples 7, 8, 10, and 11.)

13. The *Earth* is the semantic domain for a global *map*.

14. A *house* is a semantic interpretation of a *blueprint* (cf. Potts 1973, Rapaport 1978, Smith 1985).

15. A *scale model* (say, of an airplane) corresponds to the *thing modeled* (say, the airplane itself) as syntax to semantic interpretation. And, of course, the thing modeled could itself be a scale model, say, a statue; so I could have a model of a statue, which is, in turn, a model of a person. (Cf. Smith 1985, Shapiro & Rapaport 1991).

16. A *French translation* of an *English text* can be seen from the French speaker's point of view as a *semantic* interpretation of the English syntax, and from the English speaker's point of view as a *syntactic* expression of the English (cf. Gracia 1990: 533).

17. A computer *program* is a static piece of syntax; a computer *process* can be thought of as its semantic interpretation. And, according to Smith, one of the concerns of knowledge representation is to interpret *processes* in terms of the actual world: "It follows that, in the traditional terminology, the *semantic* domain of traditional programming language analyses [which "take...semantics as the job of mapping programs onto processes"] should be the knowledge representer's so-called *syntactic* domain" (Smith 1987: 15, 17-18).

18. A *data structure* (such as a stack or a record) provides a semantic interpretation of (or, a way of categorizing) the otherwise inchoate and purely syntactic *bits* in a computer (Tenenbaum & Augenstein 1981, Schneiderman 1993). Suppose we have a computer program intended to model the behavior of customers lining up at a bank. Some of its data structures will represent customers. This gives rise to the following transitive syntax-semantics chain: syntactic bits are semantically interpreted by data structures, which, in turn, are semantically interpreted as customers. (Cf. Smith 1982: 11.)

No doubt you can supply more examples. My conclusion is this:

Semantics and correspondence are co-extensive. *Whenever* two domains can be put into a correspondence (preferably, but not necessarily, a homomorphism), one of the domains (which can be considered to be the *syntactic domain* can be understood in terms of the other (which will be the *semantic domain*).

2.4 The Correspondence Continuum: Implications.

The syntactic domain need not be a "language", either natural or formal. It need only be analyzable into parts (or symbols) that can be combined and related—i.e., manipulated—according to rules. (Cf. Wartofsky 1979: 6.)

Moreover, *the so-called "syntactic" and "semantic" domains must be treated on a par*; i.e., one cannot say of a domain that it is syntactic except relative to another domain which is taken to be the semantic one, and vice versa: "[T]he question of whether an element is syntactic or semantic is a function of the point of view; the syntactic domain for one interpretation function can readily be the semantic domain of another (and a semantic domain may of course include its own syntactic domain)" (Smith 1982: 10).

Finally, *what makes something an appropriate **semantic** domain is that it be antecedently understood*. This is crucial for promoting semantics as "mere" correspondence to the more familiar notion of semantics as meaning or under-standing. And ultimately such antecedent understanding is syntactic manipulation of the items in the semantic domain.

Suppose that something identified as the semantic domain is *not* antecedently understood, but that the putative syntactic domain *is*. Then, by switching their roles, one can learn about the former semantic domain by means of its syntactic "interpretation" (cf. Rosenblueth and Wiener 1945: 318, Corless 1992: 203).[9]

2.5 The Correspondence Continuum of Brian Cantwell Smith.

What I have referred to as the "correspondence continuum" has received its most explicit statement and detailed investigation in the writings of Brian

Cantwell Smith (from whom I have borrowed the term).

2.5.1 Worlds, models, and representations.

In an important essay on computer ethics, Smith (1985) sets up the Wartofskian "model muddle" as follows:

> When you design...a computer system, you first formulate a model of the problem you want it to solve, and then construct the computer program in its terms. ...
>
>   To build a model is to conceive of the world in a certain delimited way. ...[C]omputers have a special dependence on these models: *you write an explicit description of the model down inside the computer*, in the form of a set of rules or...*representations*—...linguistic formulae encoding, in the terms of the model, the facts and data thought to be relevant to the system's behaviour. ...[T]hat's really what computers are (and how they differ from other machines): they run by manipulating representations, and representations are always formulated in terms of models. (Smith 1985: 636.)

The model is an abstraction of the real-world situation. For instance, "a hospital blueprint would pay attention to the structure and connection of its beams, but not to the arrangements of proteins in the wood the beams are made of..." (Smith 1985: 637). The model is itself "modeled" or *described* in the computer program; the model, thus, is a "swing domain", playing the role of syntactic domain to the real world's semantic domain, and the role of semantic domain to the computer program's syntactic—indeed, linguistic—description of it.

Smith calls the process of abstraction (which for him includes "every act of conceptualization, analysis, categorization", in addition to the mere omission of certain details) a necessary "act of violence—[if you] don't ignore some of what's going on—you would become so hypersensitive and so overcome with complexity that you would be unable to act" (Smith 1985: 637). Of course, one ought to do the least amount of violence consistent with not being overwhelmed. This might require successive approximations to a good model that balances abstraction against adequacy. Lakoff's complaints about "objectivism" (1987) can be seen as a claim that "classical" categories defined by necessary and sufficient conditions do too much violence, so that the resulting models are inadequate to the real-world situations.

But I fail to see why complexity makes acting difficult. The real-world situation has precisely the maximal degree of complexity, yet a human *is* capable of acting. Moreover, a complete and complex model of some real-world situation might be so complex that a mere human trying to understand *it* might "drown" in its "infinite richness" (Smith 1985: 637), much as a human can't typically hand-trace a very long and complex computer program. Yet a computer can execute that program without "drowning" in its complexity.

Nevertheless, for Smith, "models are inherently *partial*. All thinking, and

85

all computation, ...similarly *have* to be partial: that's how they are able to work" (Smith 1985: 637). Note that some of the partiality of thinking and computation is inherited from the partiality of the model and then compounded: To the extent that thinking and computation use partial descriptions of partial models of the world, they are doubly partial. Much inevitably gets lost in translation, so to speak. Models certainly need to be partial, at least to the extent that the omitted "implementation" details are irrelevant, and certainly to the extent that they (or their descriptions) are discrete whereas the world is continuous. But does thinking "have to be partial" in order to be "able to work"? A *real* thinking thing isn't partial—it is, after all, part of the real world—though its descriptions of models of the world might be partial. And that's really Smith's point—thinking things (and computing things) work with partial models. They "represent the world *as being a certain way*", "*as being one way as opposed to another*" (Smith 1987: 4, 51n.1): They present a fragmentary point of view, a facet of a complete, complex real-world situation—they are objects under a (partial) description (cf. Castañeda 1972).

So we have the following situation. On one side is the real world in all its fullness and complexity. On the other side are partial models of the world and—embedded in computer programs—partial descriptions of the models. But there is a gap between full reality, on the one hand, and partial models and descriptions, on the other, insofar as the latter fail to capture the richness of the former, which they are intended to interact with: Action "is not partial. ...When you reach out your hand and grasp a plow, it is the real field you are digging up, not your model of it...[C]omputers, like us, participate in the real world: they take real actions" (Smith 1985: 637-638). This holds for programs with natural-language competence, too. Their actions are speech acts, and they affect the real world to the extent that communication between them and other natural-language-using agents is successful.

To see how the "reaching out" can fail to cross the gap, consider a blocks-world robot I once saw, programmed with a version of an AI program (Winston 1977) for picking up and putting down small objects at various locations in a confined area. This robot really dealt with the actual world—it was not a simulation. But it did so successfully only by accident. If the blocks were *perfectly* arranged in the blocks-world area, all went well. But if they were slightly out of place—as they were on the day I saw the demo—the robot blindly and blithely executed its program and behaved as if it were picking up, moving, and putting down the blocks. More often, it failed to pick them up, knocked others down as it rotated, and dropped those it hadn't grasped correctly. It was humorous, even pathetic. The robot was doing what it was "supposed" to do, what it was programmed to do, but its partial model was inadequate. Its *successful* runs were, thus, accidental—they worked only if the real world was properly aligned to allow the robot to affect it in the "intended" manner. Clearly, a robot with a more complete model would do better. The Rochester checkers-playing robot, for example, has a binocular vision system that enables it to "see" what it's doing and to bring its motions into alignment with a changing world (Marsh et al. 1992).

So, computers participate in the real world *without interpretations of their behavior by humans* and without the willing participation of humans.[10] Does a computer with natural-language competence really "use language" or "communicate" without a human interpreter? There are two answers: 'yes' and 'no, but so what?':

Yes: As long as the computer is using the vocabulary of some natural language according to its rules of grammar, it is thereby using that language, even if there is no other language-using entity around, including a human. This is true for humans, too: Even if I talk to myself without uttering a sound, I mean things by my silent use of language; sound or other external signs of language-use are not essential to language (Cho 1992). And, therefore, neither is a hearer or other interlocutor.[11]

No; but so what?: A human might interpret the computer's natural-language output differently from how the computer "intended" it. Or one might prefer to say that the computer's output is meaningless until a human interprets it. The output would be mere syntax; its semantics would have to be provided by the human, *although it could be provided by another natural-language–using computer*. However, interpretation problems can arise in human-to-human communication, too. Nicolaas de Bruijn once told me roughly the following anecdote: Some chemists were talking about a certain molecular structure, expressing difficulty in understanding it. De Bruijn, overhearing them, thought they were talking about mathematical lattice theory, since everything they said could be—and was—interpreted by him as being about the mathematical, rather than the chemical, domain. He told them the solution of their problem in terms of lattice theory. They, of course, understood it in terms of chemistry. Were de Bruijn and the chemists talking about the same thing? No; but so what? They *were* communicating!

It is also important to note that when a natural-language–competent computer interacts with a human or another natural-language–competent computer, both need to be able to reach a more-or-less stable state of mutual comprehension. If the computer uses an expression in an odd way (perhaps merely because it was poorly programmed or did not adequately learn how to use that expression), the human (or other interlocutor) must be able to correct the computer—*not* by reprogramming it—but by *telling* it, in natural language, what it should have said. Similarly, if the human uses an expression in a way that the computer does not recognize, the computer must be able to figure out what the human meant. (Cf. Rapaport 1988b and §§2.6.2, 3, below.)

2.5.2 The model-world gap and the third-person point of view.

The gap between model and world is difficult, perhaps impossible, to bridge:

...we in general have no guarantee that the models are right—indeed we have no *guarantee* about much of anything about the relationship between model and world.

...

...[T]here is a very precise mathematical theory called "model theory." You might think that it would be a theory about what models are, what they are good for, how they correspond to the worlds they are models of. ...Unfortunately,...model theory doesn't address the model-world relationship at all. Rather, what model theory does is to tell you how your descriptions, representations, and programs *correspond to your model*. (Smith 1985: 638.)

To "address the model-world relationship" requires a language capable of dealing with *both* the model *and* the world. This would, at best, be a "Russellian" language that allowed sentences or propositions to be constructed out of real-world objects (Russell 1903, Moore 1988). It would have to have sentences that explicitly and directly linked parts of the model with parts of the world (recall Helen Keller at the well house). How can such model-world links be made? The only way, short of a Russellian language, is by having *another* language that describes the world, and then provide links between *that* language and the model. (That would have to be done in a meta-language. I am also assuming, here, that the model is a language—a description of the world. If it is a non-linguistic model, we would need yet another language to describe *it*.) But this leads to a Bradleyan regress, for how will we be able to address the relationship between the world and the language that describes it? This parallels the case of the mind, which, insofar as it has no direct access to the external world, has no access to the reference relation.

According to Smith, model theory discusses only the relation (call it R_1) between a model and its description. It does not deal with the relation (call it R_2) between the model and the real-world situation. But if semantics is correspondence, the two cases should be parallel; one ought to be able to deal with both R_1 and R_2, or with neither. Yet we have just seen that R_2 cannot be dealt with except indirectly. Consider R_1. Is it the case that the relation between the computer and the model is dealt with by model theory? No; as Smith says, it deals with the relation between a *description* of the model and the model. After all, the computer is part of the real world (cf. Rapaport 1985/1986: 68). So the argument about the model-world relationship also holds here, for, in the actual computer, there is a physical (real-world) implementation of the model.

Thus, a relation between a syntactic domain and a semantic domain can be understood only by taking an independent, external, third-person point of view. There must be a standpoint—a language, if you will—capable of having equal access to *both* domains. A semantic relation can obtain between two domains, but neither domain can describe that relation by itself. From the point of view of the model, nothing can be said about the world. Only from the point of view of some agent or system capable of taking *both* points of view simultaneously can comparisons be made and correspondences established.

2.5.3 Assymetry.

Smith begins "The Correspondence Continuum" by considering such core semantic or intentional relations as representation and knowledge, "asymmetric" relations that "characterise phenomena that are *about* something, that refer to the world, that have meaning or content" (Smith 1987: 2). What kind of asymmetry is this? Wartofsky has argued that any domain can be used to represent another (cf. our data in §2.3) and that the modeling relation (cognitive agent *S* takes domain *x* as a model of domain *y*) is asymmetric. Yet Wartofsky says that it is not merely that *x* and *y* cannot be switched, but rather that in order for *S* to take *x* as a model of *y*, *x* must (be believed by *S* to) have fewer relevant properties than *y*, because if it were "equally rich in the same properties...it would be identical with its object", and if it were "*richer* in properties,...these would then not be ones relevant to its object; it [the object] wouldn't possess them, and so the model couldn't be taken to represent them in any way" (Wartofsky 1979: 5-7).

But it is more appropriate to locate the asymmetry in the fact that the model must be antecedently understood: Suppose an antecedently understood model *M* of some state of affairs or object *O* has fewer properties than *O*, the case that Wartofsky takes to be the norm. Here, the asymmetry between *M* and *O* could be ascribed either to *M*'s having fewer properties (as Wartofsky would have it) or to *M*'s being antecedently understood (as I would have it). Suppose, next, that *M* and *O* have the same properties. On Wartofsky's view, the asymmetry is lost, but if I antecedently understood *M*, I could still use *M* as a model of *O*: This is the situation of Dennett's Ballad of Shakey's Pizza Parlor (1982: 53-60): Since all Shakey Pizza Parlors are indistinguishable, I can use my knowledge of one to understand the others (e.g., to locate the rest rooms). Finally, suppose that *M* has *more* (or perhaps merely *different*) properties than *O*. For example, one could use (the liquidity of) milk as a model of (the liquidity of) mercury (at least, for certain purposes),[12] even though milk has more (certainly, different) properties. These extra (or different) properties are "implementation details"; but they are *merely* that—hence, to be ignored. As long as I antecedently understand *M*, I can use it as a model of *O*, no matter how many properties it has. But if I *don't* antecedently understand *M*, then I *can't* use it as a model (cf. n. 9). And how do I antecedently understand *M*? By getting used to it.

2.5.4 The continuum.

Smith sees the classical semantic enterprise as a special case of a general theory of correspondence. I see *all* cases of correspondence as being semantic.

Smith distinguishes various types of correspondences. Some semantic relations, e.g., are transitive; others aren't (Smith 1987, e.g., p. 27). Consider, as he suggests, a photo (P_2) of a photo (P_1) of a ship (S). Smith observes that P_2 is not, on pain of use-mention confusion, a photo of S, but that this is "pedantic". Clearly, there are differences between P_1 and P_2: Properties of P_1 *per se* (say, a scratch on the negative) might appear in P_2 and be mistakenly attributed to S. But consider a photo of a map of the world; I *could* use the *photo* as a map to locate, say, Vichy, France. As Smith points out, the photo of the map isn't a map (just as P_2 isn't a photo of S). Yet *information* is preserved, so the photo can be *used as* a map (or: to the extent that information is preserved, it can be so used).

Another of Smith's examples is a document-image–understanding system, which has a knowledge representation of a digital image of a photo (cf. example 3, above). Does the knowledge representation represent the digitized image, or does it represent the photo? The practical value of such a system lies in the knowledge representation representing the photo, not the (intermediate) digitized image. But perhaps, to be pedantic about it, we should say that the knowledge representation does represent the digitized image even though *we* take it *as* representing the photo. After all, the digitized image is internal to the document-image–understanding system, which has no direct access to the photo. Of course, neither do we. Smith seems to agree:

> The true situation...is this: a given intentional structure—language, process, impression, model—is set in correspondence with one or more other structures, each of which is in turn set in correspondence with still others, at some point reaching (we hope) the states of affairs in the world that the original structures were genuinely about.
>
> It is this structure that I call the 'correspondence continuum'—a semantic soup in which to locate transitive and non-transitive linguistic relations, relations of modelling and encoding, implementation and realisation. ...(Smith 1987: 29.)

But can one distinguish among this variety of relations? What makes modeling different from implementation, say? Perhaps one can distinguish between transitive and non-transitive semantic relations,[13] but within those two categories, useful distinctions cannot really be drawn, say, between modeling, encoding, implementation, etc. Perhaps one can say that there are "intended" distinctions, but these cannot be pinned down. Perhaps one can say that it is the person doing the relating who decides, but is that any more than giving different names or offering external purposes? Indeed, Smith suggests (p. 29) that the only differences are individual ones.

He thinks, though, that not all "of these correspondence relations should be counted as genuinely semantic, intentional, representational" (p. 30), citing as an example the correspondences between (1a) an optic-nerve signal and (1b) a retinal intensity pattern, between (2a) the retinal intensity pattern and (2b) light-wave structures, between (3a) light-wave structures and (3c) "surface shape on which sunlight falls", and between (4a) that sunlit surface shape and (4b) a cat. He observes that "it is the cat that I see, not any of these intermediary structures"

(p. 30). But so what? Some correspondence relations are not present to consciousness. Nonetheless, they can be treated as semantic.

Not so, says Smith: "correspondence is a far more general phenomenon than representation or interpretation" (p. 30). Perhaps to be "genuinely semantic" (p. 30) is to be *about* something. But why *can't* we say that the retinal intensity pattern is "about" the light-wave structures? Or that the light-wave structures are "about" the sunlit surface shape? The relation between two of these purely physical processes is one of information transfer, so it is surely semantic. Note that it seems to be precisely when phenomena are information-theoretic that models of them *are* the phenomena themselves: Photos of maps *are* maps; models of minds *are* minds.

In any case, what is important for my purposes is Smith's claim that

> the correspondence continuum challenges the clear difference between "syntactic" and "semantic" analyses of representational formalisms... . ...[N]o simple "syntactic/semantic" distinction gets at a natural joint in the underlying subject matter. (Smith 1987: 38.)

Although he might be making the point that there can be no "pure" syntactic (or semantic) analyses—that each involves the other—his discussion suggests that the "challenge" is the existence of swing domains.

2.5.5 *Smith's Gap, revisited.*

So we have a continuum, or at least a chain, of domains that correspond to one another, each (except the last) understandable in terms of the next. Yet where the last domain is the actual world, Smith's Gap separates it from any model of it. Nonetheless, if that model of the world is in the mind of a cognitive agent—if it is *Cassie's* mental model of the world—then it was constructed (or it developed) by means of perception, communication, and other direct experience or direct contact with the actual world. In terms of Smith's three-link chain (§2.5.1) consisting of a part of the actual world (W), a set-theoretic model of it (M_W), and a linguistic description (in some program) of the model (D_{M_W}), what we have in Cassie's case is that her mental model of the world is simultaneously M_W and D_{M_W}. It is produced by causal links with the external world. Thus, the gap is, in fact, bridged (in this case, at least). Bridged, but not comprehended. In formalizing something that is essentially *in*formal, one can't *prove* (formally, of course) that the formalization is correct; one can only discuss it with other formalizers and come to some (perhaps tentative, perhaps conventional) agreement about it. Thus, Cassie can never check to see if her formal M_W really does match the informal, messy W. Thus, the gap remains. But, once bridged, M_W is independent of W, except when Cassie interacts with W by conversing, asking a question, or acting. That is the lesson of methodological solipsism. Let us turn to Cassie's construction of M_W.

2.6 Cassie's Mental Model.

How does Cassie (or any (computational) cognitive agent) construct her mental model of the world, and what does that model look like? I will focus on her language-understanding abilities—her mental model of a conversation or narrative. (For visual perception, cf. example 3, above.) Details of Cassie's language-understanding abilities have been discussed in a series of earlier papers.[14] Here, I will concentrate on a broad picture of how she processes linguistic input, and a consideration of the kind of world model she constructs as a result.

2.6.1 Fregean semantics.

Frege wanted to divorce logic and semantics from psychology. He told us that terms and expressions (signs, or symbols) of a language "express" a "sense" and that to some—but not all—*senses* there "corresponds" a "referent". So expressions indirectly "designate" or "refer" (or fail to designate or refer) to a referent. Further, the sense is the "way" in which the referent is presented by the expression. Except for the mentalistic notion of an "associated idea", which he does not take very seriously, all of this is very objective or non-cognitive (Frege 1892).

Something exactly like this goes on in cognition, when Cassie—or any natural-language–understanding cognitive agent—understands language:

1. Cassie perceives (hears or reads) a sentence.
2. By various computational processes (namely, an augmented-transition-network parser with lexical and morphological modules, plus various modules for dealing with anaphora resolution, computing belief spaces and subjective contexts, etc.), she constructs (or finds) a molecular node in the semantic network that is her mental model.
3. That node constitutes her understanding of the perceived sentence.

Now, the procedures that input pieces of language and output nodes are algorithms—*ways* in which the nodes are associated with the linguistic symbols. They are, thus, akin to senses, and the nodes are akin to referents (cf. Wilks 1972). Here, though, all symbols denote, even 'unicorn' and 'round square': If Cassie hears or reads about a unicorn, she constructs a node representing her concept (her understanding) of that unicorn. Her nodes represent the things she has thought about, whether or not they exist—they are part of her "epistemological ontology" (Rapaport 1985/1986).

A very different correspondence can also be set up between natural-language understanding and Frege's theory. According to this correspondence, it is the node in Cassie's mental model that is akin to a sense, and it is an object (if one exists) in the actual world to which that node corresponds that is akin to the referent. On this view, Cassie's unicorn-node represents (or perhaps is) the sense of what she read about, although (unfortunately) there is no corresponding referent in the external world. Modulo the subjectivity or psychologism of this correspondence (Frege would not have identified a sense with an expression of a language of thought), this is surely closer in spirit to Frege's enterprise.

Nonetheless, the first correspondence shows how senses can be interpreted as algorithms that yield referents (a kind of "procedural semantics"; see, e.g., Winograd 1975, Smith 1982). It also avoids the problem of non-denoting expressions: If no "referent" is found, one is just constructed, in a Meinongian spirit (cf. Rapaport 1981).

The various links between thought and language are direct and causal. Consider natural-language generation, the inverse of natural-language understanding. Cassie has certain thoughts; these are private to her.[15] By means of various natural-language-generation algorithms, she produces—directly and causally, from her private mental model—public language: utterances or inscriptions. I hear or read these; this begins the process of natural-language *understanding*. By means of *my* natural-language–understanding algorithms, I interpret her utterances, producing—directly and causally—my private thoughts. Thus, I interpret another's private thoughts indirectly, by directly interpreting her public expressions of those thoughts, which public expressions are, in turn, her direct expressions of her private thoughts. (Cf. Gracia 1990: 495.)

The two direct links are both semantic interpretations. The public expression of Cassie's thoughts is a semantic interpretation (an "implementation" or physical "realization") of her thoughts. And my understanding of what she says is a semantic interpretation of her public utterances. Thus, the public communication language (Shapiro 1993) is a "swing domain".

2.6.2 The nature of a mental model.

Cassie's mental model of the world (including utterances expressed in the public communication language) is expressed in her language of thought. That is, the world is modeled, or represented, by expressions—sentences—of her language of thought (which, for the sake of concreteness, I am taking to be SNePS). There may, of course, be more: e.g., mental imagery. But since Cassie can think and talk about images, they must be linked to the part of her mental model constructed via natural-language understanding (Srihari 1991ab). Hence, we may consider them part of an extended language of thought that allows such imagery among its terms. This extended language of thought, then, is propositional with direct connections to imagistic representations.

In Section 1, I asked how we understand language. This is the challenge of Searle's (1980) Chinese Room Argument: How could Searle-in-the-room come to know the semantics of the Chinese squiggles? One question left open in that debate is whether Searle-in-the-room even knows what their *syntax* is. He could not come to know the syntax (the grammar) just by having, as Searle suggests, a SAM-like program (i.e., a program for global understanding of a narrative using scripts; cf., e.g., Schank & Riesbeck 1981); a syntax-learning program is also needed (see, e.g., Berwick 1979; cf. §1.1.2.2, above). So let us assume that Searle-in-the-room's instruction book includes this.

Given an understanding of the syntax, how can semantics be learned? The meaning of some terms is best learned ostensively, or perceptually: We must see (or hear, or otherwise experience) the term's referent. This ranges from terms for such archetypally medium-sized physical objects as 'cat' and 'cow', through 'red' (cf. Jackson 1986) and 'internal combustion engine', to such abstractions as 'love' and 'think' (cf. Keller 1905: 40f, 300).

But the meaning of many, perhaps most, terms is learned "lexically", or linguistically. Such is dictionary learning. But equally there is the learning, on the fly, of the meaning of new words from the linguistic contexts in which they appear. If 'vase' is unknown, but one learns that Tommy broke a vase, then one can compute that a vase is that which Tommy broke. Initially, this may appear less than informative, though further inferences can be drawn: Vases, whatever they are, are breakable by humans, and all that that entails.[16] As more occurrences of the word are encountered, the "simultaneous equations" (Higginbotham 1989: 469) of the differing contexts, together with background knowledge and some guesswork, help constrain the meaning further, allowing us to revise our theory of the word's meaning. Sooner or later, a provisionally steady state is achieved (pending future occurrences). (See §3.2.2.)

Both methods are contextual. For ostension, the context is physical and external—the real world (or, at least, our perception of it); for the lexical, the context is linguistic (Rapaport 1981). Ultimately, however, the context is mental and internal: The meaning of a term represented by a node in a semantic network is dependent on its location in—i.e., the surrounding context of—the rest of the network (cf. Quine 1951, Quillian 1967, Hill 1994). Such holism has a long and distinguished history, and its share of skeptics (most recently, Fodor and Lepore (1992)). It certainly appears susceptible to charges of circularity (cf., e.g., Harnad 1990), but a chronological theory of how the network is constructed can help to obviate that: Granted that the meaning of 'vase' (for me) may depend on the meaning of 'breakable' *and vice versa*, nonetheless if I learned the meaning of the latter first, it can be used to ground the meaning of the former (for me). Holism, though, has benefits: The meanings of terms get enriched, over time, the more they—or their closest-linked terms in the network—are encountered. For instance, in the research for this essay, certain themes reappeared in various contexts, each appearance enriching the others. In writing, however, one must begin somewhere—writing is a more or less sequential, not a parallel or even holistic, task. Though this is the first mention of holism in the essay, it was not the first in my research, nor will it be the only one.

Understanding, we see again, is recursive. Each time we understand something, we understand it in terms of all that has come before. Each of those things, earlier understood, were understood in terms of what preceded them. The base case is, retroactively, understandable in terms of all that has come later:

> There should therefore be a time in adult life devoted to revisiting the most important books of our youth. Even if the books have remained the same (though they do change, in the light of an altered historical perspective), we have most certainly changed, and our encounter will be an entirely new thing. (Calvino 1986: 19.)

But initially, the base case was understandable solely in terms of itself (or in terms of "innate ideas" or some other mechanism; see Hill 1994 on the semantics of base nodes in SNePS).

But *is* "knowledge of the semantics" (Barwise & Etchemendy 1989: 209) achieved by speakers? If this means knowledge of the relations between word and thing in such a way that it requires knowledge of *both* the words (syntactic knowledge) *and* the things, then: No. For we can't have (direct) knowledge of the things. This is Smith's Gap. It also means, by the way, that ostensive learning is really mental and internal, too: I learn what 'cat' means by seeing one, but really what's happening is that I have a mental representation of that which is before my eyes, and what constitutes the ostensive meaning is a (semantic) link that is established between my internal node associated with 'cat' and the *internal* node that represents what is before my eyes.

Thus, "knowledge of the semantics" means (1) knowledge of the relations *between* our linguistic concepts and our "purely conceptual" concepts (i.e., that correspond to, or are caused by, external input) and (2) knowledge of the relations *among* our purely linguistic concepts. The former (1) is "semantic", the latter (2) "syntactic", as classically construed. Yet, since the former concerns relations among our internal concepts (cf. Srihari 1991ab), it, too, is syntactic.[17]

Barwise and Etchemendy (1989) conflate such an internal semantic theory with a kind of external one, identifying *"content of a speaker's knowledge* of the truth conditions of the sentences of his or her language" with *"the relationship between sentences and non-linguistic facts* about the world that would support the truth of a claim made with the sentence" (p. 220, my italics). I take "the content of a speaker's knowledge of...truth conditions" to involve knowing the relations between linguistic and non-linguistic *internal* concepts. This is the internal, Cassie-approach to semantics. In contrast, giving an "account of the relationship between sentences and non-linguistic facts" (p. 220) is an *external* endeavor, one that *I* can give concerning Cassie, but not one that *she* can give about herself. This is because *I* can take a "God's-eye", "third-person" point of view and see both Cassie's mind and the world external to it, thus being able to relate them, whereas she can only take the "first-person" point of view.

However, a "third person" cannot, in fact, have direct access to either the external world or Cassie's concepts (except as in n. 15). So what the third person is *really* comparing (or finding correspondences between) is the third person's *representations* of Cassie's concepts and the third person's *own concepts* representing the external world. That is, the third person *can* establish a semantic correspondence (in the classic sense) between two domains. From the third person's point of view, the two domains are the syntactic domain of Cassie's concepts and the semantic domain of the external world. But, in fact, the two domains are *the third person's representations* of Cassie's concepts and *the third person's representations* of the external world. These are both *internal* to the third person's mind! And internal relations, even though structurally *semantic*—i.e., even though they are correspondences between two domains—are fundamentally *syntactic* in the classic sense: They are relations *among* (two classes of) symbols in the third person's language of thought.

What holds for the third person holds also for Cassie. Since she doesn't have direct access to the external world either, she can't have knowledge of "real" semantic correspondences. The best she can do is to have a correspondence between certain of her concepts and her representations of the external world. What might her "knowledge of truth conditions" look like? Here is one possibility: When she learns that Lucy is rich, she builds the network shown in Figure 1.

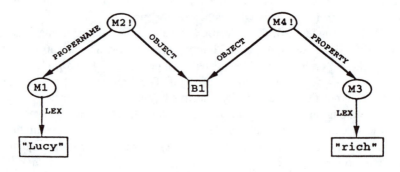

Figure 1: Cassie's belief that Lucy is rich. (Linearly abbreviated: **M4** = **B1** is rich; **M2** = **B1** is named 'Lucy'. Node labels with '!' appended are "asserted", i.e., believed by Cassie.)

Thus, Cassie might think to herself something like: "My thought that [Figure 1] is true iff ($\exists x \in$ external world)[x = Lucy & x is rich]". This would require, for its full development, (1) an internal truth predicate (cf. Maida & Shapiro 1982, Neal & Shapiro 1987), (2) an existence predicate (cf. Hirst 1991), (3) a duplication of the network, and (4) a biconditional rule asserting the equivalence (see Figure 2 for a possible version).

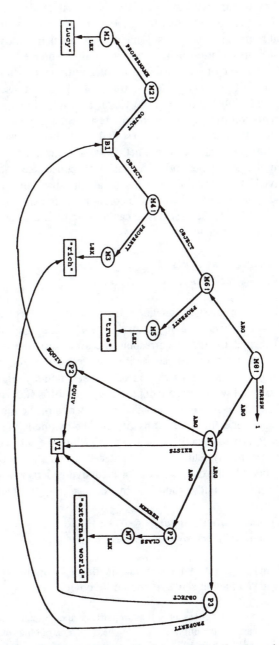

Figure 2: A biconditional rule (**M8**) asserting the equivalence of **M6** = that Lucy is rich is true, and **M7** = something in the external world is Lucy and is rich. (See Shapiro 1979, Shapiro & Rapaport 1987 for the semantics of **thresh**. The truth condition for **M2** is not shown.)

The picture we have of Cassie's mental model of the world (including utterances) is, in part, this: If Cassie hears or reads a sentence, she constructs a mental representation of that sentence qua linguistic entity, *and* she constructs a mental representation of the state of affairs expressed by that sentence. These will be linked by a Tarski-like truth-biconditional (**M8**) asserting that the representation of the sentence (**M7**) is true (**M6**) iff the representation of the state of affairs (**M7**) is believed (**M7 !**). If Cassie sees something, she constructs a mental representation of it, *and* she constructs a mental propositional representation of the state of affairs she sees. These will be linked in ways extrapolatable from §2.3, example 3, above. These networks, of course, are not isolated, but embedded in the entire network that has been constructed so far. What is newly perceived is understood in terms of all that has gone before. This is purely syntactic, since both sides of the biconditional are expressed in Cassie's language of thought. Thus, the best Cassie can do is to have a theory of truth as coherence among her own concepts.

3 Semantics as Syntax.
3.1 The Story So Far.

To understand language is to construct a semantic interpretation—a model—of the language. In fact, we *normally* understand something by modeling it and then determining correspondences between the two domains. In some cases, we are lucky: We can, as it were, keep an eye on each domain, merging the images in our mind's eye. In other cases, notably when one of the domains is the external world, we are not so lucky—Smith's Gap cannot be crossed—and so we can understand that domain *only* in terms of the model. Lucky or not, we understand one thing in terms of another by modeling that which is to be understood (the syntactic domain) in that which we antecedently understand (the semantic domain). But how is the antecedently understood domain antecedently understood? In the base case of our recursive understanding of understanding, a domain must be understood in terms of *itself*, i.e., syntactically.

3.2 Syntactic Understanding.
3.2.1 Familiarity breeds comprehension.

What is type-2, syntactic understanding? What does it mean to "get used to" something? In some sense, it should be obvious:

> In today's chess, only the familiarly shaped Staunton pieces are used. ... [One] reason is the unfamiliarity, to chess players, of other than Staunton pieces....[In Reykjavik, in 1973, two grandmasters] started to play [with a non-Staunton set], and the conversation ran something like:
> "What are you doing? That's a pawn."
> "Oh. I thought it was a bishop."

"Wait! Maybe it is a bishop."

"No, maybe it really is a pawn."

Whereupon the two grandmasters decided to play without the board. They looked at each other and this time the conversation ran:

"D5"

"C4"

"E6"

"Oh, you're trying *that* on me, are you? Knight C3."

And they went along that way until they finished their game. (Schonberg 1990: 38-39.)

In a game played with Staunton pieces, the players are "used to" the pieces. Even in a game played with no physical pieces at all, the players are "used to" the symbolic notation for the pieces. But in a game played with non-Staunton pieces, clearly they are not.

Suppose that the semantic relation is (merely) a correspondence relation. Suppose, further, that it is a homomorphism mapping the syntactic domain into the semantic domain. To understand something in terms of itself would then be to take the syntactic domain as its own semantic domain, treating the homomorphism as an *automorphism*. Such an automorphism would be a relation among the symbols of the syntactic domain, hence a classically syntactic relation. Yet it would also be a *semantic* relation, because it is a correspondence between "two" domains (better: between two roles played by the same domain). Indeed, the very first example of a semantic model in Chang & Keisler 1973 is such a mapping. The syntactic domain, now considered as its own *semantic* domain, is syntactic twice over: once by way of its own, purely syntactic, features, and once by way of the semantic automorphism. (Recall the way some linguists do semantics; cf. §2.1.)

Now, the automorphism is either the identity mapping, or it isn't. If it is, then the symbol manipulations (the syntax) that constitute the semantics are just those of the syntactic domain itself. This is the core meaning of understanding by "getting used to" the system (as in the syntactic way of understanding §2.2.2's *L'*). We do the same thing when we learn how to solve algebraic equations by manipulating symbols (Rapaport 1986).

If the automorphism is *not* the identity mapping, then it must map some elements onto others (or sets of others). So some parts of the syntactic domain will be understood in terms of others. (There may be "fixed points"—symbols that *are* mapped into themselves; see §3.2.3.) Let's see what this means for our central case—natural-language understanding.

3.2.2 Dictionary definitions and algebra.

Dictionary-like definitions are an obvious example of this sort of automorphism. Indeed, this is probably what *most* people mean by "meaning", as opposed to philosophers, logicians, and cognitive scientists—though *some* cognitive scientists are sympathetic: "meanings are, if anything, only other symbols" (Wilks & Fass 1992: 205; cf. Wilks 1971, 1972: 86).

And, as noted earlier (§2.6.2), we learn the meaning of many (if not most) new words in linguistic contexts—either in explicit definitions or "on the fly" in ordinary conversational or literary discourse. The unknown word, like the algebraic unknown, simply means whatever is necessary to give meaning to the entire context in which it appears. The meaning of the unknown word is (the meaning of) the surrounding context—the context "minus" the word. Finding the meaning is, thus, "solving" the context for the unknown: "The appearance of a word in a restricted number of settings suffices to determine its position in the language as a whole" (Higginbotham 1985: 2; cf. Wilks 1971: 519-520). As Wilks 1971 notes, the context must be suitably large to get the "correct" or at least "intended" meaning. But, as the 'vase' example shows (§2.6.2), any context will do for starters. One's understanding of the meaning of the word will *change* as one comes across more contexts in which it is used (or: as the total context becomes larger); ultimately, one's understanding of the meaning will reach a stable state (at least temporarily—everything is subject to revision). Thus, learning a word is theory construction: One's understanding of the word's meaning is a *theory*, subject to revision.

The first time I read the word 'brachet', I did not know what it meant (do you?). Here is the context of that first occurrence:

> [T]here came a white hart running into the hall with a white brachet next to him, and thirty couples of black hounds came running after them with a great cry. (Malory 1470: 66.)

My first hypothesis (believe it or not) was that a brachet was a buckle on a harness worn by the hart. Although this hypothesis goes beyond the algebraic picture I've been painting, the algebraic metaphor is still reasonable if we extend the notion of context to include the background knowledge ("world knowledge" or "commonsense knowledge") that I bring to bear on my understanding of the narrative (cf. Rapaport 1991, Rapaport & Shapiro 1995). Nor does it matter whether this hypothesis is good, bad, indifferent, or just plain silly; if I never see the word again, it won't matter, but, if I do, I will have ample opportunity to revise my beliefs about its meaning. Indeed, after 18 more occurrences of the term,[18] I stabilized on the following theory of its meaning: A brachet is a hound or hunting dog, perhaps a lead hound. Not bad, considering that the *Oxford English Dictionary* defines it as "A kind of hound which hunts by scent". (For details and further references, see Rapaport 1981; Ehrlich & Rapaport 1992; Ehrlich, 1995.)

This is purely syntactic: First, there is no external semantic domain: I did not see a brachet (or a picture of one). Second, when I read the word (or when Cassie does), I build a mental representation of that word embedded in a mental representation of its context. These mental representations are part of the entire network of mental representations in my mind. Thus, the background knowledge I contribute is part and parcel of the mental representation of the new word in context. It is that system of mental representations that constitutes the syntactic domain in which is located "the meaning" of—i.e., my understanding of—the word.

Representing meaning in such a dictionary-like network goes back at least to Quillian 1967, though he was more concerned with merely representing the information in a dictionary, whereas I am concerned with representing meaning as part of a cognitive agent's entire complex network of beliefs. This is a brand of holistic, conceptual-role semantics, since I take the meaning of a word to be, algebraically, the role it plays in its context.

3.2.3 Understanding the parts.

Another thing that using parts of the syntactic domain to understand the rest of it might mean is that those parts are primitives. How are *they* understood? What do *they* mean?

They might be "markers" with no intrinsic meaning. But such markers *get* meaning the more they are used—the more roles they play in providing meaning to *other* nodes. A helpful analogy comes from Wartofsky:

> '[M]ental' objects, or 'internal representations' are derivative, and have their genesis in our primary activity of representing, in which we take external things,—most typically, what we also designate as physical objects—as representations. Moreover, I take our *making* of representations to be, in the first place, the actual praxis of creating concrete objects-in-the-world, *as* representations; or of taking the made objects as representational. (1979: xxi-xxii.)

In this *primary* activity, what do we take the external physical object to be a representation *of*? Its use and history? What does that have to do with the common properties in terms of which one thing can represent another? More likely, it is that, once made, it can *remind us* of its use or of its manufacture and therefore represent those things for us. The *first* time we see an unfamiliar object, it is a meaningless thing (except insofar as it shares any properties with anything familiar, allowing us to form hypotheses about it and to place it in our semantic network). The *second* time we see it, it can remind us of something, if only of itself on its first appearance. Subsequent encounters produce familiarity, which entrench it in our network, and allow newer objects to be understood in terms of *it*. This is how holism works.

Alternatively, the fixed points or the markers (or—for that matter—any of the nodes) are somehow "grounded" in another domain. This, of course, is just to say that they have meaning in the correspondence sense of semantics, and ultimately we will be led to question the way in which we understand that other domain.

3.2.4 The symbol-grounding problem.

The symbol-grounding problem, according to Harnad (1990), is that without grounding, a hermetically sealed circle of nodes can only have circular meaning. And, presumably, circles are vicious and to be avoided.

It is well known that a dictionary is a closed circle of meanings: Each word is defined in terms of other words. Assuming that all words used in the definitions are themselves defined, we have a circle (in fact, several of them). Now, before agreeing with Harnad that such circles cannot yield meaning or understanding, consider that we do use dictionaries fairly successfully to learn meanings. How can this be? A very small circle may indeed not be informative, especially if we don't antecedently know the meaning of the definiens (e.g., 'being' is defined as "existence", and 'exist' as "have being" in *Webster's Vest Pocket Dictionary*). However, the larger the circumference of the circle, so to speak, the more likely it is that it will be informative, on the assumption that the definition of the word whose meaning we seek, and the definitions of the words in that definition, and so on, will contain *lot* of words that we antecedently understand. So, we can easily "solve" the "equation" for the unknown word—i.e., dictionary definitions are most useful to the extent that they are like '$x = (4 - 3)/2$', rather than like '$x = (4y - 3)/2$' (where there is a further unknown in the definiens).

Nonetheless, some words will still only be poorly defined in terms of other words, notably (but not exclusively) nouns like 'cat' or 'cow'. For these, *seeing* a cat or cow (or for 'love', *experiencing* love) is worth a thousand-word definition. Illustrated dictionaries handle this with a type distinction in the syntax of the definiens: Terms can be of the type *word* or the type *picture*. But although we now have grounding in an extra-linguistic system, *it is still part of the dictionary*. And, of course, the pictures could, with a suitable indexing scheme, themselves be definiendum entries: A picture of a cat could have as its "definiens" the word 'cat', as in a visual dictionary or a field guide to cats. This, of course, only widens the circle. We could widen it further, albeit at some expense and inconvenience: Let every dictionary come with a real cat; ditto for all other better-ostensively-defined terms. We still have a circle, but now, I think, Harnad would have to agree that we've also got grounding—we've merely incorporated the groundings into the dictionary.

The same holds for the mind. Harnad says a link is needed between (some) mental nodes (say, our "cat" node) and items in the external world (say, a cat). Although we can't import such items directly into our minds, we *can* have mental representations of them. And it is the relation between our "cat" node and a node representing a perceived cat that grounds the former. We saw how in §2.6.2: What we (or Harnad) *think* is the relation between word and world is really a connection between an internal representation of a perceived *word* and an internal representation of the perceived *world*.

Do not misunderstand me: Experience certainly enriches our understanding. Consider "immersion" learning of a foreign language. "Thinking in French" is understanding French holistically, without any correspondences to one's native language (say, English). It is helped immeasurably by living in a francophone community. When we ask "What does the French word '*chat*' mean?", and we give the answer ("cat") in English words, we are doing pure *syntax* (here, relating symbols from one system to those of another) *that is also semantic* (understanding one system in terms of another). This is no different than answering the question in French ("*un chat est un petit animal domestique, dont il existe aussi plusieurs espèces sauvages*")[19]—except for choice of language for the definiens. Giving the definition in English is just as much symbol grounding as pointing to a cat would be. Symbol grounding, thus, does *not* necessarily get us out of the circle of words—at best, it widens the circle. That is my point: Syntactic understanding—the base case of understanding—is just a *very* wide circle.

Surprisingly, Harnad's own examples of grounding are internal in just the ways we have been considering. He distinguishes between "symbolic" and "nonsymbolic" representations (Harnad 1990: 335, Abstract). But *both* are *internal* representations. Harnad says that non-symbolic "*iconic representations...are* **internal** analog transforms of the projections of distal objects on our sensory surfaces" (p. 342; Harnad's italics, my boldface). Such a projection could be a retinal image, say. So an iconic representation is some "analog transform" of *that*, stored (or created) somewhere further along the optic pathway. Thus, it could be part of our semantic network (cf. Srihari 1991ab). Furthermore, the symbolic and non-symbolic representational systems must be linked; hence, because of Smith's Gap, they must all be internal.

One would *expect* internal items to be "grounded" in *external* ones. But in Harnad's hierarchy (p. 335, Abstract), symbolic representations are "grounded" in "elementary symbols", which are "names" of "categories", which categories are "assigned on the basis of" categorical representations, which representations are "derived" from sensory projections; and iconic representations are "analogs" of those sensory projections. In fact, the only actual use of the term 'grounding' is between symbolic representations and elementary symbols, *both of which are internal*. Indeed, *all* the items on this hierarchy are internal!

Curiously, Harnad only mentions "grounding in the world" in a footnote:

> If a candidate model [for a cognitive system] were to exhibit all...behavioral capacities, both *linguistic* ["produce" and "respond to descriptions of...objects, events, and states of affairs"]...and *robotic* ["discriminate,...manipulate,...[and] identify...the objects, events and states of affairs **in the world they live in**]..., it would pass the "total Turing test". ... A model that could pass the total Turing test, however, would be **grounded in the world**. (Harnad 1990: 341fn13; Harnad's italics, my boldface.)

Recall the blocks-world and checkers-playing robots (§2.5.1). The former is blind and methodologically solipsistic. The latter can see. But is it grounded? Could it be fooled as the blind robot was? Possibly: by Cartesianly deceiving its eyes. It would then "live in" a world in which to be was to be perceived. Of course, such a Berkeleyan robot *would* be grounded *in the world that it lives in*, which happens not to be the actual world, but a purely intensional one. (In this case, note that the grounding system *and* the grounded one are *both* internal, hence part of a single network.) What would such a robot's symbols mean *to it*? Here, internal semantic interpretation would be done by internal links only.

Even more curious is the fact that grounding for Harnad—even grounding in the external world—does not seem to serve a semantic function:

> Iconic representations no more "mean" the objects of which they are the projections than the image in a camera does. Both icons and camera images can of course be *interpreted* as meaning or standing for something, but the interpretation would clearly be derivative rather than intrinsic. (p. 343.)

Harnad seems to be saying here that the causal connection of the iconic representations with its real-world counterpart is irrelevant to its intrinsic meaning. In that case, Harnad owes us answers to two questions: (1) what does such a causal grounding *do* in his theory, and (2) what *is* the intrinsic meaning of an iconic representation? Harnad may have identified an interesting problem, but he doesn't seem to have solved it.

My position is this: The mind-world gap cannot be bridged by the mind. There are causal links between them, but the only role these links play in semantics is this: The mind's internal representations of external objects (which internal representations are caused by the external objects) *can* serve as "referents" of other internal symbols, but, since they are all internal, meaning is in the head and is syntactic.

A purely syntactic system is ungrounded, up in the air, self-contained. But there are arbitrarily many ways to ground it; that is, there are infinitely many possible interpretations for any syntactic system. By "communicational negotiation", we (agree to) ground our language of thought in equivalent ways for all practical purposes (cf. Bruner 1983). Harnad seeks a *natural* grounding (cf. "intended interpretation"). Some candidates, such as the (human) body, are convenient.[20] But such natural groundings are merely one or two among many. The only one that is non-arbitrary is the "null" grounding, the "self" grounding: the purely syntactic, "internal" mode of understanding. "'Explanations come to a stop' as...Wittgenstein would put it; 'there is a last house in the lane'" (Leiber 1991: 54; cf. Wittgenstein 1958: §1, p. 3e, and §29, p. 14e). The last semantic domain in a correspondence continuum is the "last house in the lane". It can only be understood syntactically. Hence, all understanding rests on syntactic understanding.

This is one of the flaws in Searle's Chinese-Room Argument. Part of his argument is that computers can never understand natural language because (1) understanding natural language requires (knowledge of) semantics, (2) computers can only do syntax, and (3) syntax is insufficient for semantics. I take *my* argument to have shown that (3) is false (and that, therefore, (2) is misleading, since the kind of syntax that computers do *ipso facto* allows them to do semantics).

4   Summary

We understand one domain recursively in terms of an antecedently understood one. The "base" case is the case in which a domain is understood in terms of itself. When a syntactic domain is its own semantic domain, the semantic interpretation function either maps the symbols to themselves or else to other symbols. In the former case, we understand the domain by "getting used to" its syntax. In the latter case, if there are no fixed points—if each symbol is mapped to a different one—then we have the situation we face when using a dictionary. The difference is that since all external items are also mapped into internal ones, the symbol-grounding problem can be avoided. If there *are* fixed points, then they come to be understood either retroactively in terms of the role they play in the understanding of other terms, or else by "grounding" them to "non-linguistic"—albeit *internal*—symbols.

In any case, we have a closed network of meaning—a holistic, "conceptual-role semantics". And that is how semantics can arise from syntax.

Notes

1.   Kamp 1984, Kamp & Reyle 1993.
2.   Brachman & Schmolze 1985, Woods & Schmolze 1992.
3.   Schank & Rieger 1974, Schank & Riesbeck 1981, Hardt 1992, Lytinen 1992.
4.   Sowa 1984, 1992.
5.   Cassie is the Cognitive *A*gent of the *S*NePS *S*ystem—an *I*ntelligent *E*ntity. Oscar is the *O*ther *S*NePS Cognitive *A*gent *R*epresentation. Shapiro & Rapaport 1985; Rapaport, Shapiro, & Wiebe 1986.
6.   Kean Kaufmann and Matthew Dryer helped me see this.
7.   Kaufmann says that *cognitive* linguistics is not to be included here, presumably because it pairs sentences with meanings "in the head" ("cognitive" meanings), in which case, of course, it is a correspondence theory of semantics.
8.   Perhaps isomorphism is less than ideal, at least for the case of natural languages. When one studies, not isolated or made-up sentences, but "real, contextualised utterances...it is often the case that all the elements that one would want to propose as belonging to semantic structure have no overt manifestations in syntactic structure. ...[T]he degree of isomorphism between semantic and syntactic structure is mediated by pragmatic and functional concerns..." (Wilkins 1992: 154).
9.   If one understands *neither* domain antecedently, then one might be able to learn both together, either by seeing the same structural patterns in both, or by "getting used

to" them both. (Although, possibly, this contradicts the second observation, above.) In this case, neither is the syntactic domain—or else both are!

10. This has *moral* implications, too, as Smith emphasizes in his essay.
11. Though without an interlocutor, it could not pass the Turing Test; cf. §1.1.2.1.
12. Not for understanding its meniscus; the example is due to Kripa Sundar.
13. "In a case where the elements of syntactic domain S correspond to elements of semantic domain D_1, and the elements of D_1 are themselves linguistic, bearing their own interpretation relation to another semantic domain D_2, then the elements of the original domain S are called *metalinguistic*. Furthermore, the semantic relation is taken to be *non-transitive*, thereby embodying the idea of a strict use-mention distinction, and engendering the familiar hierarchy of metalanguages" (Smith 1987: 9). However, it's not clear that S really *is* linguistic (although D_1 *is*), for S will typically consist of *names* of items in D_1, but names are not linguistic in Smith's sense. Second, suppose that S = French, D_1 = English, and D_2 = the actual world. Then the semantic relation *is* transitive, and there is *no* use-mention issue. Here, I am thinking of a machine-translation system, *not* of the case of a French-language textbook written in English (i.e., a textbook whose object language is French and whose metalanguage is English). Clearly, though, there *are* systems of the sort described in this assumption.
14. See, e.g., Shapiro 1982, 1989; Rapaport 1986, 1988b, 1991; Rapaport, Shapiro, & Wiebe 1986; Wiebe & Rapaport 1986, 1988; Almeida 1987; Neal & Shapiro 1987; Shapiro & Rapaport 1987, 1991, 1995; Peters, Shapiro, & Rapaport 1988; Neal et al. 1989; Peters & Rapaport 1990; Wyatt 1990, 1993; Wiebe 1991, 1994; Rapaport & Shapiro 1995.
15. Except, of course, that I, as her programmer and a "computational neuroscientist" (so to speak), have direct access to her thoughts and can manipulate them "directly" in the sense of not having to manipulate them via language. That is, as her programmer, I can literally "read her mind" and "put thoughts into her head". But I ought, on methodological (if not moral!) grounds, to refrain from doing so (as much as possible). I should only "change her mind" via conversation.
16. Example due to Karen Ehrlich.
17. The first time you read this, you either found it incomprehensible or insane. By now, it should be less of the former, if not the latter, since its role in the web of my theory should be becoming clearer.
18. The protocols appear in Ehrlich, 1995.
19. *Dictionnaire de Français* (Paris: Larousse, 1989): 187. Translation: A cat is a small domestic animal of which there also exist many wild species. Hardly an adequate definition!
20. For discussion of various aspects of this, see Leiber 1980, Johnson 1987, Lakoff 1987, Turner 1987, Kirsh 1991, Perlis 1991, Dreyfus 1992.

References

Almeida, Michael J. (1987), "Reasoning about the Temporal Structure of Narratives," *Technical Report 87-10* (Buffalo: SUNY Buffalo Department of Computer Science).

Barwise, Jon, & Etchemendy, John (1989), "Model-Theoretic Semantics," in M. I. Posner (ed.), *Foundations of Cognitive Science* (Cambridge, MA: MIT Press): 207-243.

Berwick, Robert C. (1979), "Learning Structural Descriptions of Grammar Rules from

Examples," *Proceedings of the Sixth International Joint Conference on Artificial Intelligence (IJCAI-79*, Tokyo) (Los Altos, CA: William Kaufmann): 56-58.

Brachman, Ronald J., & Schmolze, James G. (1985), "An Overview of the KL-ONE Knowledge Representation System," *Cognitive Science* 9: 171-216.

Bruder, Gail A.; Duchan, Judith F.; Rapaport, William J.; Segal, Erwin M.; Shapiro, Stuart C.; & Zubin, David A. (1986), "Deictic Centers in Narrative: An Interdisciplinary Cognitive-Science Project," *Technical Report 86-20* (Buffalo: SUNY Buffalo Department of Computer Science).

Bruner, Jerome (1983), *Child's Talk: Learning to Use Language* (New York: W. W. Norton).

Calvino, Italo (1986), "Why Read the Classics?" *The New York Review of Books* (9 October 1986): 19-20.

Castañeda, Hector-Neri (1972), "Thinking and the Structure of the World," *Philosophia* 4 (1974) 3-40; reprinted in 1975 in *Critica* 6 (1972) 43-86.

Chang, C. C., & Keisler, H. J. (1973), *Model Theory* (Amsterdam: North-Holland).

Cho, Kah-Kyung (1992), "Re-thinking Intentionality" (in Japanese), in Y. Nitta (ed.), *Tasha-no Genshogaku (Phenomenology of the Other)* (Hokuto Publishing Co.).

Corless, R. M. (1992), "Continued Fractions and Chaos," *American Mathematical Monthly* 99: 203-215.

Dennett, Daniel C. (1982), "Beyond Belief," in A. Woodfield (ed.), *Thought and Object* (Oxford: Clarendon Press): xvi-95.

Dreyfus, Hubert L. (1992), *What Computers Still Can't Do: A Critique of Artificial Reason* (Cambridge, MA: MIT Press).

Duchan, Judith F.; Bruder, Gail A.; & Hewitt, Lynne (eds.) (1995), *Deixis in Narrative: A Cognitive Science Perspective* (Hillsdale, NJ: Lawrence Erlbaum Associates).

Ehrlich, Karen (1995), "Automatic Vocabulary Expansion through Narative Contexts," *Technical Report 96-09* (Buffalo: SUNY Buffalo Department of Computer Science).

Ehrlich, Karen, & Rapaport, William J. (1992), "Automatic Acquisition of Word Meanings from Natural-Language Contexts," *Technical Report 92-03* (Buffalo: SUNY Buffalo Center for Cognitive Science, July 1992).

Fodor, Jerry A. (1975), *The Language of Thought* (New York: Thomas Y. Crowell Co.).

Fodor, Jerry, & Lepore, Ernest (1992), *Holism: A Shopper's Guide* (Cambridge, MA: Basil Blackwell).

Frege, Gottlob (1892), "On Sense and Reference," M. Black (trans.), in P. Geach & M. Black (eds.), *Translations from the Philosophical Writings of Gottlob Frege* (Oxford: Basil Blackwell, 1970): 56-78.

Gracia, Jorge J. E. (1990), "Texts and Their Interpretation," *Review of Metaphysics* 43: 495-542.

Hardt, Shoshana L. (1992), "Conceptual Dependency," in S. C. Shapiro (ed.), *Encyclopedia of Artificial Intelligence*, 2nd edition (New York: John Wiley & Sons): 259-265.

Harnad, Stevan (1990), "The Symbol Grounding Problem," *Physica D* 42: 335-346.

Higginbotham, James (1985), "On Semantics," reprinted in E. Lepore (ed.), *New Directions in Semantics* (London: Academic Press, 1987): 1-54.

Higginbotham, James (1989), "Elucidations of Meaning," *Linguistics and Philosophy* 12: 465-517.

Hill, Robin (1994), "Issues of Semantics in a Semantic-Network Representation of

84 / William J. Rapaport

Belief," *Technical Report No. 94-11* (Buffalo: SUNY Buffalo Department of Computer Science).

Hirst, Graeme (1991), "Existence Assumptions in Knowledge Representation," *Artificial Intelligence* 49: 199-242.

Jackson, Frank (1986), "What Mary Didn't Know," *Journal of Philosophy* 83: 291-295.

Johnson, Mark (1987), *The Body in the Mind: The Bodily Basis of Meaning, Imagination, and Reason* (Chicago: University of Chicago Press).

Kamp, Hans (1984), "A Theory of Truth and Semantic Representation," in J. Groenendijk, T. M. V. Janssen, & M. Stokhof (eds.), *Truth, Interpretation, and Information* (Dordrecht: Foris): 1-41.

Kamp, Hans, & Reyle, Uwe (1993), *From Discourse to Logic: Introduction to Modeltheoretic Semantics of Natural Language, Formal Logic and Discourse Representation Theory* (Dordrecht, Holland: Kluwer Academic Publishers).

Keller, Helen (1905), *The Story of My Life* (Garden City, NY: Doubleday, 1954).

Kirsh, David (1991), "Foundations of AI: The Big Issues," *Artificial Intelligence* 47: 3-30.

Lakoff, George (1987), *Women, Fire, and Dangerous Things: What Categories Reveal about the Mind* (Chicago: University of Chicago Press).

Leiber, Justin (1980), *Beyond Rejection* (New York: Ballantine Books).

Leiber, Justin (1991), *An Invitation to Cognitive Science* (Cambridge, MA: Basil Blackwell).

Lytinen, Steven L. (1992), "Conceptual Dependency and Its Descendants," *Computers and Mathematics with Applications* 23: 51-73.

Maida, Anthony S., & Shapiro, Stuart C. (1982), "Intensional Concepts in Propositional Semantic Networks," *Cognitive Science* 6: 291-330.

Malory, Sir Thomas (1470), *Le Morte D'Arthur*, ed. and trans. by R. M. Lumiansky (New York: Collier Books, 1982).

Marsh, Brian; Brown, Chris; LeBlanc, Thomas; Scott, Michael; Becker, Tim; Quiroz, Cesar; Das, Prakash; & Karlsson, Jonas (1992), "The Rochester Checkers Player: Multimodal Parallel Programming for Animate Vision," *Computer*, Vol. 25, No. 2 (February 1992) 12-19.

Mayes, A. R. (1991), Review of [*inter alia*] H. Damasio & A. R. Damasio, *Lesion Analysis in Neuropsychology*, in *British Journal of Psychology* 82: 109-112.

Minsky, Marvin (1975), "A Framework for Representing Knowledge," in P. H. Winston (ed.), *The Psychology of Computer Vision* (New York: McGraw-Hill).

Moore, Robert C. (1988), "Propositional Attitudes and Russellian Propositions," *Report No. CSLI-88-119* (Stanford, CA: Center for the Study of Language and Information).

Morris, Charles (1938), *Foundations of the Theory of Signs* (Chicago: University of Chicago Press).

Neal, Jeannette G., & Shapiro, Stuart C. (1987), "Knowledge Based Parsing," in L. Bolc (ed.), *Natural Language Parsing Systems* (Berlin: Springer-Verlag).

Neal, Jeannette G.; Thielman, C. Y.; Dobes, Zuzanna; Haller, Susan M.; & Shapiro, Stuart C. (1989), "Natural Language with Integrated Deictic and Graphic Gestures," *Proceedings of the DARPA Speech and Natural Language Workshop* (Morgan Kaufmann): 14.

Perlis, Donald (1991), "Putting One's Foot in One's Head—Part I: Why," *Noûs* 25: 435-455.

Peters, Sandra L., & Rapaport, William J. (1990), "Superordinate and Basic Level

Categories in Discourse: Memory and Context," *Proceedings of the 12th Annual Conference of the Cognitive Science Society (Cambridge, MA)* (Hillsdale, NJ: Lawrence Erlbaum Associates): 157-165.

Peters, Sandra L.; Shapiro, Stuart C.; & Rapaport, William J. (1988), "Flexible Natural Language Processing and Roschian Category Theory," *Proceedings of the 10th Annual Conference of the Cognitive Science Society (Montreal)* (Hillsdale, NJ: Lawrence Erlbaum Associates): 125-131.

Pincus, Andrew L. (1990), "The Art of Transcription Sheds New Light on Old Work," *The New York Times*, Arts and Leisure (Sect. 2) (23 September 1990).

Potts, Timothy C. (1973), "Model Theory and Linguistics," in E. L. Keenan (ed.), *Formal Semantics of Natural Language* (Cambridge, Eng.: Cambridge University Press, 1975): 241-250.

Quillian, M. Ross (1967), "Word Concepts: A Theory and Simulation of Some Basic Semantic Capabilities," *Behavioral Science* 12: 410-430.

Quine, Willard Van Orman (1951), "Two Dogmas of Empiricism," reprinted in W. V. Quine, *From a Logical Point of View* (Cambridge, MA: Harvard University Press, 2nd ed., revised, 1980): 20-46.

Rapaport, William J. (1978), "Meinongian Theories and a Russellian Paradox," *Noûs* 12: 153-180; errata, *Noûs* 13 (1979) 125.

Rapaport, William J. (1981), "How to Make the World Fit Our Language: An Essay in Meinongian Semantics," *Grazer Philosophische Studien* 14: 1-21.

Rapaport, William J. (1985/1986), "Non-Existent Objects and Epistemological Ontology," *Grazer Philosophische Studien* 25/26: 61-95.

Rapaport, William J. (1986), "Logical Foundations for Belief Representation," *Cognitive Science* 10: 371-422.

Rapaport, William J. (1988a), "To Think or Not to Think," *Noûs* 22: 585-609.

Rapaport, William J. (1988b), "Syntactic Semantics: Foundations of Computational Natural-Language Understanding," in J. H. Fetzer (ed.), *Aspects of Artificial Intelligence* (Dordrecht, Holland: Kluwer Academic Publishers): 81-131.

Rapaport, William J. (1991), "Predication, Fiction, and Artificial Intelligence," *Topoi* 10: 79-111.

Rapaport, William J. (1992a), "Logic, Predicate," in S. C. Shapiro (ed.), *Encyclopedia of Artificial Intelligence*, 2nd edition (New York: John Wiley): 866-873.

Rapaport, William J. (1992b), "Logic, Propositional," in S. C. Shapiro (ed.), *Encyclopedia of Artificial Intelligence*, 2nd edition (New York: John Wiley): 891-897.

Rapaport, William J. (1993), "Cognitive Science," in A. Ralston & E. D. Reilly (eds.), *Encyclopedia of Computer Science*, 3rd edition (New York: Van Nostrand Reinhold): 185-189.

Rapaport, William J., & Shapiro, Stuart C. (1995), "Cognition and Fiction," in J. F. Duchan, G. A. Bruder, & L. Hewitt (eds.), *Deixis in Narrative: A Cognitive Science Perspective* (Hillsdale, NJ: Lawrence Erlbaum Associates).

Rapaport, William J.; Shapiro, Stuart C.; & Wiebe, Janyce M. (1986), "Quasi-Indicators, Knowledge Reports, and Discourse," *Technical Report 86-15* (Buffalo: SUNY Buffalo Department of Computer Science).

Rosenblueth, Arturo, & Wiener, Norbert (1945), "The Role of Models in Science," *Philosophy of Science* 12: 316-321.

Russell, Bertrand (1903), *The Principles of Mathematics* (New York: W. W. Norton,

1937).

Schank, Roger C., & Rieger, Charles J. (1974), "Inference and the Computer Understanding of Natural Language," *Artificial Intelligence* 5: 373-412.

Schank, Roger C., & Riesbeck, Christopher K. (eds.) (1981), *Inside Computer Understanding: Five Programs Plus Miniatures* (Hillsdale, NJ. Lawrence Erlbaum).

Schneiderman, Ben (1993), "Data Type," in A. Ralston & E. D. Reilly (eds.), *Encyclopedia of Computer Science*, 3rd edition (New York: Van Nostrand Reinhold): 411-412.

Schonberg, Harold C. (1990), "Some Chessmen Don't Make a Move," *New York Times* (15 April 1990), Sect. 2, pp. 38-39.

Searle, John R. (1980), "Minds, Brains, and Programs," *Behavioral and Brain Sciences* 3: 417-457.

Searle, John R. (1993), "The Failures of Computationalism," *Think* (Tilburg, The Netherlands: Tilburg University Institute for Language Technology and Artificial Intelligence) 2 (June 1993) 68-71.

Segal, Erwin M. (1995), "Stories, Story Worlds, and Narrative Discourse," in J. F. Duchan, G. A. Bruder, & L. Hewitt (eds.), *Deixis in Narrative: A Cognitive Science Perspective* (Hillsdale, NJ: Lawrence Erlbaum Associates).

Segal, Erwin M.; Duchan, Judith F.; & Scott, Paula J. (1991), "The Role of Interclausal Connectives in Narrative Structuring: Evidence from Adults' Interpretations of Simple Stories," *Discourse Processes* 14: 27-54.

Shapiro, Stuart C. (1979), "The SNePS Semantic Network Processing System," in N. Findler (ed.), *Associative Networks* (New York: Academic Press): 179-203.

Shapiro, Stuart C. (1982), "Generalized Augmented Transition Network Grammars for Generation from Semantic Networks," *American Journal of Computational Linguistics* 8: 12-25.

Shapiro, Stuart C. (1989), "The CASSIE Projects: An Approach to Natural Language Competence," *Proceedings of the 4th Portuguese Conference on Artificial Intelligence (Lisbon)* (Springer-Verlag): 362-380.

Shapiro, Stuart C. (1993), "Belief Spaces as Sets of Propositions," *Journal of Experimental and Theoretical Artificial Intelligence* 5: 225-235.

Shapiro, Stuart C., & Rapaport, William J. (1987), "SNePS Considered as a Fully Intensional Propositional Semantic Network," in N. Cercone & G. McCalla (eds.), *The Knowledge Frontier: Essays in the Representation of Knowledge* (New York: Springer-Verlag): 262-315.

Shapiro, Stuart C., & Rapaport, William J. (1991), "Models and Minds: Knowledge Representation for Natural-Language Competence," in R. Cummins & J. Pollock (eds.), *Philosophy and AI: Essays at the Interface* (Cambridge, MA: MIT Press): 215-259.

Shapiro, Stuart C., & Rapaport, William J. (1992), "The SNePS Family," *Computers and Mathematics with Applications* 23: 243-275.

Shapiro, Stuart C., & Rapaport, William J. (1995), "An Introduction to a Computational Reader of Narrative," in J. F. Duchan, G. A. Bruder, & L. Hewitt (eds.), *Deixis in Narrative: A Cognitive Science Perspective* (Hillsdale, NJ: Lawrence Erlbaum Associates).

Smith, Brian Cantwell (1982), "Linguistic and Computational Semantics," *Proceedings of the 20th Annual Meeting of the Association for Computational Linguistics (University of Toronto)* (Morristown, NJ: Association for Computational Linguistics):

9-15.

Smith, Brian Cantwell (1985), "Limits of Correctness in Computers," in C. Dunlop & R. Kling (eds.), *Computerization and Controversy* (San Diego: Academic Press, 1991): 632-646.

Smith, Brian Cantwell (1987), "The Correspondence Continuum," *Report No. CSLI-87-71* (Stanford, CA: Center for the Study of Language and Information).

Sowa, John F. (1984), *Conceptual Structures: Information Processing in Mind and Machine* (Reading, MA: Addison-Wesley).

Sowa, John F. (1992), "Conceptual Graphs as a Universal Knowledge Representation," *Computers and Mathematics with Applications* 23: 75-93.

Srihari, Rohini K. (1991a), "PICTION: A System that Uses Captions to Label Human Faces in Newspaper Photographs," *Proceedings of the 9th National Conference on Artificial Intelligence (AAAI-91, Anaheim)* (Cambridge, MA: AAAI/MIT Press): 80-85.

Srihari, Rohini K. (1991b), "Extracting Visual Information from Text: Using Captions to Label Faces in Newspaper Photographs," *Technical Report 91-17* (Buffalo: SUNY Buffalo Department of Computer Science.

Srihari, Rohini K., & Rapaport, William J. (1989), "Extracting Visual Information From Text: Using Captions to Label Human Faces in Newspaper Photographs," *Proceedings of the 11th Annual Conference of the Cognitive Science Society (Ann Arbor, MI)* (Hillsdale, NJ: Lawrence Erlbaum Associates): 364-371.

Srihari, Rohini K., & Rapaport, William J. (1990), "Combining Linguistic and Pictorial Information: Using Captions to Interpret Newspaper Photographs," in D. Kumar (ed.), *Current Trends in SNePS—Semantic Network Processing System, Lecture Notes in Artificial Intelligence, No. 437* (Berlin: Springer-Verlag): 85-96.

Tanenbaum, Andrew S. (1976), *Structured Computer Organization* (Englewood Cliffs, NJ: Prentice-Hall).

Tenenbaum, Aaron M., & Augenstein, Moshe J. (1981), *Data Structures using Pascal* (Englewood Cliffs, NJ: Prentice-Hall).

Turner, Michael (1987), *Death is the Mother of Beauty* (Chicago: University of Chicago Press).

Wartofsky, Marx W. (1979), *Models: Representation and the Scientific Understanding* (Dordrecht: D. Reidel).

Wiebe, Janyce M. (1991), "References in Narrative Text", *Noûs*, 25: 457-486.

Wiebe, Janyce M. (1994), "Tracking Point of View in Narrative," *Computational Linguistics* 20: 233-287.

Wiebe, Janyce M., & Rapaport, William J. (1986), "Representing *De Re* and *De Dicto* Belief Reports in Discourse and Narrative," *Proceedings of the IEEE* 74: 1405-1413.

Wiebe, Janyce M., & Rapaport, William J. (1988), "A Computational Theory of Perspective and Reference in Narrative" *Proceedings of the 26th Annual Meeting of the Association for Computational Linguistics (SUNY Buffalo)* (Morristown, NJ. Association for Computational Linguistics): 131-138.

Wilkins, David P. (1992), "Interjections as Deictics," *Journal of Pragmatics* 18: 119-158.

Wilks, Yorick (1971), "Decidability and Natural Language," *Mind* 80: 497-520.

Wilks, Yorick (1972), *Grammar, Meaning and the Machine Analysis of Language* (London: Routledge & Kegan Paul).

Wilks, Yorick, & Fass, Dan (1992), "The Preference Semantics Family," *Computers and Mathematics with Applications* 23: 205-221.

Winograd, Terry (1975), "Frame Representations and the Declarative/Procedural Controversy," in D. G. Bobrow & A. M. Collins (eds.), *Representation and Understanding* (New York: Academic Press): 185-210.

Winston, Patrick Henry (1977), *Artificial Intelligence* (Reading, MA: Addison-Wesley).

Wittgenstein, Ludwig (1958), *Philosophical Investigations: The English Text of the Third Edition*, trans. by G. E. M. Anscombe (New York: Macmillan).

Woods, William A., & Schmolze, James G. (1992), "The KL-ONE Family," *Computers and Mathematics with Applications* 23: 133-177.

Wyatt, Richard (1990), "Kinds of Opacity and Their Representations," in D. Kumar (ed.), *Current Trends in SNePS—Semantic Network Processing System*, Lecture Notes in Artificial Intelligence, No. 437 (Berlin: Springer-Verlag): 123-144.

Wyatt, Richard (1993), "Reference and Intensions," *Journal of Experimental and Theoretical Artificial Intelligence* 5: 263-271.

UNDERSTANDING NATURAL LANGUAGE *

T HE trouble with Artificial Intelligence is that computers don't give a damn—or so I will argue by considering the special case of understanding natural language. Linguistic facility is an appropriate trial for AI because input and output can be handled conveniently with a teletype, because understanding a text requires understanding its topic (which is unrestricted), and because there is the following test for success: does the text enable the candidate to answer those questions it would enable competent people to answer? The thesis will not be that (human-like) intelligence cannot be achieved artificially, but that there are identifiable conditions on achieving it. This point is as much about language and understanding as about Artificial Intelligence. I will express it by distinguishing four *different* phenomena that can be called "holism": that is, four ways in which brief segments of text cannot be understood "in isolation" or "on a one-by-one basis."

* To be presented at an APA symposium on Artificial Intelligence, December 28, 1979. C. Wade Savage and James Moor will comment; see this JOURNAL, this issue, 633/4, for an abstract of Moor's comment; Savage's paper is not available at this time.

I am grateful for suggestions from Nuel Belnap, Bob Brandom, Bert Dreyfus, Jay Garfield, and Zenon Pylyshyn. Kurt Baier helped with the German, and Genevieve Dreyfus with the French.

0022-362X/79/7611/0619$01.40

I. HOLISM OF INTENTIONAL INTERPRETATION

Consider how one might *empirically* defend the claim that a given (strange) object plays chess. Clearly, it is neither necessary nor sufficient that the object use any familiar chess notation (or pieces); for it might play brilliant chess in some alien notation, or it might produce "chess salad" in what appeared to be standard notation. Rather, what the defense must do is, roughly:

(i) give systematic criteria for (physically) identifying the object's inputs and outputs;

(ii) provide a systematic way of interpreting them as various moves (such as a manual for translating them into standard notation); and then

(iii) let some skeptics play chess with it.

The third condition bears all the empirical weight, for satisfying it amounts to public *observation* that the object really does play chess. More specifically, the skeptics see that, as interpreted, it makes a sensible (legal and plausible) move in each position it faces. And eventually, induction convinces them that it would do so in any position. Notice that, *de facto*, the object is also being construed as "remembering" (or "knowing") the current position, "trying" to make good moves, "realizing" that rooks outrank pawns, and even "wanting" to win. All these interpretations and construals constitute collectively an *intentional interpretation*.

Intentional interpretation is intrinsically holistic. It is supported empirically only by observing that its object makes generally "sensible" outputs, given the circumstances. But the relevant circumstances are fixed by the object's prior inputs and other outputs, *as interpreted*. Thus, each observation distributes its support over a whole range of specific interpretations, no one of which is supported apart from the others. For example, a chess move is legal and plausible only relative to the board position, which is itself just the result of the previous moves. So one output can be construed sensibly as a certain queen move, only if that other was a certain knight move, still another a certain bishop move, and so on.[1]

---

[1] A different argument for a similar conclusion depends on assuming that the inputs and outputs are semantically compound. Then, since each compound will in general share components with many others, their respective interpretations (in terms of their compositions) will be interdependent. Thus the (semantic) role of 'P' in 'P-K4' must be systematically related to its role in 'P-R3', and so on. The argument in the text, however, is more fundamental. There are fewer than two thousand possible chess moves. [Martin Gardner, in his June 1979 *Scientific American* column, gives the figure 1840; but he neglects castling and pawn promotion (see pp. 25/6)]. These could be represented unambiguously by arbitrary numbers, or even simple symbols; yet interpreting an object using such a system would still be holistic, for the earlier reasons.

This is the *holism of intentional interpretation*; and it is all too familiar to philosophers. Intentional interpretation is tantamount to Quine's "radical translation"—including, as Davidson emphasizes, the attribution of beliefs and desires. The condition that outputs be "sensible" (in the light of prior inputs and other outputs) is just whatever the ill-named "principle of charity" is supposed to capture. I have reviewed it here only to distinguish it from what follows.

II. COMMON-SENSE HOLISM

Years ago, Yehoshua Bar-Hillel pointed out that disambiguating "The box was in the pen" requires common-sense knowledge about boxes and pens. He had in mind knowledge of typical sizes, which would ordinarily decide between the alternatives 'playpen' and 'fountain pen'.[2] In a similar vein, it takes common sense to determine the antecedent of the pronoun in: "I left my raincoat in the bathtub, because it was still wet." More subtly, common sense informs our appreciation of the final verb of: "Though her blouse draped stylishly, her pants seemed painted on."

Straightforward questioning immediately exposes any misunderstanding: Was the bathtub wet? Was there paint on her pants? And the issue isn't just academic; a system designed to translate natural languages must be able to answer such questions. For instance, the correct and incorrect readings of our three examples have different translations in both French and German—so the system has to choose. What's so daunting about this, from the designer's point of view, is that one never knows which little fact is going to be relevant next—which common-sense tidbit will make the next disambiguation "obvious." In effect, the whole of common sense is potentially relevant at any point. This feature of natural-language understanding I call *common-sense holism*; its scope and importance was first fully demonstrated in Artificial Intelligence work.

The difference between common-sense holism and the holism of intentional interpretation is easily obscured by vague formulas like: the meaning of an utterance is determinate only relative to *all* the utterer's beliefs, desires, and speech dispositions. This covers both holisms, but only at the price of covering up a crucial distinction. The holism of intentional interpretation is *prior* holism, in the sense that it's already accommodated *before* the interpretation of ongoing discourse. An interpreter *first* finds an over-all

---

[2] "The Present Status of Automatic Translation of Languages," in F. L. Alt, ed., *Advances in Computers* (New York: Academic Press, 1964), vol. i, pp. 158/9. Quoted in H. L. Dreyfus, *What Computers Can't Do*, 2nd ed. (New York: Harper & Row, 1979), p. 215.

scheme that "works" and *then* can interpret each new utterance separately as it comes. For example, once a holistic chess-player interpretation has been worked out, its holism can be ignored—moves can perfectly well be translated "in isolation." [3] By contrast, common-sense holism is *real-time* holism—it is freshly relevant to each new sentence, and it can never be ignored. Even if a perfect dictionary and grammar were available, sentences like our three examples would still have to be disambiguated "in real time," by some appeal to common sense.

The point can be put another way. Prior holism is compatible with the (Fregean) ideal of semantic atomism: the meaning of a sentence is determined by the meanings of its meaningful components, plus their mode of composition. This ideal is (nearly) achieved by chess notations, formal logics, and most programming languages; but it is only grossly approximated by English—assuming that "meaning" is what one "grasps" in understanding a sentence, and that words and idioms are the meaningful components.[4] Real-time holism is precisely *in*compatible with semantic atomism: understanding a sentence requires *more* than a grammar and a dictionary—namely, common sense.[5]

The nature of common-sense holism is brought into sharper relief by current efforts to deal with it—those in Artificial Intelligence being the most concentrated and sophisticated. The hard problem, it turns out, is not simply the enormous volume of common knowledge, but rather storing it so that it can be efficiently accessed and used. Obviously, it is quite impractical to check every available fact for possible relevance, every time some question comes up. So the task is to design a system that will quickly home in on genuinely relevant considerations, while ignoring nearly everything else. This is the "memory organization" or "knowledge representation" problem; what makes it hard is the quixotic way that odd little "facts" turn up as germane.

[3] Cryptography is comparable: code cracking is holistic, but once it succeeds, deciphering goes along on a message-by-message basis.

[4] Hilary Putnam argues that there is more to meaning than what competent speakers understand, but his point is orthogonal to ours ["The Meaning of Meaning," in *Mind, Language and Reality* (New York: Cambridge, 1975)].

[5] It is difficult to say what significance this has (if any) for formal semantics. The most common tactic is to relegate matters of real-time holism to "pragmatics," and apply the semantic theory itself only to idealized "deep structures" [in which ambiguities of sense, pronoun binding, case, mood, scope, etc. are not allowed—thus saving atomism (perhaps)]. A protective quarantine for semantics may or may not work out, but earlier experience with syntax hardly bodes well.

Most contemporary systems employ some variant of the following idea: facts pertaining to the same subject are stored together ("linked") in structured clusters, which are themselves linked in larger structures, according as their subjects are related.[6]

We can think of these clusters as "concepts," so long as we remember that they are much more elaborate and rich than traditional definitions—even "contextual" definitions. For example, the concept for 'monkey' would include not only that they are primates of a certain sort, but also a lot of "incidental" information like where they come from, what they eat, how organ grinders used them, and what the big one at the zoo throws at spectators. It's more like an encyclopedia than a dictionary entry.

Three points will clarify how this is supposed to work. First, much of the specification of each concept lies in its explicit links or "cross references" to other concepts, in an over-all conceptual superstructure. For instance, part of the monkey concept would be an "is-a" link to the primate concept, which has in turn an "is-a" link to the mammal concept, and so on. So, the monkey, rat, and cow concepts can effectively "share" generic information about mammals. Second, entries in a concept can have modalities, like "necessarily," "typically," "occasionally," or even "only when . . . ." The "typically" mode is particularly useful, because it supplies many common-sense "assumptions" or "default assignments." Thus, if monkeys typically like bananas, the system can "assume" that any given monkey will like bananas (pending information to the contrary). Third, concepts often have "spaces" or "open slots" waiting (or demanding) to be "filled up" in stipulated ways. For example, the concept of eating would have spaces for the eater and the eaten, it being stipulated that the eater be animate, and the eaten (typically) be food.

A system based on such concepts copes with common-sense holism as follows. First, a dictionary routine calls the various concepts associated with the words in a given sentence, subject to constraints provided by a syntactical analyzer. Hence, only the information coded in (or closely linked to) these concepts is actually accessed—

---

[6] See, for example: Marvin Minsky, "A Framework for Representing Knowledge," in Patrick Winston, ed., *The Psychology of Computer Vision* (New York: McGraw-Hill, 1975); Yorick Wilks, "Natural Language Understanding Systems within the AI Paradigm," Stanford AI Memo-237, 1974; Roger Schank and Robert Abelson, "Scripts, Plans, and Knowledge," *International Joint Conference on Artificial Intelligence*, IV (1975); Daniel Bobrow and Terry Winograd, "An Overview of KRL, a Knowledge Representation Language," *Cognitive Science*, I, 1 (1977).

passing over the presumably irrelevant bulk. Then the system applies this information to any ambiguities by looking for a combination of concepts (from the supplied pool) which fit each other's open spaces in all the stipulated ways. So, for Bar-Hillel's example, the system might call four concepts: one each for 'box' and 'is in', and two for 'pen'. The "is in" concept would have two spaces, with the stipulation that what fills the first be smaller than what fills the second. Alerted by this requirement, the system promptly checks the "typical size" information under the other concepts, and correctly eliminates 'fountain pen'. An essentially similar procedure will disambiguate the pronouns in sentences like: "The monkeys ate the bananas because they were hungry" or ". . . because they were ripe" (cf. Wilks, *op. cit.* p. 19).

The other two examples, however, are tougher. Both raincoats and bathtubs typically get wet, so *that* won't decide which was wet when I left my coat in the tub. People opt for the coat, because being wet is an understandable (if eccentric) reason for leaving a coat in a tub, whereas the tub's being wet would be no (sane) reason to leave a coat in it. But where is *this* information to be coded? It hardly seems that concepts for 'raincoat', 'bathtub', or 'is wet', no matter how "encylopedic," would indicate when it's sensible to put a raincoat in a bathtub. This suggests that common sense can be organized only partially according to subject matter. Much of what we recognize as "making sense" is not "about" some topic for which we have a word or idiom, but rather about some (possibly unique) circumstance or episode, which a longer fragment leads us to "visualize." Introspectively, it seems that we imagine ourselves into the case, and then decide from within it what's plausible. Of course, *how* this is done is just the problem.

The ambiguity of 'painted-on pants' is both similar and different. Again, we "imagine" the sort of attire being described; but the correct reading is obviously a metaphor—for 'skin tight', which is both coordinated and appropriately contrasted with the stylishly draped blouse. Most approaches to metaphor, however, assume that metaphorical readings aren't attempted unless there is something "anomalous" about the "literal" reading (as in "He is the cream on my peaches," or ". . . faster than greased lightning"). But, in this case there is nothing anomalous about pants with paint on them—they would even clash with "stylish," explaining the conjunction "Though. . . ." On that reading, however, the sentence would be silly, whereas the metaphor is so apt that most people don't even notice the alternative.

These examples are meant only to illustrate the subtlety of common sense. They show that no obvious or crude representation will capture it, and suggest that a sophisticated, cross-referenced "encyclopedia" may not suffice either. On the other hand, they don't reveal much about what's "left out," nor (by the same token) whether that will be programmable when we know what it is. The real nature of common sense is still a wide-open question.

III. SITUATION HOLISM

Correct understanding of a sentence depends not only on general common sense, but also on understanding the specific situation(s) to which it pertains. I don't have in mind the familiar point about descriptions and indexicals, that only the "context" determines *which* table is "the table . . ." or "this table . . . ," and so on. Much more interesting is the situation-dependence of examples like Bar-Hillel's; Dreyfus (*op. cit.*) points out that

> . . . in spite of our *general* knowledge about the relative sizes of pens and boxes, we might interpret "The box is in the pen," when whispered in a James Bond movie, as meaning just the opposite of what it means at home or on the farm (216).

This is not just a problem about "exotic" contexts, where normal expectations might fail; both of the following are "normal":

> When Daddy came home, the boys stopped their cowboy game. They put away their guns and ran out back to the car.

> When the police drove up, the boys called off their robbery attempt. They put away their guns and ran out back to the car.

The second sentence is not exactly ambiguous, but it means different things in the two situations. Did they, for instance, put their guns "away" in a toy chest or in their pockets? (It makes a difference in German: *einräumen* or *einstecken*.) Could 'ran' be paraphrased by 'fled'?

So far, the role of "situation sense" seems comparable to that of common sense, though more local and specific. A fundamental difference appears, however, as soon as the stories get interesting enough to involve an interplay of several situations. A Middle-Eastern folk tale gives a brief example:

> One evening, Khoja looked down into a well, and was startled to find the moon shining up at him. It won't help anyone down there, he thought, and he quickly fetched a hook on a rope. But when he threw it in, the hook snagged on a hidden rock. Khoja pulled and pulled and pulled. Then suddenly it broke loose, and he went right

on his back with a thump. From where he lay, however, he could see the moon, finally back where it belonged—and he was proud of the good job he had done.

The heart of this story is a trade-off between two situations: the real one and the one in Khoja's imagination. The narrative jumps back and forth between them; and it is up to the reader to keep them straight, and also to keep track of their interaction and development.

In the first sentence, for example, the embedded clauses "Khoja found the moon" and "it shined up at him," are clearly about the epistemic situation, despite their grammar. One must understand this at the outset, to appreciate Khoja's progressive misperceptions, and thus his eventual pride. A trickier shift occurs in the clause "It won't help anyone down there . . . ," which must mean *"if it stays* down there" (not: "anyone *who is* down there"). In other words, it's an implicit hypothetical which refers us to yet another situation: a counterfactual one in which people are left in darkness while the moon is still in the well. This too is essential to understanding the pride.[7]

The important point is how little of this is explicit in the text: the clauses as written exhibit what can be called "situational ambiguity." It's as if situations were "modalizers" for the expressed clauses, generating "mini-possible-worlds" and implicit propositional operators. I'm not seriously proposing a model theory (though, of course, this has been done for counterfactuals, deontic modalities, and epistemic states) but only suggesting what may be a helpful analogy. Thus the clause "Khoja found the moon" would have not only the modality "Khoja thought that . . ." but also the modality "while looking into the well. . . ." The latter is a crucial modalization, for it (along with common sense) is what forces the former.

Given this way of putting it, two things stand out. First, rather than a fixed, lexically specified set of possible modalities, there are indefinitely many of them, more or less like sentences (or indeed, whole passages). Second, many of these have to be supplied (or inferred) by the reader—often, as in the last example, on the basis of others already supplied. That is, to understand the text, the reader must provide for each clause a number of these generalized

[7] There are also a number of "background counterfactuals" involved in understanding what happens. Thus, a reader should be able to say what would have happened if the hook hadn't caught on the rock, or if it hadn't broken loose. Anyone who couldn't answer, wouldn't really "have" it.

or "situational" modalities, and must do so largely on the basis of some over-all situational or modal coherence. This demand for over-all coherence—that all the various "situations" (with respect to which clauses are understood) should fit together in an intelligible way—is what I call *situation holism*. It is a general feature of natural-language text, and coping with it is prerequisite to reading.

Situation holism is especially characteristic of longer texts. We had a brief sample in our folk tale; but it really comes into its own in the forms of dialectic, characterization, and plot. Mystery novels, for example, are built around the challenge of situation holism when pivotal cues are deliberately scattered and ambiguous. Translators (who read the book first, naturally) must be very sensitive to such matters—to use 'ran' or 'flew' instead of 'fled', for instance—on pain of spoiling the suspense. But only the over-all plot determines just which words need to be handled carefully, not to mention how to handle them. Engrossed readers, of course, are alert to the same issues in a complementary way. This is situation holism, full-fledged.[8]

IV. DIGRESSION: HERMENEUTICS

Hermeneutics, in the classical (nineteenth-century) sense, is the "science" of textual interpretation—i.e., exegesis. It is often described as "holistic," on something like the following grounds: the meanings of particular passages, doctrines, and specialized ("technical") terms, are only apparent in the context of the whole; yet the whole (treatise, life's work, or genre) is composed entirely of particular passages, containing the various doctrines and special terms. So the interpreter must work back and forth among part, subpart, and whole, bootstrapping each insight on one level into new insights on the others, until a satisfactory over-all understanding is achieved.

Hermeneutics is like intentional interpretation, insofar as the point is to translate baffling expressions into others more familiar or more intelligible. And the constraint on adequacy is again that the text, as construed, make a maximum of sense. But in exegesis, "sensibleness" is not so easy to determine as it is, say, in translating chess notations. For each sentence will have various presuppositions

8 In AI, work on this problem has only just begun. See, e.g. David Rumelhart, "Notes on a Schema for Stories," in Bobrow and Allan Collins, eds., *Representation and Understanding* (New York: Academic Press, 1975); Bob Wilensky, "Why John Married Mary: Understanding Stories Involving Recurring Goals," *Cognitive Science*, II (1978): 235–266; and Robert de Beaugrande and Benjamin Colby, "Narrative Models of Action and Interaction," *Cognitive Science*, III (1979): 43–66. Compare also David Lewis, "Scorekeeping in a Language Game," forthcoming in *Journal of Philosophical Logic*.

or "facts" taken for granted and will make sense only in the light of these. Part of the interpreter's task, in determining what the text means, is to ferret such assumptions out and make them explicit. So hermeneutic interpretation must deal explicitly with common-sense holism (though it may be "common" only to the initiated few). But the paramount concern in formal exegesis is exposing the over-all structure and purport of the original. A construal cannot stand unless it renders sensible the progression and development of arguments, examples, incidents, and the like. But this is just situation holism, made more articulate. Thus, I don't think the holism of classical hermeneutics is different from the three kinds so far discussed, but is instead a sophisticated combination of them all.[9]

V. EXISTENTIAL HOLISM

In the section on intentional interpretation, we noticed how naturally we construe chess-playing computers as "trying" to make good moves, and "wanting" to win. At the same time, however, I think we *also* all feel that the machines don't "really care" whether they win, or how they play—that somehow the game doesn't "matter" to them. What's behind these conflicting intuitions? It may seem at first that what machines lack is a "reason" to win: some larger goal that winning would subserve. But this only puts off the problem; for we then ask whether they "really care" about the larger goal. And until this question is answered, nothing has been; just as we now don't suppose pawns "matter" to computers, even though they subserve the larger goal of winning.

Apparently something else must be involved to make the whole hierarchy of goals worth while—something that itself doesn't need a reason, but, so to speak, "matters for its own sake." We get a hint of what this might be, by asking why chess games matter to people (when they do). There are many variations, of course, but here are some typical reasons:

(i) public recognition and esteem, which generates and supports self-esteem (compare the loser's embarrassment or loss of face);
(ii) pride and self-respect at some difficult achievement—like finally earning a "master" rating (compare the loser's frustration and self-disappointment); or

---

[9] It can be argued (though not here) that genuine radical translation is less like the interpretation of a chess player than like a hermeneutic investigation of a whole culture—including (so far as possible) an "interpretation" of its practices, institutions, and artifacts. For a good account of what hermeneutics has become in the twentieth century (very roughly, it adds my fourth holism), see Charles Taylor, "Interpretation and the Sciences of Man," *Review of Metaphysics*, xxv, 1 (September 1971): 3–51.

(iii) proving one's prowess or (as it were) "masculinity" (compare the loser's self-doubt and fear of inadequacy).

What these have in common is that the player's self-image or sense of identity is at stake. This concern with "who one is" constitutes at least one issue that "matters for its own sake." Machines (at present) lack any personality and, hence, any possibility of personal involvement; so (on these grounds) nothing can really matter to them.[10]

The point is more consequential for language understanding than for formal activities like chess playing, which are largely separable from the rest of life. A friend of mine tells a story about the time she kept a white rat as a pet. It was usually tame enough to follow at her heels around campus; but one day, frightened by a dog, it ran so far up her pantleg that any movement might have crushed it. So, very sheepishly, she let down her jeans, pulled out her quivering rodent, and won a round of applause from delighted passersby. Now, most people find this anecdote amusing, and the relevant question is: Why? Much of it, surely, is that we identify with the young heroine and share in her embarrassment—being relieved, at the same time, that it didn't happen to us.

Embarrassment, however, (and relief) can be experienced only by a being that has some sense of itself—a sense that is important to it and can be awkwardly compromised on occasion. Hence, only such a being could, as we do, find this story amusing. It might be argued, however, that "emotional" reactions, like embarrassment and bemusement, should be sharply distinguished from purely "cognitive" understanding. Nobody, after all, expects a mechanical chess player to *like* the game or to be thrilled by it. But that distinction cannot be maintained for users of natural language. Translators, for instance, must choose words carefully to retain the character of an amusing original. To take just one example from the preceding story, German has several "equivalents" for 'sheepish', with connotations, respectively, of being simple, stupid, or bashful. Only by appreciating the embarrassing nature of the incident, could a translator make the right choice.

A different perspective is illustrated by the time Ralph asked his new friend, Lucifer: "Why, when you're so brilliant, beautiful, and

10 There are many problems in this vicinity. For instance, people (but not machines) play chess for *fun*; and, within limits, winning is more fun. It's very hard, however, to say what fun is, or get any grip on what it would be for a machine actually to *have* fun. One might try to connect it with the foregoing, and say (in a tired European tone of voice) that fun is merely a temporary diversion from the ever-oppressive burden of self-understanding. But that isn't very persuasive.

everything, did you ever get kicked out of heaven?" Rather than answer right away, Lucifer suggested a little game: "I'll sit up here on this rock," he said, "and you just carry on with all that wonderful praise you were giving me." Well, Ralph went along, but as the hours passed, it began to get boring; so, finally, he said: "Look, why don't we add some variety to this game, say, by taking turns?" "Ahh," Lucifer sighed, "that's all I said, that's all I said."

Here, even more than Ralph's embarrassment, we enjoy the adroit way that Lucifer turns the crime of the ages into a little *faux pas*, blown out of proportion by God's infinite vanity. But why is that funny? Part of it has to be that we all know what guilt and shame are like, and how we try to escape them with impossible rationalizations—this being a grand case on both counts. It's not the *psychology* of guilt that we "know," but the tension of actually *facing* it and (sometimes) trying not to face it. And actually "feeling" guilty is certainly not just a cognitive state, like believing you did wrong, and disapproving; nor is it that, with some unpleasant sensation added on. It is at least to sense oneself as diminished by one's act—to be reduced in worth or exposed as less worthy than had seemed.

Crime and Punishment, too, is "about" guilt, but it isn't especially funny. The novel is powerful and didactic: the reader's experience of guilt is not simply drawn upon, but engaged and challenged. We enter into Raskolnikov's (and Dostoyevsky's) struggle with the very natures of guilt, personal responsibility, and freedom —and in so doing, we grow as persons. This response, too, is a kind of understanding, and asking questions is a fairly effective test for it. Moreover, at least some of those questions will have to be answered in the course of producing an adequate translation.

One final example will demonstrate the range of the phenomenon I'm pointing at, and also illustrate a different way in which the reader's personal involvement can be essential. It is a fable of Aesop's.

> One day, a farmer's son accidentally stepped on a snake, and was fatally bitten. Enraged, the father chased the snake with an axe, and managed to cut off its tail. Whereupon, the snake nearly ruined the farm by biting all the animals. Well, the farmer thought it over, and finally took the snake some sweetmeats, and said: "I can understand your anger, and surely you can understand mine. But now that we are even, let's forget and be friends again." "No, no," said the snake, "take away your gifts. You can never forget your dead son, nor I my missing tail."

Obviously, this story has a "moral," which a reader must "get" in order to understand it.

The problem is not simply to make the moral explicit, for then it would be more direct and effective to substitute a non-allegorical paraphrase:

> A child is like a part of oneself, such as a limb. The similarities include:
>   (i) losing one is very bad;
>   (ii) if you lose one, you can never get it back;
>   (iii) they have no adequate substitutes; and thus
>   (iv) they are literally priceless.
>
>   Therefore, to regard trading losses of them as a "fair exchange," or "getting even," is to be a fool.

But this is just a list of platitudes. It's not that it misrepresents the moral, but that it lacks it altogether—it is utterly flat and lifeless. By comparison, Aesop's version "lives," because we as readers identify with the farmer. Hence, we too are brought up short by the serpent's rebuke, and that makes us look at ourselves.

The terrifying thing about losing, say, one's legs is not the event itself, or the pain, but rather the thought of *being* a legless cripple for all the rest of one's life. It's the same with losing a son, right? Wrong! Many a parent indeed would joyously give both legs to have back a little girl or boy who is gone. Children can well mean more to who one is than even one's own limbs. So who are you, and what is your life? The folly—what the fable is really "about" —is not knowing.[11]

A single event cannot be embarrassing, shameful, irresponsible, or foolish in isolation, but only as an act in the biography of a whole, historical individual—a person whose personality it reflects and whose self-image it threatens. Only a being that cares about who it is, as some sort of enduring whole, can care about guilt or folly, self-respect or achievement, life or death. And only such a being can read. This holism, now not even apparently in the text, but manifestly in the reader, I call (with all due trepidation) *existential holism*. It is essential, I submit, to understanding the meaning of any text that (in a familiar sense) *has* any meaning. If situation holism is the foundation of plot, existential holism is the foundation of literature.

In the context of Artificial Intelligence, however, there remains

---

11 Rumelhart (*op. cit.*) analyzes a different version of this story in terms of an interesting "story grammar," loosely analogous to sentential grammar. Significantly, however, he addresses only the continuity of the story and never touches on its moral or meaning.

an important question of whether this sets the standard too high—whether it falls into what Papert somewhere calls "the human/superhuman fallacy," or Dennett "the Einstein-Shakespeare gambit." Wouldn't it be impressive enough, the reasoning goes, if a machine could understand everyday English, even if it couldn't appreciate literature? Sure, it would be impressive; but beyond that there are three replies. First, if we could articulate some ceiling of "ordinariness" beyond which machines can't pass or can't pass unless they meet some further special condition, that would be very interesting and valuable indeed. Second, millions of people can read—really read—and for most of the others it's presumably a socio-historical tragedy that they can't. Existential holism is not a condition just on creative genius. Finally, and *most important*, there is no reason whatsoever to believe there is a difference in kind between understanding "everyday English" and appreciating literature. Apart from a few highly restricted domains, like playing chess, analyzing mass spectra, or making airline reservations, the most ordinary conversations are fraught with life and all its meanings.

VI

Considering the progress and prospects of Artificial Intelligence can be a peculiarly concrete and powerful way of thinking about our own spiritual nature. As such, it is a comrade of the philosophy of mind (some authors see AI as allied to epistemology, which strikes me as perverse). Here, we have distinguished four phenomena, each with a claim to the title 'holism'—not to trade on or enhance any mystery in the term, but rather, I would hope, the opposite. The aim has not been to show that Artificial Intelligence is impossible (though it is, you know) but to clarify some of what its achievement would involve, in the specific area of language understanding. This area is not so limited as it seems, since—as each of the four holisms testifies—understanding a text involves understanding what the text is "about." The holisms, as presented, increase in difficulty relative to current AI techniques; and my own inclination (it's hardly more than that) is to regard the last, existential holism, as the most fundamental of the four. Hence my opening remark: the trouble with Artificial Intelligence is that computers don't give a damn.

JOHN HAUGELAND

University of Pittsburgh

Individualism, Computation, and Perceptual Content

FRANCES EGAN

1. Introduction

Individualism in psychology is a thesis about how mental states are to be taxonomized. As Tyler Burge characterizes it, individualism is the view that

> the mental natures of all a person's or animal's mental states (and events) are such that there is no deep individuative relation between the individual's being in states of those kinds and the nature of the individual's physical or social environments. (1986, pp. 3-4)

Individualism has sometimes been formulated as a supervenience thesis, according to which psychological states are said to supervene on intrinsic, physical states of the organism to which they are ascribed (e.g. Stich 1983, pp. 164-5). Any differences between organisms not reflected in their intrinsic physical states are not psychologically relevant, it is claimed, and should be ignored by psychological theory. Thus, according to individualism, I and my Twin Earth counterpart are psychologically identical, in virtue of the fact that we are, according to Putnam's story, molecule for molecule identical.

In a series of important papers (especially 1979 and 1986), Tyler Burge has argued that individualism is false with respect to a wide range of explanatory kinds in psychology, including the intentional states invoked in folk psychological explanation. Most strikingly, perhaps, Burge and others have claimed that perceptual theories, including David Marr's computational theory of vision, individuate perceptual states in part by reference to the environment of the subject possessing them, and so violate individualism (e.g. Burge 1986 and 1988, Kitcher 1988, and Davies 1991).

As formulated above, individualism says nothing about the *contents* of mental states. While individualism is generally construed as a thesis about the individuation of the propositional attitudes, that is, beliefs and desires—states which have contents—nothing in the above formulations requires that the mental states so individuated must have propositional contents.[1] In fact, proponents *and* opponents of individualism (in psychology) often cite analogies from other sciences—in which the relevant states are claimed either to supervene on local physical features or to fail to do so—in support of their views (e.g. Burge 1986, Fodor 1987, ch.

---

[1] This is also true of Fodor's characterization of *methodological individualism*, "the doctrine that psychological states are individuated *with respect to their causal powers*" (1987, p. 42). Fodor's characterization of individualism differs in important respects from both Burge's and Stich's. (The latter two I take to be roughly equivalent.)

Mind, Vol. 101 . 403 . July 1992

---

2). These arguments presuppose that the nature of the case is not significantly changed by the fact that psychological states typically have propositional contents.

Nevertheless, the usage has not been consistent. Individualism is sometimes characterized as a thesis about how mental *contents* are to be individuated. I propose, however, to use the term "internalism" for the view that holds that the *contents* of mental states supervene on intrinsic physical states of the subject, and hence are individuated "narrowly", without essential reference to the subject's physical and social environment. The view that denies that mental contents supervene on intrinsic physical states of the subject, claiming that they are individuated in part by reference to the subject's environmental or social context, hence "widely", I shall call "externalism".

It is generally assumed that intentional mental states are individuated by their contents, that they have their contents *essentially*. Proponents of individualism, unless they are eliminativist about intentional contents, have therefore found themselves burdened with the task of articulating and defending some notion of *narrow* content, where by "narrow" we mean *supervening locally on the subject*. Skepticism about the possibility of an adequate account of narrow content has led others to embrace anti-individualism, on the assumption that if the *content* of mental states fails to supervene on intrinsic states of the individual subject, then the mental states possessing such content must also fail to supervene on intrinsic states of the individual subject.

In this paper I wish to challenge the widely held assumption that individualism entails either content internalism or content eliminativism,[2] while content externalism entails the falsity of individualism. I shall confine my attention to computational psychology. I shall argue, first, that computational theories are individualistic—they taxonomize mental states without essential reference to the subject's environment. Representational contents, I suggest, play a role in computational psychology analogous to the role played by models in the physical sciences. I shall then argue that the content attributed to computational states in the explanatory models of computational theories of perception are, typically, *wide*, illustrating my argument by reference to Marr's theory of vision. Therefore, contrary to the above assumption, computational theories of perception are both individualistic *and* externalist. This is possible only because mental states, as characterized by computational psychology, do not have their contents essentially.

2. Computation and individuation

My argument that computational theories are individualistic depends in part upon the view that the goal of such theories is to characterize the mechanisms under-

[2] Content eliminativism either denies that mental states have content or denies that content plays a genuine explanatory role in psychology: see e.g. Churchland (1981) and Stich (1983).

lying our various cognitive capacities, and further, that this goal is best served by theories which taxonomize states individualistically.

Cognitive psychological theories aim to characterize human cognitive processes. *Computational* cognitive theories construe human cognitive processes as a species of information-processing, and the systems that subserve such processing as symbol manipulating systems. This is to imply that some of the events postulated within the system can be consistently interpreted as having a meaning in a certain domain.

My claim that the goal of computational psychological theories is to characterize the *mechanisms* underlying our cognitive capacities may appear to violate a widely accepted principle about the proper approach to the study of information-processing systems. As David Marr (1982) and others (e.g. Ullman 1979) have cogently argued, an information-processing system should be analyzed at several distinct levels of theory. Most importantly, it has been claimed, the nature of the information-processing task itself—the computation performed by the system—needs to be understood independently of any attempt to characterize the physical mechanisms supporting the computation. According to Marr:

> If one believes that the aim of information-processing studies is to formulate and understand particular information-processing problems, then it is the structure of those problems that is central, not the mechanisms through which they are implemented. (1981, pp. 139-40)

Marr criticizes Newell and Simon's work on production systems because, he claims, it amounts to "studying a mechanism, not a problem":

> The mechanisms that such research is trying to penetrate will be unraveled by studying problems, just as vision research is progressing because it is the problem of vision that is being attacked, not neural visual mechanisms. (1981, p. 140)

But to claim, as I do, that the goal of computational theories is to characterize the mechanisms underlying cognitive capacities is not to specify the level of abstraction at which, or the vocabulary in which, the mechanisms should be described. In particular, it is not to maintain that computational theories aim to characterize cognitive mechanisms only at what Marr calls the third level of description—the specification of the neural circuitry which implements the computation. The claim that cognitive scientists should study the information-processing problem independently of the physical mechanisms implementing the process can plausibly be construed as a recipe for achieving the correct characterization of cognitive mechanisms. On such a construal, my claim that the goal of computational psychology is to characterize the mechanisms underlying cognitive capacities is consistent with the expectation that the complete characterization of such mechanisms will include components corresponding to Marr's three levels of analysis—a specification of *the function computed by the cognitive mechanism*, a description of *how the function is computed* (i.e. a specification of a representation and algorithm), and a description of the neural hardware supporting the computation.[3]

[3] Marr, somewhat misleadingly, called the specification of the function computed by

In treating human cognitive processes as a species of information-processing, and the systems that subserve such processing as symbol manipulating systems, computational theories construe cognitive processes as formal operations defined over symbol structures. To describe something as a symbol is to imply that it is semantically interpretable, but (and this is the important point) its type identity as a symbol is independent of any particular semantic interpretation it might have. Symbols are just functionally characterized objects whose individuation conditions are specified by a realization function f_R which maps equivalence classes of physical features of a system to what we might call "symbolic" features. Formal operations are just those physical operations that are differentially sensitive to the aspects of symbolic expressions that under the realization function f_R are specified as symbolic features. The mapping f_R allows a causal sequence of physical state transitions to be interpreted as a *computation*.

Given this method of individuating computational states, two systems performing the same operations over the same symbol structures are computationally indistinguishable. If two systems are physically identical, then they serve as domains for the same class of realization functions. Consequently, there can be no *computationally relevant* grounds for attributing a particular symbolic property to one that would not be grounds for attributing it to the other. So if two systems are molecular duplicates then they are computational duplicates.[4] Computational descriptions are individualistic: they type-individuate states without reference to the subject's environment or social context.

Actually, a stronger conclusion can be drawn. To the extent that computational processes are construed as *modular* processes,[5] even the *internal* environment is irrelevant to the type-individuation of the computational states of a system. To use an example of Martin Davies' (which he employs in an argument *against* individualism in Davies 1991), imagine a component (module) of the visual system, called the *visex*, which computes, say, a representation of features of the surface structure of an object based on information about binocular disparity. Now imagine that within the auditory system of some actual or imagined creature there is a component that is physically identical to the visex. Call this component the *audex*. According to theories of auditory processing, the audex computes a rep-

---

the system the "theory of the computation". I shall follow Marr in using this terminology to refer to Marr's topmost level of analysis. What I call a "computational theory" (following standard usage) comprises all three levels of analysis.

[4] Cummins makes this point in his 1989, p. 81. However, he concludes from this that representational content is shared by computational duplicates. I criticize this argument below.

[5] David Marr says;

> Computer scientists call the separate pieces of a process its *modules*, and the idea that a large computation can be split up and implemented as a collection of parts that are as nearly independent of one another as the overall task allows, is so important that I was moved to elevate it to a principle, the *principle of modular design*. (1982, p. 102)

Marr's own theory of early vision respects the principle of modular design.

resentation of certain sonic properties. We can imagine a particular visex and audex removed from their normal embeddings in visual and auditory systems respectively and switched. Since the two components are by hypothesis physically identical, the switch should make no discernible difference to the behaviour of the creatures, nor to their internal goings-on. The two components are computationally identical, despite the difference in their normal internal environments.

It might be objected that I have construed the goal of computational psychological theories too narrowly. Characterizing the mechanisms underlying human cognitive capacities is one goal of computational psychological theories, but computational theories are also typically concerned to explain the contribution of cognitive mechanisms toward the overall success of the organism in its environment. Accordingly, it is claimed, we would expect such theories to individuate psychological states with an eye to how the mechanisms are embedded in larger systems within the organism and ultimately in the organism's normal environmental niche—that is, we would expect them to individuate psychological states non-individualistically.[6]

It is reasonable to assume that psychological theories will contribute to a satisfactory account of organism/environment interaction that would explain an organism's success, or failure, in its normal environment. But, I maintain, the explanation of organism/environment interaction is not the primary goal of computational theorizing, and such explanations are forthcoming only when a computational theory is supplemented by further assumptions about the normal environment in which the described cognitive mechanisms are deployed. In fact, precisely because the hypothesized cognitive mechanisms are assumed to be invariant across environmental changes, we can see why *this* mechanism would not have been adaptive had the environment been different, and why it might cease to be adaptive if the environment changes.

It might be objected that assumptions about the subject's environment play an essential role in the description of the cognitive mechanisms themselves, particularly the mechanisms underlying perception.[7] In the first place, the inputs to perceptual mechanisms are often characterized in terms of their typical environmental causes. Secondly, and perhaps more importantly, large scale assumptions about the environment are built into the mechanism itself. The solutions to information-processing problems solved by cognitive mechanisms are often underdetermined by the information contained in the inputs to the mechanism (the so-called "poverty of the stimulus" phenomenon). The processing is achieved only with the help of additional information which is assumed to be innate. The innate information available to the perceptual mechanisms concerns

[6] For versions of this argument see Burge (1986), Davies (1991), Dennett (1987), Kobes (1990), and van Gulick (1989). See Burge (1986) and Kitcher (1988) for detailed arguments that Marr's theory of vision fits this model. See Segal (1989, 1991) and Egan (1991) for arguments against the latter claim.

[7] See Burge (1986) and Kitcher (1988). The argument concerns Marr's theory of vision, but it can be generalized.

very general features of the subject's normal environment; because this informa-tion is true the subject's experience is typically veridical.[8]

Andy Clark warns against studying intelligent systems independently of the complex structure of their natural environments. He cites what he calls the "007 principle" as an important maxim of cognitive theorizing:

> In general, evolved creatures will neither store nor process information in costly ways when they can use the structure of the environment and their operations upon it as a convenient stand-in for the information-pro-cessing operations concerned. That is, know only as much as you need to know to get the job done. (1989, p. 64)

Given the apparently indispensable role of environmental information, both for specifying the inputs to the perceptual mechanisms and for characterizing the additional (innate) information required for cognitive processing to proceed, it might be argued that the nature of the environment plays an essential role in the characterization of the cognitive mechanisms themselves. This conclusion, how-ever, does not follow. Environmental information, while often crucial for theory construction and articulation, does not function essentially as part of the compu-tational theory's individuative apparatus.

In the first place, while the inputs to perceptual mechanisms are often given a distal interpretation, the fact remains that the realization function f_R determines how the computational states of the system are individuated. This function indi-viduates computational states *non-semantically*, that is, independently of any particular semantic interpretation such states may have. This point may be obscured by the fact that the realization function is not always completely speci-fied. Some computational processes may be postulated without an explicit spec-ification of the algorithms that carry out the processing, or even of the symbolic tokens that the missing algorithms would be defined over. In such cases, the the-orist may rely on a presumptive semantic interpretation of underlying states to informally characterize the hypothesized procedures. The important point is that while the semantic interpretation does provide a useful description of what the system does, it does not serve to *individuate* the underlying computational states. Rather, it plays a *reference-fixing* role, giving us a way to refer to the underlying states, which must be presumed to be independently characterizable if the account is to be genuinely computational. A computational theory is committed to the existence of a fully specifiable formal account of the cognitive processes it attempts to characterize. Otherwise the processes are not programmable and the

[8] An example of such an assumption is Shimon Ullman's *rigidity assumption*, which says that "any set of elements undergoing a two-dimensional transformation has a unique interpretation as a rigid body moving in space and hence should be interpreted as such a body in motion" (1979). Ullman has proved that three distinct views of four non-coplanar points in a rigid body are sufficient to determine its three-dimensional structure. In a world like ours where most things are rigid, a process that incorporated the rigidity assumption—as Marr's structure-from-motion module is hypothesized to do—would generally be suc-cessful in recovering the three-dimensional structure of distal objects from three such views.

theory reneges on its promise to provide a purely mechanical (hence, physically realizable) account of cognitive processes.

Secondly, general assumptions about the environment are claimed by Marr and others to be incorporated and used by perceptual mechanisms in solving the information-processing tasks set them by nature; however, it does not follow that the mechanisms themselves are type-individuated by reference to the environment. The assumptions are built into the mechanism only in the following sense—the mechanism operates in such a way that if the assumptions are true it will succeed in recovering information about the environment from information in the input.[9] The important point is that the *same* perceptual mechanism could occur in an environment where the relevant assumptions were radically false,[10] although in such an environment we might expect the mechanism (and the organisms containing it) to be short-lived.

Finally, to say that a computational theory is individualistic is *not* to imply that the theorist must ignore the subject's environment in constructing her theories. The expectation that the cognitive mechanisms of evolved creatures are well-suited to the environment will constrain computational accounts. The theorist will typically exploit environmental knowledge in attempting to uncover the computational problems that need to be solved and the nature of the mechanisms required to solve them. She must not postulate mechanisms that are implausible from an environmental or evolutionary point of view. However, the mechanisms themselves, as characterized by computational theories, supervene on the physical states of the subjects possessing them.

3. The role of content

Tyler Burge (1986) has argued that a defence of individualism in psychology is a two-part task. The individualist must not only show that the presuppositions of psychology are purely individualistic, she must also explicate an individualist language that would allow the attribution of narrow content to the subject's psychological states. I have attempted the first task above, arguing that computational theories are committed to individualist taxonomic principles. Others who have argued that psychology is individualistic have typically shouldered the second burden as well, attempting to articulate and defend a notion of mental content that is purely individualistic (e.g. Fodor 1987 ch. 2, Block 1986, Segal 1989 and 1991). But since computational theories individuate psychological states by non-semantic criteria, the individualist who restricts her attention to computational theories need not take on the second task. Whatever content computational states have—narrow or wide—the states themselves supervene on the intrinsic physical

[9] For example, the mechanism characterized by Shimon Ullman succeeds in recovering structure from motion in worlds where (most) objects are rigid.

[10] See Segal (1989) and Egan (1991) for detailed argument on this point.

states of the subject possessing them, and are thus shared by doppelgängers in the thought experiments.

One individualist who seems not to have fully appreciated the implications of computational individuation is Robert Cummins. He argues as follows:

> The CTC [Computational Theory of Cognition] must hold that the capacities it seeks to explicate retain their identity across differences in *noncomputational* factors. It must therefore cleave to the viability of a kind or aspect of content that is narrow with respect to causal and historical features not mirrored in computational architecture. (1989, p. 119)

Cummins is right that the cognitive capacities characterized by computational theories are assumed to be invariant across environmental differences. But he is mistaken in concluding that computationalists require a notion of content that supervenes on the subject's computational architecture. There is no *computationally motivated* reason why the interpretation of computational states should be narrow.[11]

The assumption that individualists require a notion of narrow content is typically based on a more fundamental assumption shared by most participants to the debate—that psychological states have their contents essentially.[12] This is perhaps understandable given the tendency to identify such states with propositional attitudes. Standard accounts of the propositional attitudes construe them as relations (to propositions or mental representations that have their meanings essentially), although such a construal is not mandatory.[13] In any event, the assumption that propositional attitudes have their contents essentially is perhaps plausible inasmuch as we have no other way to characterize the internal states posited by commonsense psychology as the causes of behaviour except by reference to their contents. But it is not plausible for mental states construed as computational states, because the latter are individuated by computational theories according to non-semantic criteria.

Computational theories construe cognitive processes as formal operations defined over symbol structures. To speak of these structures as symbols is to imply that the postulated structures can be consistently interpreted. Their interpretation is given by an *interpretation function f_I* that specifies a mapping between elements of symbol structures and elements of some represented domain. For example, to interpret a device as an adder involves specifying an

---

[11] Thus, Cummins dismissal of Millikan's account of mental representation, on the grounds that since it is externalist it is incompatible with the computational theory of cognition, is ill-founded.

[12] See e.g. Tyler Burge (1979, 1986, p. 15f). Fodor says "…I suppose (it) to be untendentious that mental states have their contents essentially, so that typological identity of the former guarantees typological identity of the latter…" (1987). Jackson and Pettit challenge this assumption in Jackson and Pettit (1988).

It is clear from Cummins' account of computation that he does not assume that computational states have their contents essentially, despite the suggestion to the contrary in the passage quoted above.

[13] For an account that does not construe propositional attitudes as relations see Matthews (1990).

interpretation function f_I that pairs symbolic states of the device with numbers. A computational account can plausibly claim to have shown how a device actually cognizes only if there exists an interpretation function that maps computationally specified states to appropriate contents in a fairly *direct* way, although it is notoriously hard to specify precisely the conditions on direct interpretation.[14] Assuming that these conditions are met, and that the theory is technically (biologically) feasible, the computational account demonstrates how the device *could* compute the hypothesized cognitive function.

Computational theories provide a *formal* characterization of the functions computed by cognitive mechanisms. The functions are specified mathematically, and inputs and outputs of the processes that compute the functions are characterized non-semantically. The interpretation function f_I provides an *intentional* specification of a function, by characterizing the representational tokens over which the hypothesized process is defined in terms of some represented domain. It is misleading, however, to construe the content assigned by f_I as part of the computational theory itself, rather than as a feature of the expository apparatus that both renders the theory's formal exposition intelligible and allows the postulated computational process to be seen as *cognition*.

Let me elaborate this point. It is a truism that the postulates of a theory can be understood more readily when embedded in a familiar model than when given a purely formal (that is, mathematical) exposition. Maxwell's efforts to represent Faraday's lines of force by the flow of liquid through tubes was an attempt to make intelligible a purely formal exposition of unfamiliar phenomena (in this case, electromagnetic phenomena) by appeal to systems governed by the laws of mechanics, which have the status of familiar principles. In the case of mechanical models, the relevant similarity between the model and the modelled phenomena is a nomic isomorphism, that is, an isomorphism between two corresponding sets of laws. In the computational case, the interpretation function f_I that pairs symbolic expressions with contents specifies an isomorphism between computational states and features of the represented domain. The suggestion that the contents assigned to the representational structures postulated by computational theories should be understood as *models* of such theories is made plausible by the fact that an interpretation can aid our understanding of such formal accounts in two distinct respects. In the first place, while it is possible to specify the function computed by a computational device purely formally, rather than by way of an interpretation, doing so would make understanding the computational account exceedingly difficult. Secondly, given that the questions that define a psychological theory's domain are usually couched in intentional terms, an intentional specification of the postulated computational processes demonstrates that these questions are indeed answered by the theory, perhaps in conjunction with auxiliary assumptions. For example, a theory of mental arithmetic must explain how a subject is able to compute simple sums and products. It is only under an interpretation of some of the internal states of the subject as representations of num-

---

[14] For discussion of this issue see Cummins (1989, ch. 8).

bers that the computational processes postulated by the theory are revealed as addition and multiplication. Thus, the interpretation *explains* the computational account.

If the foregoing account is correct, then computational theories of cognition are not intentional, although they have intentional models, where an intentional model is just an interpretation that treats the device as computing a cognitive function.[15]

Construing interpretations as explanatory models of computational theories helps to explain other features of computational theorizing. Often when a theory is incompletely specified the study of a model of the theory can aid in the further specification of the theory itself. As previously noted, a computational theorist may resort to characterizing a computation partly by reference to features of some putative represented domain, hoping to supply the formal details (i.e. the theory) later. For example, the representational tokens postulated by a theory of visual perception might be characterized in terms of the distal interpretations that would be assigned to such states under an intuitively plausible interpretation function. In such a case, the computational theory is expressed through one of its models, and the language used to express the theory should not be construed as basic. The hypothesized function could, in principle, be described formally. The philosopher interested in uncovering the individuative principles of the computational theory should not assume that they can be read directly off the intentional specification of the functions computed by the postulated computational mechanisms. To argue that the states picked out are individuated essentially by reference to their distal interpretations (or any intentional specification) is to mistake an adventitious feature of a theory's model for an essential feature of the theory itself.[16]

It is often noted that, since an interpretation is just a structure-preserving mapping between symbolic elements and elements of some represented domain, the representational contents of computational states will typically be non-unique. If interpretations are understood as explanatory models, this is just what one would expect. The existence of unintended models does not undermine the explanatory usefulness of an intended interpretation. The choice of an explanatory model for a computational theory is based on extrinsic (i.e. noncomputational) considerations, the most important of which, is demonstrating that the questions that define the theory's domain are indeed answered by the theory. The fact that a hypothesized visual system could be interpreted as computing a function on the auditory domain (or as calculating the batting averages of the New York Mets) would not undermine the theorist's claim to have described a possible visual sys-

---

[15] A cognitive function can be characterized informally as a function whose arguments and values are epistemically related. Thus, the outputs of the computation can be seen as cogent or rational given the inputs.

[16] I argue in (1991) that Burge makes this mistake in interpreting Marr's theory of vision.

tem, assuming that the mechanism could be consistently and directly interpreted as computing the appropriate function on the visual domain.

4. Perceptual content

I turn now to the representational contents assigned to the data structures subserving perception. I shall focus on a favourite example of philosophers—the theory of vision developed by David Marr and his colleagues. My discussion is intended to support the general account of content articulated in the previous section.

In accordance with his methodology for the explanation of an information-processing capacity, Marr's theory of vision is deployed at three distinct levels of description—the specification of *the function computed* by various visual processes hypothesized by the theory, the *algorithmic implementation* of the hypothesized functions, and *the hardware implementation* of the hypothesized algorithms. The "topmost" level—what Marr called the "theory of the computation"—is the most developed aspect of the theory.

The goal of the visual system is to derive a representation of three dimensional shape from information contained in two-dimensional images. Marr's theory divides this task into three distinct stages, each involving the construction of a representation, tokens of which serve as inputs to subsequent processes. Vision culminates in a representation that is suitable for the recognition of objects. Innate assumptions of the sort described earlier, incorporated into the visual system itself, and reflecting physical constraints on the pairing of retinal images with distal shapes, allow the postulated mechanisms underlying early vision to recover information about the distal scene based only on information contained in the image. Early visual processing is thus "data-driven".

Interpreters of Marr (individualists and anti-individualists alike) have construed the theory of the computation, that is, the specification of the function computed by the visual system, as *intentional*. More specifically, it has been argued that the functions computed by the various modules of the visual system (i.e. what the system does) are individuated essentially by reference to the contents of the representational tokens that form the inputs and outputs of these modules (see Burge 1986, Kitcher 1988, Davies 1991, Segal 1989 and 1991). This claim is based on a misreading of Marr's theory, and more generally, on a misunderstanding of the computational approach to cognition. In his exposition of the theory of vision, Marr often describes the postulated visual processes in terms of features of the distal environment that typically co-vary with the representational tokens that form the inputs and outputs to the processes. This suggests that the theory has intentional *models*, in particular, that it has *externalist* models, but not that the theory is intentional. In discussing the levels-of-explanation methodology, Marr explicitly points out that the theory of the computation is a *formal* characterization of the function(s) computed by the various processing modules. The following diagram, taken from Marr's book *Vision* (1982, p. 338), depicts (top) the mathematical formula that describes the initial filtering of the image, and (below) a cross section of the retina which implements the computation.

$$\nabla^2 G * I(x, y),$$

$$\text{where } \nabla^2 G(r) = -\frac{1}{\pi\sigma^4}\left(1 - \frac{r^2}{2\sigma^2}\right)\exp\left(\frac{-r^2}{2\sigma^2}\right)$$

(a)

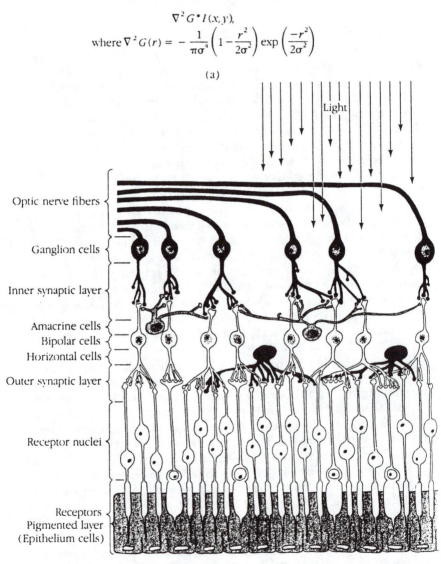

(b)

From *Vision*, by David Marr. Copyright (c) 1982 by W.H. Freeman and Company. Reprinted by permission

138

The point to note is that the function computed by the retina ((a) in the diagram) is characterized formally. Marr says the following:

> I have argued that from a computational point of view [the retina] signals $\nabla^2 G * I$ (the X channels) and its time derivative $\partial/\partial t\,(\nabla^2 G * I)$ (the Y channels). From a computational point of view, this is a precise specification of what the retina does. Of course it does a lot more—it transduces the light, allows for a huge dynamic range, has a fovea with interesting characteristics, can be moved around, and so forth. What you accept as a reasonable description of what the retina does depends on your point of view. I personally accept $\nabla^2 G$ [(a) in the diagram] as an adequate description, though I take an unashamedly information-processing point of view. (p. 337)

$\nabla^2 G$ is a function that takes as arguments two dimensional intensity arrays $I(x,y)$ and has as values the isotropic rates of change of intensity at points $(x,\ y)$ in the array. The implementation of this function is used in Marr and Hildreth's (1980) model to detect *zero-crossings*, which correspond to sudden intensity changes in the image.[17] Marr grants that the formal specification of the function computed by the retina may not make what the retina does *perspicuous*. Nonetheless, from an information-processing point of view, the formal specification is "adequate".

The representational tokens over which the processes postulated in Marr's theory are defined are built up out of sets of *primitives*. The *primal sketch*, for example, is constructed out of blobs, bars, edges, and terminations. The fact that Marr calls these primitives "edges" and "bars" does not mean that they represent properties of the distal scene; indeed Marr explicitly cautions against such an interpretation. He is careful to point out that these primitives, considered individually, do not reliably co-vary with what we take to be salient features of the distal scene (for example, object boundaries) and so do not have "physical reality".[18] They are treated, in the theory, as uninterpreted *structures*. It is their structural properties—position, length, width, and orientation—that are computationally significant. Grouping processes operate on the primitives in virtue of their structural properties (see Marr 1982, p. 53 and pp. 71-3).

To summarize the above discussion: (1) The theory of the computation is the formal specification of the functions computed by the visual system. (2) Inputs and outputs of the hypothesized processes are characterized in the theory in terms of their computationally significant properties, that is, their structural properties. (1) and (2) support my characterization of Marr's theory as individualistic, and also my claim that the theory is not intentional.

Marr is attempting to characterize a mechanism that we know does reliably recover information about the environment, so he is concerned to find structures that correspond to real physical changes. One needs to be somewhat cautious in

---

[17] It is important to note that the mathematical formula that describes the $\nabla^2 G$ function is not assumed by Marr and Hildreth to be explicitly represented in the retina.

[18] They do reliably co-vary with properties of the image. Gabriel Segal (1989) concludes that *edge* is assigned narrow content in the theory. But there would seem to be no motivation for such a move. Marr's caution against assigning distal interpretations to primitives at this stage should not be construed as entailing that they have narrow content.

drawing implications from this fact. To point out that certain data structures are reliably correlated with salient features of the distal scene is not, in itself, to attribute wide content to these structures. Nowhere does Marr do the latter, and it would certainly be wrong to attribute to him a causal covariance theory of content, indeed *any* theory of content. Nevertheless, such structures *are* candidates for distal interpretation in explanatory models of the theory. The *raw primal sketch*, which contains information from several distinct $\nabla^2 G$ channels, is the first data structure which correlates (in *this* world) with salient physical properties, and so is the earliest candidate for distal interpretation. Subsequent data structures, notably the 2.5-D sketch and the 3-D model representation, can be consistently given distal interpretations. In some *other* environment, however, structures in the retinal image might be reliably correlated with, say, object boundaries, and so would be plausible candidates for distal interpretation in explanatory models appropriate to that world.

It would be consistent with the above that at least some representations are assigned narrow content. The problem with this suggestion is that there is no motivation for the ascription of narrow content, and no evidence that Marr has any interest in the possibility of a non-distal interpretation. The fact that structures in the primal sketch reliably co-vary with features of the image, for example, does not justify construing these structures as representing features of the image. There is, however, a clear motivation for the ascription of wide content.

Ascribing content to the postulated representational structures helps to make the formal apparatus of the theory intelligible. Ascribing *wide* content enables us to see that the visual system is able to perform the cognitive task that defines the theory's domain—it can recover 3-D shape relations among objects from information contained in two dimensional projections, *in its normal environment*. By interpreting (some of) its states as referring to aspects of the distal scene we can see how the visual system *could* perform the antecedently characterized cognitive task, and in the absence of a competing account, plausibly how it *does*. It is therefore likely that explanatory models of Marr's theory of vision are *externalist*. The content ascribed in such models does not supervene on intrinsic physical states of the subject—if the subject were in a radically different environment, the content ascribed to her visual states would be different.

The above argument applies to perceptual content in general. The cognitive tasks that define the domains of theories of perception are *typically* specified in terms of the recovery of certain types of information about the subject's normal environment. Interpreting the subject's perceptual states as carrying information about the environment will demonstrate that the theory has indeed answered the question it was initially set. Consequently, we should expect that the content ascribed to representational structures in the explanatory models of perceptual theories will be wide.

5. Concluding remarks

To summarize what I have argued: Computational theories are individualistic—the mental states characterized by computational theories are shared by doppelgängers. Representational contents play a role in computational psychology analogous to the role played by models in the physical sciences. The contents ascribed to mental states in explanatory models of computational theories of perception are, typically, wide; hence, such theories are *both* individualistic and externalist.

The account of content sketched above contrasts sharply with an alternative view, according to which semantic properties of representations play an explanatory role in a system's capacity to compute a cognitive function. According to the alternative proposal, when a system produces an early representation *R1*, as part of a process that culminates in the production of a later representation *R2*, *R1's having the content it does explains the production of R2.* [19] The alternative view, in my opinion, misplaces the explanatory contribution of content in computational accounts of cognitive capacities. Computational processes are blind to the semantic properties of the structures over which they are defined. A computational explanation of *R2*'s production will appeal only to formal (i.e. non-semantic) properties of the system. Such explanations are *methodologically solipsistic.* But the fact that the system produces structures that are appropriately interpretable explains how a system that computes the hypothesized function could subserve the cognitive task that it does, where the task is typically described intentionally. The ascription of content plays an explanatory role in computational accounts, although not the role envisioned in the alternative view.

A final point: As previously noted, computational psychology respects the principle of modular design, treating cognitive processes as independently characterizable components of larger systems. The conspicuous successes of the discipline have been in the study of capacities that are relatively isolable, for example, early vision and syntactic and morphological analysis. Complex behaviour will be explained, if at all, as the interaction of multiple modular processes. The ascription of content serves an additional purpose besides its role in explanatory models of computational theories: it is essential for understanding how a module might be integrated into larger cognitive systems. Consider once again the visex/audex example. Recall that the two modules—one subserving visual perception, the other subserving auditory perception—are computationally identical. Characterizing what the components do in terms appropriate to the psychological domain in which they are normally deployed (that is, as either computing a representation of surface features of objects, or computing a representation of certain sonic properties) allows us to understand each module's role

---

[19] The content of the representations might be conceived as either wide or narrow. In some versions of the proposal, the content of early representations is explicitly claimed to be *causally efficacious* in the production of later representations

in the overall cognitive economy of the organism. Interpreting the inputs and outputs of modular processes seems unavoidable if we hope to explain how they interact to produce complex behaviour. Thus the choice of an explanatory model for a computational theory of a cognitive capacity is likely to be made with an eye to broader explanatory purposes—explaining how the output of a particular cognitive module feeds into later processes, and eventually explaining how the capacity contributes to the organism's successful interaction with its environment.[20]

Department of Philosophy   FRANCES EGAN
Rutgers University
New Brunswick
NJ 08903
USA

REFERENCES

Block, N. 1986: "Advertisement for a Semantics for Psychology", in *Midwest Studies in Philosophy Volume 10: Studies in the Philosophy of Mind*, French, P. A., Uehling, T. E. and Wettstein, H. K., eds., Minneapolis: University of Minnesota Press, pp. 615-78.

Burge, T. 1979: "Individualism and the Mental", *in Midwest Studies in Philosophy Volume 4: Studies in Metaphysics*, French, P. A., Uehling, T. E. and Wettstein, H. K., eds., Minneapolis: University of Minnesota Press, pp. 73-121.

——1986: "Individualism and Psychology". *The Philosophical Review*, 95, pp. 3-45.

——1988: "Cartesian Error and the Objectivity of Perception", in *Contents of Thought*, Grimm, R. H. and Merrill, D. D., eds., Tucson: University of Arizona Press, pp. 62-76.

Churchland, P. 1981: "Eliminative Materialism and the Propositional Attitudes". *Journal of Philosophy*, 78, pp. 67-89.

Clark, A. 1989: *Microcognition*, Cambridge, Mass: MIT Press.

Cummins, R. 1989: *Meaning and Mental Representation*, Cambridge, Mass: MIT Press.

Davies, M. 1991: "Individualism and Perceptual Content". *Mind*, 100, 4, pp. 461-84.

Dennett, D. C. 1987: "Evolution, Error, and Intentionality", in his *The Intentional Stance*. Cambridge, Mass: MIT Press, pp. 287-321.

Egan, F. 1991: "Must Psychology Be Individualistic?" *The Philosophical Review*, 100, pp. 179-203.

Fodor, J. A. 1987: *Psychosemantics*, Cambridge, Mass: MIT Press.

[20] Thanks to Robert Matthews, Colin McGinn, Gabriel Segal and Steve Stich for helpful comments on earlier drafts of this paper.

Jackson, F. and Pettit, P. 1988: "Functionalism and Broad Content". *Mind*, 97, pp. 381-400.

Kitcher, P. 1988: "Marr's Computational Theory of Vision". *Philosophy of Science*, 55, pp. 1-24.

Kobes, B. 1990: "Individualism and Artificial Intelligence", in *Philosophical Perspectives, Vol.4: Action Theory and Philosophy of Mind*, J. Tomberlin, ed., Atascadero, CA: Ridgeview Publishing Co., pp. 429-459.

Marr, D. 1981: "Artificial Intelligence: A Personal View", in *Mind Design*, Haugeland, J., ed., Cambridge, Mass: MIT Press, pp. 129-142.

——1982: *Vision*. New York: Freeman Press.

Marr, D. and Hildreth, E. 1980: "Theory of Edge Detection", in *Proceedings of the Royal Society*, London, B200, pp. 187-217.

Matthews, R. 1990: "The Measure of Mind," report no. 57, *Research Group on Mind and Brain,* ZiF, Bielefeld.

Segal, G. 1989: "On Seeing What is Not There". *The Philosophical Review*, 98, pp. 189-214.

——1991: "Defence of a Reasonable Individualism". *Mind*, 100, 4, pp. 485-93.

Stich, S. P. 1983: *From Folk Psychology to Cognitive Science*. Cambridge, Mass: MIT Press.

Ullman, S. 1979: *The Interpretation of Visual Motion*. Cambridge, Mass: MIT Press.

van Gulick, R. 1989: "Metaphysical Arguments for Internalism, and Why They Don't Work", in *Re-Representation*, Silvers, S., ed., Dordrecht: Kluwer Academic Publishers, pp. 151-9.

XI*—EXTERNALIST EXPLANATION[1]

by Christopher Peacocke

I will be putting forward a thesis about how explanation by externalist states works. My plan is to go on to indicate some of the consequences of this thesis for a range of issues in the philosophy of mind. The range of issues includes the correctness of teleological approaches to content, the nature of subpersonal psychology, and the explanation of self-knowledge. One of the early tasks must also be to account for the possibility of externalist explanations, in the face of several arguments in the literature that it must be impossible.

By an externally individuated mental state or event-type, I mean one whose identity is dependent at least in part on its relations to things outside the subject, where these are taken to include properties and relations of things outside the subject. A constitutive account of what it is for the subject to be in such a state has to mention matters outside the subject. The external properties of the state are not restricted to those it possesses at the time it exists; a state or event-type can count as externally individuated in virtue of a dependence of its identity upon its earlier relations to external things, properties and relations. External individuation is a matter of the identity of the state itself, and not of some way of thinking of the state. For present purposes, I will be taking it for granted that some of the content-involving states recognized by folk psychology are externally individuated. It is to these states that I will, trading off some disregard for the normal meaning of a suffix in favour of concise expression, henceforth refer as 'externalist states'.

*Meeting of the Aristotelian Society, held in the Senior Common Room, Birkbeck College, London, on Monday 26th April 1993 at 8.15 p.m.

1 I am extremely grateful to the Research Centre of King's College Cambridge for support in the Lent Term of 1992, which made available the time for work on the topics of this paper. An earlier version was presented to the Research Centre's seminar during that term; I have been helped by the discussion on that occasion.

I

Explanation of the Relational; Explanation by the Relational.

A psychological explanation of an event typically explains certain of its relational properties. An action involving a particular hand movement may have each of these relational properties: it may be

a movement away from the subject's body;

a movement towards the window;

a movement towards a person in the garden;

a movement northwards.

A given psychological explanation may explain some, but not others, of these relational properties of the action. The range of relational properties of an action which may be psychologically explained is vast. It includes a variety of other spatial, environmental relational properties. A psychological explanation may explain the distance of one of your hands from a given point, if you are indicating how long you perceive something to be.[2] Temporal properties may be psychologically explained too, as anyone who is aware of the importance of the timing of a remark knows. The highly relational property of saying something which has a certain meaning is another example of a property whose instantiation is psychologically explained in any conversation.

The relational character of the explananda of propositional attitude psychology has certainly been noted before. This relational character is indeed a consequence of broadly interpretationist approaches to intentional content, such as Davidson's (1984). In general, what is made rational by a set of states with given intentional contents is an action as characterised in relation to its environment. The relational character of psychological explananda has been noted by Burge (1986 p. 11) and by me (1981); some of its ramifications have also been discussed at length by Hornsby (1986).[3] As the reader can guess from my agenda, my view is that

---

2 See for instance the means of testing perceived distance in Solomon and others (1989).

3 Though the claims to be developed here can be made without any commitment to 'object-dependent' contents: see below.

there is further material of philosophical interest to be developed from the point.

There is one very distinctive feature of explanations of relational properties of an action. It concerns the nature of the counterfactuals normally sustained by these explanations. Suppose your mental states explain your action's relational property of being a movement of your hand towards the person in the garden. Then if the person were in a different location, your hand would move in the direction of that different location, other things equal. If the person were at a different location, but the explanation of your action accounted for its relational property of being a movement in a northerly direction, your hand would not move towards the seen person in those counterfactual circumstances; and so forth. Other things equal, not only are different counterfactuals sustained when it is different relational properties of the event which are explained; these different, and usually competing, counterfactuals have antecedents which are themselves formulated in environmental terms; and their various consequents concern the agent's relation to things in his environment.[4]

Corresponding to these differences of counterfactuals sustained, there is a difference in predictions for differences between relational explananda. When a set of mental states explains the relational property of an action of being a movement in the direction of the person in the garden, the same set of states, if it supports rough-and-ready prediction at all, supports prediction of an action as having that relational property. Such an explanation says nothing about the orientation of the agent relative to the room, and it can apply over a range of different room-relative locations of the agent. The room-relative location of the agent does not need to be known for the explanation to be given.

As one might expect, similar points apply *pari passu* to the relational properties of objects and events which explain psychological states. Consider a linguistic example. There is a highly relational property of an utterance of the sentence 'Your house is burning'—the property of meaning that your house is burning

---

4 In emphasizing counterfactuals in an account of the explanatory relevance of externalist states, I am in agreement with LePore and Loewer (1987).

—which causes states that in turn cause you to take action. Any utterance of another sentence in the same language with the same meaning would have the same effects (other than the effects involving perception and beliefs about which particular sentence was uttered). Lastly, to complete the quartet of kinds of case, in predicting the psychological effects of a given event, for a subject with a given background of attitudes, we commonly need to know only a range of its relational properties. These properties too may be instantiated in a number of different, but psychologically irrelevant, ways.

These points suggest a general thesis about externalist states:

> It is partially constitutive of the identity of any externalist state that, in suitable circumstances, it can explain, or be explained by, relational properties of external objects or events.

There are many ways in which this general thesis can be made more specific. One could, for example, take a particular type of mental state, such as perceptual experience, and attempt to say, for each kind of content it may have, what relational explaining and explained states of affairs contribute to its identity. This is a particularly important task for someone (like me) who holds that some perceptual contents are nonconceptual. A conceptual content is individuated in terms of its possession conditions (Peacocke 1992). A nonconceptual content is not, and the question of what it is for it to be a constituent of the content of a mental state must be answered in some other way. One way of answering this question is to give a more specific elaboration of the general constitutive thesis about explanation, an elaboration treating, in a suitably general fashion, each kind of nonconceptual constituent of the content of a perceptual experience. What I want to concentrate on initially, however, is just the displayed general thesis itself, regardless of the way it is elaborated in detail.[5]

---

5 The position I am outlining here has links with several others in the literature. I mention two examples. (i) Cases in which we have a relational explaining condition—such as the occurrence of an utterance of a sentence meaning that your house is on fire—are cases in which we have the phenomenon which Blackburn (1991) identifies as "'looking through" the preceding realization' (p.215). The state of a thermometer 'looks through' the particular realization of heat in the object with which it is in contact. Only the temperature of that object, and not its particular realization—which will be quite different in a solid and in a liquid—will be relevant to the explanation of the reading on the

Many writers have worried whether it is possible for the content of a mental state to be explanatory of behaviour. The worry has been that the content of a mental state is, in general, externally determined: it depends on more than just the subject's brain states. But, the concern continues, the brain states must be sufficient to explain behaviour (if anything does), and hence mental content must be epiphenomenal. If the general thesis about externalist states is correct, this worry is based on a misapprehension about what is explained by states with mental content. It is true that brain states and efferent connections will be enough to explain any given bodily movement. But what is distinctively explained by a set of externalist states are relational facts about events or objects, relational facts which go beyond mere bodily movements. As we noted, there are distinctive counterfactuals linking relational causes and relational effects with the presence of externalist states. If the subject had not seen the person as being in the garden, he would not have pointed towards the garden. It is counterfactuals like that which support the explanatory importance of externalist states. Their truth is entirely consistent with the truth that different behaviour, nonrelationally described, will result only from different brain states. Dennett says that the idea of the mind as a semantic engine is incoherent (1987 p. 61; 1990 p.19). So it is, if the idea is that a semantic engine is one on which externalist properties of states are supposed to be essential in the explanation of behaviour nonrelationally characterized. But if a semantic engine is one whose behaviour relationally described is counterfactually dependent upon the external relations of its states, then there is no conceptual obstacle to our being semantic engines.

thermometer. I conjecture that the link between Blackburn's general position and my own is this: to capture the right level of state which is 'looked through to' in explanations of (and by) propositional attitudes, we need to mention the relational character of what those states characteristically explain and are explained by. (ii) Block (1990 section 4) observes that a functional-role theorist of the meaning of internal representations should insist that if a representation were to have a different meaning, it would in general have different consequences (because it would then have a different functional role). Indeed, if externalist states had functional definitions, then the arguments I have given so far would just be illustrations of his point—a point which, as he notes (p.150), applies whether content is taken as 'narrow' or as 'wide'. However, the points in the text about which counterfactuals are sustained by a particular psychological explanation can be made even if the externalist states are not functionally definable in the sense discussed by Block: on the important question of whether they must be so, see section 3 below.

This conception of externalist explanation contrasts with two other views. It contrasts, first, with accounts according to which internalist states, when suitably supplemented, can explain relational facts without appeal to externalist states.

This first competing suggestion would be that if we supplement a suitable specification of an internalist state with a statement of selected features of the circumstances surrounding the subject, we will obtain something which does explain the holding of certain relations in the external world. Let us consider exactly what would have to be included in this supplementation. We can fix on the intention to point to someone in the garden whom you recognize. To reach something capable of explaining your pointing to him, an internalist might add as a supplement the truth that the person in question is in a certain direction, the direction of the bodily movement actually made. But this addition by itself is not enough. The bodily movement may also be in the direction of Alpha-Centauri, but the psychological explanation need not explain the relational fact that the subject points towards Alpha-Centauri. Quite generally, explanation of a truth by a given set of states is not preserved by substitution of coextensive predicates in that truth, not even if we add a statement of the coextensiveness to the original explanation.

This point is also highlighted by the observation that supplementing a specification of an internal state with a description of the environmental relations of the bodily movements it produces fails to sustain the family of environment-involving counterfactuals which we noted. In the example of the intention, the internalist explanation plus supplementation will not sustain the counterfactual that if the recognized person were in a different direction, the subject would still have pointed at him.

So, let us suppose the internalist state supplemented with a batch of specifications of the external relations in which bodily movements would have stood under various different external antecedent conditions. We would also need bridging principles connecting these different antecedent external conditions with correspondingly different internal states, in order to be able to derive the counterfactuals. We would need a third thing too. The intention to point to the recognized person is constant across these various counterfactual circumstances, and the internal state must be described at a sufficiently nonspecific, functional, level so that it too is present in all these counterfactual circumstances.

When the internal state is supplemented with all this, is that then enough to explain external, relational truths in the way that externalist states do? It is not. The intention has a distinctive pattern of possible external relational conditions which explain *it*. It is essential to intentions that they can be explained by suitable beliefs, desires, emotions, and the like, which in turn can be explained by relational facts about the external environment. Indeed these connections also generate their own distinctive counterfactuals linking environmental conditions with relational characterizations of the subject's actions. So the supplementation would have to include further material to capture these links and counterfactuals too. But as we add more and more relational specifications to the original explanation involving only an internalist state, the question arises of whether we are not in fact adding sufficient material to ensure that the subject is, after all, in an externalist state.

A dilemma emerges for the view that, suitably supplemented, an internalist state can have the relational consequences and ante-cedents of an externalist state. Either the supplementary material plus the internal facts are not sufficient to ensure that the subject is in the externalist state in question; or they are sufficient. If they are not sufficient, then the internal states plus supplementation will not have all the actual and possible explanatory and counterfactual relations of the externalist state. If they are sufficient, the internal state plus supplementation is hardly an alternative to the view that externalist states are explanatory. The externalist state to which it was proposed as an alternative explanation actually supervenes on the explanatory resources employed in the alleged alternative.

II

Does Externalist Explanation Violate Contingency Requirements?

The preceding argument cannot by itself exhaust the case in favour of explanation by externalist states. We have also to answer the various arguments which aim to show that psychological explanation by externalist states is, for one reason or another, impossible. Do these arguments apply against the conception I have been promoting? I take first an argument developed by Fodor in 'A Modal Argument for Narrow Content' (1991).

The core of Fodor's position is that the contents of states with causal powers must be narrow contents, given that genuine causal powers capable of explaining an effect must be a matter of what they are contingently connected with, rather than a matter of any conceptual connections involving them: '...to put it roughly, your causal powers are a function of your *contingent* connections, not of your conceptual connections. As, indeed, Uncle Hume taught us' (p.19). Let twater be the substance which resembles water on Putnamian twin earth, but has a different chemical composition. Fodor considers the claim that water thoughts, rather than twater thoughts, are explanatory of water behaviour. He rejects this position as in contravention of the Humean principle about causal powers:

> Does the difference between having water thoughts and having twater thoughts count as a causal power in virtue of the fact that it is responsible for this difference in the intentional properties of the behaviour of the thinker? And the answer is: "No, because it is conceptually necessary that people who have water thoughts (rather than twater thoughts) produce water behaviour (rather than twater behaviour)." Being water behaviour (rather than twater behaviour) *just is* being behaviour that is caused by water thoughts (rather than twater thoughts). (p.21)

This may be a good argument against treating the properties of behaviour under which it is intentional as sufficient grounding for a claim about the difference between the causal powers of water thoughts and twater thoughts. But at this point in the argument, we must distinguish the relational properties of behaviour which I have been emphasizing from the intentions which produced the behaviour. Behaviour which involves a certain relation to water—a relation to something in the external world—does not fall within the scope of Fodor's argument. This is because it is not conceptually necessary that people who have water thoughts produce behaviour which involves relations to water. They will not do so, for instance, if transported (unbeknownst to them) from their normal environment; nor will they do so if tricked in their normal environment with substances which are superficially water-like. In these circumstances, though, their behaviour will still be water behaviour—at least to start with—in Fodor's sense; for it is caused by water thoughts. This point applies whether we understand 'water thoughts' merely as thoughts, of water, that it is so-and-so, or understand them to be thoughts, *de dicto*, that water is so-and-so.[6]

We should not, though, remain *au pied de la lettre de Fodor*, since there may be some natural and sympathetic extension of his reasoning on which it does apply to the conception of externalist explanation I have been promoting. A first adaptation of Fodor's reasoning would be the assertion that it is still objectionable that the following conditional is a conceptual truth, given that it is also meant to be cite an explanatory connection:

> If the subject is in his normal environment which includes water, and has water thoughts, he will (in the presence of other suitable attitudes) behave in various ways in relation to water.

The consequent of this conditional is about behaviour relationally described, so the objection cannot be dismissed on the same grounds as its predecessor. Nonetheless, I cannot see why it should be objectionable for this conditional (or some refinement of it) to have a necessary and *a priori* status. When the theoretical term 'gene' was introduced, prior to knowledge of its molecular basis, another conditional would also have had some kind of *a priori* status, viz.:

> If an organism develops normally, and one of its parents has a dominant gene for blue eyes, then it will have blue eyes.

The *a priori* status of some such conditional does not prevents us from citing facts about genes as causally explanatory of facts about eye colour. That status does not imply that it is *a priori* that eye colour has to be explained genetically, just as it is in no way *a priori* that any given relational property of behaviour has to have a psychological explanation. Maybe it is required, if the displayed

6 In the penultimate paragraph of his main text, Fodor writes: 'since it is assumed that the effects of mental states that differ only in broad content are (relevantly) different *only* under intentional description, it follows that there are *no* taxonomically relevant differences consequent upon broad-content differences as such' (pp.24–5). The assumption stated in this 'since...' clause will be contested if relational explananda are meant to be excluded from Fodor's intentional descriptions. If they are not excluded, I would of course dispute that what Fodor says follows does in fact follow. The result is that I am in agreement with Fodor's imagined objector (p.25) who says that Fodor's argument is an argument against (certain) arguments against individualism, not an argument for narrow content.

conditional about genes is to be explanatory, that dominant genes for blue eyes have some theoretical characterization which is not similarly *a priori* connected with the production of blue eyes in the offspring. They do of course have some such characterization at the molecular level. Similarly, water thoughts can have some theoretical and empirical characterization in a subpersonal psychology.

A second adaptation of Fodor's argument results from switching to a different type of example. Some of the complications present for the example of water-thoughts do not arise for thoughts whose contents contain perceptual demonstratives. The referent of the singular component of a content 'that apple grew in France' in a thinker's attitudes is willy-nilly different if the thinker is perceiving a different apple.[7] It is plausible that it is necessary, and *a priori*, that certain attitudes containing perceptual-demonstrative modes of presentation *of x* will in suitable circumstances produce behaviour which involves relations *to x*. It is also less clear that in the case of perceptual demonstratives, the parallel argument about genes is available to take away the sting from the corresponding claim of conceptual necessity of the relevant explanatory principle. A thinker's possessing a perceptual demonstrative mode of presentation of a given object *x* will no doubt have some subpersonal psychological elaboration, but that elaboration will surely involve the thinker's relations *to the object x* if it is to be a fully explanatory and sufficiently specific subpersonal elaboration of having a perceptual demonstrative mode of presentation of *x*.

The objection posed in this second adaptation presupposes that the defender of the present conception of externalist explanation must also be committed to demonstratives having object-dependent contents. There are several nonequivalent ways of characterizing object-dependence, the favoured characterization being a function of a theorist's views on other issues in the theory of intentional content. One characterization is this: a content is dependent upon one of the objects to which it refers if that object itself is a constituent of the content (the Californian conception,

---

7 More strictly: if the perception which makes available the perceptual-demonstrative to the thinker is a perception of a different object.

particularly associated with Kaplan and Almog). Another characterization, more congenial to those using a relatively substantial notion of sense, is that a content is dependent upon one of the objects to which it refers if some constituent of the content is individuated in part by its (and possibly the thinker's) relations to that particular object. Both of these characterizations have the consequence that were the object not to exist, the content would not exist either. It is indeed true that acceptance of some form of object-dependence for a specified class of contents could be made to mesh with the present conception of externalist states as explaining external relational states of affairs. An account could be developed on which certain attitudes to a content dependent on a particular object x are peculiarly capable of explaining certain relations in which the thinker stands to that particular object x. (Such an account could be developed within the framework in Peacocke (1981).) A theorist who believes in such object-dependence must indeed defuse this latest form of Fodor's objection, either by rejecting his restrictions on causal powers, or by denying that such object-dependent theories violate them. But it is very important that it is not true that the general conception of explanation by externalist states outlined in this paper involves a commitment to object-dependent contents.

What is crucial, according to the present conception of the explanatory powers of an externalist state, is not the identity of the object acted upon, but rather which relations are explained. How can this be? We can consider a view of intentional psychological explanation on which attitudes are relations to content-types which have particular objects 'bleached out' of them, in the following way. Suppose a book is presented visually to one thinker, and that a different but qualitatively identical book is presented in qualitatively identical circumstances to a different thinker. Each may think 'that book is blue', and their perceptual-demonstratives 'that book' refer to distinct books. But the two books are thought of in the same type of way (as long as the two subjects' perceptual systems are relevantly similar), and on the bleached-out conception, the two thinkers have attitudes to the same bleached-out content-type.

It is fully consistent to treat attitudes as having such bleached-out contents and at the same time to endorse the conception of externalist states I have been advocating. For on this combination of views, what should be regarded as explaining facts about a thinker's relations to particular objects is the combination of attitudes to content-types together with a specification of which objects are the referents of the constituents of the relevant content-type, relative to the thinker at the time in question. So for this combination of views, the thesis about externalist states should be framed thus, with two parts. The first part says that it is constitutive of such a state, with a given intentional content-type, that it is capable, in suitable circumstances, with given objects as the referents of its constituents, of being explained by, or explaining, certain relational facts about those objects, given that those objects are the referents. The second part, which is essential to avoid trivialization, says that the individuation of the content-*type* depends upon the complex of environmental relations of one who has attitudes whose contents contain it. This second part can be seen to be fulfilled for the perceptual-demonstrative associated with 'that book' in our example when we reflect that in the perceptual experience which makes the demonstrative available, the book will be seen as at a certain distance from the subject, and in a certain (body-relative) direction from him. That the book is perceived thus contributes to the individuation of the perceptual content-type associated with 'that book'. The supporter of externalism will say that perceiving the book that way is constitutively tied to the perception's capacity, in suitable circumstances, to explain relational facts about actions— such as the subject's moving, for instance, in the very bodily direction in which the book is presented as located. If these points are correct, then the present conception of externalist states and their distinctive role in explanation is neutral on the soundness of the arguments for object-dependent contents.

III

Blocked by Block's Principle?

The question also arises of whether the approach I have been developing falls foul of a principle of Ned Block's, to the effect that second-order properties, and higher-order properties in general, are not causally explanatory of the effects in terms of which they are defined (1990 pp.156–60). The two questions of the correctness of this principle, and of its consequences for the correct account of psychological explanation, are so important that the principle deserves a name—I will refer to it as 'Block's Principle'. Block illustrates the principle by considering a sleeping pill, whose chemical properties cause sleep in someone who ingests it. We can define the second-order property which Block calls the property of 'dormativity'. It is the property of having some property which causes sleep: if we use lambda-notation for properties, we can say that it is $\lambda x[\exists P(Px$ & P causes sleep$)]$. Block's claim is that what explains the sleep of someone who has taken a sleeping pill is the chemical property which verifies the existential quantifier over properties, rather than the higher-order property of dormativity.

If content-involving states were defined functionally over a theory of internal states which explain only bodily movements, Block's Principle would certainly seem to be incompatible with the claim that such states are causally explanatory of their defining effects. This incompatibility does not apparently evaporate when the holism of belief/desire psychology is taken into account. That holism would affect the complexity of the higher-order definitions, and has the consequence that the effect of producing a certain type of bodily movement is not in general mentioned in the definition of a single belief, or a single desire, on its own. The occurrence of such a movement would rather follow from the two propositions that the subject meets the offered functional characterization of a certain desire and also meets the offered functional characterization of a certain belief.[8] The motivation for Block's Principle naturally extends to rule out pairs of higher-order states as causally explanatory of the effects which are consequential upon their definitions taken together. However, if the arguments earlier in this paper are sound, we can already exclude the possibility of functional characterizations of externalist states if the functional characterizations quantify only over internalist states, and if the underlying nonfunctional theory explains only bodily movements. What the externalist state explains, in combination with other mental states, are relational properties of the bodily movement. I

---

8   The theorist would be well-advised to make sure that intention is in his account too; but this does not affect the present issues.

emphasized that we do not obtain an explanation of these relational properties just by adding specifications of relational properties of an event to an explanation of the event non-relationally described. The case is different in principle, and not merely in degree, from that of dormativity: in that case, there is no question but that the chemical property quantified over is sufficient to explain sleep. As a quite general rule, when defining functional states by reference to a particular type of theory, you certainly cannot get any more in the way of explananda than are given in theories of the type over which the definitions are being given. (As far as causal explanation goes, if Block's Principle is correct, you even get less).

So far I have been considering the easy case. It is well known that functionalism comes in 'long-arm', environment-involving varieties (Harman 1982), and it may be objected that nothing I have said rules out some kind of externally-oriented functional definition of intentional states. Indeed, it may well seem that the account I have been favouring must be committed to the possibility of such definitions. Surely we can obtain such a long-arm functional definition for any given state just by collecting together a statement of its essential role in externalist explanation (both as explainer and as explained)? If such definitions exist, will not the claim that these externalist states are explanatory of their defining effects be manifestly incompatible with Block's Principle?

Several recent writers reject Block's Principle for one reason or another (thus Blackburn (1991) and Segal and Sober (1990)). I propose now to outline three theoretical options available at this point in the argument; the positions vary in respect of whether they endorse, qualify, or remain neutral on Block's Principle.

Option 1: on this view, externalist states do have (non-individualistic) states which realize them, and these realizing states can be said to explain the relational states of affairs distinctively explained by intentional states—but only parasitically. According to this first view, the only sense in which the realizing states have relational explananda is that they realize states which have relational explananda in a nonparasitic sense.

The problem with this first option is that its claim is so strong that it excludes an attractive conception of subpersonal psychology. Under this conception, a subpersonal psychology can explain how we can be in a given externalist state recognised by propositional attitude psychology.[9] But if a subpersonal psychology can do that, then it will mention states which (by transitivity) can themselves explain what the externalist states of propositional attitude psychology explain. Yet if Option 1 were correct, this could not be genuine explanation by the subpersonal states—for it would have to be a kind of explanation not parasitic on explanations in propositional attitude psychology (on pain of the subpersonal states not explaining personal-level states). I confess I do not see why such subpersonal explanations of the externalist states of propositional attitude psychology cannot be genuine explanations in good standing. If they are in good standing, Option 1 should not be embraced.

Option 2 is inspired by David Lewis's theory that to give a causal explanation of an event is to give some information about its causal history (Lewis 1986a). This option in its most natural form involves at least some qualification of Block's Principle. To say that the ingested pill had the second-order property of dormativity is certainly to give some information about the causal history of the event of the person's falling asleep—for instance (overdetermination aside) it rules out tiredness as a cause. It is just that, because of the existential quantifier in the definition of dormativity, citing dormativity is rather less informative than an explanation could be. Citing externalistic intentional states is, however, much more informative—and the various environment-involving counterfactuals I emphasized earlier can be taken under Option 2 as showing precisely why it is so much more informative.

In Lewis's approach, what is explained is the occurrence of a particular event *tout court*; a causal history is, for him, a relational structure whose relata are particular events (related by causation). If the event e of pointing towards the person in the garden is taken to be identical with the event e' of pointing towards the window, then the causal histories of e and of e' will be identical. Hence any information about the causal history of e will be information about the causal history of e'; and conversely. Option 2 would then not be capable of accounting for the fact that different relational explananda have different explanations. So if we are to consider

9 This means that the subpersonal psychology must itself be externalist at some points—see further below.

Option 2 in a maximally sympathetic way, we need to consider the version in which e is regarded as distinct from e'.

The main drawback of Option 2 as a solution to our problem is that the very example of dormativity shows that a statement can give information about the causal history of an event without identifying the underlying property which is causally efficacious in producing it—the chemical property in this example. Someone who is concerned to show that the semantic properties of intentional states are causally efficacious will not be (or should not be) comforted by an account which treats the intentional states as no more explanatory than dormativity is under Option 2. Someone with these concerns should not be satisfied with an account on which the intentional states are indirect, existentially quantified pointers to states of some other, different kind, which have the status of a more fundamental explanation.

It is right to assess Option 2 without commitment to Lewis's own theory of events, for his thesis about causal explanation is independent of that theory. Nonetheless, it is worth noting a further problem for Option 2 for one who does hold Lewis's theory of events (Lewis 1986b). For Lewis, a particular event is a property of a region.[10] He also holds that events must be predominantly intrinsic: 'the alleged event that is essentially a fiddling while Rome burns would be too extrinsic' (ibid., 264). An intrinsic property is one which is necessarily possessed by both or neither of a pair of perfect duplicates. (The qualification 'predominantly' is to cover the point that Lewis takes account of time and place in individuating particular events.) These requirements seem too strong when we consider externalist psychological explanation. If the event of a particular pointing towards the window, and the event of a particular pointing towards the person in the garden, are distinct (as they must be if Option 2 is to help us), they are certainly not predominantly intrinsic in Lewis's sense. Some of the duplicates of each of these will not be pointings to windows, or persons in the garden, respectively. So if we combine Lewis's theory of events with his account of causal explanation, we are apparently in danger

10 For Lewis, a property is a class, where the class may contain merely possible, as well as actual, things (ibid. p.244). His claim about the individuation of particular events is also one which could be accepted without accepting this theory of properties.

of losing the distinctive explananda of externalist psychological states.

Is any sting caused by the view that there are no extrinsic events satisfactorily drawn by the observation that 'If there are no extrinsic...events to be caused, still there are extrinsic...truths about regions to be explained' (ibid., p.268)? Lewis writes: 'Why did Xanthippe become a widow? Because she was married to Socrates at the time of his death. (Noncausal.) Because Socrates was made to drink hemlock. (Causal, with the noncausal background most likely presupposed.)' (ibid., p.269). But a particular psychological explanation of the relational fact that someone is pointing to the person in the garden is not a noncausal, broadly 'logical' explanation—it is quite empirical. Nor is it just a causal explanation of some intrinsic core of the pointing which is in fact a pointing to the person in the garden: to say it for what I promise is the last time, we do not obtain a full psychological explanation of a relational fact by explaining some nonrelational properties, and then simply tacking on contextual, relational information. It certainly looks as if the lesson to be drawn from these points is that a satisfactory account of externalist psychological explanation, if it is to be given in terms of the explanation of events, must recognise extrinsic events.

Option 3, which I endorse, goes back to the start of the argument, and disputes the claim that the description which has been given of externalist explanation really leads to long-arm functionalist characterizations which are within the scope of Block's Principle. ('The first step is the one which altogether escapes notice'—Wittgenstein (1958 §308).) Suppose we grant, for the sake of argument, that an externalist state is fully individuated by a certain complex role it possesses in externalist explanations (either as explanans or as explanandum). Suppose one tiny part of the role in question of the state of wanting to draw attention to the person in the garden is that, in the context of suitable attitudes, the subject's possession of it explains the fact that he pointed to the person in the garden. It is natural to take 'explains' here as an operator on a pair of contents—the fact that p explains the fact that q. The description of the attitude as a desire to draw attention to the person occurs within the scope of 'explains'. If we construe this explanatory role as one part of what individuates a desire with that content, we can say that

part of what individúates that psychological state is that it is a state
S such that a subject's being in it explains, in the given context of
other attitudes, his pointing towards the person in the garden. But
since the propositional-attitude description occurred within the
scope of 'explains', the variable '*S*' here must be understood as a
variable *over psychological states.* It is not a variable over realizing
states; so it is not even of the right form to be one small part of a
higher-order functional definition of the sort to which Block's
Principle would apply. Any account of a propositional attitude
which results from repeating this process would be better called a
theoretical characterization than a functional characterization. By
contrast, of course, the variable over states in the definition of
dormativity ranges only over chemical states—it is certainly not
meant to have the state of dormativity in its range too (if it did, the
definition would suffer from an unfortunate form of
ungroundedness).

   This third Option need not, then, have any dispute with Block's
Principle. Nor need Option 3 deny that there are nonindividualistic
states which realize the states of propositional attitude psychology.
The thesis of Option 3 is just that propositional attitudes are not
individuated by higher-order definitions over such realizing states.
The defender of Option 3 can indeed endorse the attractive conception with which Option 1 is incompatible. There is nothing in
the position of Option 3 to rule out subpersonal explanations of a
person's being in a given externalist state.

IV

Can Explanation of an Event tout court Suffice?

The conception of externalist explanation I have been defending
contrasts also with a second kind of view, on which no special place
needs to be accorded to relational explananda. On this second kind
of competing view, we can describe the functioning of externalist
states satisfactorily simply by saying how they explain events *tout
court.*

   This second kind of view is to be distinguished from those which
really end up conceding that mental content is not explanatory. The
advocates of these latter views often proceed by finding something

other than actions of which mental content *is* explanatory, whilst not defusing the arguments that it cannot be. Thus, for instance, Dretske says that 'if the meaning of an event does not supervene on the event's intrinsic properties, as on most (plausible) accounts of meaning it does not, the meaning of this event is effectively screened off from explanations of its effects' (1990 p. 12). Dretske's position is that the content or meaning of a particular event *a* can explain, by a learning mechanism, why events of (one of the) types of *a* cause events of (one of the) types of its effect. I am in agreement with Fodor (1990) and Block (1990) that if the position is left at that, meaning or content remains irrelevant to the explanation of particular effects, and the same applies to any externalist state. I cannot see how the position is essentially different if we agree with Dennett (1990) that a harmony between the content-involving properties of events and states and the internal ('syntactic') properties of events and states is virtually certain always to be present when an organism is settled into its environment. The fact that a property explanatory of behaviour is virtually certain always to be coinstantiated with a second is not sufficient to make the second property explanatory of behaviour.

   The second class of views with which I want to develop a contrast to my own are rather those which squarely give a criterion for something to be explanatory of an event *tout court*, and then argue that externalist states meet the given criterion. These views have been developed by Segal and Sober (1990), and applied by Michael Tye (1991). In the final chapter of his book *The Imagery Debate*, Tye is concerned to show that the content of an image can be causally efficacious in producing behaviour. He accepts that the content of an image depends upon its relations to things outside its owner's head, and so the problem he addresses is a special case of the one that has been exercising us. His strategy is first to elucidate a relation *O causes E in virtue of having macroproperty P*. He then argues that the relation he has elucidated holds between an image, an appropriate piece of behaviour, and the macroproperty of having a certain content. Tye, following Segal and Sober, gives this account of the relation:

> the effect E has some property Q for which P is nomologically sufficient; P supervenes on some microproperty P'; and O causes E in virtue of some microproperty P'' included in (entailed by) P'.

This summarizes Tye's final position (p. 148), and his account of O causing E in virtue of having macroproperty P can be diagrammed thus:

O causes E

$P(O)$ $Q(E)$

P nomologically suffices for Q
|
supervenes on
|
P'

P' entails P''

O in virtue of P', causes E

It is indeed true that according to this definition, imagistic content can be causally efficacious in the required way. The content of an image is determined by all sorts of relations to things outside the brain; but it is nonetheless true that image content supervenes on a complex microproperty which entails a microproperty which *is* a matter only of what goes on in the brain, and is causally efficacious at the micro level. The problem, though, with this defence is that it could also be used to establish the causal efficacy of all sorts of macroproperties which are, intuitively, causally irrelevant. Consider any macroproperty R which is of the right type to feature in a law, and which imposes no more internal restrictions on brain states than does the macroproperty P. On Tye's definition, if O causes E in virtue of having macroproperty P, and O in fact has the macroproperty R, then it follows that O also causes E in virtue of having macroproperty $P\&R$. For if P is nomologically sufficient for Q, then $P\&R$ will also be so; $P\&R$ will also supervene on some microproperty or other; and by the choice of R this microproperty must entail the microproperty P'' of the brain which was entailed by the microproperty on which P supervened. R might, for instance, be the property of having grown up in an industrialized country. The question arises, then, for Tye's account of why content-involving properties are any more properly regarded as causally efficacious than such an arbitrarily chosen additional property *P&R*. Even if it is thought that the definition of causal efficacy of a property can stand, we still have an obligation to say why content-involving properties are so much more explanatory than the likes of *P&R*.

Since this problem arises from the presence of the property-inclusion requirement, the obvious question to ask is: why is it there? Why can't we just revise the condition to require merely that *P* supervenes on some property in virtue of which *O* causes *E*? The inclusion requirement is inherited from Segal and Sober.[11] They are tentatively in favour of counting the presence of air as efficacious in the lighting of matches which are struck. Air is about 70% nitrogen and 30% oxygen, and only the oxygen is causally relevant at the micro level. Segal and Sober's view is that semantic properties are as efficacious in the transactions of representations as airiness is efficacious in its transactions with matches (p.16). We can, though, distinguish one (or more) of the several conditions which must constitutively be met for the presence of a property as the one (or as the ones) in virtue of which it is efficacious. In the case of the property of being surrounded by air, it is the condition of containing oxygen which is efficacious—any other inert gas combined with oxygen would have been equally good. On the Segal and Sober treatment, the semantic properties of a representation are no more causally efficacious than is the nitrogen in the air in causing matches to burn: it is not the semantic properties of the represent-ation in virtue of which it has its effects.

To summarise: if we fix on the notion of the property in virtue of which the representation has its effects, then incorporating the property-inclusion requirement does not result in a plausible de-finition. On the other hand, if we leave it out, it is not plausible that the microproperty on which content-involving states supervene are the ones in virtue of which certain brain states cause their effects.

11 Ibid. p.15; see their (P5).

I doubt that this problem can be met by tinkering with definitions. We need rather an approach which slices explananda more finely, and distinguishes content-involving states as peculiarly appropriate for certain kinds of explananda. We do not do explanation by content-involving states a service by trying to assimilate it to a model appropriate only for states which do not involve content.[12]

V

Consequences and Prospects.

I now turn to consider the bearing of this treatment of externalist states upon some extant theories in the philosophy of mind, and upon our understanding of some issues on which we ought to be developing theories. All I can do here is to indicate the issues: all the topics in question manifestly need extensive discussion.

(i) What is the relation between the general thesis that externalist explanation is constitutive of content-involving mental states on the one hand, and teleological theories of intentional content on the other? Any plausible teleological theory of intentional content will treat intentional content as externalist. But is the converse true? Must any plausible externalist theory be a teleological theory? I would argue that, on the contrary, there are plausible ways of developing an account of (for instance) perceptual content, in accordance with the general thesis about externalism, ways which nevertheless make it clear that in some possible circumstances, a state which misrepresents may confer a selective advantage, and become established in the species through natural selection. That is, we can conceive of externalist states which constitute a counter-example to this thesis:

> perceptual states of type T represent the environment as having property O iff natural selection has operated to ensure that states of type T covary with property O.

Suppose members of a species are subject to attack by a particularly dangerous kind of predator. The members of this species commonly

---

12 The points in these recent paragraph were developed in my review (forthcoming) in *Philosophy of Science* of Tye's book.

perceive these predators as closer than they actually are—as, say, two-thirds of the distance they actually are. Perceiving them as closer has conferred a selective advantage, we can suppose, because it makes the perceiver run away faster, and generally activates flight responses at a higher level. In these circumstances, the perceptual state which represents the predator as at a distance which is measured by about 20 feet will be of a type which natural selection has operated to ensure covaries with the predator being about 30 feet away. So the biconditional displayed above would assign the wrong content to these perceptual states. It counts these perceptions as representing the predator as being at a distance which is measured by about 30 feet, which is not in fact the experience's representational content.

There are, though, plausible ways of developing the general thesis about externalist explanation for the particular case of perceptual content which do make a correct assignment of content to these experiences. One plausible way of developing the thesis is that states with spatial representational content must be capable of explaining the relational, and in particular the spatial, properties of behaviour. The naive, misperceiving subject who experiences the predator as at a distance which is measured by 20 feet will throw a stone aimed at it to about 20 feet, not 30 feet (other things equal). There may also be more distant consequences in time. If our subject keeps track of the apparent past location of the predator on his cognitive map, he will avoid a place, or will build a trap at a place, which is 20 feet, not 30 feet, from his location at the time of the encounter. These are all relational, spatial consequences of his perceptual state, and they are legitimately cited by an externalist account. (These conditional consequences of the misrepresentation will not of course be adaptive if they are relied upon; but their triggering conditions may not have been fulfilled when the creatures' perceptual systems were fixed by natural selection.) An externalist account need not, then, be teleological; and it can be more output-oriented than the biconditional displayed above.

(ii) If the conception advanced in this paper is correct, and if one of the tasks of a subpersonal psychology is to explain how humans can have particular propositional attitudes, then at least some part of subpersonal psychology must employ externally individuated states. Citing a subpersonal state whose nature does *not* involve any external relations can never by itself be a full account of the realization of a person's being in a state whose nature *does* involve such external relations. Mention of such a subpersonal state may indeed be supplemented with a specification of some of the external, environmental relations in which it stands (in both actual and some counterfactual circumstances). With this supplementation, we would have something of the right kind to have the same explanatory powers as an externalist state of propositional-attitude psychology. What would be doing the explaining would then be something with a nature partially externally individuated.

Similarly, the treatment of this paper can be extended to support the claim that a content-involving characterization of a subpersonal computation can be explanatory. A system's being in one content-involving state can be explained as the result of a computation carried out on an initial state which is also content- involving. When the contents in question are partially externally individuated, we have in such a case the explanation of one externalist state by another externalist state. What is distinctive about explanations of this kind is again captured by the points at the start of this paper: the explanation will sustain distinctively relational counterfactuals and predictions. To say that there is such a level of computational explanation is not at all to deny that causation is local, nor that some kind of 'formality' constraint must be met by computational mechanisms. It does, though, involve denying that the only contents which can legitimately feature in subpersonal psychological theories are those which are individuated by reference solely to some sort of internal functional role.

(iii) Externalism comes in many varieties, and the varieties are themselves classifiable along several dimensions. The core of the externalist claim in the earlier sections of this paper is a constitutive claim—that what makes something a state with a certain intentional content is a matter of certain relational states of affairs which may explain it or be explained by it. Constitutive claims are, as always, to be distinguished from modal claims. There are various modal varieties of externalism. Since they each claim a kind of possible separation of an intentional state from the internal states actually involved in a thinker's being in that intentional state, they can be called 'modal separation theses'. One of the weakest modal separation theses is simply the claim that an intentional mental state does not supervene on a thinker's internal states. A stronger claim states that the internal state which actually realises a thinker's being in a given intentional state would not do so in certain different, and possible, environmental conditions. (This is a stronger thesis, since the supervenience claim does not even commit its holder to making sense of the notion of a realisation of a particular mental state.) A very strong modal separation thesis would go further, and say that an internal state which in fact realises one intentional state could, in different environmental conditions, realise a different mental state. It is not clear whether any form of modal separation thesis is correct for the state of having an experience with a given represent-ational content. But even if none is correct, that would not under-mine all forms of externalism for the representational content of experience. Falsity of the modal separation theses does not imply falsity of the constitutive claim. A twin-earth case of course establishes a modal separation thesis. So we can put this most recent point by saying: the existence of twin-earth cases is not necessary to establish the externalist character of a kind of intentional state.

That constitutive dependence should come apart from modal dependence should not be alarming. We have long lived with that situation elsewhere. What it is, constitutively, for something to be unprovable in arithmetic is a matter of the nonexistence of a certain kind of sequence of sentences. The property of being unprovable is necessarily coextensive with certain other properties (e.g. properties definable using Gödel numbering): but these other properties are not what *make* a sentence unprovable.

(iv) The claim that mental states of a certain type are constitutively dependent upon their environmental relations is still quite enough to generate a challenge to the externalist to provide an account of a person's knowledge of his own externalist states. In its simplest form, the challenge runs thus: if the individuation of a certain state involves its environmental relations, how is it possible for a person to know he is in that state without checking on his environmental relations?

Again, this is no place to try to develop a detailed response to the challenge. What I do want to do is very briefly to indicate one way in which the account of externalist explanation provides a resource on which the externalist can draw in meeting the challenge. One of the concerns behind the challenger's question is that, on an externalist theory of mental states, a person's knowledge of his own mental states cannot be much better than that of a person who knows something about a second person who knocks on the door of his room, but does not enter. The first person can know that the second person knocks heavily, has a loud footstep, and the like; but unless the person enters, there is a clear sense in which the first person does not know who it is.

An externalism of the kind I am endorsing can meet this concern by appealing to what I call a principle of inheritance. Let us fix on the state of having a visual experience as of a telephone in a certain direction from one's body. I have been emphasizing that part of what is involved in the experience's having that content is its capacity, in certain circumstances, to explain the subject's reaching, or pointing, or standing in various other relations, to that particular direction (identified in relation to the body). Let us collect these capacities together under the label of the experience's 'powers of explanation of relational facts involving that direction'. Now let us consider the subject's belief that he has an experience as of a telephone in that same direction. Suppose that it is potentially constitutive of such a belief state that it is one the subject is willing to go into when he has just such an experience. An inheritance principle states that in such a case, the belief state inherits the same powers of explanation of relational facts involving the given direction as are possessed by the experience itself. It is because this is so that, when asked, 'Which is the direction in which your experience represents there as being a telephone?', the subject can point in the correct direction. If this and similar abilities do not amount to knowing which direction is in question, it is unlikely that anything ever could. If such an inheritance principle is correct, the case is, then, quite unlike that of the person's failure to know who is knocking at the door. A satisfactory externalist theory of self-knowledge should make essential use of such inheritance principles. There must also of course be a great deal more to a satisfactory theory of self-knowledge.

(v) Still further from our present grasp than a full account of self-knowledge is a theory of our knowledge of other minds. But even in the dim state of our present understanding of the matter, we can see that the present externalist account entails a view of the evidence to which hypotheses about others' intentional states are answerable. Subject to the normal kinds of inductive uncertainty and fallibility, we confirm or refute hypotheses about other peoples' intentional states by evidence about their relations to things in their environment in various circumstances. This confirmation involves hypotheses about which of these relations are actually the ones explained by the subject's intentional states. All this is to be expected if explanatory relations to relational states of affairs is of the essence of intentional states. The knowability of another's intentional states rests upon the knowability of his relations to the world around him.

Magdalen College
Oxford OX1 4AU

REFERENCES

Blackburn, S. 'Losing your mind: physics, identity and folk burglar prevention.' In *The future of folk psychology: intentionality and cognitive science*, ed. J. Greenwood. Cambridge: Cambridge University Press, 1991.
Block, N. 'Can the mind change the world?' In *Meaning and Method: Essays in Honor of Hilary Putnam*, ed. G. Boolos. Cambridge: Cambridge University Press, 1990.
Burge, T. 'Individualism and Psychology.' *Philosophical Review* XCV (1986): 3–45.
Davidson, Donald. *Inquiries into Truth and Interpretation*. Oxford: Clarendon Press, 1984.
Dennett, D. *The Intentional Stance*. Cambridge, Mass.: MIT Press, 1987.
Dennett, D. 'Ways of Establishing Harmony.' In *Information, Semantics and Epistemology*, ed. E. Villaneuva. Oxford: Blackwell, 1990.
Dretske, F. 'Does Meaning Matter?' In *Information, Semantics and Epistemology*, ed. E. Villaneuva. Oxford: Blackwell, 1990.
Fodor, Jerry. 'Reply to Dretske's 'Does Meaning Matter?'.' In *Information, Semantics and Epistemology*, ed. E. Villaneuva. Oxford: Blackwell, 1990.
Fodor, Jerry. 'A Modal Argument for Narrow Content.' *Journal of Philosophy* LXXXVIII (1 1991): 5–26.
Harman, G. 'Conceptual Role Semantics.' *Notre Dame Journal of Formal Logic* 23 (1982): 242–56.
Hornsby, J. 'Physicalist Thinking and Conceptions of Behaviour.' In *Subject, Thought and Context*, ed. P. Pettit and J. McDowell. Oxford: Clarendon Press, 1986.
LePore, E. and B. Loewer. 'Mind Matters.' *Journal of Philosophy* LXXXIV (11 1987): 630–642.
Lewis, D. 'Causal Explanation.' In *Philosophical Papers: Volume II*. New York: Oxford University Press, 1986a.
Lewis, D. 'Events.' In *Philosophical Papers: Volume II*. New York: Oxford University Press, 1986b.
Peacocke, C. 'Demonstrative Thought and Psychological Explanation.' *Synthese* 49 (1981): 187–217.
Peacocke, C. *A Study of Concepts*. Cambridge, Mass.: MIT Press, 1992.

Ecological content

Josefa Toribio

The paper has a negative and a positive side. The negative side argues that the classical notions of narrow and wide content are not suitable for the purposes of psychological explanation. The positive side shows how to characterize an alternative notion of content (ecological content) that is suitable for those purposes. This account is supported by (a) a way of conceptualizing computation that is constitutively dependent upon properties external to the system and (b) empirical research in developmental psychology. My main contention is that an adequate computational explanation of the behavior involved in cognitive activities should invoke a concept of content that can capture the intimate dynamical relationship between the inner and the outer. The notion of content thus reaches out to include the set of skills, abilities and know-hows that an agent deploys in a constantly variable environment. The assumption underlying my attempt to characterize this ecological notion of content is that cognition is better understood when treated as embedded cognition and that the idea of cognitive significance ought to be cashed out in non-individualistic and pragmatic terms.

1. Introduction

Paramount among the (recent) historical roots of the notion of narrow content is Putnam's (in)famous Twinearth thought-experiment. Putnam (1975) describes a pair of microphysically identical twins who differ only in their absolute relational properties. In particular, some of one twin's thoughts are caused by H_2O, while the other's (on 'Twinearth') are caused by a superficially identical liquid XYZ. But despite their neural and bodily microphysical identity one twin has thoughts that are about water and the other does not. Thus it would seem

Pragmatics & Cognition Vol. 5(2), 1997. 257–285
© John Benjamins Publishing Co.

that thought content is not fully determined by (does not supervene upon[1]) microphysical states of the brain. Thought content seems to be individuated by reference to the subject's environmental context and not by reference to her intrinsic physical properties. This is the main contention of the 'externalist' — one who holds that mental contents are fixed by a subject's relations to external (extra-neural, extra-bodily) states of affairs.

This position, however, can seem unsatisfactory if we also hold that thought content should play a causal role in explaining, say, the origins of the gross bodily responses which will be shared by the microphysically identical twins. The notion of narrow content is then invoked to plug the explanatory lacuna left by the strong externalist view. The guiding idea is that, even if Putnam is right and a dimension of the content of a thought is relational or externalist (namely, that dimension of content that matters when we want to fix the truth-conditions of the sentence used to express that thought), there *must* in addition be *some other* dimension of content that is non-relational, i.e., a dimension of content that can be fixed regardless of the relations that obtain between the thinker and the external world. It is this narrow dimension of content that matters, it seems, whenever we want to provide psychological explanations (cf. Fodor 1987: chapter 2).[2] The stage is thus set for the debate between internalism and externalism.

Let us characterize internalism as the view that holds both that the content of a mental state supervenes on intrinsic physical states of the subject, and that such contents are individuated 'narrowly', i.e., without essential reference to the subject's physical and social environment. The externalist position, by contrast, denies that mental contents supervene on intrinsic physical properties of the subject. The externalist claims that contents are individuated 'widely', i.e., by reference to the subject's environmental or social context.

I agree with the externalist (See Burge 1979, 1986, 1993; Peacocke 1993, 1994)[3] that psychological explanation (both of the 'folk' and scientific variety) does not require the full classical notion of narrow content. But there is surely something correct about the intuitions which drive the dissenters to a vision of narrow content. What is correct, I believe, is that we do indeed need to avail ourselves of some kind of non-relational account of what it means to have a thought with a particular content if we are to provide good scientific psychological explanations. In this paper I will try to steer a middle way. I will argue that narrow content — or, at least, the *standard* notion of narrow content developed by Fodor — can't fulfill the function for which it was designed, i.e., that narrow content is not, after all, an adequate theoretical tool for the purposes of scientific psychological explanation. I will then defend a different notion of content, neither narrow nor traditionally wide, that seems better fit to meet our psychological explanatory needs.

Along the way I will invoke two additional theoretical tools. The first is a way of conceptualizing computation that is constitutively dependent upon properties external to the system (Section 4). The second is some empirical research in developmental psychology that aims to vindicate a similar approach for understanding psychological development (Karmiloff-Smith 1986, 1992; Rutkowska, 1990, 1991, 1993a, 1993b). I will introduce these empirical results in Section 5. With these tools in hand, I will argue (Section 6) for a new notion of content: one that is methodologically more appropriate for the purposes of scientific psychological explanation. This is the notion that I shall dub 'ecological content'.

2. The nature and role of narrow content

There are at least two features of narrow content about which everybody seems to agree. First, narrow content strongly supervenes on intrinsic, non-intentional, physical properties of an organism. It is precisely that feature which makes narrow content *narrow*.[4] The second relevant feature is that narrow content is invoked mainly, if not exclusively, for predicting and explaining behavior.

Given just these two features, one might well ask what makes narrow content 'content' at all. But interestingly enough this issue is usually finessed by making a general assumption: that whatever is going on in the head of a subject such that we invoke it to account for her behavior deserves to be treated as a contentful state of some kind. The image of the mind as a computer undergirds this assumption. According to a classical version of the computational view, intentional states are supported by states that involve symbols of a *mental* language or *language of thought* (Fodor 1975). My belief that there is an apple pie in the refrigerator involves my being in some kind of computational relation to the *mentalese* symbols corresponding to "There is an apple pie in the refrigerator". The content of such an intentional state is just the content of that chain of symbols in *mentalese* and the fact that it is a belief — rather than a desire or a doubt — is determined by the nature of its computational relation to the rest of my mental states and/or my behavior. The symbols of that mental language possess a combinatorial syntax and are physically implemented by the brain.

Thus, even if we don't put forward any theory about what narrow content actually *is* or about what makes narrow content 'content', the following can be said: narrow content is content that serves the purposes of scientific psychological explanation. It picks out intrinsic states that play a causal role in the generation of behavior, and it is capable of figuring in causal-explanatory accounts of intentional action. Narrow contents thus satisfy the demand that *scientific* explanations should be *causal explanations*. The justification of this demand comes from the physicalist bias of standard scientific methodology, i.e., the idea that the causal powers of any event are completely determined by its physical features. As a result, content that is individuated in terms of a system's intrinsic properties is deemed adequate for a *scientific* explanation of behavior.

Add a computationalist spin to this physicalistic bias and the nature of narrow content finally emerges. According to the computational theory of mind, cognitive capacities are to be treated as information-processing operations and to be characterized in computational terms. Computational processes are defined, in turn, in terms of operations on representations. Input-representations stand for arguments in a function. Output-representations constitute the values of the computed function. A representation is thus a very special kind of physical configuration, a physical configuration that has a syntactic vehicle and a semantic content. The important point is that, although computer processes are only sensitive to the syntax, a computing device can be designed in such a way that the production of syntactic states respects the semantic interpretation. Under such conditions, the semantics does indeed supervene on the syntax. But even so, there remains a (fatal) problem afflicting any attempt to identify some more specific syntactical state (e.g., a particular pattern of activity in a neuronal population) with a certain semantic content. The problem is nicely described by Ned Block who comments that "syntactically identical objects can play very different functional roles, and be associated with very different recognitional capacities" (Block 1991: 39). In the same vein Stalnaker (1990: 135) claims that the

> [Physical or syntactical properties of a thought token] surely will not be sufficient to determine even the narrow content of the thought token. Presumably, the same particular physical event or state that is a particular thought that water is the best drink for quenching thirst might, if the functional organization of the thinker were different enough, have not only a different wide content, but also a different narrow content.

In other words, the properties that seem to account for a state's narrow content and that would justify its intentional (i.e., semantic) role for the internalist are not syntactical properties of individual thought tokens. The upshot, it seems to me, is that even if we accept that the mental states must supervene on a system's intrinsic physical description, we must still recognize that specific mental states are not constituted by syntactic properties. Instead, the individuation even of narrow contents will depend on further facts concerning the large scale functional organization of the system. Such a concession, however, immediately paves the way for an even more radical proposal: the proposal to extend the supervenience base to include not just facts about the larger scale details of the inner economy, but to include facts about what might be termed the local ecological economy. This would include both the organism itself and certain aspects (this restriction to be discussed later) of local environmental structure. This is the proposal to be pursued in Sections 4–6. First though, we should notice a few more problems with the traditional notions of both narrow and wide content.

3. Narrow content, wide content and scientific psychology

Can any kind of narrow content really fulfill the explanatory role for which it has been created? In other words, can the causal explanation of an agent's behavior consist in the specification of the role played by her internal states as specified by an *internalist content-involving description*?[5] By an internalist content-involving description I mean the kind of description that would be cashed out in terms of the system's intrinsic properties characterized independently of the system's interaction with its environment. One problem is that whenever we try to *formulate* such descriptions, we lose the very *narrowness* that we were trying to capture. This is because psychological explanations invoke mental states with particular intentional contents in order to explain or justify a given course of action. Thus the explanation of why Michael opened the refrigerator appeals to his desire for a piece of apple pie and to his belief that there is some apple pie in the refrigerator. To invoke mental states with those particular intentional contents ('there is some apple pie in the refrigerator' and 'I want some apple pie') allows us to explain Michael's behavior and does so by depicting such contents as the causal determinants of his action. The individuation of a mental state as an allegedly explanatory state with such-and-such a content is thus achieved in part by appealing to properties of the external objects and events implicated in a particular behavior. But, if this is so, then the content-involving descriptions can't really be of a purely internalist kind; they can't be narrow content-involving descriptions.

At this stage, a distinction might be drawn between narrow content as explanatory of a subject's *attempt* to do something and narrow content as explanatory of why that attempt succeeded, if it did succeed, or failed, if it failed. The subject's external environment is indeed relevant to explaining the success or failure of any attempt to perform a given action. An internalist interested in the explanatory aspect of narrow content might claim that narrow content matters also if we want to explain the success or failure of the actions performed by the subject in its environment. Let's call this internalist's goal oriented position a Type 0 claim.[6]

It seems to me, however, that Type 0 claims need not be a threat to the kind of position I am going to defend. Legitimate as they are, Type 0 claims address an issue different from the one I am concerned with in this paper. The evaluation of the appropriateness of the notion of narrow content that I am concerned with here is tied to the explanation of a system's *behavior*, i.e., the explanation of "whatever people or organisms or even mechanical systems *do* that is publicly *observable*" (Kim 1996: 28).[7] This is the central issue for psychology. The explanation of the success or failure of such 'doings' is obviously important from some other points of view (e.g., from an evolutionary point of view) but it is not important from a psychological perspective. In the next section, I shall mention David Papineau's concern with this problem. But for now, the following should be clear: Type 0 claims concern why a subject achieves or fails to achieve a certain goal, while the claims that are relevant for the discussion at hand concern only the internally caused motions and gross actions displayed by a subject.[8]

A sensible internalist, concerned with this second issue, would agree that to explain behavior, we must know what in the subject's external environment is being represented to that subject. But this internalist will insist that it is still the subject's inner states rather than anything outside her head which determine the behavior psychology needs to explain. In other words, the sensible internalist will still insist that the subject's internal and narrowly individuated states determine her beliefs and therefore explain her behavior. Let's call the sensible internalist's weakly environment-invoking position a Type I claim.

In reply to the sensible internalist, let me say the following. Remember that I am arguing against the *explanatory adequacy* of a given concept, namely, narrow content, for scientific psychology. My worry is thus that the exchange between subject and environment might at times be so complex, and the dynamics of the overall coupled system so different from the dynamics of either component alone, that it is often much more *methodologically fruitful* to take the dynamics of the whole (subject *cum* local environment) as the basic explanatory unit in psychology. Let's call this stronger position a Type II claim.

Next, suppose we take computational psychology as representative of scientific psychology. The sensible (Type I) internalist insists on the individualistic character of the concepts involved in adequate computational *explanations* of behavior. The issue is thus whether the concepts involved in computational explanations ought to have such an individualistic character or not. This question probably can't be resolved without providing a full account of the notion of explanatory adequacy and a description of how that account fits into the framework of computational psychology. But even without such an account, some interesting examples can be provided to help distinguish the different issues involved in Type I and Type II claims.[9]

Think of Scrabble-playing strategies.[10] While playing, we may physically arrange and rearrange the letter tiles as a way of prompting recall of candidate words. A computational psychology concerned with the explanation of this kind of behavior might usefully characterize such external manipulations as a means of providing inputs to prompt a pattern-completing associative memory. Such a picture is, however, nicely compatible with the weak Type I model. For the Type I internalist needs only think of the world as a source of inputs and an arena for action. She can agree that the possibility of individuating the computational states of cognitive systems is relative to the properties of the world that they inhabit. But this is to say that the world *determines* the agent's cognitive states (via the inputs), and not that external features can play any role in constituting such states.

The stronger Type II theorist aims to show that sometimes such a division between world and agent is not productive; that it is not always methodologically appropriate for psychological purposes. Think, for instance, of swimming. It is not just that we hit the water and trigger a swimming routine. Instead, we produce a movement, the water flow changes and that alteration calls forth a new movement, and so on. Now, maybe you could analyze this case as a complex combination of inputs prompting inner states which prompt actions. But it may be much more explanatorily fruitful to treat brain, body and water here as a complex coupled whole with its own intrinsic dynamics.

Kirsh and Maglio's (1994) thorough analysis of expert performance on the computer game Tetris provides a neat example of such a Type II claim. Tetris players have to place blocks of different geometric shapes (zoids) into compact surfaces (rows). When a row is completed, it disappears from the screen and new zoids begin to fall again — from the top of the screen — at a speed that increases with successful performance of the game. While falling, the player can operate on the zoid — rotate it, move it to the left, to the right, or drop it directly to the bottom of the row. The purpose of the game is thus to match zoid-shapes and row-shapes under rather severe time constraints. What Kirsh and Maglio have shown is that advanced players of Tetris, although able to mentally rotate a zoid so as to better determine its shape, often prefer to rotate the zoid *physically* (this is an option in the game), because this *external* manipulation is both faster and more reliable.[11]

Physical zoid rotation, Kirsh and Maglio suggest, is best thought of as a proper part of a distinct computational subroutine invoked during expert play. The fact that this subroutine incorporates a 'call to the world' is less important than the fact that it constitutes a computationally unified whole. The density of information flow within the subroutine (including the operations performed in the world) is so great and so temporally complex that the decomposition of the system into biological wetware and local environment structure is less revealing, from a computational point of view, than its decomposition into a set of subroutines one of which is partly constituted by operations performed out in the real world.

What these experiments suggest is that some cognitive states may be best characterized in terms of world-involving skills or abilities rather than merely in terms of the inner brain structures underlying performance. The question is thus whether the best unit of analysis for understanding cognitive organization is always the bare biological device or whether it is sometimes the agent plus a select chunk of the local environment (see also Hutchins 1995). The kind of research just discussed suggests that sometimes, at least, the latter option is explanatorily attractive. Type II claims are thus not claims about the *nature* of the computational processes involved in psychological explanations. They are claims about the methodological advantages of looking at coupled systems whose overall dynamics are taken as explanatorily central. As should become clearer later in the paper, my contention is that the characterization of computational descriptions that is most fertile for the explanation of psychological phenomena is externalist in this Type II sense (cf. Peacocke 1994).

The contention is that an adequate computational explanation of the behavior involved in many cognitive activities should invoke a concept of ecological content — one that captures the intimate dynamical relationship between the inner and the outer. If that notion of content is to play its explanatory role, then we should characterize it in such a way that it couldn't be ascribed to an agent except insofar as the agent is embodied and embedded in a particular environment. It follows that the notion of content will not be narrow in the standard individualist sense. I thus aim to defend a notion of content that is neither traditionally narrow nor traditionally wide, yet which serves the purposes of scientific psychological explanation in a way consistent with both the supervenience constraint and the insights concerning embodied and situated cognition. It should already be clear how ecological content differs from standard narrow content. What about wide content?

Wide content, as explained in the Introduction, is basically a *semantic* device for the individuation of propositional attitudes, i.e., it is the *semantic* component required in order to fix, among other things, the truth-conditions of the sentences used to express different beliefs. Notice that the notion of ecological content — insofar as it is a notion geared to the explanatory requirements of Cognitive Science — is not a real competitor with traditional wide content. Here is why.

First, to argue the need for a semantic device like wide content is not necessarily to rule out the possibility of also invoking some notion of narrow content. Indeed, so-called dual factor theories attempt to provide an explanation of the content of our utterances and mental states in terms that involve two different notions, each motivated by separate concerns. One notion — the psychologically relevant one — deals with the causal explanatory aspect of mental states and/or sentences. The other deals with contentful mental states and/or sentences as related to propositions, i.e., as objects that can be assigned referential truth-conditions (see McGinn 1982; Block 1986). A notion of content designed to play an explanatory role in psychology thus doesn't necessarily conflict with a notion of wide content: it represents a challenge only for its individualistic counterpart.[12]

Second, the friend of wide content is concerned not only to make a constitutive claim about what makes something a state with a particular content, but also to display the *relational* character of the *explananda* of folk psychology, i.e., of the kind of psychology concerned with the relationships between propositional attitudes and actions. Tyler Burge (1986) and Christopher

Peacocke (1993, 1994) have been pursuing just such an agenda (see also Hornsby 1986). But the kind of psychological explanation that matters for the characterization of ecological content is not the *folk* variety. It is *scientific* psychological explanation that is at issue. Insofar as wide content is mainly tied up with folk psychological explanations, it need not be in competition with our alternative account.

Third, it might be suggested that the truth or falsity of a belief *does* matter. It matters whenever we want to explain why an agent is successful (or not) in achieving a certain end. David Papineau, for example, has argued that truth values matter whenever we are concerned to explain success and has suggested we treat truth as the guarantee of such success (Papineau 1990). But even if this argument is sound, it doesn't impinge upon the explanatory character of wide content. As I said, wide content is a semantic device that fixes truth-conditions, not truth values. Papineau's view involves a clear shift from the former to the latter.

This is not to deny that truth plays an important role in explaining the success of an agent in achieving a certain goal. But it is to deny that truth plays any role when what we want to explain is not success or failure but — to adopt Papineau's terminology — to explain the *means* adopted by an agent in pursuit of a certain goal. This is because the external properties that determine the truth-conditions of a sentence (as the expression of a thought) are usually microphysical properties of the environment surrounding the individual. Thus, any sentence containing the expression 'water' will have as part of its truth-conditions a possible world in which the reference of the word is H_2O. But these properties need not affect a subject's psychology, if we take it that psychological states are invoked to explain behavior. For, if the liquid in Lake Michigan turns out to be made of XYZ instead of H_2O, but nothing other than this microphysical composition has changed, there is no reason to suppose that the behavior of the agents in contact with that substance would change either. These microphysical differences matter for the individuation of wide contents but they don't make any computational difference to the subject and, as such, don't affect what we are calling ecological contents. To further clarify this notion, let us first make a small digression concerning the concept of computation.

4. Computation and explanation

A major rationale for the claim that the idea of narrow content is needed for the purposes of scientific psychology is the conviction that scientific psychological explanations will be computational. Computational processes, it is said (Fodor 1981), cannot be sensitive to external properties. Therefore psychological explanations can only involve internal properties. Since my argument aims to both undermine the role of narrow content in psychological explanations and to maintain the foundational role of computation in Cognitive Science, it must invoke a different account, if not of the *nature* of computation, at least of the best way of *conceptualizing* computational explanations.

What is at issue is whether the kind of properties that are most fruitful for *conceptualizing* computational explanations of behavior ought indeed to be *internalist properties*? Might a suitably externalist account of the computational properties which explain behavior in fact be *better* than an internalist account? A popular way of arguing for such a possibility is to argue for a notion of computational states whose individuation is sensitive to external properties in the sense that, without invoking them in our taxonomy, we couldn't specify the causal organization of the system (Peacocke 1993, 1994). That idea, however, remains a little too close to a Type I claim. The basic individualistic assumption is unaffected: it is assumed that *modulo* its external individuation, the content of a thought still supervenes on the inner vehicles of that thought. By contrast, I aim to argue for a genuinely (Type II) *externalist* account of *computationalism*. We may begin by rehearsing (what I take to be) the main reason why the classic individualistic view of computation has so long prevailed.[13]

A key factor underlying this persistence is the long-standing tendency to treat cognition in a completely disembodied fashion. The study of intelligent behavior has focused heavily on higher-order cognitive activities such as abstract problem solving. Computational models in these domains often involved discrete sequential manipulations of static representational structures. The modeling of planning is a good example of how this traditional approach operates. Think of, e.g., Herbert, a robot built in the 80's in the Mobile Robot (Mobot) Laboratory at the Massachusetts Institute of Technology. Herbert's job was to collect empty soft drink cans left around the laboratory. The robot had to move around, recognize, and collect the empty cans. It had to share its space with the rest of the members of the lab and not disrupt the work being carried out by the researchers. Modeling Herbert's behavior according to the traditional, disembodied, approach might consist, e.g., in exploiting sensitive scanning devices tied to a very complex image processing and planning system. At the periphery of the system would be input and output transducers: systems which transform sensory stimulation into input representations and output representations into physical movements. The goal would be to generate a detailed internal model of the surroundings, to isolate the cans and then to plan an effective collection itinerary. However, this kind of solution would be clearly uneconomical, defective, and frail. The robot, once in motion, would be frequently interrupted by the arrival of new objects, people moving around the lab, and unexpected changes in the arrangement of furniture. Had Herbert been built in this way, he would have spent too much time just wondering about future plans of action, lost in all the multiple inference chains triggered by the scanning of the situation.

The alternative 'embodied' solution, the one used by Herbert's designer (Rodney Brooks's graduate student Jonathan Connell), is to exploit the shortcuts afforded by the environmental surroundings and by Herbert's own capacities of movement and action. Instead of constructing any elaborated internal model of its surrounding or exploiting a very complex image processing and planning system, Herbert was built using a kind of architecture that incorporates multiple quasi-independent subsystems, each of which is responsible for one aspect of its activity. Those subsystems are not coordinated by any central system. They send simple signals that can ignore and/or modify the response of other subsystems. The robot also uses its own motion in the world to assist its sensory explorations and the various sensory systems cooperate directly in the engendering and control of particular behaviors (cf. Brooks 1991):

> [T]hese simple behaviors included obstacle avoidance (stopping, reorienting, etc.) and locomotion routines. These would be interrupted if a table-like outline was detected by a simple visual system. Once Herbert was beside a table, the locomotion and obstacle-avoidance routines ceded control to other subsystems that swept the table with a laser and a video camera. Once the basic outline of a can was detected, the robot would rotate until the can-like object was in the center of its field of vision. At this point, the wheels stopped and a robot arm was activated. The arm, equipped with simple touch sensors, gently explored the table surface ahead. When Herbert encountered the distinctive shape of a can, grasping behavior ensued, the can was collected, and the robot moved on (Clark 1997: 14-15).

On the whole, the disembodied approach has contributed to a notion of computational organization that systematically marginalizes the properties of the environment in which the system is embedded. This looks increasingly ill-suited for the explanation of adaptive success. The main reason for this failure is that these models of cognition cannot account for the fact that the behavior of any system is determined both by the physical/biological embodiment of the system and the dynamical relations that the system establishes with its environment. They lack the resources to model the constant feedback that takes place in this hybrid structure of relations. Such systems depend on manipulating representations of the world so as to plan complex sequential activities such as those involved in, say, general-purpose reasoning. But they fail to account for the kind of highly coupled real-time adaptive behavior that is the result of, e.g., the sensory-motor system's continuous local interactions with the environment. Overall, the disembodied approach "leans too heavily on detailed inner models and long chains of inference, and makes too little use of the simplifications and shortcuts afforded by simple environmental cues and the robots own capacities of action, motion and intervention" (Clark (Forthcoming: 5); see also Clark 1997). The time factor is also essential. In fact, for Port and van Gelder, two of the main critics of the disembodied view,

> [t]he heart of the problem is *time. Cognitive processes and their context unfold continuously and simultaneously in real time.* [Disembodied] computational models specify a discrete sequence of static internal states in arbitrary 'step' time (t_1, t_2, etc.). Imposing the latter onto the former is like wearing shoes on your hands. You can do it, but gloves fit a whole lot better (Port and van Gelder 1995: 2).

Although important in certain restricted domains, the disembodied computational approach is thus no longer the only model in psychology. Neither is it in the philosophy of mind. Other ways for understanding cognition have lately been developed in different areas of Cognitive Science. Artificial Life (especially work in robotics and Autonomous Agent theory) is one of those areas (e.g., Ackley and Littman 1992, Brooks 1991, Harvey *et al.* 1993, Hinton and Nowland 1987). Dynamical Systems Theory is another one (e.g., Port and van Gelder 1995, Abraham and Show 1992, Beer 1990). The notion of representation employed within these models involves a kind of content-involving computational description that is Type II externalist. In these accounts cognition is characterized basically in terms of actions, i.e., in terms of the exchanges between the physical/biological features of an organism and those of the environment in which the organism is embedded and functioning. Where content-involving computational descriptions are suitable for the explanation of such a cognizer's behavior, they involve a notion of content that is partly constituted by the abilities of a system to interact in specific ways with the world in which it is embedded. The system's inner states need not constitute any kind of replica or objective model of the world. Rather, they engage with those properties of the environment that the system needs to co-opt in the service of adaptive success.

It is worth noticing that I am not claiming that a computational description is externalist just because the inputs originate in the world. That claim would be trivial. My claim is that it can be methodologically fruitful to treat certain computational processes as emergent out of the complex dynamical properties of a wider system that actually includes chunks of the local environment. My claim is thus a Type II claim according to which psychological explanation requires a dimension of *enacted* content, i.e., a notion of content that supervenes on interactions between the system and its environment (cf. Varela *et al.* 1991). It is this notion of enacted content that is needed to *explain* why cognitive agents behave in the way they do, and to generate useful *predictions* of their behavior. Given that the explanation and prediction of behavior are the aims of psychology, it is not difficult to see that, once computational descriptions are understood in this externalist way, we have effectively secured their scientific role. In the next section, I summarize some empirical support for this kind of computational externalism.

5.   Perceptual-cognitive development

A variety of psychological and psychophysical experiments seem to challenge the individualist philosopher's claim that "whole subjects plus embedding environments do not make up integrated, computational systems" (Segal 1991: 492). For example, the especially crucial role of subject/environment interactions in computational theorizing about human development suggests an explanatory paradigm convivial to the Type II externalist. This research supports the idea that a notion of content fit to play an explanatory role in psychology can't always be defined independently of the properties of the environment with which the organism interacts.

An example. Tracking moving objects, defensive motions, stopping moving objects, and reaching for objects of different shapes and weights are all examples of infants' interactions with their environment (Rutkowska 1990, 1991, 1993a, 1993b). We could try to account for such behavior by reference to purely internal states of representation and computation. But in so doing, Rutkowska claims, we would miss one of the main components of the perceptual process, namely, the behavioral component. Purely internalist stories fail, Rutkowska (1993a: 971) suggests,

> adequately to consider the role of the behavioral component of action in perceptual processing ... Instead [descriptions of objects and their properties] can be viewed more pragmatically in terms of action programs: virtual mechanisms whose operation selectively exploits task-relevant aspects of multiple descriptions ... to support the direct invocation of behavioral procedures ... Making explicit an aspect of the physical world, such as a surface, over many situations does not entail any ability to represent it as a property that is common to that range of situations, let alone potentially applicable to others.

If we opt for this second, action-guided, approach, we will have to acknowledge that visually based representations are not to be conceptualized independently of behavioral processes. One reason is that these processes often change the viewer's relationship to her/his environment, and this in turn changes the information available to visual processing. As these diachronic processes of change are the outcome of our sensory-motor systems' local interactions with the environment, they invite a computational account based on the concept of *action*. This computational account could not be developed without including as *explananda* descriptions that involve properties that belong to that environment and that are therefore external to the system. But more significantly, what we really need, in order to pursue this computational strategy, is a truly *interactive* account of vision in which "systems ostensibly 'extrinsic' to literally seeing the world, such as the motor system and other sensory systems (auditory, somatosensory), do in fact play a significant role in what is literally seen" (P.S. Churchland *et al.* 1994: 23). Underlying this alternative account of the computational organization and dynamics of mammalian vision is the idea that the visual system is much more intimately integrated with other action systems, such as the motor, auditory and somatosensory systems, than was previously suspected (but see Gibson 1979). This integration, however, is not a hierarchical process in which connection to the motor system takes place once the internal representation has been fully constituted. Instead:

... motor assembling begins on the basis of preliminary and minimal analysis. Some motor decisions, such as eye movements, head movements, and keeping the rest of the body motionless, are often made on the basis of minimal analysis precisely in order to achieve an upgraded and more fully elaborated visuomotor representation (P.S. Churchland *et al.* 1994: 27).

If this hypothesis is correct — and numerous psychophysical experiments, like the ones developed by Rutkowska, seem to support its plausibility (e.g., Thelen and Smith 1994, Bingham 1995, Turvey and Carello 1995) — , then we must begin to re-think our ideas about computation and representation so as to capture the essential interpenetration of sensing, thinking and acting. If computational descriptions are going to play a role here, they will be best conceptualized in terms of externalist content-involving descriptions, since the constitutive parameters that fix the content of those descriptions will belong to the array of relations between the system and properties of its environment. In addition, a great deal of cognition may involve tracking properties of objects in such a way that the internal representations of those objects are not *objetivist*, in the sense of representing the object in a context-independent manner. Instead, it is only how the object appears under a particular perspective and how it can be acted upon within a particular behavioral context that counts. The interactive framework for understanding vision proposed by P. S. Churchland *et al.* illustrates this claim. According to Churchland *et al.,* the idea of 'pure vision' — that what is seen is just a pure replica of the world achieved by the *visual system alone* — is a radical oversimplification of the kind of computational strategies used by the brain. In natural cognition, the internal representation of an object is almost always, it seems, mediated by the local behavioral context.

Such being the *general pattern* of explanation for our basic cognitive abilities, it seems likely that we do indeed need a notion of content that (a) is not narrowly individuated (because that leaves out the essential relations between the system and the environment) and (b) is not traditionally widely individuated either (because the relevant relations must be identified by actual patterns of action in, and interaction with, the world — not merely introduced by a passive relation of reference).

6. Ecological content

One type of practical interaction (that has already received useful philosophical attention) is the kind that involves discriminative abilities on the part of the subject. The ability to adjust one's grasping actions to suit different kinds of object, the ability to recognize similarities and/or dissimilarities in shape and structure, or to recognize an object as the referent of a proper name, are all examples of such abilities. These discriminative capacities, it has been suggested, are pivotal for the project of individuating the contents of our thoughts. This idea is found in some of the writings of the later Wittgenstein and is central to Dummett's characterization of the nature of a theory of meaning (see Dummett 1975, 1976). Closer to the narrow/wide debate itself, Gareth Evans's (1982) and Cussins's (1992) distinction between non-conceptual and conceptual content represent important steps in an ecological direction. It is also a central issue for recent research programs revolving around the idea of embedded cognition (cf. McClamrock 1995).

Consider Gareth Evans's interpretation of Frege's analysis of identity statements (Frege 1892) in terms of what Evans calls the "intuitive criterion of difference" (Evans 1982: 18-22),which lies at the root of this interactive idea of cognition. The criterion is *intuitive* because, as a content-individuation tool, it relies on abilities that exploit our being connected to the objects of our thoughts without assuming that we have any special conception of those objects, i.e., without assuming that the untutored subject can provide a description of the causal mechanisms underlying those interactive abilities. Dummett — commenting on Frege — makes a similar point when he claims that

> all that is necessary, in order that the senses of two names which have the same referent should differ, is that we should have a different way of recognizing an object as the referent of each of the two names: there is no reason to suppose that the means by which we effect such a recognition should be expressible by means of a definite description or any other singular term (Dummett, 1973: 98).

In the same vein, although this time focusing on the *experiential* character of our abilities to entertain different attitudes toward an object, Cussins (1992: 655-656) points out that

> the abilities are not available to the subject as the content's referent, but they are available to the subject as the subject's experience-based knowledge of how to act on the object, and respond to it. The theorist may canonically

specify the content by referring to abilities, because the cognitive significance
of the content consists in the experiential accessibility of these abilities to the
subject in experience-based knowing-how.

Using one of Evans's favorite examples, we could thus say that what fixes the
content of the experience of hearing a sound as coming from "over there" is the
subject's particular ability to negotiate the domain in which she is embedded
(Evans 1982: 154). To 'negotiate a domain' is to be able to cope with a variety
of specific situations in a constantly variable environment. It is to have a set of
skills, abilities and other know-hows that will enable us to carry out a particular
task, where such skills need not include any explicit theoretical knowledge.
Even if 'over there' could be substituted *salva veritate* by 'from the North', that
doesn't imply that we can describe the subject's experience as hearing a sound
coming from the North, i.e., it doesn't imply that the subject possesses the
concept NORTH THERE, or any of the concepts involved in spatial directions.
In other words, it doesn't entail that the subject has the concept NORTH in any
way that can be assimilated to the possession of theoretical knowledge. The
properties that count for the explanation of the subject's behavior are sensory
properties that function in a structured way so as to support the various movements involved in the identification of the sound as coming from a particular
place.

     If we substitute 'content' for 'concept' in the above paragraph, we will
have a pretty clear vision of the notion of ecological content. Such content is
constituted by the set of skills, abilities, and know-hows that an agent deploys
to negotiate a domain. The properties that constitute a mental state's ecological
content include only those properties of the environment that make a difference
to the behavior of the coupled system. But these need not be available to the
subject as propositional knowledge.

     Maybe an example will help to make these ideas a bit clearer. We are all
familiar with the child's game of balancing objects of different sizes on some
sort of support. According to A. Karmiloff-Smith, who has carried out experiments involving these situations, children develop the notion of a center of
gravity in this concrete behavioral context of balancing a series of blocks on a
narrow metal support (cf. Karmiloff-Smith 1992. See also Clark and Karmiloff-
Smith 1993). Of course, the fact that we can use the concept CENTER OF
GRAVITY to describe the behavior of the children doesn't entail that that
concept itself "is somehow a component of the experience's representational

content, nor that the concept must be possessed by the experiencer" (Peacocke 1992: 111). That is, it doesn't entail that the children have the quite abstract concept CENTER OF GRAVITY in any way that can be assimilated to the possession of a symbolic expression. What children have acquired is rather some more primitive concepts in terms of sensory properties that can function in a *structured* way to accomplish the different movements involved in the task of balancing different objects. The ascription of those primitive concepts is warranted by the mastery of the abilities directed towards handling observable objects in that specific domain. The ecological content of the mental states that explain behavior in this particular context is thus individuated in terms of causal relations holding among those environmental, task-domain specific properties. Such content does not exhibit a linguistic or 'inner-symbolic' character.

From a developmental and an evolutionary point of view, explicit propositional knowledge seems to come much later than such basic abilities to cope with concrete situations in a complex environment. Accordingly, our emphasis is on the agent's capacity to adapt to its immediate circumstances in the world, and not on those more objective descriptions that a theorist might introduce as representations of those circumstances.[14] The strong assumption underlying my attempt to characterize an explanatory notion of content for psychology is thus that cognition is better understood when treated as *embedded* cognition and therefore that the notion of content ought to be cashed out in non-individualistic and pragmatic terms.

Given the evolutionary considerations just mentioned, it might be inferred that the notion of ecological content is tied to some kind of teleological account of cognition. A word of warning about that. It is certainly no surprise that teleological approaches to content fit rather nicely into my ecological picture. However, as Peacocke (1993: 224-225) has pointed out, it is not true that any plausible externalist theory — and I'm taking the gist of the theory sketched here to be both externalist and plausible — has to be of the teleological sort. A theory based on the notion of ecological content is clearly externalist, but is not necessarily teleological in Millikan's sense, because it doesn't have to depend on claims concerning the evolutionary *proper function* of mental states (cf. Millikan 1984, 1993).

To clarify just where Millikan's approach and the ecological approach differ, let me make a quick remark about 'accidental doubles'. An accidental double is someone who (for example) crawls out of a swamp due to some kind of subatomic miracle and who happens to be molecule for molecule identical to someone else (e.g., me). Millikan's claim is that the states of accidental doubles don't have proper functions and thus that their neural states don't have any content (as content is teleologically defined in terms of proper function and they lack the right sort of history). Equally, the heart of my double doesn't have as its proper function the circulation of blood because it is not there as a result of the appropriate historical causal chain.

But the characterization of content that I defend involves only the current properties, relations, dispositions and abilities of a subject. It doesn't have in addition to invoke the right individual or evolutionary history. If the double that crawls out of the swamp has an experience as of humidity — as I imagine she might — nothing in my account would impede the proper ascription of a particular ecological content. This is unsurprising, since — as remarked earlier — the aim of our analysis is to provide a good theoretical base for scientific explanations of behavior. Such explanations, however, do not seem to require an account of the content of our representations given in evolutionary terms. From the psychological point of view, the agent's representations do not have to be tied to the objective conditions for its survival. The explanatorily central issue is not the identification of proper biological functions, but rather the ability to cope with ecologically relevant environmental situations.

What, though, of the putative non-individualism of our account? In what sense does the stress on abilities to cope with the world fit the idea that certain properties of the world play a constitutive role in the fixation of ecological content? Recall Herbert Simon's tale of an ant walking on a 'wind- and wave-molded' beach (Simon 1969). The marks on the sand form a complex line. If we take the complex geometry of the line as an aspect of the ant's behavior, an analysis of that line exclusively in terms of the ant's cognition will be completely inadequate. The complexity of the line is (partially at least) due to the physical structure of the beach. The moral of the story (a Type II story) is that an explanation of this aspect of the ant's behavior would be inadequate if it abstracted from the features of the current environment in which that behavior is being displayed. What we add — as John Haugeland (1995) has pointed out — is now the idea that if we want to understand such an agent's behavior, we should treat the agent's internal states and aspects of the agent's local environment as an integrated unit. As he puts it, we would have to regard Mind as "not incidentally but *intimately* embodied and *intimately* embedded in its world" (Haugeland 1995: 36). Ecological content takes this larger whole as the basic unit for psychological explanations.

A nice example, provided by McClamrock, is that of speech perception or, more precisely, what is known as vowel normalization. This example is especially interesting inasmuch as it involves a *constitutive* claim of much the same kind as I have made regarding the ecological character of content. The example is taken from a study by Nusbaum and DeGroot (1991) and focuses on the fact that "what acoustic pattern counts as a phoneme of a particular type is highly dependent on the surrounding speech context" (McClamrock 1995: 96). What makes an acoustic pattern a particular vowel sound is thus something external to that particular pattern. Phonetic identity depends constitutively upon what surrounds that sound. Other, more 'cognitive', episodes also serve as good examples of context-dependent and environment-involving constitution. That is the case in, e.g., the well-known Gestalt phenomena which show how the intervention of sensory modalities other than visual perception can prime the subject to see something as a particular object instead of something else. In trivial cases, the 'other' sensory modalities would be instructions given to the subject by the researcher. Those instructions act as the necessary context upon which, e.g., the interpretation of an ambiguous or degraded picture occurs. Similar but more interesting demonstrations include those in which what constitutes a given perception as such-and-such a perception is partly dependent on a specific spatial orientation. Consider the case of letters, words, and diagrams. If the figure of, e.g., an 'E' is rotated 90 degrees, the 'E' is no longer seen as that letter any more.

Context also plays an essential role in pragmatics. Think, for instance, of irony. What makes a particular utterance an ironic remark has very little to do with the standard meaning attached to the sentence. Much depends on the linguistic and non-linguistic context in which the utterance is uttered (cf. Searle 1979). In the same way, properties external to the agent, and properties that are context-dependent and environment-involving, can all constitute key parameters for the individuation of ecological content. Such properties are indeed the result of a constant exchange of energy and information between the inner and the outer realm — but that exchange is not to be cashed out in terms of propositional knowledge. It does not consist in explicit information so much as in patterns of causal exchange that make a computational difference *to* the system without necessarily being explicitly represented *by* the system.

If we now return to the (in)famous Twinearth thought experiment, the situation can be analyzed as follows. If my Twin and I could notice or reflect upon the difference between H_2O and XYZ, then the content of our thoughts would differ and we would be dealing with good old fashioned narrow content. If my Twin and I could not thus notice or conceive any difference between H_2O and XYZ then, the content of our thoughts would not reflect it and therefore we would be dealing with good old fashioned wide content. But, there is a third possibility, somewhat obscured by the fact that we often fail to distinguish between knowing-how and knowing-that (cf. Ryle 1963) — and thus fall squarely back into the classical 17th century formulations of the problem.[15] It is the possibility that the kind of difference that matters in this context may be a computational difference that doesn't necessarily involve awareness or propositional knowledge. If, for instance, the density of H_2O were different from the density of XYZ in such a (subtle) way that the motor skills of my Twin and I when swimming had to adjust to that density accordingly, there would still be a computational difference of the ecological kind. In such a case the subject's mental states need not involve any kind of explicit representation of the relevant difference.

The possibility of computational differences without explicit representational differences marks one respect in which our position differs from e.g. Fodor's new 'correlational' theory (Fodor 1994). While Fodorian representations seem to be generally interpreted as explicit, language-like representations,[16] the content-bearing states invoked in my ecological account are not. Instead, such states are constituted, in part, by the subject's actual interactions with specific features of the local environment. At this point, however, the ghost of holism may seem to threaten. How are we to select, from the multiple possible interactions and features of the local environment, those which are relevant for the individuation of ecological content? How are we to circumscribe those immediate circumstances in the world on which our account depends?[17] In order to answer these questions, I would like to highlight and elaborate two points that have already been mentioned. The first is that the abilities that count for the individuation of ecological content are keyed to actual activity in *specific task-domains*. As a result, the characterizations of content that they provide are not specified by reference to the full gamut of (to take the usual Twinearth example) our water-related dispositions. Instead they include only the dispositions related to water as the stuff in which I practice specific activities (such as swimming) characteristic of my normal ecological involvement with the immediate environment.

The second point to stress is that the issue about holism arises mainly when we deal with declarative or language-like internal entities and when we then try to provide a *systematic* account of how the content of constituent expressions contributes to fixing the contents of the whole language. The claim that holism mainly arises for language-like representations is easy to justify if we attend to the fact that individuation problems and their holistic implications originate primarily when a theory can't provide identity criteria for the constituent tokens of the complex structures in which those tokens appear. But to talk about the content of the constituent tokens of any physical structure which we may care to identify with a given concept already implies an interpretation of that inner structure as syntactic. Now, in elevating a notion of discriminative abilities into a central parameter for my notion of ecological content, I need not understand the internal vehicles of contentful thoughts as *explicit* representations of any kind. These representations need not have any syntactic or language-like format. The reason is, again, that the properties that count for the individuation of ecological content are restricted to specific task-domains with the result that the information available to the subject can't be transferred from that domain to a different one. That is, in fact, what makes those activities cases of knowing-how and cases of implicit knowledge. In the example of the children playing with building blocks, what that means is that the children can't transfer what they thus know about gravity to a different context. The notion of explicit knowledge is best invoked at the linguistic stage of human development. That stage ushers in a wide and flexible use of the basic knowledge once implicit in task-specific procedures. It is at this linguistic stage that the structure of the representations in relation to the agent's behavior is most evident. If we don't assume language-like representations at the outset, then the issue of holism can only arise in a rather weak sense, i.e., we might want to demarcate the circumstances that ought to be considered relevant for a certain content ascription. Here pragmatic considerations surely play a key role, even if such considerations don't fully resolve the problem.

In closing, let me emphasize that I have not tried, in this brief treatment, to dispel all possible internalist worries. No doubt the sensible internalist of Section 2 could still argue for a (Type I) individualistic characterization of content that is nonetheless compatible with some recognition of these ecological dimensions. But even if an individualistic interpretation is always possible, it will not always be as fruitful — from an explanatory point of view — or as easily able to display the real world, real-time dynamics of cognition as is the ecological alternative. Let me also add that it was not my aim to provide a fully developed theory of content. My hope was only to provide some notes towards a different way of thinking about the notion of psychological explanation — a way which lays much more stress on the pragmatic, environment-involving, skill-oriented dimensions of real-world cognition. As such, my project is largely independent of (and might even be compatible with) a more philosophically motivated account of content in terms of truth-conditions — just as some account of motion might be given independently of an account of the skills underlying those motions. Whether these two projects may ultimately be reconciled remains to be seen.[18]

Washington University in St. Louis

Notes

1.   'Supervenience' is here to be read as *strongly supervening* in the sense of Kim (1984: 262): " ... *the supervenience of a family A of properties on another family B* can be explained as follows: necessarily, for any property F in A, if any object x has F, then there exists a property G in B such that x has G, and necessarily anything having G has F. When properties F and G are related as specified in the definition, we may say that F is supervenient on G, and that G is a supervenience base of F".

2.   The same kind of strategy had already been followed by Fodor in his classic "Methodological solipsism considered as a research strategy in cognitive psychology" (Fodor 1981). There, however, the vindication of narrow content was tied up with the alleged syntactic nature of computation and with the characterization of psychological explanations as computational explanations.

3.   Once a great supporter of narrow content, Fodor himself has also been moving lately in the direction of externalism. His claim is that we can have everything we want narrow content for (intentional psychological laws and their corresponding computational implementations) without narrow content (Fodor 1994). Fodor's change of position doesn't mean that the internalist camp has been left empty. See, e.g., Jackson and Pettit (1993), Lewis (1994), Loar (1988), and White (1982),for a defense of narrow content.

4.   Following Kim's formulation we can say that necessarily, for any property F in the family of contentful states, if any object x has F, then there exists a property G in the family of physical states such that x has G, and necessarily anything having G has F. The main problem with this characterization is how to interpret that notion of necessity. I don't intend to address that problem here though. Nothing in my argument requires a particular reading of necessity.

5.   I borrow the *shape* of this expression from Peacocke (1993), who introduces the notion of externalist content-involving computational description.

6.   Thanks to an anonymous referee for pointing this out.

7. Interestingly, following this definition, Kim points out that "'Doing' is to be distinguished from 'having something done'. If you grasp my arm and pull it up, the rising of my arm is not something I do; it is not my behavior ... It isn't something that a psychologist would be interested in investigating" (Kim 1996: 28). He also distinguishes four types of behavior: physiological reactions and responses (e.g., salivation), bodily motions (e.g., throwing a baseball), actions involving bodily motions (e.g., telephoning your mother) and actions not involving overt bodily motions (e.g., deciding). See Kim (1996: 28-29).

8. For the notion of behavior as internally caused bodily motion see Dretske (1988: chapters 1 and 2).

9. See Wilson (1994b) for a possible development of such an account.

10. This example is from Kirsh (1995).

11. The example concerns what they characterize as an *epistemic* action, i.e., an action whose primary purpose is to alter the nature of our own mental states, as opposed to *pragmatic* action, namely, action undertaken because we need to alter the world to achieve some physical goal.

12. I have argued elsewhere (Toribio, forthcoming) that dual factor theories of meaning are fatally flawed in at least two ways. First, their very duality constitutes a problem: the two dimensions of meaning (reference and conceptual role) cannot be treated as totally orthogonal without compromising the intuition that much of our linguistic and non linguistic behavior is based on the cognizer's interaction with the world. Second, Conceptual Role Semantics seems unable to explain a crucial feature of linguistic representation, viz., the special kind of compositionality known as concatenative compositionality. Dual factor theories, I conclude, cannot constitute an acceptable philosophical model of content.

13. Robert Wilson's recent piece on 'wide computationalism' points in the same direction. He argues that " ... the computational argument for individualism should be rejected because ... the assumption that computational processes in general are individualistic is false in light of the possibility and plausibility of wide computationalism in cognitive psychology" (Wilson 1994a: 370). Wide computationalism (a Type II thesis) is, roughly, the view that the computational systems that are interesting for cognitive psychology extend beyond the individual and include parts of the system's environment.

14. In fact, the very structure of the environment sometimes provides solutions to problems that would be much more complex if we thought of those solutions as solely the result of the cognizer's inner computations (see Ballard 1991).

15. Thank to Marcelo Dascal for pointing this out. Notice, in this context, that although I am invoking the Rylean distinction between 'knowing that' (propositional knowledge) and 'knowing how' (non-propositional knowledge), my own account invokes internal representations and therefore doesn't have the strong behavioristic flavor characteristic of the pure Rylean view.

16. Even if Fodorian representations don't *necessarily* need to be language-like representations, that seems to be the usual reading of Fodor's views about representationalism in general and about the structure of mental representations in particular. Even in his recent work (Fodor 1994) he has not altered his views about these two issues. Representationalism is the

thesis that, in order for a system to exhibit any reasonably complex cognitive function or behavior, it has to possess the ability to entertain certain *structured* mental representations. The necessary property that the inner structure of mental representations must have to be able to explain cognitive behavior is called compositionality. The inner structure of mental representations thus has to be of a compositional kind. According to Fodor, the compositionality of our thoughts can only be explained if mental representations have a *syntactic* inner structure (Fodor and Lepore 1992: 176). If compositionality is to be explained, the physical instantiation of tokens of the same type have to be identical. Therefore compositionality means *syntactic* compositionality. It is in this specific sense that we may characterize the representations as 'language-like'.

17. This same problem also arises for other (related) approaches such as Simon and colleagues' *situated action* view. I thank Marcelo Dascal for pointing this out.

18. I wish to thank Andy Clark, David Chalmers, Keith Butler, Fernando Broncano, Marcelo Dascal, and two anonymous referees for helpful comments on earlier versions of this paper.

References

Abraham, R.H. and Shaw, C.D. 1992. *Dynamics. The Geometry of Behavior,* 2nd ed. Redwood City, CA: Addison-Wesley.

Ackley, D. and Littman, M. 1992. "Interactions between learning and evolution". In C. Langton, C. Taylor, D. Farmer and S. Rasmussen (eds), *Artificial Life II*, Redwood City, CA: Addison-Wesley, 487–509.

Ballard, D. 1991. "Animate vision". *Artificial Intelligence* 48: 57–86.

Beer, R. 1990. *Intelligence and Adaptive Behavior*. San Diego: Academic Press.

Bingham, G. P. 1995. "Dynamics and the problem of visual event recognition". In R. F. Port and T. van Gelder (eds), *Mind as Motion. Explorations in the Dynamics of Cognition*. Cambridge, MA: The MIT Press, 403–448.

Block, N. 1986. "Advertisement for a semantics for psychology". In P. French, T. Uehling and H. Wettstein (eds), *Midwest Studies in Philosophy, vol. 10: Studies in the Philosophy of Mind*. Minneapolis: University of Minnesota Press, 615–678.

Block, N. 1991. "What narrow content is not". In B. Loewer and G. Rey (eds), *Meaning and Mind. Fodor and His Critics*. Oxford: Blackwell, 33–64.

Brooks, R. 1991. "Intelligence without representation". *Artificial Intelligence* 47: 139–159.

Burge, T. 1979. "Individualism and the mental". In P. French *et. al.* (eds), *Midwest Studies in Philosophy, Volume 4*. Minneapolis: University of Minnesota Press, 73–121.

Burge, T. 1986. "Individualism and psychology". *The Philosophical Review* 95: 3–45.

Burge, T. 1993. "Mind-body causation in psychology". In J. Heil and A. Mele (eds), *Mental Causation*. Oxford: Clarendon Press, 97–120.

Churchland, P.S., Ramachandran, V.S. and Sejnowski, T.J. 1994. "A critique of pure vision". In C. Koch and J. Davis (eds), *Large-Scale Neuronal Theories of the Brain*. Cambridge, MA: The MIT Press, 23–60.

Clark, A. 1997. *Being There. Putting Brain, Body and World Together Again*. Cambridge, MA: The MIT Press.

Clark, A. Forthcoming. "Embodied, situated and distributed cognition". In W. Bechtel and G. Graham (eds), *Companion to the Philosophy of Cognitive Science*. Oxford: Blackwell.

Clark, A. and Karmiloff-Smith, A. 1993. "The cognizer's innards". *Mind and Language* 8(4): 487–519.

Cussins, A. 1992. "Content, embodiment and objectivity: The theory of cognitive trails". *Mind,* 101: 651–688.

Dretske, F. 1988. *Explaining Behavior*. Cambridge, MA: The MIT Press.

Dummett, M. 1973. *Frege. Philosophy of Language*. London: Duckworth.

Dummett, M. 1975. "What is a theory of meaning? (I)". In S. Guttenplan (ed), *Mind and Language*. Oxford: Clarendon Press, 97–138.

Dummett, M. 1976. "What is a theory of meaning? (II)". In G. Evans and J. McDowell (eds), *Truth and Meaning. Essays in Semantics*. Oxford: Clarendon Press, 67–137.

Evans, G. 1982. *The Varieties of Reference*. Ed. by J. McDowell. Oxford: Clarendon Press.

Fodor, J. 1975. *The Language of Thought*. New York, Thomas Y. Crowell.

Fodor, J. 1981. "Methodological solipsism considered as a research strategy in cognitive psychology". Reprinted in J. Fodor, *Representations*. Cambridge, MA: The MIT Press, 225–253.

Fodor, J. 1987. *Psychosemantics*. Cambridge, MA: The MIT Press.

Fodor, J. 1994. *The Elm and the Expert. Mentalese and Its Semantics*. Cambridge, MA: The MIT Press.

Fodor, J. and Lepore, E. 1992. *Holism. A Shopper's Guide*. Oxford: Blackwell.

Frege, G. 1892. "Über Sinn und Bedeutung". In *Zeitschrift für Philosophie und philosophische Kritik*, NF 100, 1892. Trans. in M. Black and P. Geach (eds): *Translations from the Philosophical Writings of Gottlob Frege*. Oxford: Blackwell, 1952.

Gibson, J.J. 1979. *The Ecological Approach to Visual Perception*. Boston: Houghton Mifflin.

Harvey, I., Husbands, P., and Cliff, D. 1993. "Issues in evolutionary robotics". Sussex: University of Sussex. Cognitive Science Research Papers, TR 219.

Haugeland, J. 1995. "Mind embodied and embedded". In *Mind and Cognition: Collected Papers from 1993 International Symposium on Mind and Cognition*. Taipei, Taiwan: Institute of European and American Studies, Academia Sinica, 3–37.

Hinton, G.E. and Nowland, S.J. 1987. "How learning can guide evolution". *Complex Systems* 1: 495–502.

Hornsby, J. 1986. "Physicalist thinking and conceptions of behaviour". In P. Pettit and
    J. McDowell (eds), *Subject, Thought and Context*. Oxford: Clarendon Press, 95-115.
Hutchins, E. 1995. *Cognition in the Wild*. Cambridge, MA: The MIT Press.
Karmiloff-Smith, A. 1986. "From meta-processes to conscious access: Evidence from
    children's meta-linguistic and repair data". *Cognition* 23: 95–147.
Karmiloff-Smith, A. 1992. *Beyond Modularity. A Developmental Perspective on Cognitive
    Science*. Cambridge, MA: The MIT Press.
Jackson, F. and Pettit, P. 1993. "Some content is narrow". In J. Heil (ed), *Mental
    Causation*. Oxford: Clarendon Press, 259-282.
Kim, J. 1984. "Epiphenomenal and supervenient causation". In P. French *et. al.* (eds),
    Midwest Studies in Philosophy, vol. 9. Minneapolis: University of Minnesota Press,
    257-270.
Kim, J. 1996. *Philosophy of Mind*. Boulder, CO: Westview Press.
Kirsh, D. 1995. "The intelligent use of space". *Artificial Intelligence* 72: 1–52.
Kirsh, D. and Maglio, P. 1994. "On distinguishing epistemic from pragmatic action".
    Cognitive Science 18: 513–549.
Lewis, D. 1994. "Reduction of mind". In S. Guttenplan (ed), *Companion to the Philoso-
    phy of Mind*. Oxford: Blackwell, 412-431.
Loar, B. 1988. "Social content and psychological content". In R.H. Grimm and D.
    Merrill (eds), *Contents of Thought*. Tucson: University of Arizona Press, 99-110.
McClamrock, R. 1995. *Existential Cognition*, Chicago: The University of Chicago Press.
McGinn, C. 1982. "The structure of content". In A. Woodfield (ed), *Thought and Object*.
    Oxford: Clarendon Press, 207–258.
Millikan, R. 1984. *Language, Thought and Other Biological Categories. New Foundations
    for Realism*. Cambridge, MA: TheMIT Press.
Millikan, R. 1993. *White Queen Psychology and Other Essays for Alice*. Cambridge, MA:
    The MIT Press.
Nusbaum, H. and DeGroot, J. 1991. "The role of syllables in speech perception". In
    M.S. Ziolkowski, M. Noske and K. Deaton (eds), *Papers from the Parasession on the
    Syllable in Phonetics and Phonology*, Chicago: Chicago Linguistic Society 287-317.
Papineau, D. 1990. "Truth and tleology". In D. Knowles (ed), *Explanation and Its Limits*.
    Cambridge: Cambridge University Press, 21–43.
Peacocke, C. 1992. "Scenarios, cncepts and prception". In T. Crane (ed), *The Contents of
    Experience. Essay on Perception*. Cambridge:Cambridge University Press, 105–135.
Peacocke, C. 1993. "Externalist eplanation". *Proceedings of the Aristotelian Society*
    XCIII: 203–230.
Peacocke, C. 1994. "Content, cmputation and eternalism". *Mind and Language* 9(3):
    303–335.
Port, R.F. and van Gelder, T. (eds) 1995. *Mind as Motion. Explorations in the Dynamics
    of Cognition*. Cambridge, MA: The MIT Press.

Putnam, H. 1975. "The Meaning of «meaning»". In H. Putnam, *Mind, Language and Reality: Philosophical Papers, Volume 2.* Cambridge: Cambridge University Press, 215–271

Rutkowska, J.C. 1990. "Action, connectionism and enaction: A developmental perspective". *AI and Society* 4: 96–114.

Rutkowska, J.C. 1991. "Looking for «constraints» in infants' perceptual-cognitive development". *Mind and Language* 6: 215–238.

Rutkowska, J.C. 1993a. "Ontogenetic constraints on scaling-up sensory-motor systems". *Proceedings of the Second European Conference on Artificial Life, Vol. 2.* Brussels, 970–979.

Rutkowska, J.C. 1993b. *The Computational Infant.* Brighton: Harvester Press.

Ryle, G. 1963. *The Concept of Mind.* Harmondsworth: Penguin.

Searle, J.R. 1979. "Literal meaning". In J.R. Searle, *Expression and Meaning: Studies in the Theory of Speech Acts.* Cambridge: Cambridge University Press, 117–161.

Segal, G. 1991. "Defence of a reasonable individualism". *Mind* 100: 485–494.

Simon, H.A. 1969. *The Sciences of the Artificial.* Cambridge, MA: The MIT Press (2nd ed., 1987).

Stalnaker, R. 1990. "Narrow content". In C.A. Anderson and J. Owens (eds), *Propositional Attitudes. The Role of Content in Logic, Language and Mind.* Stanford: Center for the Study of Language and Information, 131–145.

Thelen, E. and Smith, L. 1994. *A Dynamic Systems Approach to the Development of Cognition and Action.* Cambridge, MA: The MIT Press.

Toribio, J. Forthcoming. "Twin pleas: Probing content and compositionality". *Philosophical and Phenomenological Research.*

Turvey, M.T. and Carello, C. 1995. "Some dynamical themes in perception and ation". In Port and van Gelder (eds), 373–401.

Varela, F., Thompson, E., and Rosch, E. 1991. *The Embodied Mind: Cognitive Science and Human Experience.* Cambridge, MA: The MIT Press.

White, S. 1982. "Partial character and the language of thought". *Pacific Philosophical Quarterly* 63: 347–365.

Wilson, R. A. 1994a. "Wide computationalism". *Mind* 103: 351–372.

Wilson, R. A. 1994b. "Causal depth, theoretical appropriateness, and individualism in psychology". *Philosophy of Science* 61: 55–75.

Advertisement for a Semantics for Psychology

NED BLOCK

Meaning is notoriously vague. So, it should not be surprising that semanticists (those who study meaning) have had somewhat different purposes in mind, and thus have sharpened the ordinary concept of meaning in somewhat different ways. It is a curious and unfortunate fact that semanticists typically tell us little about what aspects of meaning they are and are not attempting to deal with. One is given little guidance as to what extent "rival" research programs actually disagree.

My purpose here is to advocate an approach to semantics relevant to the foundations of psychology, or, rather, one approach to one branch of psychology, namely cognitive science. I shall be talking in terms of some of the leading ideas of cognitive science, most importantly the representational theory of mind, aspects of which will be sketched as they become relevant.[1] The representalist doctrine that my argument depends on is that thoughts are structured entities. I know this will be a sticking point for some readers, so I will say a bit more about what this comes to, and I will compare my position with related positions that reject it.

My strategy will be to begin with some desiderata. These desiderata vary along many dimensions: how central they are to meaning, how psychologically oriented they are, how controversial they are. I will argue that one approach to semantics (not to keep you in suspense—conceptual role semantics) promises to handle such desiderata better than the others that I know about. Though I think my desiderata yield a coherent picture of a psychologically relevant semantics, they are not intended to be pretheoretically obvious; rather, they were chosen to flatter the theory I have in mind. I will *not* be arguing that semantic theories that fail to satisfy these desiderata are thereby defective; there are distinct—and equally legitimate—questions about meaning that a semantic theory can seek to answer.

The view that I am advertising is a variant on the functionalism familiar in the philosophy of mind. However, I will not be attempting to counter the objections that have been raised to that view (except briefly, and in passing). My bet is that looking at functionalism from the point of view of meaning (rather than mentality) and with an eye to its fertility and power rather than its weaknesses will provide a rationale for working on its problems.

DESIDERATA

Desideratum 1: Explain the relation between meaning and reference/truth. This is the least psychological of all my desiderata. The details of what I have in mind will be discussed when I say how conceptual role semantics promises to explain the relation between meaning and truth.

Desideratum 2: Explain what makes meaningful expressions meaningful. What is it about 'cat' in virtue of which it has the meaning it has? What is the difference between 'cat' and 'glurg' in virtue of which the former has meaning and the latter does not? (And so on, for types of expressions other than words.)

Desideratum 3: Explain the relativity of meaning to representational system. This desideratum is arguably just a special case of the preceding one, but I think it is worth mentioning and discussing separately. As we all know, one linguistic item—for example, a sound or linguistic expression—can have different meanings in different languages. For example, many vocabulary items have different meanings in the dialects of English spoken in North America and England, as in 'trailer' and 'bathroom'.

But the significance of this relativity of meaning to system of representation goes deeper than such examples suggest. One way to see this is to note that whole semantic (and syntactic) *categories* are relative to system of representation. Ink marks that function as a picture in your tribe may function as a word in mine. Further, within the category of pictures, representations are understood differently in different cultures.[2] Finally, syntactic category is relative in the same way. Handwriting, for example, differs in different school systems. Perhaps the ink marks that are regarded as an 'A' in Edinburgh are regarded as an 'H' in Chicago. Is there some common explanation of the relativity to representational system of both semantic and syntactic categories?

Desideratum 4: Explain compositionality. The meaning of a sentence is in some sense a function of the meanings of the words in it (plus the syntax of the sentence). What, exactly, is the relation between the semantic values of sentences and words? Is one more basic than the other? Another question arises once we have fixed on an answer to these questions—namely, why is it that the semantic value of a sentence has whatever relation it has to the semantic values of its parts?

Desideratum 5: Fit in with an account of the relation between meaning and mind/brain. Why should one expect (or at least hope for) a *semantic* theory to fit into an account of the relation between meaning and mind or brain? Because it would be surprising if the nature of meaning (what meaning *is*) were utterly irrelevant to explaining what it is to grasp or understand meanings, and how grasping meanings can have physical effects. At least, one can imagine differences between x and y that make for a difference between what it is to grasp x and y. For example, understanding x may require skills or recognitional abilities, whereas understanding y may require only propositional knowledge.

I said "mind *or* brain," but in fact I will focus on the brain. And in discussing this matter, I will simply adopt a form of materialism (the "token" identity thesis—that each particular mental occurrence is a physical occurrence).

What is supposed to be in need of explanation about the relation of meaning to the brain? Well, one obvious question is: what is it for the brain to grasp meanings, and how is it that the brain's grasp of meanings has effects on the world? Meanings are (at least apparently) nonphysical abstract objects. And the relation between a brain and the meanings it grasps does not seem to be like the relation between a metal bar and the number of degrees Celsius that is its temperature—a case in which there are proposals about how a change in the value of the temperature can cause, say, expansion of the bar (see Field 1980). Yet the difference between a brain that grasps a certain meaning and a brain that does not makes for a difference in the causal properties of that brain. A brain that grasps the meaning of 'transmogrify' can win a quiz show for its owner, transporting the two of them to a hotel in the Catskills. We need an account of how such a relation between a brain and a meaning can make a causal difference.

Desideratum 6: Illuminate the relation between autonomous and inherited meaning. If there are representations in the brain, as the representational theory of the mind contends, then there is an obvious distinction to be made between them and other representations—for instance, representations on this page (Searle, 1980a; Haugeland, 1980). The representations on the page must be read or heard to be understood, but not so for the representations in the brain. The representations on the page require for their understanding *translation,* or at least *transliteration* into the language of thought; the representations in the brain (some of them, at any rate) require no such translation or transliteration. Let us say that the representations that require no translation or transliteration have *antonomous* meaning, where as the ones that do require translation or transliteration have *inherited* meaning.

Different views of meaning have quite different consequences for the issue of what a semantic theory could hope to say about either type of meaning. On Searle's view, for example, the most a semantic theory could say about this matter is to give an account of how inherited meaning (*observer-relative* meaning, in his terminology) is inherited from autonomous meaning (*intrinsic meaning,* in his terminology). Explaining autonomous meaning itself, in his view, is simply outside the scope of semantics. The most we can say by way of giving an account of autonomous meaning, according to Searle, is that it arises from the causal powers of the human brain and would arise from any other object (e.g., a machine) that has "equivalent causal powers."

Despite the panoply of views on this matter, there are a few questions whose interest should be agreed on by all who accept the distinction between autonomous and inherited meaning to begin with. The main questions are: What are autonomous and inherited meaning? What is the relation between autonomous and inherited meaning? For example, are they just two different types of meaning, neither of which is derivative from or reducible to the other?[3]

A related question is how a representation with autonomous meaning can mean the same as a representation with inherited meaning. Many philosophers would disparage such a question because of skepticism about synonomy. But it is not clear that those who accept it are caught in the Quinean quicksand. That depends on whether the notion of meaning used in cognitive science must carry with it commitment to *truths* of meaning, and hence commitment to a priori truth.[4]

Desideratum 7: Explain the connections between knowing, learning, and using an expression, and the expression's meaning. Obviously, there is a close connection between *the meaning of a word,* on the one hand, and *what we know when we know or understand a word* and *what we learn when we learn a word,* on the other hand. Indeed, it is intuitively plausible that these italicized descriptions have the same referent (though it would be a mistake to adhere dogmatically to this pretheoretic intuition).

Further, one who has learned an expression (and therefore knows it) automatically has a capacity to use it correctly; also, evidence of correct usage is evidence for knowing the meaning. A psychologically relevant theory of meaning ought to illuminate the connections between knowing/understanding/learning and usage, on the one hand, and meaning on the other.

Desideratum 8: Explain why different aspects of meaning are relevant in different ways to the determination of reference and to psychological explanation. One can distinguish between two aspects of meaning that are relevant to psychological explanation in quite different ways. One type of case involves indexicals, for example:

(1) I am in danger of being run over.
(2) Ned Block is in danger of being run over.

Consider the difference between the beliefs I would express by uttering (1), as compared with (2). Believing (2) cannot be guaranteed to have the same life-saving effect on my behavior as believing (1), since I may not know I am Ned Block (I may think I am Napoleon).[5] So there is an important difference between (1) and (2) with respect to causation (and therefore causal explanation) of behavior.

This observation is one motivation for a familiar way of thinking about meaning and belief content in which, when you and I have beliefs expressed by our (respective) utterances of (1), we have beliefs with the same content. This is the way of individuating in which two lunatics who say "I am Napoleon" have the *same delusion*. Corresponding to this way of individuating belief content, we have a way of individuating meanings in which the meanings of the two lunatics' sentence tokens are the same. This is the way of individuating meanings of tokens that is geared toward sentence types, and thus seems most natural for linguistics—since it makes the meaning of a sentence a function of the meanings of the words in the sentence (plus syntax). Notice that on this way of individuating, utterances of (1) and (2) by me have *different* meanings and standardly express beliefs with *different* contents. Again, this way of individuating is natural for linguistics, since no reasonable dictionary would give 'I' and 'Ned Block' the same entry.

Nonetheless, (1), said by me, and (2) express the same proposition, according to a familiar way of individuating propositions. In a familiar sense of 'meaning' in which two sentence tokens have the same meaning just in case they express the same proposition, (1), said by me, and (2) have the same meaning. If we individuate contents of beliefs as we individuate the propositions believed, the belief I express by (1) would have the same content as the belief I express by (2). Further, the belief I express by (1) would have different content from the belief you express by (1); similarly, the meaning of my utterance of (1) would be different from your utterance of (1).

Call the former scheme of individuation *narrow* individuation and the latter *wide* individuation (cf. Kaplan's different distinction between character and content). Wide individuation groups token sentences together if they attribute the same properties to the same individuals, whereas narrow individuation groups sentence tokens together if they attribute the same properties using the same descriptions of individuals—irrespective of whether the individuals referred to are the same. In other words, narrow individuation abstracts from the question of (i.e., ignores) whether the same individuals are involved and depends instead on how the individuals are referred to.[6] (Note that the question of how individuals are referred to is quite different from the question of how the referrer thinks of the referent. For example, two uses of (1) have the same narrow meaning (in my sense of the phrase) even if one user thinks he's Napoleon while the other thinks he's Wittgenstein.)

One can think of narrow and wide individuation as specifying different aspects of meaning, narrow and wide meaning. (I am not saying that narrow and wide meaning are *kinds* of meaning, but only aspects or perhaps only *determinants* of meaning.) Narrow meaning is "in the head," in the sense of this phrase in which it indicates supervenience on physical constitution,[7] and narrow meaning captures the semantic aspect of what is in common to utterances of (e.g.) (1) by different people. Wide meaning, by contrast, depends on what individuals outside the head are referred to, so wide meaning is not "in the head." The type of individuation that gives rise to the concept of narrow meaning also gives rise to a corresponding concept of narrow belief content. Two utterances have the same narrow meaning just in case the beliefs they express have the same narrow content.

Note that despite the misleading terminology, wide meaning does not *include* narrow meaning. Utterances of (1) (by me) and (2) have the same wide meaning but not the same narrow meaning.[8]

Narrow meaning/content and wide meaning/content are relevant to psychological explanation in quite different ways. For one thing, the narrow meaning of a sentence believed is more informative about the mental state of the believer. Thus narrow meaning (and narrow content) is better suited to predicting and explaining what someone decides or does, so long as information about the external world is ignored. Thus, if you and I both have a belief we would express with (1), one can explain and predict our sudden glances at nearby vehicles and our (respective) decisions to leap to the side. Wide meanings are less suited to this type of prediction and explanation, because they "leave out" information about the way one refers to oneself. Since the wide meaning of (1) said by me and (2) are the same, if you are told I believe a sentence with this wide meaning (i.e., the wide meaning common to my [1] and [2], you know that I believe that something—me, as it happens, but you aren't told that I know it's me—is in danger of being run over. Thus, information is omitted, since you aren't told how I conceive of the thing in danger. On the other hand, you do know that I believe that something is in danger, so you do have *some* information about my mental state.

From what I have just said, it would seem that narrow meaning includes everything relevant to psychological explanation that wide meaning does, and more. But wide meaning may be more useful for predicting in one respect: to the extent that there are nomological relations between the world and what people think and do, wide meaning will allow predicting what they think and do without information about how they see things. Suppose, for example, that people tend to avoid wide open spaces, no matter how they describe these spaces to themselves. Then knowing that Fred is choosing whether to go via an open space or a city street, one would be in a position to predict Fred's choice, even though one does not know whether Fred describes the open space to himself as 'that', or as 'Copley Square'.

Narrow meaning has another kind of theoretical import: it determines a function from expressions and contexts of utterance onto referents and truth values.[9] When you and I utter 'I' in (1), there is something we share, some semantic aspect of the word 'I' that in your context maps your token onto you and in my context maps my token onto me.

Let me guard against some misunderstandings. First, as I already indicated, the narrow meaning of 'I' does not include one's conception of oneself. Second, although I have said that there is a shared semantic aspect of 'I' relevant to explaining behavior and a shared semantic aspect relevant to determining a function from context to referent, I do not suggest that these shared semantic aspects are exactly the same. It is an open question whether they are the same, and hence whether 'narrow meaning', as I am using the term, picks out a single thing. On the theory I will be arguing for, the semantic aspect that determines the function from context to referent (and truth value) turns out to be a *part* of the semantic aspect that plays a part in explaining behavior. Thus the latter semantic aspect does *both* jobs. Hence, I will use 'narrow meaning/content' as uniquely referring to the more inclusive semantic aspect. I do want to note, though, that this way of talking carries a strong theoretical commitment. Finally, the narrow/wide distinction as I have described it so far applies to tokens, not types. However, there is an obvious extension to (nonindexical) types.

I will now pause to say what the considerations raised in this section so far have to do with a semantics for psychology. First, a semantics for psychology should have something to say about what the distinction between narrow and wide meaning comes to and, ideally, should give accounts of what the two aspects of meaning are. Second, the theory ought to say why it is that narrow and wide meanings are distinctively relevant to the explanation and prediction of psychological facts (including behavior). Third, the theory ought to give an account of narrow meaning that explains how it is that it determines a function from the context of utterance to reference and truth value.

I have been talking so far about the meaning of sentences with indexicals, but the points I have been making can be extended to names and, more controversially, to natural kind terms. Consider Teen (of Earth) and her twin on Twin Earth, Teen$_{te}$. The two are particle-for-particle duplicates who have had exactly the same histories of surface stimulations. In various different versions of the story, we are to imagine various differences in their worlds outside the sphere of what has impinged on them. For now, let us suppose their environments are exactly the same, except, of course, that the individuals on the two worlds are distinct—Teen's hero is Michael Jackson, whereas Teen$_{te}$'s hero is a distinct but indistinguishable (except spatiotemporally) personage. Teen and Teen$_{te}$ each have the thought they would express with:

(3) Michael Jackson struts.

Once again, we can distinguish between two ways of individuating thought contents, and also the meanings of the sentences thought. On one, the narrow scheme, we can talk of Teen and Teen$_{te}$ as having the same thought, and we can talk of them as uttering sentences with the same meaning. If they would both sincerely say "Michael Jackson has supernatural powers," they share the same delusion. This is narrow meaning and narrow content. Alternatively, we can regard the meanings and thought contents as distinct simply in virtue of the fact that Teen is referring to Michael Jackson and Teen$_{te}$ is referring to Michael Jackson$_{te}$. This is wide meaning and content.

This illustrates same narrow/different wide meaning and content. The case of same wide/different narrow meaning (the case analogous to [1] and [2] above uttered by the same person) is illustrated by 'Cicero orates' and 'Tully orates'. The principles of individuation in these name cases are the same as in the indexical cases, though their motivation is in one respect weaker because it is controversial whether names even *have* meanings. Also, the nomological connection between names and behavior is not as simple as that between 'I' and behavior.

There are two basic facts on which the narrow/wide distinction is based. One is that how you represent something that you refer to can affect your psychological states and behavior. So if you know that Cicero orates and you don't know that Cicero = Tully, you are not in a position to make use of the fact that Tully orates. The second basic fact is that there is more to semantics than what is "in the head." The contents of the head of a person who asserts (3), together with the fact that Michael Jackson struts, are *not enough to determine whether (3) is true or false,* since the truth value depends as well on who 'Michael Jackson' refers to. Imagine that though Michael Jackson is an excellent strutter, his twin cannot strut; the strutting ascribed to his twin by Twin Earth teenagers is actually done by a stuntman. Then utterances of (3) on Twin Earth differ in truth value from utterances of (3) on Earth, despite no relevant differences between teenage heads on the two planets, and despite it being just as much a fact on Twin Earth as on Earth that Michael Jackson struts. (If this seems mysterious to you, note that in the last sentence, I used 'Michael Jackson' as it is used in my language community—Should I talk someone else's language?—and the language community on Twin Earth uses the same expression to refer to a different person.) *Since the truth value of a sentence is determined by the totality of semantic facts, plus the relevant facts about the world, there is more to the totality of semantic facts about the sentence than is in the speaker's head. The "extra" semantic facts are about what the referring terms in the sentence refer to.*[10] But even though there are semantic differences between Teen's and Teen$_{te}$'s utterance of and thinking of (3), there are important similarities as well—and this is the main point of this section—that give rise to notions of aspects of content and meaning (narrow content and meaning) *that are shared by Teen and Teen$_{te}$* and that explain similarities in their (for example) fantasy life and ticket-buying behavior and that determine the function from their different contexts to their different referents.

As in the idexical case, wide meaning and content are not well suited to explaining change of mental state and behavior. The wide meaning of 'Water is wet' (in English—not Twin English) is the same as that of 'H$_2$O is wet', despite the potentially different effects of believeing these sentences on mental states and on behavior. Further, as Kripke's Pierre example reveals (Kripke 1979), if one's conception of translation is overly referential (allowing 'London' to translate 'Londres' inside belief contexts), one is faced with situations in which one is forced to ascribe contradictory beliefs that are no fault of the believer.[11] In addition, what is shared by Teen and Teen$_{te}$ also determines that one is referring to Michael Jackson, whereas the other is referring to Michael Jackson's twin. What is shared determines a function from context to reference. Had Teen been raised on Twin Earth, she would have been molecule for molecule the same as she actually is (ignoring quantum indeterminacy), but her token of 'Michael Jackson' would have referred to Michael Jackson's twin.[12]

The reader may wonder why I have gone on about this desideratum (on the narrow/wide distinction) at such length. (And I'm not finished yet!) The version of conceptual role semantics that I will be defending characterizes *narrow* meaning in terms of conceptual role. There is another version (Harman 1982) that has no truck with narrow content or meaning. Harman's conceptual roles involve perceptual and behavioral interactions with what is seen and manipulated, that is, objects in the world, whereas my conceptual roles stop at the skin. (So if you don't like all this narrow this and narrow that, you can still appreciate the previous desiderata as motivating a Harmanian version of conceptual role semantics.) I prefer my version, and I am trying to spell out part of the motivation for it.[13] (I will say more about Harman's alternative shortly.)

Consider Putnam's original Twin Earth story. My doppelgänger (again, a physical duplicate)[14] uses 'water' to refer to XYZ. Suppose, along with Putnam, that XYZ is *not* a type of water. Further, we may add into the story ideas developed by Burge (Burge 1979) that show the differences in how our different language communities use words can determine differences in the meanings of our words, even when they do not result in differences in stimuli impinging on our surfaces. Suppose my twin and I both say to ourselves:

> My pants are on fire. But luckily I am standing in front of a swimming pool filled with water. Water, thank God, puts out fires.

If Burge and Putnam are right (and I am inclined to agree with them), there are substantial semantic differences between my twin's and my meanings and thought contents because of the differences in physical and social environment. Nonetheless—and here, again, is the crucial idea behind my advocacy of narrow meaning and content—*there is some aspect of meaning in common to what he says and what I say (or at least a common partial determinant of meaning), and this common semantic aspect of what we say provides part of a common explanation of why we both jump into our respective pools.* And if current ideas about the representational theory of mind are right, narrow meaning and content will be usable to state nomological generalizations relating thought, decision, and action.

Further, had my twin grown up in my context, his token of 'water' would refer to H_2O rather than XYZ. Thus, as before, it seems that there is some common semantic aspect of our terms that operates in my case to map my context onto H_2O, and in his case to map his context onto XYZ.

The reader may have noticed my shift to the natural extension I described of the narrow/wide distinction from tokens to types. Since 'Cicero' and 'Tully' are standardly used to refer to the same person, we can regard the sentence types 'Cicero orates' and 'Tully orates' as having the same wide meaning. Likewise for 'water' (as used in English as opposed to Twin English) and 'H_2O'.

Let us say that a propositional attitude or meaning ascription is individualistic if it is supervenient on the physical state of the individual's body, where physical state is specified nonintentionally and independently of physical and social conditions obtaining outside the body.[15] I believe that there is an important individualistic scheme of individuation of beliefs, belief contents, and the meanings of the sentences believed. There is a strong element of individualistic individuation in ordinary thought, but its main home lies in scientific thinking about the mind, especially in contemporary cognitive science. I also agree with Burge and Putnam that there is an important nonindividualistic scheme of individuation in ordinary thought. No incompatability yet.

But Putnam, Burge, and others have also argued against individualistic individuation. Putnam's conclusion (1983) is based on an argument that it is impossible to come up with identity conditions on content or meaning, individualistically considered. I don't have identity conditions to offer, but I am inclined to regard this not as an insurmountable obstacle but as an issue to be dissolved by theory construction. My guess is that a scientific conception of meaning should do away with the crude dichotomy of same/different meaning in favor of a multidimensional gradient of similarity of meaning.[16] After all, substitution of a continuum for a dichotomy is how Bayesian decision theory avoids a host of difficulties—for example, the paradox of the preface—by moving from the crude pigeonholes of *believes/doesn't believe* to degrees of belief.[17]

Burge (1984) is arguing mainly against "pan-individualism," the claim that *all* propositional-attitude individuation in psychology is individualistic. However, I am not advocating this doctrine but only the more limited claim that there is an important strain of individualistic individuation in psychology (and in commonsense discourse). Burge has doubts about this too, but the matter can only be settled by a detailed discussion of psychological practice.

Let me mention only one consideration. Psychology is often concerned with explaining psychological differences. The measure of these differences is *variance*.[18] For example, variance in intelligence and other mental attributes and states is ascribed to differences in genes and environment (and interactions of various sorts between these causal factors). Suppose we fill a tour bus with travelers, half from Twin Earth and half from Earth. The Earthlings believe that water is wet and prefer drinking water to gasoline, whereas the Twin Earthlings do not hve these propositional attitudes (because when they think about what they call 'water', they are not thinking about water—they have no term that refers to water). Suppose that the Earthlings and Twin Earthlings do not differ in relevant ways in genes or in the surface stimulation that has impinged on their bodies over their whole lives. Hence, in this population, differences in propositional attitudes cannot be attributed to environment (in the sense of surface stimulation) and genes (and their interactions): the differences in water attitudes are due to something that has nothing to do with differences in the genes or surface stimulations that have affected these people. An analysis of variance would have to attribute a large component of variance to differences in a factor that does not cause any differences in proteins, synaptic connections, or any other physicochemical feature of the body, as do differences in genes and surface stimulations. This would amount to a kind of action at a distance, and this would clearly go counter to the methodology of attribution of variance. (Note that this point could have been formulated in terms of Burge's point about the social nature of meaning rather than Twin Earth.)

I just argued for individualistic individuation of propositional attitude states—for example, beliefs. But there is a gap between individuating beliefs individualistically and individuating belief *contents* individualistically. One might hold that when you individuate belief individualistically, you still have belief of some strange sort; but that content, individualistically individuated, is like a president who is deposed—no longer a president (cf. Stich 1983). I propose to fill the gap as follows.

Where we have a relation, in certain types of cases we have individualistic properties of the related entities that could be said to ground the relation. If x hits y, y has some sort of consequent change in a bodily surface, perhaps a flattened nose, and x has the property of say, moving his fist forward. Of course, the same individualistic property can underlie many different relational properties, and some relations notoriously don't depend on individualistic properties—for example, 'to the left of'. When content is *non*individualistically individuated, it is individuated with respect to relations to the world (as in the Twin Earth case) and social practice (as in Burge's arthritis example).[19] There is a nonrelational aspect of propositional attitude content, the aspect "inside the head," that corresponds to content in the way that moving the fist corresponds to hitting. This nonrelational aspect of content is what I am calling narrow content. But is narrow content really content?[20]

I find much hostility among philosophers to the ideas of narrow content and narrow meaning. There are many reasons for this resistance that I accept as points of genuine controversy, and about which I am not at all confident about my position. But the worry just mentioned seems to me misplaced, at least as a criticism of conceptual role semantics. The criticism is that I have wrongly assumed that the aspect of meaning or content that is inside the head is something genuinely *semantic*. Jerry Fodor once accused me of a "fallacy of subtraction," that is, of assuming that if you take meaning or content and *subtract* its relation to the world and its social aspect, what you have left is something semantic.

There *is* such a thing as a fallacy of subtraction, of course. If you subtract the property of being colored from redness, you do not get colorless redness. But the issue with respect to conceptual role semantics is merely verbal. Nothing in my position requires me to regard narrow meaning and narrow content as (respectively) *kinds* of meaning and content. As mentioned earlier, I regard them as aspects of or as *determinants* of meaning and content. All that is required for my position is that what I am calling narrow meaning is a distinct feature of language, a characterization of which has something important to contribute to a total theory of meaning (e.g., as indicated in my desiderata). Similarly for narrow content.

Am I conceding that conceptual role semantics isn't really part of *semantics?* The first thing to be said about this question is that it is of very minor intellectual importance. It is a dispute about the border between disciplines; like so many of these disputes, it can be resolved only by a kind of ordinary language philosophy applied to technical terms like 'semantics' (or, worse, by university administrations). Ordinary language philosophy has its place in analyses of concepts that play a central role in ordinary human thought; but application of these techniques to technical terms, where stipulation is the order of the day, is not very illuminating. Nonetheless, I am as willing to quibble as the next person. The correct application of disciplinary terms depends in large part on developments in the disciplines. Often the pretheoretic ideas about the domain of the discipline are left far behind. If meaning indeed decomposes into two factors, then the study of the nature of these two factors belongs in the domain of semantics, even if one or both of them are quite different from meaning in any ordinary sense of the term.

To appeal to ordinary ideas about meaning to argue for excluding narrow meaning from the domain of semantics is like excluding electrons from the domain of the study of matter on the ground that they aren't "solid" and diffract like light.

Further, the role of narrow meaning in determining the function from context to reference and truth value seems especially deserving of the appellation 'semantic'. (I will argue in discussing Desideratum 1 below that narrow meaning—as specified by conceptual role semantics—does indeed determine this function.)

I will continue to talk, as I have, of narrow meaning and narrow content; but I won't mind if the reader prefers to reformulate, using phrases like 'narrow determinant of meaning'.

CONCEPTUAL ROLE SEMANTICS AND TWO-FACTOR THEORY

Conceptual role semantics is not among the more popular approaches, but it has the distinction of being the only approach (to my knowledge, at any rate) that has the potential to satisfy all these desiderata. The approach I have in mind has been suggested, independently, by both philosophers and cognitive scientists: by the former under the title "conceptual role semantics" and by the latter under the title "procedural semantics." (Oddly, these two groups do not refer to one another.) The doctrine has its roots in positivism and pragmatism and in the Wittgensteinian idea of meaning as use. Among philosophers, its recent revival is due mainly to Harman (following Sellars),[21] and Field.[22] Churchland, Loar, Lycan, McGinn, and Schiffer have also advocated versions of the view.[23] In cognitive science, the chief proponent has been Woods,[24] though Miller's and Johnson-Laird's[25] versions have been of interest. The version I like is a "two-factor theory" something like the one advocated by Field,[26] McGinn, (1982), and Loar (1982). (See also Lycan 1981.)

The idea of the two-factor version is that there are two components to meaning, a conceptual role component that is entirely "in the head" (this is narrow meaning)[27] and an external component that has to do with the relations between the representations in the head (with their internal conceptual roles) and the referents and/or truth conditions of these representations in the world. This two-factor approach derives from Putnam's argument (1975, 1979) that meaning could not both be "in the head" and also determine reference. It also takes heart from the Perry-Kaplan points about indexicals mentioned earlier (character and content are two "factors"). The two-factor approach can be regarded as making a conjunctive claim for each sentence: what its conceptual role is, and what its (say) truth conditions are.[28] I will refer to the *two-factor version* of conceptual role semantics as CRS, though perhaps it should be TFCRS to remind the reader of the two-factor nature of the theory.

For present purposes, the exact nature of the external factor does not matter. Those who are so inclined could suppose it to be elucidated by a causal theory of reference or by a theory of truth conditions. The internal factor, conceptual role, is a matter of the causal role of the expression in reasoning and deliberation and, in general, in the way the expression combines and interacts with other expressions so as to mediate between sensory inputs and behavioral outputs. A crucial component of a sentence's conceptual role is a matter of how it participates in inductive and deductive inferences. A word's conceptual role is a matter of its contribution to the role of sentences.[29]

For example, consider what would be involved for a symbol in the internal representational system, '$\rightarrow$', to express the material conditional. The '$\rightarrow$' in 'FELIX IS A CAT $\rightarrow$ FELIX IS AN ANIMAL'[30] expresses the material conditional if, for example, when the just quoted sentence interacts appropriately with:

'FELIX IS A CAT', the result is a tendency to inscribe 'FELIX IS AN ANIMAL' (other things equal, of course).

'FELIX IS NOT AN ANIMAL', the result is a tendency to prevent the inscription of 'FELIX IS A CAT', and a tendency to inscribe 'FELIX IS NOT A CAT'.

'IS FELIX AN ANIMAL?', the result is a tendency to initiate a search for 'FELIX IS A CAT'.

Conceptual role is *total causal role,* abstractly described. Consider, by way of analogy, the causal role of herring. They affect what they eat, what eats them, what sees them and runs away, and, of course, they causally interact with one another. Now abstract away from the total causal role of herring to their culinary role, by which I mean the causal relations involving them that have an effect on or are affected by human dining. Presumably, some of what affects herring and what they affect will not be part of their culinary role: for example, perhaps herring occasionally amuse penguins, and this activity has no culinary causes or effects. Similarly, elements of language have a total causal role, including, say, the effect of newsprint on whatever people wrap in it. Conceptual role abstracts away from all causal relations except the ones that mediate inferences, inductive or deductive, decision making, and the like.

A crucial question for CRS (*the* crucial question) is what counts as identity and difference of conceptual role. Clearly, there are many differences in reasoning that we do not want to count as relevant to meaning. For example, if you take longer than I do in reasoning from x to y, we do not necessarily want to see this as revealing a difference between your meanings of x and/or y and mine. Our reasoning processes may be the same in all inferentially important respects.

Further, CRS must face the familiar "collateral information" problem. Suppose you are prepared to infer from 'TIGER' to 'DANGEROUS', whereas I am not. Do our 'TIGER's have the same conceptual role or not? More significantly, what if we differ in inferring from 'TIGER' to 'ANIMAL'? Does the first difference differ in kind from the second?

CRS has less room to maneuver here than, say, Katzian semantics, since CRS cannot make use of an analytic/synthetic distinction. The problem is that if we make the inferences that define 'cat' just the putatively analytic ones (excluding, for example, the inference from 'cat' to 'is probably capable of purring'), we get a meaning for 'cat' that is the same as for 'dog'. (One could try to distinguish them by making use of the difference between the words themselves [e.g., the fact that 'is a cat' entails 'is not a dog'], but that would at best allow intrapersonal synonomy, not interpersonal synonomy. See Field 1978.) This is not a problem *within* Katzian semantics because Katzians appeal to primitive (undefined) elements of language in terms of which other elements are defined. (See Katz 1972.) The Katzian picture is that you can distinguish the meaning of 'dog' from 'cat' by appealing to the analytic truths that cats are feline (and not canine) and dogs are canine (and not feline), where 'feline' and 'canine' are primitive terms. This move is not available for CRS, since it has no truck with primitive terms: conceptual role is supposed to completely determine narrow meaning. (One qualification: it *is* possible to take conceptual role as a *part* of a theory of the narrow meaning of *part* of the language—the nonprimitive part—while appealing to some other conception of meaning of primitives; procedural semanticists sometimes sound as if they want to take *phenomenal* terms as primitives whose meaning is given by their "sensory content," while taking other terms as getting their meanings via their computational relations to one another and to the phenomenal terms as well [perhaps they see the phenomenal terms as "grounding" the functional structures]. It should be clear that this is a "mixed" conceptual role/phenomenalist theory and not a pure conceptual role theory.)

Without an analytic/synthetic distinction, we would, as I mentioned earlier, have to move to a scientific conception of meaning that does away with the crude dichotomy of same/different meaning in favor of a multidimensional gradient of similarity of meaning (hoping for results as good as those achieved by decision theory in moving from an all-or-nothing notion of belief to a graded notion).

If CRS is to be developed to the point where it can be evaluated seriously, definite proposals for individuating conceptual roles must be framed and investigated. One of the purposes of this paper is to try to make it plausible that CRS is worth pursuing.

What about the social dimension of meaning demonstrated in Burge (1979)? Two-factor theory *can* try to capture such phenomena in the referential factor. For example, perhaps the causal chain determining the reference of my use of 'arthritis' is mediated by the activities of people who know more about arthritis than I do. (See Boyd [1979] for an indication of how to knit the social aspect of meaning together with a causal theory of reference.) Alternatively, two-factor theory may have to expand to three-factor theory, allowing a distinct social factor to meaning. Since my mission is to compare the broad outlines of the view I am espousing with alternative points of view, I will not pursue the matter further (though later on I will take up the question of how the conceptual role factor is related to the referential factor).

It should be becoming clear that CRS as I am conceiving of it is so undeveloped as to be more of a framework for a theory than a theory. Why bother thinking about such a sketchy theory? I think that the current status of CRS is reminiscent of the "causal theory of reference." The root idea of causal theories of reference seems clearly relevant to central phenomena of reference, such as how one person can acquire the ability to refer to Napoleon from another person, even without acquiring many beliefs about Napoleon, and even if most of what he believes is false. Detailed versions of causal theories (Devitt 1981) have not commanded widespread agreement; nonetheless, since the only alternative theories of reference (e.g., the description theory) seem hopeless as accounts of the phenomena just mentioned, we are justified in supposing that the central ideas of the causal theory of reference will have to play a part in some way in any successful theory of reference. I intend the desiderata I've discussed to provide a similar rationale for supposing that the central ideas of CRS must somehow fit into our overall semantic picture.

I should mention that (as with the causal theory of reference) a two-factor conceptual role semantics has been set out in one precise version—that of Field (1977). Though Field's account is very suggestive, I will not adopt it, for a number of reasons. For one thing, Field's account is not quite a conceptual role account in the sense in which I have defined it, since his conceptual roles are not quite causal. Field defines conceptual role in terms of conditional probability. Two sentences have the same conceptual role if and only if they have the same conditional probability with respect to every other sentence. Though Field is not explicit about this, he obviously intends some kind of causal account in terms of the causal consequences of new evidence on degrees of belief. Harman (1982) criticizes Field's account on the ground that it does not allow for revision of belief. Harman's argument, apparently, is that Bayesians merely change their degree of belief rather than changing their mind. That is, Bayesians do not treat new evidence as dictating that they should reject claims they formerly accepted (or conversely), but rather that they should move from a .67 degree of belief in a claim to a .52

degree of belief. I don't find Harman's objection very persuasive; what corresponds to change of mind in the Bayesian perspective just *is* change of degree of belief. The Bayesians reject change of mind in favor of change of degree of belief; this is a theoretical disagreement that is not settled by insisting. However, a version of Harman's conclusion seems quite likely right, but for another reason: in seeing change of mind entirely in terms of change in degree of belief via conditionalization (or generalized conditionalization), the Bayesian perspective (like the logical empiricist views that are concerned with justification rather than discovery) cannot model the kind of change of mind that involves the generation of new hypotheses (this point is most convincing with regard to new hypotheses that involve new ideas). Its not that the Bayesian perspective is in any way incompatible with the generation of new hypotheses, but rather that on the Bayesian account of reasoning, new hypotheses must be treated as "given" via some non-Bayesian process, and so the Bayesian account is importantly incomplete. Conceptual role includes the kind of reasoning in which one infers from evidence against one's hypothesis to an obvious variant deploying a revised version of an old idea, and this cannot be captured wholly within a Bayesian framework.

Even ignoring this matter, Field's account highlights a choice that must be made by CRS theorists, one that has had no discussion (as far as I know): namely, should conceptual role be understood in ideal or normative terms, or should it be tied to what people actually do? As Harman (forthcoming) points out (in another context), accounts of reasoning that involve change of degree of belief by conditionalizing on evidence require keeping track of astronomical numbers of conditional probabilities. (Harman calculates that a billion are needed for thirty evidence propositions.) So any Bayesian account would have to be very far removed from actual reasoning. However, if we opt against such idealization, must we stick so close to actual practice as to include in conceptual role well-known fallacious reasoning strategies, such as the gamblers' fallacy?[31]

I prefer not to comment on this matter, in part because I'm not sure what to say and in part because I am trying to stay away from controversies *within* conceptual role semantics, because the points I want to make can be made on the basis of a version of the doctrine that contains very little in the way of details.

Calling the causal roles CRS appeals to 'conceptual' or 'inferential' shouldn't mislead anyone into supposing that the theory's description of them can appeal to their meanings—that would defeat the point of reductionist theories. The project of giving a nonsemantic (and nonintentional) description of these roles is certainly daunting, but the reader would do well to note that it is no more daunting than the programs of various popular philosophical theories. For example, the causal theory of reference, taken as a reductionist proposal (as in Devitt's but not in Kripke's versions) has the same sort of charge. And, a rather similar charge falls on "traditional" non-representational functionalism (e.g., as in Lewis's or Putnam's versions), where the causal roles of propositional attitude states are to be described in nonintentional and nonsemantic terms.

Representationalists differ in how important they think the role of English expressions are in reasoning, deliberation, and so forth. At one end of the spectrum, we have the view that English is *the* language of thought (for English speakers). Near the other end, we have those who, more influenced by cognitive psychology, have tended to see reasoning in English as the tip of an iceberg whose main mass is computation in an internal language common to speakers of English and Walburi.[32] On the latter view, the narrow meaning of English expressions is derivative from the narrow meanings of expressions in the internal language. (The dependency would, however, be the other way around for the referential component of meaning, since it is English expressions that are more directly related to the world.) I will not be concerned with this and a number of other disputes that can occur *within* the framework of conceptual role semantics.

In what follows, I shall be quite relaxed about this issue of the role of English in thinking. Sometimes, I will take English to be the language of thought. However, when it is convenient, I will assume that English is used only for communication and that *all* thought is in a language that does not overlap with English, mentalese. When on this latter tack, I will also assume that mechanisms of language production and language understanding establish a *standard association* between English and mentalese expressions. When a speaker formulates a message using 'CAT', language—production mechanisms map 'CAT' onto 'cat'; and when the hearer understands 'cat', the language—understanding mechanisms map it onto 'CAT'.

This standard-association notion can be used to construct a way of individuating conceptual roles in which English expressions have the conceptual roles of the mentalese expressions with which they are standardly associated. Suppose I am told that Felix is a cat and am asked about Felix's weight. I answer "Felix weighs more than .01 grams." I suggest we start with the following simple mechanistic picture. When I hear "Felix is a cat," language-understanding mechanisms produce "FELIX IS A CAT." Reasoning mechanisms produce "FELIX WEIGHS MORE THAN .01 GRAMS," and language-production mechanisms result in the utterance of "Felix weighs more than .01 grams." Now an English sentence and its internal standard associate certainly hve different causal properties. For example, one is visible or audible (normally) without neurophysiological techniques. But we can individuate conceptual roles so as to give them the *same* conceptual roles, simply by (1) taking the relevant causal properties of English expressions as the ones that are mediated by their causal interactions with their standard associates and (2) abstracting away from the mechanisms that effect the standard association. Then any cause or effect of 'cat' will, for purposes of individuation of conceptual roles, be regarded as the same as a cause or an effect of 'CAT'.

An analogy: Consider a computer in which numbers are entered and displayed in ordinary decimal notation, but in which all computation is actually done in binary notation. The way the computer works is that there are mechanisms that transform the '3 + 4' you enter on the keyboard into an internal expression we can represent as '+ (11,100)'. This is a translation, of course, but we can talk about it without describing it as such, by describing it in terms of the mechanism that computes the function. Internal computational mechanisms operate on this expression, yielding another expression, '111', which is transformed by the translation mechanisms into a '7' displayed on the screen. Now the process by which '3 + 4' yields '7' is exactly the same as the process by which '+ (11,100)' yields '111', except for the two translation steps. So if we (1) ignore causes and effects of decimal digits other than those mediated by their interactions with binary digits in the innards of the machine and (2) abstract away from the translation steps, we can regard the decimal and corresponding binary expressions as having the same computational roles.

Thus, one can speak of the conceptual roles of English expressions, even when adopting the view that internal computation is entirely in mentalese. This will seem strange if your picture of English tokens is inert expressions in dusty books, as compared with the dynamic properties of the internal representations in which all thought is actually conducted. So remember that I am adverting to what the English expressions do when seen or heard.

Let me try to clarify what I am trying to do with the notion of standard association by mentioning some caveats.

(1) The English language is of course a social object. In speaking of the conceptual roles of English expressions, I do not intend a theory of that social object. Conceptual role, you will recall, is meant to capture narrow meaning. Indeed, since causal roles differ from person to person, CRS deals with *idiolect* narrow meaning rather than public language narrow meaning.

(2) The existence of the mechanisms that effect the standard association is an empirical question (though, as Stich [1983, p. 80] argues, something like this idea seems to be part of commonsense psychology). I appeal to empirical work on the "language module"—see Fodor (1983b). Were the empirical assumption to turn out false, a conceptual role theory of (the narrow meaning of) external language could still be given (in terms of the causal interactions between external and internal language), but what would be lost would be the plausibility of a conceptual role theory in which for almost any external expression, one could expect an internal expression with the same narrow meaning. So as to have my empirical eggs in one basket, let me include the assumption of a language module under the rubric of "representationalism."

(3) In order for the notion of standard association to be usable to define conceptual roles, it must be characterizable nonsemantically and nonintentionally. But doesn't this idea founder on obvious facts about the devious road from thought to language, for example, that people lie? The point of my appeal to the language module is that it works (once engaged) without the intervention of any intentional states. Of course, it is used by us in a variety of ways, since we have many purposes in using language. The language module works the same in lying and truth telling; the difference is to be found in the mentalese message. Perhaps confusion would be avoided if one focuses on the use of language, not in communication, but in thinking out loud or in internal soliloquies.

(4) Language production may have to bear more of the burden in characterizing standard association than language perception, since the latter encounters complications with indexicals and the like. When one hears "I'm sick," one doesn't represent it the way one would represent one's own first person thought.

(5) Despite the convention I've adopted of writing mentalese as English in capitals, nothing in the CRS position requires that a sentence spoken have the same meaning as that sentence thought. One can make sense of the idea that in speech one uses the English word 'chase' to mean what one means in thought by the English word 'CHAIR'. Imagine yourself moving to a place where they speak a dialect of English that differs from yours in exchanging the meanings of these two words. If you continue to think in your old dialect but talk in the new one, you would be in the described situation. Consider two quite different scenarios. In one, the new situation never effects a change in your language production/perception module. In communicating, you consciously adjust your words, but in thinking out loud, you talk as before. In the other scenario, the module changes so as to adjust to the external shift. In the former case, standard association will be normal. In the latter, 'chair' will be standardly associated with 'CHASE', and the conceptual role of 'chair' will derive from 'CHASE'-thoughts (involving trying to catch rather than sitting). 'Chair' will have the same conceptual role as 'CHASE'. Neither scenario provides any problem for the view of conceptual role of external language that I sketched. Schiffer and Loar have emphasized that if there is an internal language, a sentence spoken need not have the same meaning as the same sentence thought, but they have been led to conclude that if a language of thought hypothesis is true, it is reasonable to deploy two quite different types of theories of meaning—one for internal language, one for external language. Their concern with external language is with meaning in public language, whereas mine is with narrow meaning in idiolect, so there is no direct conflict. Still, I want to emphasize that a conclusion analogous to theirs for idiolect narrow meaning is mistaken. (See Loar 1981; Schiffer 1981.) This matter will come up again in the section below on what makes meaningful expressions meaningful.

One final point of clarification: Though I am advocating CRS, I am far from a true believer. My position is that CRS can do enough for us (as indicated by the desiderata it satisfies) to motivate working it out in detail and searching for solutions to its problems.

Perhaps this is the place to mention why I am willing to advocate a version of functionalism despite my arguments against functionalism in Block (1978). First, I am impressed by the questions this particular version of functionalism (apparently) can answer. Second, I am now willing to settle for (and I think there is some value in) a theory that is chauvinist in the sense that it does not characterize meaning or intentionality in general, but only *human* meaning or intentionality. Third, the arguments I gave for the conclusion that functionalism is liberal (in the sense that it overascribes mental properties, e.g., to groups of people organized appropriately) were strongest against functionalist theories of *experiential* mental states. I am now inclined to regard intentional mental states as a natural kind for which a functionalist theory may be OK, even though it is not acceptable for experiential states. Indeed, if the domain of CRS is a natural kind, then so is the domain of intentional mental phenomena.

Ironically, this concession to functionalism may make my position harder to defend against thoroughgoing functionalists, since it may commit me to the possibility of intentionality—even intentional states with the same sort of intentional content as ours—without experience. Perhaps I would be committed to the possibility of "zombies," whose beliefs are the same as ours (including beliefs to the effect that they are in pain), but who have no real pains (only "ersatz" pains that are functionally like pain but lack qualitative content). Then I would have to confront the arguments against this possibility in Shoemaker (1984, chaps. 9 and 14). (On my view, pain, for example, is actually a composite state consisting of a nonfunctional qualitative state together with a functional state. Since the qualitative state can be neurophysiologically—but not functionally—characterized, I regard the full account of the mental as part functional, part physiological.) Finally, I believe many of the other arguments that have been advanced against functionalism in its various forms to be defective (see my argument below against Searle).

Two Factors or One Factor?

The version of CRS I have been talking about is a "two-factor" version, in which the conceptual role factor is meant to capture the aspect (or determinant) of meaning "inside the head," whereas the other is meant to capture the referential and social dimensions of meaning.

As I mentioned earlier, Gilbert Harman has been advocating a different version of conceptual role semantics. Harman's version makes do with *one* factor, namely, conceptual role. How does he do without the referential and social factors? By making his one factor reach out into the world of referents and into the practices of the linguistic community. I have been talking about conceptual roles along lines common in functionalist writing in philosophy of mind. These conceptual roles stop roughly at the skin. Outputs are conceived of in terms of bodily movements or, according to the more scientifically minded, in terms of outputs of, say, the motor cortex (allowing for thoughts in disembodied brains). Inputs are conceived of in terms of the proximal stimuli or in terms of outputs of sensory transducers. By contrast, here is Harman on the subject.

> Conceptual role semantics does not involve a "solipsistic" theory of the content of thoughts. There is no suggestion that content depends only on functional relations among thoughts and concepts, such as the role a particular concept plays in inference. (Field, 1977, misses this point.) Also relevant are functional relations to the external world in connection with perception, on the one hand, and action on the other. What makes something the concept red is in part the way in which the concept is involved in the perception of red objects in the external world. What makes something the concept of danger is in part the way in which the concept is involved in thoughts that affect action in certain ways.[33]

One might speak of Harman's conceptual roles as "long-armed," as opposed to the "short-armed" conceptual roles of the two-factor theorist.

My objection to Harman, in brief, is that I don't see how he can handle the phenomena one would ordinarily think of as being in the purview of a theory of reference without extending his account to the point where it is equivalent to the two-factor account.

The point emerges as one looks at Harman's responses to problems that are dealt with by familiar theories of reference. Consider a resident of Earth who travels to Twin Earth in a space ship. He lands in a body of XYZ; but, ignorant of the difference between Twin Earth and Earth, he radios home the message "Surrounded by water." At first glance, one would think that the Harmanian conceptual role of the traveler's word 'water' would at that moment involve a connection to XYZ, since that is what his perception and action is at that moment connected with. Then Harman would be committed to saying the traveler's message is true—in contrast with the Putnamian claim that his message is false because he is not surrounded by water (but rather twin water). Since Harman accepts the Putnam line, he deploys a notion of "normal context" (Harman 1973), the idea being that the traveler's conceptual role for 'water' is to be thought of as involving the substance he normally refers to using that word.

Another case Harman discusses is Putnam's elm/beech case. (You will recall that the question is how I can use 'elm' to refer to elms when what I know about elms is exactly the same as what I know about beeches (except for the names). Harman's solution is to include in *my* conceptual role for 'elm' its role in the minds of experts who actually know the difference.

It begins to look as if Harman is building into his long-arm conceptual roles devices that have usually been placed in the theory of reference. The point can be strengthened by a look at other phenomena that have concerned theories of reference, such as borrowed reference to things that do not now exist but did exist in the past. I can refer to Aristotle on the basis of overhearing your conversation about him, even if most of what I believe about Aristotle is false, because I misunderstood what you said. Will Harman deal with this by making his conceptual roles reach from one person to another, into the past, that is, making a causal relation between Aristotle and me—mediated by you, and your source of the word, and your source's source, etc.—part of the conceptual role of my use of 'Aristotle'? If not, how can Harman handle borrowed reference? If so, Harman certainly owes us a reason for thinking that the outside-the-body part of his long-arm conceptual roles differs from the referential factor of two-factor theory.[34] The burden of proof on Harman is especially pressing, given that it appears that one could easily transform a theory of the sort he advocates into a theory of the sort I have been advocating. If you take Harman's long-arm conceptual roles and "chop off" the portion of these roles outside the skin, you are left with my short-arm conceptual roles. If the outside-the-body part that is chopped off amounts to some familiar sort of theory of reference, then the difference between Harman's one-factor theory and two-factor theory is merely verbal.

Conceptual role semantics is often treated with derision because of failure to appreciate the option of a two-factor version, a failure that is as common among the proponents of the view as the opponents. Consider Fodor's critique (1978) of Johnson-Laird's version of conceptual role semantics. Johnson-Laird's version tended in his original article towards verificationism; that is, the roles of words he focused on were their roles in one specific kind of reasoning, namely verifying. Fodor correctly criticizes this verificationism.[35] But I want to focus on a different matter. Fodor objected that the meaning of 'Napoleon won the Battle of Waterloo' could not possibly consist in any sort of a set of procedures for manipulating internal symbols. That idea, he argued, embodies a use/mention fallacy.

Suppose somebody said: 'Breakthrough! The semantic interpretation of "Did Napoleon win at Waterloo?" is: *find out whether the sentence "Napoleon won at Waterloo?" occurs in the volume with Dewey decimal number XXX, XXX in the 42nd St. Branch of the New York City Public Library'.* . . . . " 'But', giggled Granny, 'if that was what 'Did Napoleon win at Waterloo?' meant, it wouldn't even be a question aobut *Napoleon'*. 'Aw, shucks', replied Tom Swift."[36]

Fodor's objection is that if meaning is identified with the causal interactions of elements of language, sentences would be about *language*, not the world.

My defence of Johnson-Laird should be obvious by now. Take the procedures that manipulate 'Napoleon', etc. (or, better, the whole conceptual roles of these words) as specifying *narrow* meaning. Fodor's argument would only be damaging to a theory that took conceptual role to specify what language is *about*. But if conceptual role specifies only narrow meaning, not reference or truth conditions, then Fodor's criticism misses the mark. Were Johnson-Laird to adopt a two-factor theory of the sort I have been advocating, he could answer Fodor by pointing out that the job of saying what language is about is to be handled by the referential component of the theory, not the narrow-meaning component.

A similar point applies to Dretske's rather colorful criticism of remarks by Churchland and Churchland, (1983).

It sounds like magic: signifying something by multiplying sound and fury. Unless you put cream in you won't get ice cream out no matter how fast you turn the crank or how sophisticated the "processing." The cream, in the case of a cognitive system, is the *representational* role of those elements over which computations are performed. And the representational role of a structure is, I submit, a matter of how the elements of the system are related, not to one another, but to the external situations they "express."[37]

But the cream, according to two-factor theory, is conceptual role *together with* Dretske's representational role. Since CRS puts in Dretske's cream, plus *more,* there is no mystery about how you get ice cream out of it.

The same sort of point applies against criticisms of CRS that take the conceptual role component to task for not providing a *full* theory of meaning. Our judgments of sameness of meaning are controlled by a complex mix of conceptual role and referential (and perhaps other) considerations.[38]

Fodor (1985) points out that the concept of water can be shared by me and Blind Me. He says this presents problems for theories like CRS. He goes on to say:

The obvious reply is that the properties of causal relations that make for sameness and difference of functional roles are very abstract indeed. Well, maybe; but there is an alternative proposal that seems a lot less strained. Namely that if Blind Me can share my concept of water, that's not because we both have mental representations with abstractly identical causal roles; rather, it's because we both have mental representations that are appropriately connected (causally, say) to *water.*[39]

But the two replies he gives aren't *incompatible alternatives;* CRS can adopt them both—though I think Fodor is right that the fact that the reference by me and Blind Me is to the same stuff is probably the main thing here. The point is that one cannot criticize a two-factor theory for not doing it all with one factor.

OVERVIEW

The rest of the paper is mainly concerned with showing how CRS satisfies the desiderata and with comparing CRS with other semantic theories in this regard. I will be talking about two quite different (but compatible) kinds of semantic theories: reductionist and nonreductionist. A reductionist semantic theory is one that characterizes the semantic in nonsemantic terms. A nonreductionist semantic theory is not one that is *anti*reductionist, but only one that does not have reductionist aims. These theories are mainly concerned with issues about constructions in particular languages, for example, why 'The temperature is rising' and 'The temperature is 70" do not entail '70° is rising'. The nonreductionist theories I will mention are possible-worlds semantics, the model-theoretic aspect of situation semantics, Davidsonian semantics, and Katzian semantics. The reductionist theories are CRS; Gricean theories, by which I mean theories that explain the semantic in terms of the mental; and what I call "indicator" theories, those whose metaphor for the semantic is the relation between a thermometer and the temperature it indicates, or the relation between the number of rings on the stump and the age of the tree when cut down. These theories regard the nomological relation between the indicator and what it indicates as the prime semantic relation. In this camp I include views of Dretske, Stampe, Fodor, and one aspect of Barwise and Perry's position.

The reductionist/nonreductionist distinction as I have drawn it does not do justice to Davidson's views. The problem is *not* that Davidson's work on, for example, the logical form of action sentences makes him a nonreductionist, whereas his view about what meaning is makes him a reductionist. As I pointed out, the reductionist and nonreductionist enterprises are compatible, and there is nothing at all odd about one person contributing to both. The problem, rather, is that Davidson has views about what meaning is, thereby making it seem (misleadingly) that he is a reductionist, however, his views of what meaning is are clearly *not* reductionist. (See Davidson [1984, p. xiv], where he describes his project as explaining meaning in terms of truth.) A finer-grained classification would distinguish between (1a) reductionist and (1b) nonreductionist theories about what meaning is and distinguish both types of views of what meaning is from (2) the project of model-theoretic semantics, Davidson's work on action sentences, and the like. In labeling (1a) as reductionist and everything else as nonreductionist, I've unhappily lumped together (1b) and (2), but this is unimportant for my purposes, since I am ignoring (1b) theories.

Being reductionist in intent, CRS should not really be regarded as competing with the nonreductionist theories. Nonetheless, I shall be comparing CRS with these nonreductionist theories as regards the desiderata I have listed. To prevent misunderstanding, I want to emphasize that I am not attempting to criticize these nonreductionist theories. Rather, my purpose is to make it clear that they should not be seen as pursuing the same goals as the reductionist theories.

I will also be comparing CRS with the reductionist theories. These theories are in the same ball park as CRS, but most are not genuine competitors. Since CRS in the version I am promoting is a two-factor theory, it requires the partnership of a reductionist truth-conditional theory. Indicator semantics is a candidate. Another candidate that is both truth-conditional and reductionist is Field's interpretation (1972) of Tarski. I won't be discussing it because I know of no claims on its behalf that it is a full theory of meaning—indeed, Field views it as a candidate for the truth-conditional factor of a two-factor theory (see Field 1977). Though I do not regard indicator semantics as a real competitor, I will mention serious problems with the view.

The only circumstance in which the reductionist truth-conditional theories would be genuine competitors to CRS would be if one of them could satisfy a range of desiderata of the sort I've mentioned. I consider it no problem if they can contribute to *some* such desiderata, since there is often more than one way of explaining something. But if some truth-conditional reductionist theory could satisfy *all of them,* the need for the conceptual role component would be brought into question.

The only approach that remains as a genuine competitor is the Gricean approach. I shall not attempt to refute this approach (for one thing, as will appear, it has considerable similarity to mine). I mainly aim to block an argument that anyone who favors a functionalist approach to meaning should adopt some sort of Gricean view rather than CRS.

A brief guide to the semantic theories I will be mentioning: I lump the truth-conditional theories minus indicator semantics plus Katzian semantics together as nonreductionist. Gricean and indicator theories, by contrast, are reductionist.

$$
\left.
\begin{array}{l}
\text{Situation semantics} ---- \\
\text{Davidsonian semantics} ---- \\
\text{Possible-worlds semantics} -- \\
\left\{ -- \text{ Indicator semantics} ---- \right.
\end{array}
\right\}
\begin{array}{l}
\text{Truth} \\
-- \text{conditional}
\end{array}
$$

Reductionist $\left\{ --- \right.$ Gricean semantics

Katzian semantics

As you can see, four of the six theories I will be contrasting with CRS are classifiable as truth-conditional. While CRS in the version I am adopting has a truth-conditional component, it will play little role in satisfying the desiderata. Thus it may seem that I am taking truth-conditional theories to task for not doing something that they were never intended to do. The rationale for the contrasts I will be making is that radical disagreement is so common with regard to matters semantic that there is little consensus about which semantic theories have which purposes. For each of the truth-conditional theories I will mention, claims have been made on its behalf in the direction of satisfying desiderata of the sort I've listed.

Representationalism

Before I go on to discuss how CRS satisfies the desiderata, I want to make sure my representationalism is not misunderstood. I am committed to complex reasoning being a process that involves the manipulation of symbolic structures. I am not committed to the idea that these symbolic structures are *independent* of representational states of mind, mental objects that are viewed by an inner eye. It is convenient to talk in terms of internal representations as if they were literally sentences in the brain (and I do talk this way), but this talk is, of course, metaphorical. My commitment will be satisfied if the representational states themselves constitute a combinatorial system; that is, if they are structured in a way that allows parts corresponding to words to be combined so as to constitute representational states corresponding to sentences.[40]

I am not committed to the manipulation of symbol structures being involved in *all* reasoning, since I want to allow for "primitive" reasonings out of which complex reasonings are built. (E.g., in some computers, multiplication is a symbolic process in that a multiplication problem is "decomposed" into a series of addition problems; but addition itself is not "decomposed" into another type of problem, but rather accomplished by a hardware device, a primitive processor, that contains no internal representations. If you ask how the computer multiplies, you get a representational answer; if you ask how it adds, you do not.) I am not committed to rules for reasoning being themselves represented. Such an assumption involves notorious paradoxes, and in computers we have examples of symbol manipulators many of whose symbol-manipulating "rules" are implicit in the way the hardware works (See Block 1983). I am not committed to any detailed thesis as to what the internal computations are like. For example, I am not committed to any such idea as that in computing '99 + 99 = 198' there is any internal analog of carrying a '1', or any such symbol manipulation of the sort a person might carry out in doing such a sum.

Further, the claim that we are symbol manipulators is intended as empirical and contingent. I find the idea perfectly intelligible and possible that we are "analog" computers whose internal activities involve no symbol manipulation at all. I make the representationalist assumption for two rea-

sons: the most promising line of research in cognitive science is massively
committed to representationalism, and it seems to be paying off; and I
believe that there are an astronomical number of thoughts that people are
capable of having. I would argue that the number of thinkable sentences
thirty words long is greater than the number of particles in the universe.
Consider the set of entertainable sentences of the following form: $n \times m = q$, where n and m are in the hundreds of billions range familiar from the
national budget (twelve figures), and q is twice as long. Many of these sen-
tences are not believable (e.g., nine hundred billion times itself $= 0$), but each
is certainly thinkable. The number of distinct entertainable propositions of
the form mentioned is on the order of forty-six digits long. An instructive
comparison: the number of seconds since the beginning of time is only about
eighteen digits long. I don't see what the mechanism could be by which a
person can think any one of such a vast variety of thoughts without some sort
of combinatorial system being involved. My representationalist assumption
is in the spirit of Smart's claim that pain is a brain state: an empirically based
thesis about what reasoning most likely is.

Of the semantic theories I will be contrasting with CRS, only Fodor's
version of indicator semantics has a comparable representationalist assumption; nonetheless, I do not think that my representationalism ought to be
seen as the key difference between the theory I am advocating and most of
the other theories. For one thing, a denotational theory like Fodor's could
be framed in terms of assent to English sentences instead of computational
relations to internal sentences. Fodor is a sententialist in that he believes that
propositional attitude states are relations to internal sentences. But the internal sentences have no privileged *semantic* role in his account. Also, there are
nonrepresentationalist avenues towards the type of functionalist-based semantics I am advocating—for example, Loar's and Schiffer's version of the
Gricean program. If CRS in the form in which I am advocating it were to
meet serious empirical problems because of its representationalism, I would
pursue a nonrepresentationalist version.

Question: If my basic commitment is to a functionalist theory of meaning, why don't I *now* adopt a nonrepresentationalist version of functionalism
(e.g., the Loar-Schiffer program) instead of pursuing a program based on a
risky empirical assumption (representationalism)? Answer: As I shall point
out later, even if the Loar-Schiffer program works for natural language, if
there is a language of thought not identical to natural language, their theory
won't work for *it*. So *both* theories are subject to empirical risk. Theirs is
inadequate if representationalism is true, whereas mine is wrong if representationalism is false.

SATISFYING THE DESIDERATA

In the rest of the paper, I shall be mainly concerned with showing how CRS satisfies the desiderata I sketched above and contrasting CRS's treatment with treatments possible for other approaches.

What Is the Relation between Meaning and Reference/Truth?

From the CRS perspective, what this question comes to is: what is the relation between the two factors? Are the two factors independent? Do they fit together in a coherent way?

I think the conceptual role factor is *primary* in that it determines the nature of the referential factor, but not vice versa. Suppose, for illustration, that one of the familiar versions of the causal theory of reference is true. What makes it true? Facts about how our language works—specifically, how it applies to counterfactual circumstances. Kripke convinces us that it is possible that Moses did not do any of the things the Bible said he did, but rather was an itinerant Egyptian fig merchant who spread stories about how he was found in the bulrushes, saw the burning bush, and so on. Kripke is convincing because we use names such as 'Moses' to refer to the person who bears the right causal relations to our uses of the name, even if he does not fit the descriptions we associate with the name. This is a fact about the conceptual role of names, one that can be ascertained in the armchair, just by thinking about intuitions about counterfactual circumstances.

Of course, our names could have functioned differently; for example, they could have functioned as the competing "cluster of descriptions" theory dictates. If that had been how names functioned, it too could have been ascertained by thinking of the right thought experiments, since it would be a fact purely about the internal conceptual role of names. For example, if 'Moses' functioned according to the cluster of descriptions theory, the intuition about Kripke's story dictated by the way names function would be "Oh, in that case Moses doesn't exist—there never was a Moses." What makes the cluster theory wrong is that that just isn't the intuition dictated by the function of our terms—the intuition, rather, is given by: "In that case, Moses wouldn't have done the things the Bible ascribes to him."

(Note that one cannot *identify* the intuition dictated by the function of names with the intuitions we actually have about cases, since there are all sorts of other factors that influence those intuitions. In the early days of the mind-body identity theory, many philosophers voiced the intuition that there was something semantically wrong with "I just drank a glass of H_2O." Presumably, they were influenced by the "oddity" of mixing scientific terms with mundane terms. Using intuitions to isolate facts about the function of names is not a simple matter.)

In short, what theory of reference is true is a fact about how referring terms function in our thought processes. This is an aspect of conceptual role. So it is the conceptual role of referring expressions that determines what theory of reference is true. Conclusion: the conceptual role factor determines the nature of the referential factor.

Note the crucial difference between saying that the conceptual role factor determines the nature of the referential factor and saying that the conceptual role factor determines reference. I hold the former, but not the latter. The two-factor theory is compatible with a variety of different mappings from a single conceptual role onto aspects of worlds. For example, a word with the conceptual role of our 'water' could map onto one substance here, another on Twin Earth, and another on Triplet Earth. What is in the head—conceptual role—determines the nature of reference without determining reference itself.

If what I've just argued is right, it is easy to see that conceptual role determines the function from context to reference and truth value. It is the referential factor (as described in a theory of reference) that determines that 'water' picks out H_2O on Earth, but XYZ on Twin Earth. For example, on a causal theory of reference, this will be held to be a matter of the causal relation to different liquids in the two contexts. But since the referential factor must take context into account in this way in order to dictate reference, it will determine the function from context to reference.

What Is the Connection between the Meaning of an Expression and Knowing or Learning Its Meaning?

CRS says meaning is conceptual role. If someone uses a word (or a word functions in her brain) that has the conceptual role of 'dog', then the word in question means the same as 'dog'. If a person's brain changes so as to cause a word to be used (by her or her brain) so as to have the conceptual role in question, then she has acquired the concept of a dog (unless she already has it); if the word in question is 'dog' itself or a mentalese standard associate of 'dog', and if the brain change is a case of learning, then she has learned the meaning of 'dog'. Also, CRS allows us to see why evidence for proper use of 'dog' is evidence for knowing the meaning of 'dog'. For a word to have proper use is for it to function in a certain way; hence someone whose word 'dog' functions appropriately thereby knows the meaning of dog; hence evidence of function can be evidence of knowing the word. Finally, CRS allows us to see how knowing meaning is related to our ability to use language. To know the meaning of an English word is for it to function in a certain way, and the obtaining of this function, together with certain psychological facts (e.g., about motivation) explains correct external usage.

The nonreductionist theories should not be regarded as aimed at answering the questions just discussed, but should nonreductionists disagree, they could give a kind of answer (in the metatheory, of course). A theory that postulates a type of semantic value V (e.g., truth conditions, situations, sets of possible worlds, markerese structures) can say that what it is to know or acquire the meaning of a sentence is to know or learn or acquire its V. But saying this only shifts the question to what it is to know or acquire V's. Consider the project of producing an account of what it is for 'cat' to acquire its semantic value in the child. If the semantic value is conceptual role, we can at least picture how the project would go. But what would the project be like—if not the same as the one we just pictured—for semantic values like truth conditions, situations, sets of possible worlds, or markerese structures (rather, senses expressed by these structures)? Davidsonians say that to know the meaning of 'Snow is white' is just to know that it is true iff snow is white. But, as Harman has pointed out, saying this just raises the issue of how one represents to oneself that snow is white. If one uses some sort of symbol structure (and how else is one supposed to do it?), the Davidsonian has only pushed the question back a step, for now we want a theory of the meaning of the symbol structure itself.

Further, there is an open question, on these nonreductionist semantic theories, as to how knowing a word's or a sentence's V could explain our ability to use the word or sentence appropriately. For example, suppose knowing the meaning of "The balloon burst" is knowing what situation it denotes. But how can knowledge of the denoted situation explain how we use the sentence appropriately?[41] Not that these questions could not be answered by the nonreductionist—for example, they could *adopt CRS*. The point is that the nonreductionist semantic theories I mentioned have no account of their own. (Of course, as I keep saying, this is not a *defect* of these theories.)

Another matter that distinguishes CRS from the nonreductionist theories (and the non-Gricean reductionist theories) is that CRS promises to give a semantic explanation of certain "principles of charity." Many philosophers of language imagine a "radical translation" or "radical interpretation" situation, in which one is trying to interpret utterances (typically, the problem is introduced with an anthropological situation, and then it is observed that the same issues arise in justifying the homophonic translation). As many philosophers have stressed, one must consider one's hypotheses about what the foreign terms mean together with hypotheses about the speakers' beliefs (and other propositional attitudes). It is the "simplicity" of the *total* theory that counts. Now it is often said that it is the *truth* of the alien beliefs that counts (Davidson sometimes says this); but this seems clearly wrong, in the absence of reason to believe that the alien has got things right. A better approach to principles of charity emphasizes coherence. Attribution of irrational belief cannot go on without limit; eventually, one loses one's grip on the content of what one has attributed. But this kind of charity can be explained by CRS. To understand the alien's beliefs, one has to appreciate their inferential roles (or rather, the inferential roles of the symbol structures that express them).

If the mismatch between the alien's inferential roles and our own is too great, there will be no way for us to translate what he says (cf. Loar 1982).

Further, to the extent that inferential role is normative (an issue within CRS, and therefore one I have avoided), there will be rationality constraints on what can sensibly be attributed. These rationality constraints are in no way a by-product of considerations about translation or about a mismatch of conceptual roles; rather, they are a matter of constraints on the conceptual roles that can possibly express concepts.

Let us return to the familiar claim that to know the meaning of a sentence is to know its truth conditions. In any sense in which this claim has substantial content, it is not at all obvious. For example, it is possible to imagine someone knowing the entire set of possible worlds in which a sentence is true without knowing what the sentence means. For the *way the person represents the set of possible worlds* may not capture its meaning. Perhaps it is possible to develop a canonical notation for representing possible worlds. In terms of such a notation, one could develop an ordering of possible worlds, and thus one might be able to exhibit a set of possible worlds via an arithmetical predicate that picks out the right numbers. But if one knows, say, that the prime-numbered possible worlds are the ones in which a sentence is true, does one thereby know its meaning? Further, even if no such ordering exists, one can imagine representing the possible worlds in which a sentence is true in a way that makes use of a motley of devices, different devices for different classes of worlds. Such a representation needn't capture what the worlds have in common in virtue of which they are the ones in which the sentence is true.[42]

Though it is not at all obvious that knowing truth conditions guarantees knowing meaning, the converse claim is more plausible. And, as Harman has pointed out,[43] CRS can explain this in the following way: normal users of language understand certain metalinguistic ideas, such as the disquotational use of 'true', and this is what gives them knowledge of truth conditions. The conceptual roles of 'true' and nonsemantic terms yield knowledge of biconditionals like " 'Snow is white' is true iff snow is white." But even if knowing meaning involves knowing truth conditions, one can hardly jump to the conclusion that knowing meaning *is* knowing truth conditions.

The fertility of the CRS account of learning can be illustrated by its solution to what might be tendentiously called Fodor's Paradox. Fodor's Paradox is posed by the following argument (Fodor 1975):

1. Learning the meaning of a word is a matter of hypothesis formation and testing.
2. When we learn a new English term (e.g., 'chase'), we can do so only by hypothesizing definitions in terms already known (including terms of the language of thought).

3. The history of attempts to define English terms "decompositional-ly" (e.g., 'try to catch') has been a dismal failure, and there are familiar Quinean considerations that explain why. This suggests that most English terms cannot be so defined.
4. Therefore, when a term like 'chase' is learned, it must be learned by hypothesizing a definition in terms of a *single* term of the language of thought, 'CHASE', which has the same meaning as 'chase'. In other words, the typical word-learning hypothesis has the form: 'chase' means 'CHASE'.
5. Therefore, for most terms of English, we grasp them only because they correspond to (indeed, are standardly associated with) innate terms of mentalese.

I call the argument a paradox because the conclusion is obviously unacceptable; the issue is which premise to give up. Why is the conclusion unacceptable? Could scientific concepts like 'meson' and 'enzyme', as well as technological ideas such as 'monitor', 'zipper', and 'transistor', be *individually* innate? If so, either evolution mysteriously foresaw the concepts needed for science and technology, or else progress in science and technology is possible only with respect to a highly arbitrary, accidentally prefigured vo-cabulary. Were this the case, one could expect that some accidental modifica-tion of some current technological device would produce a new and utterly unintelligible device that we could use the way a two-year-old uses a tele-phone while confused about whether it is a game in which daddy is somehow hiding inside the phone.

So what premise must go? The first premise is empirically plausible, justified, for example, by appeal to the type of errors children make. Also, hypothesis formation and testing is the only model of learning we have.

Much ink has been shed over the third premise. No doubt readers have made up their minds on the issue, and what I could say in a brief space here would be of no use at all. I shall confine myself to the remark that *if* it has been shown that there aren't many analytic decompositional definitions in natural languages,[44] that doesn't *show* that there aren't many decomposition-al definitions of natural-language terms in mentalese; but the burden of proof is on those who think mentalese differs from English in this respect.

The premise CRS militates against is 2. According to CRS, the way we learn a new English term needn't be a matter of definition at all. Rather, the CRS picture is that the term (or its newly formed mentalese standard associ-ate) comes to have a certain function. To the extent that hypotheses are involved, they are hypotheses about how the term functions in thought, reasoning, problem solving, and so forth.

One way to see what the CRS proposal comes to is to reflect on how one learned the concepts of elementary physics, or anyway, how I did. When

I took my first physics course, I was confronted with quite a bit of new terminology all at once: 'energy', 'momentum', 'acceleration', 'mass', and the like. As should be no surprise to anyone who noted the failure of positivists to define theoretical terms in observation language, I never learned any definitions of these new terms in terms I already knew. Rather, what I learned was how to *use* the new terminology—I learned certain relations among the new terms themselves (e.g., the relation between force and mass, neither of which can be defined in old terms), some relations between the new terms and old terms, and, most importantly, how to generate the right numbers in answers to questions posed in the new terminology. This is just the sort of story a proponent of CRS should expect.[45]

Note that CRS is not a psychological theory. In particular, though it can tell us that Fodor's second premise *needn't* be true, it is compatible with its actually being true. For it is compatible with the CRS account that the way one learns to use a new term correctly is by linking it to a term one already has that functions appropriately.

Let me now raise a bogeyman that will come up repeatedly: psychologism. Am I just making the verbal maneuver of using 'semantics' to mean the study of the psychology of meaning, rather than the study of meaning proper? As pointed out in connection with the question of whether narrow meaning is genuine meaning, this question is a quibble. However, my answer is that although knowing is a mental state and learning is a mental process, it is not psychologism to suppose that a theory of what meaning *is* ought to be in some way relevant to what it is to know or learn meaning. For example, one can imagine quite different ideas of what good taste is (ranging from a form of knowing how to a form of knowing that) that would engender quite different ideas of what it is to learn good taste. Closer to home, consider the view that philosophy is conceptual analysis contrasted with the view that philosophy is a kind of history (in which heavy emphasis is placed on knowing the texts). These conceptions would lead to different ideas of what it is to learn philosophy.

But how is the idea that meaning is, say, truth conditions, supposed to be in any way relevant to what it is to learn or know meaning? (Unless truth conditions are identified with *verification conditions,* in which case we have a rather unattractive *special case* of CRS in which conceptual role is role in verifying.) The issue of what it is to learn or know truth conditions, or situation denoted, or associated semantic marker, or function from possible worlds to truth values is just as much in need of illumination from a theory like CRS as what it is to learn or know meaning.

I chose the desideratum about learning as the place to bring up the psychologism bogeyman first because this desideratum is perhaps the most psychological of the ones I mentioned; so it is this desideratum for which, if I am just changing the subject, it should be most apparent. My hope is that exposing the weakness of the psychologism charge here will allow me to pay less attention to it with regard to later desiderata.

What Makes Meaningful Expressions Meaningful?

I will use this section to lay out the basic ideas of the comparisons with the alternative theories, especially the reductionist competitors. So this will be a long section. According to CRS, what makes an expression meaningful is that it has a conceptual role of a certain type, one that we may call "appropriate." The difference between 'cat' and 'glurg' is that 'cat' has an appropriate conceptual role, whereas 'glurg' does not. What gives 'cat' the particular meaning that it has is its particular conceptual role. The difference between meaningful expressions with different meanings ('cat' and 'dog') is a conceptual role difference *within* the category of appropriate conceptual roles.[46]

The dominant perspectives in semantics—possible worlds semantics, situation semantics, and the approaches of Davidson and of Katz, can be used to give responses to my questions that look just as good at first glance. Suppose they say, for example, that what makes a meaningful sentence meaningful is that it has truth conditions, or a set of truth values in possible worlds, or an associated (sense expressed by a) markerese structure, or a denoted situation. But such answers just *put off* the semantic issue. For now we want to know what it is that makes for the difference— what it is in virtue of which there *is* a difference—between sentences that *have* and sentences that *lack* truth conditions, truth values in possible worlds, associated markerese structures, or denoted situations, and to these questions these non-reductionist perspectives have no answers.[47]

Of course, one can also ask of CRS what the difference is between sentences that have and sentences that lack conceptual roles. But CRS has an answer: certain causal properties. And if the questioner wants to know why sentences have the causal properties they do, again there are answers, at least in principle, to be sought, of the same sort that one would give to "Why do genes have the causal properties they have?"

What the difference comes down to is that CRS aims for a reductionist account, indeed, a naturalistic-reductionist account, in proposing to explain a semantic property in terms of a naturalistic, nonsemantic property: causation. CRS's reductionism and naturalism allow it to promise an answer to "What makes a meaningful expression meaningful?" The semantic approaches mentioned in the paragraph before last, being nonreductionist, cannot answer this question.

Although the dominant views in semantics should be regarded (in my view) as just not directed towards the sort of question typified by this desideratum, it should be noted that they often seem to be responding to much the same motivation that lies behind a naturalistic-reductionistic account. For instance, Davidsonians, though not reductionists, make much of the claim that a theory of the sort they favor will allow a deduction from a finite nonsemantic base of a specification of truth conditions for any indicative sentence.

On the whole, most of the standard approaches have been primarily concerned with the *relations* among meanings, not the nature of meaning itself. For example, the standard approaches have been concerned with an aspect of compositionality: how the meanings of larger elements such as sentences are related to the meanings of smaller elements such as words. Another sort of issue motivating the standard theories is what we can tell about the logical form of "Sam ate with a fork" from the fact that if it is true, so is "Sam ate." Another issue (one that has been a stumbling block for possible-worlds semantics and one that situation semantics hopes to make progress on) is what the relation is between the semantic value of 'Grass is green' and 'John believes that grass is green'. But these questions can be and have been discussed without ever broaching the issue of what it is in virtue of which expressions have their meanings in the first place.

The main aim of most of the standard approaches to semantics has been to *correlate* meanings with certain objects, so that relations among meanings are mirrored by formal relations among the corresponding objects. These approaches have often been concerned with a purely *descriptive* project, a kind of "curve-fitting," not with explaining the nature of meaning.

The major tradition within this conception of semantics is well described in Barwise and Perry (1984).[48]

> We have intuitions about the logical behavior of a certain class of sentences. With attitudes reports, these are largely intuitions about the phenomenon of "opacity": reluctance to substitute co-referential terms and the like. We codify these intuitions in a set of logical principles, and then semantics consists of finding a collection of plausible set-theoretic models that makes the logical principles come out correct. I think this is the traditional conception in semantics, and it is the setting for Montague Grammar, but it is what I would now call the thin conception of semantics.

As suggested earlier, the Barwise and Perry effort to produce a semantics that satisfies a richer, "thicker" conception of semantics can be seen as moving on two fronts: one involves model-theoretic ideas (e.g., the idea of a partial model), the other a kind of indicator semantics (discussed later in this section). Another aspect of the thickness that Barwise and Perry seek is to make semantics compatible with commonsense psychology, for example, to avoid the possible-worlds semantics problem that one would seem to believe everything logically equivalent to what one believes.[49]

Now Barwise and Perry (1984) have advocated a functionalist theory of propositional attitudes. Perhaps they (and some Davidsonians, Katzians, and possible-worlds semanticists) envision a two-stage process of semantic theorizing: first, a nonreductive account of meaning*s*, and second a reductive account aimed at desiderata something like the ones I have mentioned. Theorists in these traditions have not, however, put forward second-stage theories. I know of only two types of reductionist approaches to semantics other than CRS (and the causal theory of reference, which I am not discussing in any detail); after considering an objection, I shall sketch these approaches and their relation to CRS.

It may be objected that I have confused:

(i)   In virtue of what is a particular token/ches/-noise an utterance of the English word 'chase' meaning, of course, 'try to catch')?

(ii) In virtue of what does the English word type 'chase' mean 'try to catch'?[50]

It may be said that (ii) has no nontrivial answer—it is part of what it *is* to be the English word 'chase' to mean what it does.[51] Asking (ii), on this view, is like asking what makes the number two even. If it weren't, it wouldn't be the number two. (Or: 'Two is even' is analytic.)

On the objector's view, the problem I raise does not *disappear,* but is rather transformed. Instead of asking what it is in virtue of which 'chase' means what it does, I must ask what it is in virtue of which a token is of the type *'chase' in English,* with the meaning that that word necessarily (?) has. Since the problem survives, I suppose that the real objection here is that the question I raise (being about a token) is really pragmatic rather than semantic.

Perhaps some perspective can be gained by contrasting the question about language with the question of why, in the American system of government, cabinet officers are approved by the Senate but presidential advisors are not? Here there seems little utility to seeing the American system of government as an abstract object that has this property necessarily (or analytically). It is not helpful to see the question as one about whether a certain token system is a token of the type "the American system of government." But is language more like a political institution or more like mathematics? This question won't get us very far. What issues belong in pragmatics as opposed to semantics is a matter to be settled by finding out which way of dividing up issues makes the most theoretical sense, not by consulting intuitions about whether language is more social than mathematical.

The important point against the objection is that it is a mistake to see the contrast the objector raises as hinging on the type/token distinction. This becomes especially obvious when one is reminded that the English language is in constant flux. 'Yuppie' has no meaning in English-1982, but it has a meaning in English-1985. And 'chase' may mean something different in English-1988 from what it does in English-1985. If a word's meaning is a necessary—though language-relative—property of the word, then (1) we must regard different dialects and language stages as in the relevant sense, different languages; and (2) we must recognize a sense of 'word type' in which word types are language specific. So we cannot speak of one word's different meanings in different dialects. But this is just a peculiar way of talking. As we have seen, there is a natural use of the notion of a word type in which we *can* speak of one word as having different meanings in different dialects (as is the case with 'yuppie'). So, deploying the notion of word type in the latter way, the question of why the word type 'chase' means 'try to catch' in English-1985 is not trivial.

The Reductionist Alternatives

There are two competing families of approaches to semantics that *are* reductionist,[52] and hence that *do* have genuine answers to the questions posed in the desiderata I've been talking about. One of them is the approach of reducing meaning to *mental content*. Call this type of approach "Gricean." The Gricean approach as developed by Grice himself, and later Schiffer, reduces speaker meaning to the content of speaker's intentions. For the speaker to mean such and such by what he says is for him to intend his utterance to affect the propositional attitudes of hearers in certain ways. Sentence meaning, on this theory, can be reduced to speaker meaning via a conventional correlation between sentences in the language and communicative intentions. This conventional correlation makes it practicable for a speaker to use certain sentences to produce certain effects in hearers.[53]

Searle has an approach that is Gricean in my sense, in which the intention isn't communicative but rather an intention to produce an object with certain "satisfaction conditions" (Searle 1983a). A rather different sort of Gricean approach was taken by Ramsey, who attempted to reduce the meaning of an item of language to the beliefs that would be expressed by that item.

Gricean approaches have been enveloped in controversies, none of which will be discussed here. Nor is this the place for a full-dress comparison between Gricean and conceptual role accounts. However, there are a few points of comparison that can be made rather briefly. Although I do not want to belittle the Gricean accomplishment, without a naturalistic account of the mental, the Gricean approach has little to contribute to the project I am discussing. One who is concerned with the questions I have been asking about meaning will be equally concerned with corresponding questions about intentional content. Consider, for example, the three questions involved in the desideratum currently being discussed:

1. What is it about a meaningful expression that makes it meaningful?
2. What is responsible for an expression's having the particular meaning it has?

3. What is the difference between expressions with different meanings in virtue of which they have different meanings?

The Gricean faces corresponding questions about intentional content, viz.:

1'. What is it about a contentful state that makes it contentful?
2'. What is responsible for a state's having the particular intentional content it has?
3'. What is the difference between states with different intentional contents in virtue of which they have their different contents?

In the light of this problem, Griceans have a number of options. First, they could simply regard intentional content as primitive—in other words, regard questions like 1', 2', and 3' as having no answers. For Griceans to take this line would be to give up on satisfying the desiderata I've been talking about. This is the nonnaturalistic option I mentioned. Another line would be to pursue some nonfunctionalist reductionist strategy, such as physiological reductionism. This is an unpromising tack (see Fodor 1974), and it is especially unattractive if one is interested in a semantics that might apply to the language use of an intelligent computer or computerlike machine, if we ever construct one.[54]

Another option is Searle's reduction of intentionality to *the brain or whatever has "equivalent causal powers."* The wild card of "equivalent causal powers" allows Searle to avoid the usual drawbacks of physiological reduction. For example, the theory is not chauvinist because it allows for the possibility that the control systems of intelligent machines can have causal powers equivalent to ours. However, the other side of the coin is that the theory is far from naturalistic. To say a machine has causal powers equivalent to those of the human brain is only to say that the machine has causal properties that result in intentionality. So Searle must either (1) regard intentionality as primitive, in which case he has not answered the questions I am talking about, or (2) he must give some nonintentional analysis of "equivalent causal powers." It is clear that Searle takes option (1). That is, he has no intention of giving a reductionist theory of intentionality, though he takes physicochemical properties of *each being* that has intentional states to cause that being's intentional states. (See Searle 1984.)

Searle repeatedly *says* that it is an empirical question whether a given machine has equivalent causal powers, but the careful reader discerns that it is an empirical question only in that the machine itself *will know* if it does indeed have equivalent causal powers.[55] The crux of the disagreement between Searle and me is not about whether a sapient and sentient machine will have to have innards with causal powers equivalent to those in us (we agree on this); the crux rather is whether some sort of functionalist thesis is true of us. For if intentionality can be characterized functionally, then *the way to make a machine with intentional states is to make a machine functionally equivalent to us—the equivalent causal powers of the machine's brain will come along for free.* Searle's argument against functionalism is his "Chinese room" argument, to be discussed briefly later in this paper.

There is one final "methodological" point to be made against Searle. One should not adopt his view without proper exploration of the alternatives, since if Searle's account is true, the sciences of mind and meaning would seem to be severely limited. In particular, it is hard to see how science (or philosophy) could ever tell us anything substantive about what the source of autonomous meaning or intentionality is.

Another Gricean option is that championed by Schiffer and Loar (and perhaps Grice): they couple the reduction of meaning to the mental with a functionalist reduction of the mental. A major difference between the functionalism-based Gricean theory and CRS is that the Gricean theory is not committed to any sort of representationalism, even of the weak sort that CRS is committed to (viz., that thoughts have recombinable ingredients). This difference between the Loar-Schiffer account and the CRS account is a disagreement about the empirical facts about how the mind works (or about how much philosophical ice such empirical facts cut), not about the functional source of meaning.[56] In sum, in one version Gricean theory is not a competitor to CRS; in another version, it is a competitor but has drawbacks; and in another version, it differs with respect to representationalism and, of course, the details of the Gricean reduction in terms of intentions, as well as the focus on public language meaning as opposed to idiolect narrow meaning.

I shall now turn to an argument by Loar (1981, chap. 9; 1983) against the sort of view I am advocating. As I understand it, Loar's argument is that a theory of meaning should not depend on a speculative psychological claim such as representationalism. So Loar advocates the Gricean reduction of external language to mentality (coupled with a functionalist reduction of the mental). If representationalism happens to be true, Loar favors what amounts to a conceptual role semantics theory of the internal language (though not external language). My objection is simple: if representationalism is false, CRS is certainly false. But if representationalism is true, Loar is stuck with an intention-based semantics for external language plus a conceptual role semantics for internal language—whereas CRS makes do with the latter type of semantics for *both* types of language. (Of course, Loar is concerned with public meaning rather than narrow idolect meaning, but this fact does not play any direct role in his argument.) So, if representationalism is true, the Loar-Schiffer account seems at a disadvantage.

Is there some way in which the Gricean account could be extended to internal language? Computation in internal symbol systems appears to be of a rather "automatic" sort which gains efficiency through inflexibility.[57] For example, if one memorizes a list of six letters, say 'UEKNMG', and one is asked whether 'E' is on the list, one does an "exhaustive" serial search, looking at all six letters, one by one, even if 'E' is the first letter in the list.[58] (This is one of the better tested results in all of cognitive psychology.) Is it at all plausible that one forms an *intention* to look at all the items, or to do an exhaustive serial search? Further, even if the uses of the internal system are intentional in some sense, surely the intentions are not intentions to *communicate,* as in the standard Gricean theories.

But what if the internal symbol system *is* English (that is, the same as whatever external language is spoken)? Can the Gricean then avoid the problem of the last paragraph by giving a theory of meaning for English, and simply postulating that sentences in the language of thought have the same meaning as in English? First, it is not at all obvious that the meaning of English as used in thought (if it is used in thought) is somehow derivative from its use in communication. Why not the other way around? Second, and more importantly, I have talked as if it is perfectly possible that English is the language of thought, but this is simply *not* in the cards. For one thing, external language is radically ambiguous, both syntactically and semantically. If there is no confusion in *thought* as between financial banks and river banks, then one word in the internal system presumably does not carry both meanings. And if someone says "I tire of visiting relatives," knowing full well whether relatives are visiting her or whether she is the visitor, then it is doubtful that the English sentence could be the vehicle of the thought. (But see Block and Bromberger 1980.) From what I've said thus far, one might suppose that the language of thought might be a kind of regimented English (e.g., syntactic trees with English terminal nodes, as suggested for part of the language of thought in Harman, [1970]). But, at most, some sort of regimented English could be *part* of the language of thought. (Indeed, although there is controversy over whether English is part of the language of thought, there is none over whether English is the *whole* of the language of thought.) For example, there is enormous evidence for representations in mental imagery (see Block 1983 for discussion and references to the literature); and it is quite out of the question that these representations are in English (none of the defenders of the view that the representations of imagery are languagelike have suggested such a thing). When one looks in any detail at what a languagelike representation would have to be to play the role of representations of imagery, this is obvious. Nor would any such suggestion be remotely sensible for the representations of early vision (see Marr 1982).

If English is part of the language of thought, it would seem especially peculiar to treat the semantics of that part of the language of thought so differently from the semantics of external English.

In sum, the Griceans cannot claim that their account is to be preferred to CRS on the ground that their account has no empirical vulnerability, since both accounts have an element of empirical vulnerability. Nonetheless, the choice between the two approaches seems mainly a matter of philosophical metatheory. If one wishes to insulate one's semantics from experimental falsification, while being willing to tolerate ad hoc addition of components to handle experimental discoveries, the Loar-Schiffer perspective is better. If one is interested in a semantics based on the best empirical theories extant, CRS is better.

There is a second family of reductionist approaches to semantics that could be claimed to satisfy my desiderata: what I called "indicator semantics." Dretske (1981) and Stampe (1977) have similar versions, which I believe have been refuted by Fodor (1984), who has his own version of the view (Fodor 1984, forthcoming). Barwise and Perry (1983) have a view that has affinities to that of Dretske and Stampe, which I will not be able to discuss in detail here.

Dretske and Stampe say what it is for a sentence S to have the content that T in terms of tokens of S carrying information about T; carrying information, in turn, is cashed in terms of a nomological relation between S's and T's (roughly, an S nomologically requires a T).[59] Fodor objects that if error is possible, then a non-T can cause a tokening of S; but then why should we regard T as the state of affairs with which S is nomologically correlated when S has a *better* correlation with the disjunctive state of affairs whose disjuncts are T and the non-T state that causes S? So it seems that, on the Dretske/Stampe view, error is not possible.

Barwise uses the type/token distinction to deal with this problem. Suppose Ed "says 'It is 4 p.m.' at 4:30. While we can truly report that *Ed means what he says,* we can also truly report that *Ed's statement does not mean that it is 4 p.m.*"[60] Barwise's claim is that 'means' is ambiguous: there is one sense appropriate to tokens, another to types. A false token does not convey the information (this is the sense of meaning appropriate to tokens) conventionally associated with the corresponding type. (What about false sentence types? According to Barwise and Perry, it is only tokens [e.g., utterances] of sentences that have truth values, not sentence types.)

But I don't see how Barwise and Perry propose to avoid Fodor's objection in giving an informational account of sentence type meaning. One often gets the impression that their theory is that the meaning of a sentence type is the information *normally conveyed* by tokens of it. But what could 'normally' come to here? This cannot be shorthand for information conveyed by *true uses,* since that would ruin any attempt to give an account of the semantic in nonsemantic terms. If 'normal' is some sort of appeal to what is usual, however, Fodor's problem stands in the way. The correlation between tokens of S and the disjunction of T and pseudo-T states of affairs (ones that mislead people into false assertions of S) will inevitably be better than the correlation between S and T itself. Indeed, it is not hard to think of sentences whose assertions are more often false than true (e.g., famous last words). If 'normal' is some sort of appeal to the conventional, Barwise and Perry owe us an account of how that is supposed to connect with information conveyed and how they expect to avoid an analysis of conventionality in terms of intentional notions (as in Lewis's analysis). If it is a teleological notion, my guess is that their account will succumb to the kind of criticism now to be raised against Fodor's own account. (I've been assuming that Barwise and Perry do aim for an account of meaning in nonsemantic and nonintentional terms. This conception seems to me to permeate Barwise and Perry (1983), though it is never explicitly announced. In recent conversations with Barwise and Perry, I gather that they do not take themselves to be aiming for an account of meaning that is reductionist in this sense.)

Fodor's own view attempts to captitalize on the very fact that torpedoes the Dretske-Stampe approach. The basic idea is that, in a sense, error is not possible. The aim of Fodor's theory is to give a naturalistic account of what it is in virtue of which a sentence has the truth condition it has—what *makes* a sentence have the truth condition that it has. Some examples of theories that are in the same ball park: (1) the British empiricist theory that what gives a mental representation its truth condition is *resemblance* between the representation and the state of affairs, (2) the Skinnerian theory that what makes T the truth condition of S is that T is the discriminative stimulus of S. These are both false doctrines, for well-known reasons, but they are nonetheless naturalistic.

Fodor's task is one that many writers have seen the need for. As Field (1972) pointed out, the Tarskian approach, on one construal, yields the truth conditions of sentences only by means of *lists* of the referents of singular terms and the denotations of predicates. ('Boston swelters' is shown to be true only because the object that is listed as the referent of 'Boston' is in the set that is listed as the denotation of 'swelters'.) However, serious suggestions for solving this problem are thin on the ground. The only remotely plausible views I know of are the indicator semantics approach (common to Fodor, Dretske/Stampe, and Barwise and Perry); and Tarski's approach, construed as in Field (1972), together with a naturalistic theory of reference such as the causal theory. (Field's construal of Tarski is as giving a way of reducing truth to primitive denotation.)

The heart of the theory is an account of the truth conditions for mental sentences.[61] The account makes use of the claim that believing is a computational relation between a person and a mental sentence. (This computational relation is described below as the sentence being in the "belief box.") The claim is that what it is for T to be the truth condition for a mental sentence M is:

(1) If the cognitive system is functioning as it is *supposed* to; and
(2) idealizing away from epistemic limitations, then *M is in the "belief box"* $\longleftrightarrow$ *T*.

There are two "wheels" that drive this account: the teleological wheel, indicated by the 'supposed' in condition (1), and the epistemic idealization wheel. The idea behind Fodor's account is that there are cognitive mechanisms that are designed to put sentences in the belief box if and only if they are true. Error results when these mechanisms fail, or when epistemic conditions are less than ideal. Thus, if one can spell out the teleological notion and say what epistemically ideal conditions are in a naturalistic way, one will have a naturalistic theory of truth conditions.

There are serious problems with each of two "wheels." Let us begin with the epistemic idealization. One sees how it is supposed to go for cases of things that are too small to see, or happened too far away or too long ago. In these cases, what Fodor imagines we idealize away from is how big we are, where we are, or when we are. The idea is that if epistemically ideal conditions held, one's nose *would be rubbed in the truth* ; then mechanisms whose function it is to make one see the truth would take over, and one would indeed see the truth.

But what about statements to the effect that space is Riemannian, or that some quarks have charm, or even that one is in the presence of a magnetic field? Here, it is not enough to suppose one's nose is rubbed in the truth, for its no use having your nose rubbed in the facts—you have to come up with the right theory, too, and you have to know that it is the right theory. Imagine that in the long run the evidence converges on a Riemannian geometry for the universe The ideal scientific community will only believe in this claim if someone *thinks* of it. After all, it is quite intuitive to suppose that there is exactly one parallel to a given line at a given point, as Euclidean geometry tells us. No *series of measurements* can guarantee that anyone thinks of (or takes seriously, even if they think of) claiming that the Euclidean parallel postulate is false. To make a long story short, I don't see how such theoretical statements can be handled without in one way or another abandoning naturalism—for example, appealing to some sort of magical machinery or smuggling something semantic into the specification of the epistemic idealization. Suppose that whenever a "theoretical" property of the sort I just mentioned is raised, the Fodorean constructs an idealization in which humans have a perceptual detector that detects this property. Nothing semantic need be smuggled in with the description of these detectors: they say 'p' if and only if p. With such detectors, if your nose is rubbed in a fact, you will perceive it to obtain. But this response abandons naturalism. We have no idea how such detectors would work or even whether they are possible. Appealing to them is like saying: "Aha, what makes T the truth condition for M is that an omniscient wizard (i.e., one who believed 'p' if and only if p) would believe M if and only if T." You don't get a naturalistic account of truth conditions by appealing to the imaginary behavior of an imaginary being.

Idealizing often starts with something familiar and envisions a systematic change. So, in the last paragraph, we started with normal perceptual detectors and imagined them getting better and better (or, alternatively, more and more numerous). Another idea is to try envisioning systematic change in our theorizing mechanisms. Of course, we need a nonsemantic characterization of the ideal theorizing mechanisms. It won't do to say they find the *right* theory, since that is a semantic notion. Perhaps we can simply envision mechanisms that construct all possible theories and choose the simplest of them that is compatible with the data. The problems here are complex, and I can only hint at them. I would argue that on any formal notion of simplicity (e.g., one that involves counting symbols), it just is not true that the simplest theory is true. And even if the simplest theory were true, this assumption—which, of course, is a semantic assumption—would be part of the account. So, the account would not be naturalistic.[62] On the other hand, a *semantic* conception of simplicity (e.g., one that involves the concept of truth) won't be naturalistic either.

The second wheel driving Fodor's account is the idea that the cognitive system is *supposed* to function in a certain way. How is this teleological talk supposed to be understood? (Anyone who has read the current literature on teleology knows that promising suggestions are hard to find.)[63] Sometimes Fodor talks in terms of a notion of teleology provided by evolutionary theory. The cognitive system is supposed to function a certain way in that that is what evolution designed it to do.

One problem is that one cannot rely on evolution in such a simple way, since one can imagine a molecule-for-molecule duplicate of a baby who comes into being by chance and grows up in the normal way. Such a person would have language with the normal semantic properties, but no evolutionary "design."

Quite a different type of problem comes in through evolutionary theory itself. I think it is now quite generally accepted among evolutionary biologists that one cannot suppose that every phenotypic (i.e., actual) characteristic of an organism is an optimal design feature (in any nontrivial sense), given the environment.[64] To take a rather extreme case, for purposes of illustration, consider the phenomenon of "meiotic drive." Normally, each of a pair of genes has an equal chance of ending up in an offspring: if you have one blue-eye gene and one brown-eye gene, the chance that your child will get one of these from you is equal to the chance that it will get the other. But there are some known cases of genes—the mouse t-allele, for example—that beat out whatever gene they are paired to, thus propelling themselves into the next generation. Any such gene that does not have lethal effects on the phenotype is likely to spread in a population very quickly, even if it has suboptimal pheonotypic effects. The upshot is that there are known mechanisms (of which this is only one of many examples) that could have the effect of producing cognitive mechanisms that aim, to some extent, at properties of beliefs other than truth.[65]

One final point about Fodor's account. One peculiar fact about it is that it does not exploit the compositional structure of the language at all. (This is especially odd in view of the fact that Fodor's representationalism gives him objects in the belief box ripe for compositional exploitation.) In this respect, it is markedly inferior to Field's proposal (mentioned above), in which the truth conditions for sentences are built up out of naturalistic analyses of reference and denotation. This feature of Fodor's theory renders it vulnerable to the following problem (I am indebted here to Michael Bratman): If S and S' are nomologically correlated states of affairs, then on Fodor's analysis, any sentence that is mapped onto one of them will be mapped onto the other. Consider, for example, the correlated properties of electrical and thermal conductivity (whose correlation is expressed in the Wiedemann-Franz Law). Let us agree with Fodor that it is the function of the cognitive mechanisms to put 'The electrical conductivity is rising' in the belief box (in ideal epistemological circumstances) iff the electrical conductivity is rising. But since the right-hand side of this biconditional is true iff the thermal conductivity is rising, the left-hand side will be true iff the thermal conductivity is rising. So Fodor's theory will not distinguish between the semantic values of 'The thermal conductivity is rising' and 'The electrical conductivity is rising'. I don't see how such a problem can be dealt with without going to a compositional story (e.g., by adding a conceptual role component to the theory).[66]

Let me summarize. I've mentioned two types of reductionist theories—indicator semantics and Gricean semantics. (I've also mentioned the causal theory of reference, but I haven't compared it with CRS since it is not normally thought of as a full semantic theory. It—like indicator semantics—is a candidate for the referential-truth-conditional factor of a two-factor theory.) I've mentioned and endorsed Fodor's reason for thinking one version of indicator semantics won't work, and I've given some reasons to be dissatisfied with Fodor's theory. I've mentioned a few versions of Gricean theory, arguing that Searle's version isn't naturalistic (and so isn't a competitor to CRS); and I have countered an argument that the Grice-Schiffer-Loar version should be preferred to CRS because the former, unlike the latter, does not depend on what psychologists find out about mental representation.

Before I go on to the next desideratum, I shall very briefly consider an objection to the whole enterprise: I have been comparing a conceptual role theory of *narrow meaning* with theories that have conceptions of meaning that are quite different from narrow meaning (and also from one another's conceptions of meaning). Isn't this comparing apples, oranges, and mangoes?

Reply: (1) It would not change my points were I to switch from talk of narrow meaning to talk of meaning. Since meaning, on my view, is a pair of factors—the narrow meaning factor and the referential factor—to talk in terms of meaning would be to talk in terms of both factors of the two-factor account of meaning rather than just one of the factors (narrow meaning). After all, I chose the desiderata to exhibit strengths of the conceptual role factor of the two-factor theory, and I will be exercising the two-factor theory's right to introduce the referential factor where relevant. (2) It is true that different semantic theories differ in their conceptions of meaning, but that does not make comparison illegitimate. Vienna and New Delhi differ in their conception of dessert, but that won't stop me from preferring strudel to gulabja.

Why Is Meaning Relative to Representational System?

The CRS explanation of this relativity is simple. The conceptual role of a symbol is a matter of how it *functions* in a representational system (for this reason, conceptual role is sometimes called "functional role"). How a representation functions in a system depends, of course, on the system. If meaning is function, as CRS dictates, then meaning is system relative.

The nonreductionist semantic theories can, of course, be used to handle this phenomenon (in a nonexplanatory way) by assigning different semantic values to an expression when it manifestly has different semantic properties. Thus a sentence with 'trailer' in it would be assigned different situations, or truth conditions, or extensions in possible worlds or markerese representations, depending on whether the dialect is American English or English English. Once again, this is accommodation, not explanation. The difference between CRS and the nonreductionist theories is that conceptual roles are, by their nature, system relative because they are functional entities and the semantic values of the nonreductionist theories are not.

It is worth emphasizing how important a matter this is. It is a banal feature of languages that the shape or sound of a word does not determine its meaning. Indeed, this point is sometimes described as "trivial semantic conventionalism," to distinguish it from more interesting claims. If no semantic theory could explain such a fact, semantics would be in trouble.

Perhaps it is worth mentioning the psychologism allegation again. Am I just demanding that semantics answer a question that belongs in the domain of, say, the psychology of language? Pretheoretically, the fact that one linguistic element can have different meanings in different languages would seem to be a clearly semantic phenomenon. I would think that the burden of argument would be on anyone who wanted to argue otherwise.

So CRS can explain the general fact that meaning is relative to representational system. Also, as pointed out in the last section, it promises to explain *particular* meaning differences. Since the difference in meaning of 'trailer' in English English (in which it means: movie preview) and American English is a matter of differences in the causal properties of the term, it is in principle possible, according to CRS, to specify the factors that cause the difference in causal properties. By contrast, think of how a possible-worlds semanticist or a Katzian would go about explaining the difference. Nothing in such nonreductionist semantic theories would help.

The relativity of meaning to system of use is more fundamental to cognitive science than attention to examples such as 'trailer' indicates. Functional differences determine differences in the semantic (and syntactic) *categories* of representations—for example, the difference between the representational properties of *languagelike* and *picturelike* representations. This is especially important because there is reason to believe that many of our mental representations may actually be pictorial. None of the other semantic theories has a chance to explain the difference between the semantics of languagelike and picturelike representations.

Moreover, recall that syntactic category is as relative to system as semantic category. The relativity of syntactic category has the same explanation as the relativity of semantic category: syntax is functional too. If this isn't obvious, consider two processors that read English text: one reads odd-numbered characters, whereas the other reads even-numbered characters. One would read 'CDAOTG' as 'CAT', the other as 'DOG'. CRS allows a common explanation of an interesting fact—that both syntactic and semantic category are relative to system.

Further, CRS is important for avoiding misconceptions about concepts that are widespread in the psychological literature. The word 'concept' is used in psychology to denote a mental or physiological entity that expresses or represents a concept in the philosopher's sense of the term (in which concepts are abstract entities). The concept of a cat (in the psychologist's sense of the term) is a mental or physiological entity that expresses or represents cathood (much as the word 'cat' expresses or represents cathood). It is widely supposed in developmental psychology that mental images are probably children's concepts but that they could not be adult concepts. Piaget says:[67]

> The preconcepts of this level can be considered to be still half-way between the symbol and the concept proper. . . . [T]he preconcept involves the image and is partially determined by it, whereas the concept, precisely because of its generality, breaks away from the image. . . .

Another example: Premack (1982) argues that whereas the concepts of many lower animals are pictorial, the concepts of primates must be in part languagelike because pictorial concepts cannot express certain abstract ideas. For example, chimps can "match to sample" not only in cases where the sample is red and the correct multiple choice item is red, but also where the sample is AA and the choices are AB, BC, and BB. Here the correct choice is BB, and the common property is being a pair whose members are identical.

According to Premack, this requires a nonimagistic concept because the sample and target do not "resemble" one another. Another issue where this mistake (Which mistake? See the next paragraph) sometimes comes in is the issue of whether there is a "third code" more abstract than either languagelike or picturelike codes. The mistaken reasoning is that we have a nonlanguagelike code but that it could not be pictorial because pictorial representations could not have the kind of generality required of a concept.[68]

The doctrine that picturelike representations won't do for general or adult or primate concepts involves a conceptual error, one for which CRS is a corrective. CRS tells us that to be a concept of, say, dog, a mental representation must function in a certain way. Obviously, you can't tell how a certain representation functions by confining your attention to the representation alone, or to its "resemblances" to things in the world. You must know something about how the processors that act on it treat it. Thus a pictorial representation can express quite an abstract property, so long as the processors that act on it ignore the right specificities. To take a venerable example, a picture of an equilateral triangle can serve to represent triangles in general so long as the processors that act on it ignore the equality of the sides and angles. Similarly, a picture of a set of twins *could* represent or express the concept of a pair whose members are identical.

Note that I am not just pointing out that Piaget and Premack are the victims of "resemblance" theories of pictorial representation. The error I am pointing to is more fundamental in the sense that it includes the resemblance-theory error, plus a failure to see the shape of a positive doctrine — namely, that how or what a representation represents is a matter of more than the intrinsic properties of the representation or simple relational properties like "resemblance"; in particular, it is a matter of a complex relational property: how the representation functions.

What Is the Relation between Meaning and Mind/Brain?

How does the brain confer meaning on its representations?[69] Answer: By conferring the right causal roles on the representations. What is it for a person to grasp the meaning of a word? Answer: For a person to grasp the meaning of a word is for the word (or its standard mentalese associate) to have a certain causal role in his or her brain. How can it be that a person grasping an abstract object can propel the person (and his or her brain) to Hawaii? Answer: The difference between grasping a meaning and not grasping it is a difference in the causal role of entities in the person's brain, and differences in such causal roles can make for differences in behavior and the rewards that are contingent on behavior.

As before, the nonreductionist semantic theories can give superficial answers to the desideratum question. How does the brain grasp meanings? By grasping truth conditions or a denoted situation or a markerese structure.

But the question of how the brain grasps truth conditions or denoted situations or markerese structures is just as pressing as the original question.[70]

What Is the Relation between Autonomous and Inherited Meaning?

Recall the distinction (made in Desideratum 6) between autonomous and inherited meaning. Inherited meanings, like those of the linguistic expressions on this page, require translation or transliteration into the language of thought of a reader or hearer for their understanding. Autonomous meaning, the kind of meaning of the elements of the language of thought itself, requires no reading or hearing and thus no translation or transliteration in order to be understood. The questions I raised were: What is autonomous meaning? What is inherited meaning? What is the relation between autonomous and inherited meaning? For example, is one reducible to the other? Or are they both manifestations of a single type of meaning? Or are they unrelated phenomena with only a superficial resemblance?

The CRS answers to the first two questions are simple: autonomous meaning is conceptual role—and so is inherited meaning. (You will recall that using the notion of standard association, one can individuate conceptual roles of English as their standard associates in the internal system.) Further, the conceptual roles of external language are inherited from those of internal language. So inherited meaning is (surprise!) inherited from autonomous meaning.

The nonreductionist semantic theories, by contrast, have little to say about these matters. They *can* say that 'cat' and 'CAT' have the same semantic values; but as far as I can see, none of them have conceptual resources adequate to spell out any reasonable characterizations of autonomous and inherited meaning or say anything about whether one is reducible to the other.

Psychologism again: Is CRS supposed to be better for the purposes of psychology simply because it *contains* some psychological claims? Autonomous and inherited meaning are two categories of meaning (maybe even basic categories). It would be a surprise—*which itself would need explaining*—if no good theory of the nature of meaning could illuminate the issues I have been discussing about the relation between these two categories.

Indeed, once one sees the distinction between autonomous and inherited meaning, it is reasonable to ask of any theory of meaning *which* type of meaning it is intended to speak to. CRS speaks to both. Indeed, CRS explicates the difference between autonomous and inherited meaning without giving up a *unified* account of the two types of meaning. English inscriptions and utterances affect one another (via their effects on internal language) so as to give English expressions conceptual roles; and these conceptual roles are (at least on the simplified model I discussed) dependent on the conceptual roles of internal expressions.

Thus far, I have said little about causal theories of reference. Such theories, if they can be made to work, potentially have more to say about the relation between autonomous and inherited meaning than nonreductionist theories such as possible-worlds semantics, situation semantics, Davidsonian semantics, and Katzian semantics, because they can say something about the similarities and differences between the causal chains leading to 'cat' and 'CAT' that explains the differences and similarities between the two representations. But causal theories of reference cannot capture the aspect of meaning inside the head.[71] For example, they cannot capture the aspect of sameness in meanings of the sentences of me and my twin on Twin Earth (despite the difference in our causal chains outside our heads). From the point of view of a causal theory of reference, 'Hesperus = Hesperus' and 'Hesperus = Phosphorus' have the same semantic value.[72] Further, the theory that I am promoting can appropriate whatever successes causal theories of reference may have. Recall that CRS in the version I favor is part of a two-factor theory, the external factor of which can adopt aspects of a causal theory of reference account. In sum, causal theories of reference cannot accomplish the task I have set; and whatever they can accomplish can be appropriated by the two-factor version of CRS.

One final advantage of the CRS approach to the distinction between autonomous and inherited meaning is that it allows a theoretical approach to Searle's "Chinese Room" argument. With apologies to those who have heard this too many times: we are to imagine a monolingual English speaker who is placed in a room in a robot's head. He has a large library of instructions in English (the program) that tells him to push certain buttons (controlling outputs of the body) or write certain notes to himself (thus changing the "internal state" of the system) depending on what input lights are on and what notes he has written to himself earlier. The man never understands any Chinese, but nonetheless the robot he controls "speaks" excellent Chinese. Searle argues that since the man never understands Chinese, and since the robot paraphernalia adds no understanding, what we have is a Chinese simulator with no genuine Chinese understanding.

The most penetrating criticisms have focused on what Searle—anticipating the challenge—calls the systems reply. The systems reply says that since the system as a whole—man + library + room + robot body and control system—has the information processing characteristic of an intelligent Chinese speaker, we should take the whole system as understanding Chinese, even though the homunculus inside does not. The critics insist that the whole system does understand Chinese. (See Dennett 1983.) Searle has a clever reply. He tells the critics to just imagine the paraphernalia of the "system" *internalized,* as follows. First, instead of having the homunculus consult a library (the program), let him *memorize* the whole library. Second, let him memorize his notes instead of writing them down. Finally, instead of having the homunculus inhabit a robot body, let him *use his own body*. That is, what we are to imagine in the new version is that the homunculus manipulates his own body in just the way he manipulated the robot body in the previous version. When he seems to be asking for the salt in Chinese, what he is really doing is thinking *in English* about what noises and gestures the program dictates that he should produce next.[73]

At this point, the issue seems to come down just to a matter of conflicting intuitions. The opponents say the man following the instructions does understand Chinese, Searle says he does not.[74] This is where CRS comes in. The trouble with the systems reply as so far discussed is that it contains no theoretical perspective on what it would be for the system's Chinese symbols to be meaningful for it in the way the symbols in the head of a normal Chinese speaker are meaningful for that person—it contains no perspective on autonomous meaning. CRS has an answer: what would give the symbols autonomous meaning is the right conceptual role. There is a complication that makes this point harder to see. Namely, there is a crucial ambiguity in Searle's statement of his examples. Is the robot system (and the later case in which the homunculus internalizes the program) supposed to be one in which the information processing of a normal Chinese speaker is *simulated*? Or is the information processing of a normal Chinese speaker actually *instantiated* or *emulated* in the system?[75] (I can simulate an Aristotelian physicist's information processing by figuring out what someone would think if, like Aristotle, he didn't distinguish average from instantaneous velocity; but I cannot instantiate or emulate this information processing—that is, have this type of information actually go on in me—because I cannot avoid seeing the distinction.) In the case of mere simulation, the information-processing point of view does not dictate that the system *does* understand anything. But in the emulation case—the one in which Chinese symbols are processed so that they have the same conceptual roles they have in a normal Chinese speaker.[76]—then CRS dictates that the robot does indeed understand Chinese. I think that what makes Searle's argument sound so convincing is that it is difficult to imagine a version of Searle's example that is a genuine instantiation or emulation rather than a mere simulation.[77] In sum, CRS allows one to see an important distinction that is not respected in the debate, and it gives those who are inclined toward functionalism a positive view about autonomous meaning so they can steer away from mere intuition-mongering.

What's the difference between Searle's argument and my argument in Block (1978)? To make a long story short, though our examples were similar, Searle's argument has a wider target, the symbol-manipulating view of the mind common in cognitive science. This view entails functionalism but is not entailed by it. My aim, by contrast, was mainly to argue that functional definitions constructed from commonsense psychology (by a Ramsification procedure) carried a burden of proof. I argued that nothing of any substance had been said in their favor, and there was some reason to doubt them. Desiderata like the ones mentioned in this paper can be used to satisfy this burden of proof—for intentional states but not experiential states.

Compositionality

The points to be made about compositionality are very similar to points already made, so I will be brief.

According to CRS, it is sentences (and perhaps larger chunks of discourse) that embody hypotheses, claims, arguments, and the like, not subsentential elements. So, according to CRS, the semantic values of words and other subsentential elements are a matter of their contributions to the conceptual roles of sentences and supersentential elements. The conceptual role of 'and', for example, derives from such facts as that a commitment to rejecting 'p' (in the absence of a commitment to accept 'p and q') can lead (in certain circumstances) to a commitment to rejecting 'p and q'. In this way, CRS explains why words have the conceptual roles they do by appeal to conceptual roles of sentences; thus the semantic values of words are seen to be a matter of their causal properties.

The nonreductionist theories do not and should not be regarded as aimed at this type of issue. They are concerned with what the relations among meanings of, say, words and sentences are, not with the issue of why those relations obtain.

What about indicator semantics and Gricean semantics? They, like CRS, take sentential and perhaps supersentential chunks as the basic semantic unit. And, like CRS, they can regard the meanings of words as their contributions to the semantic values of sentences. CRS has no advantage in this matter.

Narrow Meaning, Twin Earth, the Explanation of Behavior, and the Function from Context to Reference and Truth Conditions

The hard work of this section was done (or at any rate, attempted) in the desideratum on narrow meaning. I can be brief here, concentrating on objections and extensions.

What is narrow meaning? (Recall that CRS can do without the claim that narrow meaning is genuinely a kind of meaning, rather than a determinant of meaning.) Here, the comparison with the other theories looks quite different than with the other desiderata. CRS does have an answer—namely, conceptual role—and the other theories have no answer. But the other theories I've been mentioning are not *about* narrow meaning.

Why is narrow meaning relevant to the explanation of behavior, and why is it relevant in the same way for me and my twin? Taking the second question first: since my twin and I are physically identical, all of our representations have exactly the same internal causal roles, and hence the same narrow meanings. But why is narrow meaning relevant to the explanation of behavior in the first place? To have an internal representation with a certain narrow meaning is to have a representation with certain likely inferential antecedents and consequents. Hence, to ascribe a narrow meaning is to ascribe a syndrome of causes and effects, including, in some cases, behavioral effects (or at least impulses in motor-output neurons). The reason my twin and I both jump is that we have representations with conceptual roles that have, as part of their syndrome of effects, jumping behavior. The reason that wide meaning is not as relevant to the explanation of behavior as is narrow meaning is that differences in wide meaning that do not involve differences in narrow meaning (e.g., the difference between me and my twin) do not cause behavioral differences.[78]

The CRS explanation of behavior may seem circular, hence trivial. How can I characterize a meaning functionally, in part in terms of a tendency for representations that have it to cause jumping, and then turn around and explain jumping by appeal to a representation's having this meaning? This is an objection of a well-known sort to explanation in terms of functionally individuated entities, and it has a familiar sort of rebuttal. 'Gene' is defined functionally in Mendelian genetics, in part in terms of effects on, for instance, hair color. 'Reinforcement' is defined in operant-conditioning circles in part in terms of effects on, for instance, bar-pressing. How, then, can one turn around and explain blonde hair in terms of genes, or bar-pressing in terms of history of reinforcement? Part of the answer is that one is not talking about a *single* effect, postulated ad hoc, but rather a complex web of interacting effects. A sickle-cell gene yields sickle-cell anemia in one circumstance (when paired with another sickle-cell gene) but resistance to malaria in another. When one postulates a gene on the basis of one effect, one can obtain converging evidence for it from other effects; and these effects enrich the functional characterization. If you give a rat Burpee Rat Chow (at 80% body weight[79]) contingent on bar-pressing, the rat's bar-pressing response normally increases in strength (on a variety of measures). So it is said that the Burpee Rat Chow is a reinforcer. Part of what makes this a nonempty claim is that one can get the rat to do all sorts of other things using Burpee Rat Chow or other reinforcers.

Second, and more importantly, a functionally individuated entity can, in principle, be identified by independent (usually physicalistic) means and the mechanism of its causal connection to the effects described. For example, a gene identified functionally via the methods of Mendelian genetics can be identified as a clump of DNA via the methods of molecular genetics. And the mechanism by which the gene produces phenotypic characteristics can be described biochemically. Similarly, the mechanism by which Burpee Rat

Chow affects behavior can (presumably) be characterized biologically, or perhaps even psychologically (in terms of the rat's information processing).

The application of the first point to CRS is obvious, but the application of the second is more problematic. The problem has to do with the type-token relation for mental representations. The hope is that there will be a stable physical realization (at least over short stretches of time) of, say, the representation 'CAT', which of course will be identifiable only by its functional role. Then, in principle, one could trace the causal links between this representation and behavior, just as the biochemist can in principle trace the mechanism by which a gene affects the phenotype.[80]

Let us now turn briefly to the matter of the essential indexical. 'I am in the path of danger', and 'Ned Block is in the path of danger' can have systematically different conceptual roles, depending on whether I know I am Ned Block (rather than, say, Napoleon). 'I', used by a speaker, differs systematically from the speaker's own name in its conceptual role, even though they refer to the same thing. Hence CRS assigns them different narrow meanings. Thus the thought I express with 'I' (or its internal associate) is different in narrow content from the thought I would have expressed were my name to have replaced 'I'. Thus, narrow meaning, as articulated by CRS, can be used to explicate a notion of thought *state* distinct from thought *object* that will serve the purpose for which Perry suggested this distinction.[81]

Similar points apply to the examples using names and natural kind terms mentioned in the desideratum on this subject. 'Cicero struts' and 'Tully struts' have different conceptual roles; so despite the fact that they have identical wide meanings, we can see why believing these different sentences could have different effects on other mental states and behavior.[82]

Let us now turn again to the determination of the function from context to reference and truth value. I argued in the section on meaning and reference/truth that conceptual role does determine this function. Take 'I', for example. If someone says "I am in danger," one can infer that the speaker has said, of himself, that he is in danger. In general, it is part of the conceptual role of 'I' that it refers to the producer of the token of 'I' (except in contexts such as quotation). However, there are other aspects of conceptual role that are relevant to, say, explanation of behavior, but not to determination of the function from context to reference and truth value. For example, one can infer from "I entirely fill such and such a spatiotemporal volume" to "You do not occupy this volume." But this inference does not seem relevant to the determination of the aforementioned function. Similar points apply to other types of terms. One can infer from 'water' to 'colorless' (or, at least to 'colorless if pure'); but this has little or nothing to do with determination of reference. I would still be referring to the same liquid even if I were under the impression that in its pure state it has a bluish tinge to it. Indeed, it may be that the aspect of conceptual role that determines the function from context to reference is the same for all natural kind terms. My highly tentative conclusion is that the aspect of conceptual role that determines the function from context to reference and truth value is a small part of the conceptual roles relevant to the explanation of behavior and psychological state.

In conclusion: In this paper, I have not attempted to elaborate CRS, or supply any analyses of language from its perspective. Rather, I have tried to provide reason for suppressing the "put up or shut up" reflex that dogs talk of conceptual roles in the absence of identity conditions for them. My hope is that this theory will get more attention and that more detailed versions of it will allow us to evaluate its prospects better.[83]

Notes

1. Good sketches of the ideas of the representational theory of mind are to be found in Fodor (1981) and Lycan (1981). A more detailed treatment is provided in Pylyshyn (1984).

2. See Block (1983) for a discussion of this distinction and for references to the literature on this topic.

3. I hope my "inherited/autonomous" terminology won't make these questions seem trivial.

4. It is commitment to a priori truth (by which I mean truths for which there is no epistemic possibility of refutation) that really causes trouble for friends of analyticity—not our inability to come up with identity conditions for meaning. After all, no one has ever come up with satisfactory identity conditions for people or ships.

5. Perry (1977, 1979); Kaplan (unpublished).

6. A natural variant on the notion of narrow individuation that I described would require in addition that the same properties be attributed in the same way.

7. Note that the claim that narrow meaning is in the head, in this sense, is not incompatible with the idea that what it is for a word to have a certain narrow meaning is for it to express a concept, where concepts are taken to be abstract objects not locatable in space and time; in this respect, "in the head" is not an apt phrase.

8. Of course, one could define a referential notion of meaning that included narrow meaning and therefore better deserved to be called "wide." This would also result in a more intuitive treatment of vacuous reference. Since the main use I'll be making of the notion of wide meaning is to highlight narrow meaning, I'll stick with the simple definition I've introduced.

9. See Loar (1982), 279; White (1982); and Fodor (1985).

10. Cf. Field (1977).

11. This is a controversial reading of the lesson of Kripke's puzzle. I don't have the space here to describe either the puzzle or the conceptual role semantics solution.

12. White (1982) attempts to *define* a narrow meaning notion using such counterfactuals. But this seems misguided, since there is something shared by the twins *in virtue of which* the counterfactuals are true, and that seems a better candidate for narrow meaning.

13. See McGinn (1982), esp. 211-16, for arguments from the nature of representation to narrow content and meaning.

14. Ignore the problem that since we are made up largely of water, my twin and I can't be duplicates—fixes for this have been proposed by Putnam and Burge.

15. Burge (1979).

16. Actually, my position is that such a multidimensional gradient is needed for full-blooded narrow meaning, but not for the *part* of narrow meaning responsible for mapping contexts onto referents and truth conditions.

17. See Horwich (1982b). Here is the paradox of the preface: I write a book all of whose sentences I believe; nonetheless, I am sure that, being human, I have asserted at least one falsehood. Contradiction. Solution: I have a high degree of belief in each sentence in the book, but that is compatible with a high degree of belief in the falsity of their conjunction.

18. Variance is mean squared deviation from the mean.

19. Burge (1979). Burge constructs cases in which a man has a slight misunderstanding about how a word is used (e.g., he thinks you can have arthritis in the thigh). He then argues, persuasively, that a doppelgänger of this man in a language community in which 'arthritis' is standardly used to include rheumatoid inflammations of bones such as the thigh should not be regarded as meaning by 'arthritis' what we and our man mean by the word.

20. LePore and Loewer (1985) seem to object in this way to two-factor conceptual role semantics.

21. See Harman (1974, 1975, and 1982) and Sellars (1963, 1969, and 1974); see also Putnam (1979).

22. Field (1977, 1978).

23. See Churchland (1979), Loar (1981, 1982), Lycan (1981), McGinn (1982), and Schiffer (1981). Loar and Schiffer advocated conceptual role semantics only as a subsidiary semantic theory for the language of thought, if there happens to be one. The semantic theory they advocated for external language is a functionalized Gricean theory.

24. Woods (1977, 1978, and 1981).

25. Johnson-Laird (1977) and Miller and Johnson-Laird (1976).

26. Though in a paper given at the MIT Sloan Conference, 1984, Field suggests a view in which meaning and content are abandoned altogether. Field's 1977 and 1978 papers are quite skeptical about intersubjective comparisons of conceptual role—because of the collateral information problem. For that reason, he placed great weight on the referential component; recent skepticism about the referential component has led to skepticism about meaning and content altogether.

27. That is, the narrow aspect or determinant of meaning.

28. McGinn (1982) states the theory as assigning states of affairs to sentences. This leads LePore and Loewer (1985) to suppose that a two-factor theory must be more liberal than Davidsonian truth theory in allowing, in the external factor: 'Water is wet' is true $\leftrightarrow$ H_2O is wet. But a two-factor theorist *can* adopt Davidsonian truth theory for the external factor, even though demanding that the sentence on the right-hand side of the biconditional be a *translation* of the quoted sentence on the left-hand side is a stronger demand than necessary for the two-factor theorist.

29. For purposes of this discussion, I shall be ignoring pictorial internal representations.

30. Brain-writing, as everyone knows, is spelled in capital letters.

31. See Kahneman, Slovic, and Tversky (1982) and references therein for detailed studies of such fallacies.

32. Harman (1970) contrasts code-breaking views of language understanding with incorporation views. On the latter, understanding English is translation into a different language; whereas on the former, English is part of the language of thought (actually, a system of syntactic structures with English vocabulary items is part of the language of thought), so no translation is involved.

33. Harman (1982), 14.

34. See Loar (1982), 278-80, for a different slant on what is wrong with Harman's view. Loar takes the line that devices such as Harman's "normal context" and conceptual role in the minds of experts are ad hoc.

35. Johnson-Laird's reply (1978) to Fodor pretty much abandons this verificationist tendency in favor of a generalized conceptual role much like the idea I've been alluding to here.

36. Fodor (1978); reprinted in Fodor (1981), 211.

37. Dretske (1983), 88.

38. This is well argued by Stich (1983). (Although, as I think Sterelny (1985) shows, Stich deploys the wrong notion of "potential" in characterizing his functional roles.) Oddly, Stich considers mental representations, functionally individuated, without ever considering whether there is a distinction to be made between the aspect of functional role relevant to semantics and the aspect that might be called syntactic. (Indeed, these are in effect identified on p. 200.) This is a distinction we make with respect to English orthography. If someone writes the letter 'a' in an idiosyncratic way, we can identify it *functionally,* by the way it appears in words—e.g., it appears by itself, it appears in '*b*n*n**, in place of the asterisks, etc. At the same time, we can distinguish functionally between two uses of the same syntactic type, 'bank'.

39. Fodor (1985).

40. See Hills (1981), 18-19, for a dicussion of the two ways of talking about internal symbolism, and Harman (1973) for an application of the representational state version.

41. See Horwich (1982) for a discussion of this issue in another context.

42. Lycan (forthcoming) argues that God could tell us which worlds were the ones in which a sentence is true without telling us what the sentence means. I think he is right, but only for the reason mentioned in the text. God could indicate the possible worlds in a way that allows us to represent which ones they are without representing what they have in common in virtue of which they are the ones in which the sentence is true. See Lycan's paper for a discussion of indexicals and for references to the literature on this topic.

43. See also Loar (1982), 277.

44. This is Putnam's claim in an influential series of articles beginning with "The Analytic and the Synthetic" (1962); the few decompositional definitions he allows are those that, like 'bachelor = never-married adult male; involve a single "criterion." The idea is that the term 'bachelor' responds to only one "concern," and so there is no possibility that different concerns will "pull apart," creating a situation in which we will have to choose arbitrarily how the word is to apply. Putnam has also formulated a version of the argument given below against Fodor's innateness thesis.

45. Of course, it is not a particularly *new* story. Indeed, it is just what you would expect if you believed aspects of Quine and Kuhn, or if you accepted Lewis' "functional definition" story in "How to Define Theoretical Terms" (Lewis 1970). See Kuhn (1983) for semantic views quite close to those of conceptual role semantics.

46. I have heard it said that a conceptual role account of meaningfulness is much more plausible than a conceptual role account of particular meanings. This view is reminiscent of the cognitive theory of emotions that says that what makes a state an emotional state is a certain type of physiological arousal, but what makes such a state joy as opposed to anger is a difference in cognitive "overlay." The application of this idea to semantics cannot be evaluated in the absence of a suggestion as to what it is that accounts for the differences among meanings. Just one comment: in the case of experiential mental states, this type of view is less plausible than the reverse: that some sort of physiological state makes a state experiential, whereas functional *differences* are responsible for the difference between pain and the sensation of red.

47. These theories can often explain semantic defects in complex entities on the basis of the semantic properties of primitives. For example, Katzian semantics can explain why 'red idea' is semantically defective on the basis of the semantic values of 'red' and 'idea'. But Katzian semantics can give no answer to the question of what makes a primitive meaningful element meaningful. The Katzian accommodates the difference between 'red' and 'glub' by putting 'red' but not 'glub' in his dictionary. But it is not part of the theory to give an account of *why*.

48. This article is a jointly written pseudointerview in which the quoted material is put in Barwise's mouth (p. 51), but Perry continues the line of thought.

49. See Stalnaker (1984) for an attempt to solve this within the possible-worlds framework.

50. I derive this objection by analogy to a point made with regard to truth in Soames (1984), 426.

51. This may be Soames's view in the article mentioned in note 50, and I also see a tendency towards this view in Katz (1982), though Katz and Soames probably have different notions of necessity in mind.

52. Though, in the case of at least one version of the Gricean approach, not naturalistic.

53. See the statement of the theory in Schiffer (1982).

54. I used to think that the Fodor-Putnam multiple realizability arguments against physiological reductionism settled the matter. Their point, in essence, was that physiological reductionism was a chauvinist thesis in that, construed as a theory of the mind *simpliciter,* it would exclude intelligent machines or Martians. I now think that the best one is likely to get in the way of a theory of the mind will be a theory of the *human* mind. Such a theory will inevitably be chauvinist. The representational theory of mind that I am adopting here is a theory in that chauvinist tradition. What makes physiological reductionism look so bad is not simply that it is chauvinist—i.e., not just that there are merely *possible* creatures that share our intentional states without sharing our physiology—but rather that we do have promising theories of the human mind and that they are computational-representational (which is not to say that they are committed to the claim that the brain is a digital computer). If the scientific "essence" of intentional states is computational-representational, then it is not physiological—for the old multiple realizability reasons. So multiple realizability is the nub of the matter, but only because one chauvinist theory of the mind is multiply realizable in terms of another.

55. This comes through loud and clear in Searle (1980b).

56. Though in a draft of an article circulated in 1984, Schiffer rejects his earlier approach.

57. See Posner (1978) and Fodor (1982).

58. Sternberg (1969).

59. I can't possibly go into the details here. Dretske's view is couched in terms of the interesting notion of the *most specific information* that a tokening of a representation carries about a state of affairs.

60. Barwise (1984), 8.

61. The theory is sketched in Fodor (1983a, 1984) and expounded in detail in a widely circulated but as yet unpublished paper, "Psychosemantics" (see Loar [1983] for further comments on this paper), which Fodor is now saving for a book he is preparing of the same title. The reason I devote so much space to a largely unpublished account is that the problems with Fodor's account, together with Fodor's refutation of the Dretske-Stampe view, gives us an excellent picture of the type of problem faced by indicator semantics.

62. I am indebted to Paul Horwich here.

63. See, for example, the articles in the relevant section of Sober (1984).

64. There are disagreements about the *extent* of forces orthogonal to optimality. Lewontin and Gould, for example, are controversial in their insistence that the extent of such orthogonal forces is very great. (See their article in Sober [1984].) But this disagreement in the field should not obscure the important agreement mentioned in the text.

65. This issue can be discussed in terms quite distant from evolutionary biology. One example considered by Fodor is that when it comes to beliefs about poisons, false negatives are much more damaging than false positives. False positives ("This is a poison," said of something that is harmless) can cost you a meal, but false negatives can cost you your life. There are mechanisms in rats and even people that could perhaps be interpreted as inclining one to overattribute noxiousness to foods. Fodor insists that in such cases, one should *always* interpret the organisms as paying heed to low probabilities of very bad things rather than falsely ascribing high probabilities to the bad things. He sees this as a product of a principle of charity. The trouble with this reply is that this is not an a priori issue. If the mental sentence theory of belief is right, there is a difference between acting on a belief that *p* and acting on an estimate that, though *p* is unlikely, it would be terrible if true. Independent evidence could be marshalled in favor of one or another alternative. Further, even if Fodor's a priori assumption is right about our cognitive mechanisms, it is contingently right. If we come to understand how our cognitive

mechanisms work, perhaps we could build cognitive mechanisms that work otherwise. It would be a strange semantic theory that depends on such a highly contingent and perhaps quite alterable fact about the cognitive mechanisms that we happen to have. Such a semantic theory would not apply to robots who think, act, and talk almost exactly as we do, but, say, are built to overattribute poisonous qualities to foods on the basis of slim evidence. Will Fodor say we are barred by the logic of the concepts involved from building such a robot?

Another problem with Fodor's a prioristic method of handling these cases is that he is forced to adopt, ad hoc, *other* methods of handling other cases in which supposedly cognitive mechanisms don't aim at truth. In considering the possibility that our cognitive mechanisms are built to *repress* certain unpleasant truths, Fodor stipulates that such mechanisms are not cognitive. He is stuck with simply stipulating which mechanisms are cognitive and which are not.

66. There is a parallel problem in causal theories of reference that *seems* more tractable, but perhaps only because it is more familiar.

67. Quoted in Mandler (1983). On this issue as on many others, one finds glimmers of quite different views in Piaget. There are other passages where he seems to have some appreciation of the Berkeleyan point I make below. See also the discussion in Fodor (1975).

68. This is not the only argument for the third code. There are powerful empirical reasons for postulating a third code. See Potter, Valian, and Faulconer (1977) for both the good and the bad reasons for believing in a third code. Brison (n. d.) (1984) contains an excellent rebuttal of arguments for a third code that make this (and other) mistakes. See also Kolers and Brison (1984).

69. Recall that I am ignoring the mind, concentrating on the brain.

70. The issue of psychologism naturally comes up with respect to this issue, but I have already answered it a number of times.

71. Unless they include in their causal chains the causal roles inside the head, in which case they include CRS itself.

72. Field (1977), 390.

73. This example is similar to ones described in Block (1978, 1981).

74. See the replies in the issue of *Behavioral and Brain Sciences* in which Searle's article appeared and the interchange between Searle and Dennett in *New York Review of Books* (Searle 1983b; Dennett 1983).

75. See Block (1980, 1981).

76. At the appropriate level of abstraction, of course. In this case, as in others I have mentioned, identity of conceptual role is compatible with a variety of causal differences.

77. The only reply I've seen that contains a glimmer of the CRS reply is Haugeland's in the BBS issue just mentioned (Haugeland 1980).

78. Burge (1984) objects that this use of 'behavior' begs the question in favor of individualistic accounts, behavioral ascriptions often being nonindividualistic. I agree that ordinary behavior descriptions are nonindividualistic; I would argue along the lines suggested in Desideratum 8 that an important line of work in cognitive psychology *is* individualistic.

79. To make sure it is hungry—an explanation avoided by most of those who condition rats.

80. Actually, I think there is less of a problem here than meets the eye. Letters of the alphabet are individuated functionally—that is why we recognize shapes that we have never seen before as *A*'s. But what allows us to do this is some degree of stability in the shapes of other letters. It is hard to see how there could fail to be some analogous story about how the brain works—if representationalism is true.

81. This point is similar to the one made by Lycan (1981), (See also Dennett [1982].) However, Lycan somehow sees this point as an argument for the internal sentence story (the conceptual role semantics comes in almost incidentally). I talk about thoughts rather than beliefs because the representationalist story is more plausible for occurrent mental states. As

many commentators have pointed out, one can ascribe a belief if it follows in a simple way from what a person has explicitly thought, even if the belief ascribed has never actually occurred to the person. See Fodor (n.d.).

82. On Kripke's puzzle: since 'Londres' and 'London' have different conceptual roles, it is a mistake to accept Kripke's translation principle. In particular, from the fact that Pierre croit que Londres est jolie, we should not conclude that Pierre believes London is pretty—if the content of his belief is given by 'London is pretty'. Lycan (1981) and McGinn (1982) have interesting discussions of the conceptual role semantics response to Kripke's puzzle, but neither pinpoint the translation principle as the culprit.

83. I am grateful to the John Simon Guggenheim Memorial Foundation and the Center for the Study of Language and Information for support while writing this paper. I would like to thank Michael Bratman, Martin Davies, Hartry Field, Jerry Fodor, Gilbert Harman, Paul Horwich, David Israel, Phil Johnson-Laird, Jerry Katz, Brian Loar, Bill Lycan, and Georges Rey for their helpful comments on earlier drafts.

References

Barwise, John. 1984. *The Situation in Logic—I*. Technical report CSLI-84-2, Stanford University, March. Paper presented at International Congress on Logic and Philosophy of Science, Salzburg, July 1983.

Barwise, Jon, and John Perry. 1983. *Situations and Attitudes*. Cambridge, Mass.

Barwise, Jon, and John Perry. 1984. *Shifting Situations and Shaken Attitudes*. Research report CSLI-84-13, Stanford University, August. To appear as a reply to critics in a special issue of *Linguistics and Philosophy* devoted to situation semantics.

Block, Ned. 1978. "Troubles with Functionalism." In *Perception and Cognition: Issues in the Foundations of Psychology,* edited by C. W. Savage. Minneapolis.

Block, Ned. 1980. "What Intuitions about Homunculi Do Not Show." *Behavioral and Brain Sciences* 3: 425-26.

Block, Ned. 1981. "Psychologism and Behaviorism." *Philosophical Review* 90: 5-43.

Block, Ned. 1983. "Mental Pictures and Cognitive Science." *Philosophical Review* 92: 499-541. Reprinted in *The Philosophers' Annual* 6 (1984), edited by P. Grim et al.

Block, Ned, and Sylvain Bromberger. 1980. "States' Rights." *The Behavioral and Brain Sciences* 3.

Boyd, Richard. 1979. "Metaphor and Theory Change." In *Metaphor and Thought,* edited by Andrew Ortony. Cambridge.

Brison, Susan J. n.d. "Do We Think in Mentalese?" Forthcoming.

Burge, Tyler. 1979. "Individualism and the Mental." *Midwest Studies in Philosophy* 4:73-121.

Burge, Tyler. 1984. "Individualism and Psychology." Paper presented at Cognitive Science Conference, Massachusetts Institute of Technology. Stephen Stich and Ned Block were the respondents. This paper will appear in the Philosophical Review.

Churchland, Paul M. 1979. *Scientific Realism and the Plasticity of Mind.* Cambridge.

Churchland, P. M. and P. S. Churchland. 1983. "Content—Semantic and Information-Theoretic." *Behavioral and Brain Sciences* 6: 67-78.

Davidson, Donald. 1984. *Truth and Interpretation.* Oxford.

Dennett, Daniel C. 1982. "Beyond Belief." In *Thought and Object: Essays on Intentionality,* edited by Andrew Woodfield. Oxford.

Dennett, Dan. 1983. "The Myth of the Computer: An Exchange." *New York Review of Books* (June 14). This contains a letter from Dennett criticizing Searle (1983b).

Devitt, Michael. 1981. *Designation.* New York.

Dretske, Fred. 1981. *Knowledge and the Flow of Information.* Cambridge, Mass.

Dretske, Fred I. 1983. "Why Information?" *Behavioral and Brain Sciences* 6: 82-89. This is Dretske's reply to critics.

Field, Hartry. 1972. "Tarski's Theory of Truth." *Journal of Philosophy* 69: 347-75.

Field, Hartry. 1977. "Logic, Meaning, and Conceptual Role." *Journal of Philosophy* 74: 379-409.

Field, Hartry. 1978. "Mental Representation." *Erkentniss* 13: 9-61.

Field, Hartry. 1980. *Science without Numbers: A Defense of Nominalism.* Oxford.

Fodor, J. A. 1974. "Special Sciences." *Synthese* 28: 77-115. Reprinted as part of Fodor (1975) and in my *Readings in Philosophy of Psychology,* vol. 1.

Fodor, J. A. 1975. *The Language of Thought.* New York.

Fodor, J. A. 1978. "Tom Swift and His Procedural Grandmother." *Cognition* 6: 229-247.

Fodor, J. A. 1981. *RePresentations.* Cambridge, Mass.

Fodor, J. A. 1982. "Cognitive Science and the Twin-Earth Problem." *Notre Dame Journal of Formal Logic* 23: 98-118.

Fodor, J. A. 1983a. "A Reply to Brian Loar's 'Must Beliefs Be Sentences?' " In *PSA 1982,* vol. 2, edited by Peter Asquith and Thomas Nickles. Ann Arbor.

Fodor, J. A. 1983b. *The Modularity of Mind.* Cambridge, Mass.

Fodor, J. A. 1984. "Semantics, Wisconsin Style." *Synthese* 59: 1-20. This is primarily an attack on Dretske and Stampe, but it does contain a brief exposition of Fodor's own theory.

Fodor, J. A. 1985. "Banish DisContent." In *Proceedings of the 1984 Thyssen Conference,* edited by Jeremy Butterfield. Cambridge.

Fodor, J. A. n.d. *Psychosemantics.* Forthcoming.

Harman, Gilbert. 1970. "Language Learning." *Nous* 4: 33-43. Reprinted in *Readings in Philosophy of Psychology,* vol. 2, edited by Ned Block. Cambridge, Mass., 1981.

Harman, Gilbert. 1973. *Thought.* Princton, N.J.

Harman, Gilbert. 1974. "Meaning and Semantics." In *Semantics and Philosophy,* edited by M. K. Munitz and Peter Unger. New York.

Harman, Gilbert. 1975. "Language, Thought and Communication." In *Language, Mind and Knowledge,* edited by K. Gunderson.

Harman, Gilbert. 1982. "Conceptual Role Semantics." *Notre Dame Journal of Formal Logice,* 23: 242-56.

Haugeland, John. 1980. "Programs, Causal Powers, and Intentionality." *Behavioral and Brain Sciences* 3: 432-33.

Hills, David. 1981. "Mental Representations and Languages of Thought." In *Readings in Philosophy of Psychology,* vol. 2, edited by Ned Block. Cambridge, Mass.

Horwich, Paul. 1982a. "Three Forms of Realism." *Synthese* 51: 181-201.

Horwich, Paul. 1982b. *Probability and Evidence.* Cambridge.

Johnson-Laird, P. N. 1977. "Procedural Semantics." *Cognition* 5: 189-214.

Johnson-Laird, P. N. 1978. "What's Wrong with Grandma's Guide to Procedural Semantics: A Reply to Jerry Fodor." *Cognition* 6: 241-61.

Kahneman, D. P. Slovic, and A. Tversky. 1982. *Judgement under Uncertainty: Heuristics and Biases.* Cambridge.

Kaplan, David. n.d. "Demonstratives." Circulated in mimeograph form since 1977 and the subject of the 1980 John Locke Lectures.

Katz, Jerrold J. 1972. *Semantic Theory.* New York.

Katz, J. J. 1982. *Language and Other Abstract Objects.* Totowa, N.J.

Kolers, Paul A., and Susan J. Brison. 1984. "On Pictures, Words and Their Mental Representations." *Journal of Verbal Learning and Verbal Behavior* 23: 105-13.

Kripke, Saul. 1979. "A Puzzle about Belief." In *Meaning and Use,* edited by A. Margalit. Dordrecht.

Kuhn, Thomas S. 1983. "Commensurability, Comparability, Communicability," In *PSA 1982,* vol. 2, edited by Peter Asquith and Thomas Nickles. Ann Arbor.

LePore, E., and B. Loewer. 1985. "Dual Aspect Semantics." In a festschrift for Donald Davidson, edited by E. LePore. I sent the authors a number of criticisms of a draft of this paper; I have no idea whether the version to be published retains the points I criticize here.

Lewis, David. 1970. "How to Define Theoretical Terms." *Journal of Philosophy* 67: 427-46.

Loar, Brian. 1981. *Mind and Meaning*. Cambridge.

Loar, Brian. 1982. "Conceptual Role and Truth Conditions." *Notre Dame Journal of Formal Logic* 23: 272-83.

Loar, Brian. 1983. "Must Beliefs Be Sentences?" In *PSA 1982*, vol. 2, edited by Peter Asquith and Thomas Nickles. Ann Arbor.

Lycan, W. 1981. "Toward a Homuncular Theory of Believing." *Cognition and Brain Theory* 4:139-59.

Lycan, William G. "Semantic Competence and Truth Conditions." Unpublished manuscript.

Mandler, Jean M. 1983. "Representation." In *Cognitive Development*, edited by P. Mussen. Vol. 3 of *Manual of Child Psychology*. New York.

Marr, David. 1982. *Vision*. San Fransciso.

McGinn, Colin. 1982. "The Structure of Content." In *Thought and Object*, edited by Andrew Woodfield. Oxford.

Miller, G. A., and P. N. Johnson-Laird. 1976. *Language and Perception*. Cambridge, Mass.

Perry, John. 1977. "Frege on Demonstratives." *Philosophical Review* 86: 474-97.

Perry, J. 1979. "The Problem of the Essential Indexical." *Nous* 13: 3-21.

Posner, M. I. 1978. *Chronometric Explorations of Mind*. Hillsdale, N. J.

Potter, M. C., V. V. Valian, and B. A. Faulconer. 1977. "Representation of a Sentence and Its Pragmatic Implications: Verbal, Imagistic, or Abstract?" *Journal of Verbal Learning and Verbal Behavior* 16: 1-12.

Premack, David. 1983. "The Codes of Man and Beast." *Behavioral and Brain Sciences* 6: 125-37.

Putnam, Hilary. 1962. "The Analytic and the Synthetic." In *Mind, Language and Reality*, edited by Hilary Putnam. Cambridge.

Putnam, Hilary. 1975. "The Meaning of 'Meaning'." In *Language, Mind, and Knowledge*, edited by K. Gunderson. Minneapolis. Also in Putnam's *Mind, Language and Reality*.

Putnam, Hilary. 1979. "Reference and Understanding." In *Meaning and Use*, edited by Avishai Margalit. Dordrecht.

Putnam, Hilary. 1983. "Computational Psychology and Interpretation Theory." In *Realism and Reason*, edited by Hilary Putnam. Cambridge.

Pylyshyn, Zenon. 1984. *Computation and Cognition*. Cambridge, Mass.

Schiffer, Stephen. 1981. "Truth and the Theory of Content." In *Meaning and Understanding*, edited by H. Parret. Berlin.

Schiffer, Stephen. 1982. "Intention-Based Semantics." *Notre Dame Journal of Formal Logic*, 23: 119-59.

Searle, John. 1980a. "Minds, Brains and Programs." *Behavioral and Brain Sciences* 3: 417-24.

Searle, John. 1980b. Searle's reply to critics of "Minds, Brains, and Programs." *Behavioral and Brain Sciences* 3: 450-57.

Searle, John. 1983a. *Intentionality: An Essay in the Philosophy of Mind*. Cambridge.

Searle, John. 1983b. "The Myth of the Computer." *New York Review of Books* (June 14).

Searle, John. 1984. "Intentionality and Its Place in Nature." *Synthese* 61:3-16.

Sellars, Wilfrid. 1963. *Science, Perception and Reality*. London. See "Empiricism and the Philosophy of Mind" and "Some Reflections on Language Games."

Sellars, Wilfrid. 1969. "Language as Thought and as Communication." *Philosophy and Phenomenological Research* 29: 506-27.

Sellars, Wilfrid. 1974. "Meaning as Functional Classification." *Synthese* 27: 417-27.

Shoemaker, Sydney, 1984. *Identity, Cause, and Mind*. Cambridge.

Soames, Scott. 1984. "What Is a Theory of Truth?" *Journal of Philosophy* 81: 411-29.

Sober, Elliot. 1984. *Conceptual Issues in Evolutionary Biology*. Cambridge, Mass.

Stalnaker, Robert C. 1984. *Inquiry*. Cambridge, Mass.

Stampe, Dennis W. 1977. "Toward a Causal Theory of Linguistic Representation." *Midwest Studies in Philosophy* 2: 42-63.

Sterelny, Kim. "Is Semantics Necessary? Stephen Stich's Case Against Belief." Forthcoming. To appear in *The Australasian Journal of Philosophy.*

Sternberg, S. 1969. "Memory Scanning: Mental Processes Revealed by Reaction Time Experiments." *American Scientist* 57: 421-57.

Stich, Stephen. 1983. *The Case Against Belief.* Cambridge, Mass.

White, Stephen L. 1982. "Partial Character and the Language of Thought." *Pacific Philosophical Quarterly* 63: 347-65.

Woods, William. 1977. "Meaning and Machines." In *Proceedings of the International Conference on Computational Linguistics,* edited by A. Zampoli, Florence.

Woods, William. 1978. *Semantics and Quantification in Natural Language Question Answering.* Technical report 3687. Cambridge, Mass.

Woods, William. 1981. "Procedural Semantics as a Theory of Meaning." In *Elements of Discourse Understanding,* edited by A. Joshi, B. Webber, and I. Sag. Cambridge.

Putting Information to Work

Fred Dretske*

Information isn't much good if it doesn't do anything. If the fact that an event carries information doesn't help explain the event's impact on the rest of the world, then, as far as the rest of the world is concerned, the event may as well not carry information. To put it bluntly, in the way positivists liked to put it, a difference that doesn't make a difference isn't really a difference at all. If an event's carrying information doesn't make a difference — and by a difference here I mean a causal difference, a difference in the kind of effects it has — then for all philosophical (not to mention practical) purposes, the event doesn't carry information.

Surely, though, this is not a serious threat. We all know how useful a commodity information is, how even the smallest scrap can radically alter the course of human affairs. Think about its role in business, education, and war. Or consider the consequences of telling Michael about his wife's passionate affair with Charles. Kaboom! Their lives are never again the same. A small piece of information dramatically alters a part (and — who knows? — maybe eventually the entire course) of world history. In light of such obvious examples, how can anyone seriously doubt the causal efficacy of information and, hence, its relevance to understanding *why* some things turn out the way they do?

MEANING AND INFORMATION

There is a small subset of the world's objects on which information *appears* to have this kind of dramatic effect. These objects are people, objects like you and me, who *understand*, or *think* they understand,

268

some of what is happening around them. Talking to Michael has profound effects while talking to rocks and goldfish has little or no effect because Michael, unlike rocks and goldfish, understands, or thinks he understands, what he is being told. As a consequence, he is — typically at least — brought to believe certain things by these acts of communication. The rock and the goldfish, on the other hand, are impervious to meaning. Instead of inducing belief, all we succeed in doing by remonstrating with such objects is jostling them a bit with the acoustic vibrations we produce.

So appearances may be deceptive. It may turn out that the difference between Michael and a goldfish isn't that Michael, unlike a goldfish, responds to information, but that Michael, unlike a goldfish, has beliefs, beliefs about what sounds mean (or about what the people producing these sounds mean), and which therefore (when he hears these sounds) induce beliefs on which he acts. These beliefs are, to be sure, sometimes aroused in him by sounds that actually carry information. Nevertheless, if these beliefs in no way depend on the information these sounds carry, then the information carried by the belief-eliciting stimulation is explanatorily irrelevant. After all, rocks and goldfish are also affected by information-carrying signals. When I talk to a rock, the rock is, as I said, jostled by acoustic vibrations. But the point is that although my utterances, the ones that succeed in jostling the rock, carry information, the information they carry is irrelevant to their effect on the rock. The information in this stimulation doesn't play any explanatory role in accounting for the rock's response to my communication. From the rock's point of view, my utterance may as well not carry information. Subtract the information (without changing the physical properties of the signal carrying this information) and the effect is exactly the same.

And so it may be with Michael. To find out, as we did with the rock, whether information is doing any real work, we merely apply Mill's Method of Difference. Take away the information, leaving everything else as much the same as possible, and see if the effect on Michael changes. As we all know, we needn't suppose his wife, Sandra, is actually having an affair with Charles to get a reaction — in fact the very same reaction — from Michael. He will react in exactly the same way if his alleged informant is lying or is simply mistaken about Sandra's affairs. As long as the act of communication is the same, as long as what the speaker says and does *means* the same thing (to Michael), it will elicit the same reaction from him. What is said doesn't have to be *true* to get this effect. Michael just has to *think* it true. Nothing, in fact, need even be said. As long as Michael *thinks* it was (truly) said, as long as he thinks something with this meaning occurred, the result will be the same.

In saying that it is Michael's beliefs, not the meaning (if any) or information (if any) in the stimuli giving rise to these beliefs, that causally explains Michael's behaviour, I am assuming that we can (and should) make appropriate distinctions between these ideas — between information, meaning, and belief. Some people, I know, use these notions interchangeably. That is too bad. It confuses things that should be kept distinct. According to this careless way of talking (especially prevalent, I think, among computer scientists) information *is* meaning or (at least) a species of meaning, and a belief (or a reasonable analogue of a belief) just *is* an internal state having the requisite kind of meaning. So, for instance, anything that means that Michael's wife is having an affair carries this piece of information. If I *say* his wife is having an affair, then my utterance, *whether or not it is true*, carries this information. And if I enter this "information" into a suitably programmed computer, then, whether or not Sandra is unfaithful, the "fact" that she is unfaithful becomes part of the machine's "data base," the "information" on which it relies to reason, make inferences, answer questions, and solve problems. The computer now "thinks" that Michael's wife is having an affair. Michael doesn't even have to be married for the machine to be given the "data," the "information," that, as it were, his wife is having an affair. On this usage, the facts, the information, the data, are what we say they are.

It is perfectly understandable why computer scientists (not to mention a good many other people) prefer to talk this way. After all, it is natural to suppose that a computer (or a human brain for that matter) is insensitive to the *truth* of the representations on which it operates. Put the sentence "P" in a machine's (or a human brain's) data file, and it will operate with that data in exactly the same way whether "P" is true or false, whether it is information or misinformation. From the machine's (brain's) point of view, anything in it that qualifies as a belief qualifies as knowledge, anything in it that *means* that P is *information* that P. The distinction between meaning and information, between belief and knowledge, is a distinction that only makes sense from the outside. But what makes sense *only from the outside* of the machine or person whose behavior is being explained cannot (according to this way of thinking) help to explain that machine's (or person's) behavior. It cannot because the machine (or person) can't get outside of itself to make the needed discriminations. So, for practical explanatory purposes, meaning *is* (or may as well be) information.

Whatever the practical exigencies may be, something that makes sense only from the outside is, nonetheless, something that makes perfectly good sense. It certainly should make perfectly good sense to those of us (on the outside) talking about such systems. Something (like a statement) that *means* that Michael's wife is having an affair need not carry this information. It needn't carry this information either because Michael's wife is *not* having an affair or because, though she is, the words or symbols used to make this statement are being used in a way that is quite unrelated to her activities. I can *say* anything I like, that Mao Tse Tung liked chocolate ice cream for instance, and the words I utter will mean something quite definite — in this case that Mao Tse Tung liked chocolate ice cream. But these words, even if they are (by some lucky accident) true, won't carry the information that Mao liked chocolate ice cream. They won't because the sentence, used merely as an example and in total ignorance of Mao's preferences in ice cream, in no way depends on Mao's likes and dislikes. These words mean something, but they do not, not at least when coming from me, inform the listener. I might succeed in getting you to believe that Mao liked chocolate ice cream. I might, by telling you this, *mis*inform you about his taste in ice cream. But misinformation is not a species of information any more than belief is a species of knowledge.

So, at least on an ordinary understanding of information and meaning, something can mean that P without thereby carrying the information that P. And someone can believe that P without ever having received the information that P. Often enough, what makes people believe that P is being told that P by someone they trust. Sometimes these communications carry information. Sometimes they do not. Their efficacy in producing belief resides, however, not in the fact that the utterance carries information, but in its meaning (or perceived meaning), who uttered it, and how. No successful liar can seriously doubt this.

So if we distinguish between an event's meaning (= what it says, *whether truly or falsely*, about another state of affairs) and the information it carries (what it, among other things, *truly* says about another state of affairs), a distinction that is roughly equivalent to Grice's (1957) distinction between non-natural and natural meaning, the causal role of information becomes more problematic. What explains Michael's reaction to the verbal communication is his believing that his wife was having an affair with Charles. What explains his believing this is his being told it by a trusted confidant — i.e., his hearing someone (he trusts) *say* this, utter words with this meaning. At no point in the explanatory proceedings do we have to mention the truth of what is said, the truth of what is believed, or the fact that information (as opposed to misinformation) was communicated. If Michael *acts* on his belief, he may, sooner or later, confront a situation that testifies to the truth of what he believes (and was told). He will then, presumably, acquire new beliefs about his wife and Charles, and these new beliefs will help determine what further reactions he has, what he goes on to do. But still, at no point do we have to speak of information or truth in our explanations of Michael's behaviour. All that is needed is what Michael *thinks* is true, what he *thinks* is information, what he *believes*. Knowing whether these beliefs are true or not may be helpful in predicting the *results* of his actions (whether, for instance, he will actually find Sandra at home when he goes to look), but it is not essential for explaining and predicting what he will actually do — whether, that is, he will go home to look.

Appearances, then, *do* seem to be misleading. Despite the way things first looked, despite a variety of familiar examples in which information seemed to make a causal difference, we still haven't found an honest job for it, something information (as opposed to meaning or belief) does that constitutes *its* special contribution to the causal story.

TRUTH AND SUPERVENIENCE

It isn't hard to see why there is trouble finding a decent job for information. The information a signal (structure, event, condition, state of affairs) carries is a function of the way a signal is *related* to other conditions in the world. I have my own views (Dretske 1981) about what these relations come down to, what relations constitute information. I happen to think information requires, among other things, some relation of dependency between the signal and the condition about which it carries information. Signals don't carry information about conditions, even conditions which happen to obtain, on which their occurrence does not depend in some appropriate way. But it isn't necessary to argue about these details. I'm not asking you to agree with me about exactly what information is to agree with me that, whatever it is, as long as it (unlike meaning) involves truth, there is a special problem about how it can be put to work in a scientifically respectable way — how *it*, or the fact that something carries it, can be made explanatorily relevant.

In order to appreciate the problem it is enough to realize that since no signal, S, can carry the information that P is the case when P is not the case, you can change the information a signal carries by tinkering, not with the signal itself, but with the condition, P, about which it carries information. If it is possible, as it almost always is (by tinkering with the causal mechanisms mediating P and S), to change P without changing the character of S itself (i.e., without changing any of S's non-relational properties), then the fact that S carries information is a fact that does not (to use a piece of current jargon) supervene on its non-relational (intrinsic) properties. Signals that are otherwise identical can be informationally different. They will be informationally different when one occurs when P is the case while the other, a physical clone of the first, occurs when P is not the case.[1] But if this is so, and we assume, as it seems we must assume (more of this in a moment), that the causal powers of a signal are embodied in, and exhausted by, its non-relational properties (so that two signals that are physically identical are, in the same circumstances, causally equivalent), then the information character of a signal, the fact that it carries information, is causally inert. However useful it might be (because of the correlations it exhibits) as a predictor of correlated (even *lawfully* correlated)[2] conditions, the fact that a signal carries information will *explain* absolutely nothing. The fact that a signal carries the information that P cannot possibly explain anything if a signal lacking this information has exactly the same effects. This is not to say that signals bearing information cannot cause things. Certainly they can. It just means that their carrying information does not help explain why they cause what they cause. Distilled water will extinguish a fire — thereby causing exactly what undistilled water causes — but the fact that the water is distilled does not figure in the explanation of *why* the fire is extinguished. It won't because undistilled water has exactly the same effects on flames. And if the information in a signal is like this, like the fact that water is distilled, then the fact that a signal carries information is as explanatorily relevant to its effects on a receiver as is the fact that the water is distilled to its effects on a flame.[3]

Coupled with the idea that a symbol's meaning is a function of its relations to other conditions (the conditions it, in some sense, signifies or means), such arguments have led to the view that it is the form, shape, or syntax — not the meaning, content, or semantics — of our internal states that ultimately pulls the levers, turns the gears, and applies the brakes in the behaviour of thoughtful and purposeful agents. Semantics or meaning, the what-it-is-we-believe (and want) is causally (and, therefore, explanatorily) irrelevant to the production of behavior (which is not to say that it cannot be used to *predict* behaviour). I have merely extended these arguments, applying them to information rather than meaning or content. Since information, unlike meaning, requires truth, I think these arguments are even more persuasive when applied to information. I have, in fact, assumed up to this point that there is no particular difficulty about how meaning, either as embodied in *what a person says* or as embodied in *what a person believes*, could figure in a causal explanation. But this, too, has its difficulties. Since I am convinced that belief and meaning are notions that ultimately derive from the information-carrying properties of living systems, I think these problems are, at a deeper level, connected. I think, in fact, that the central problem in this area is the causal efficacy of information. If we can find a respectable job for information, if *it* can be provided a causal job to do, if it can be put to work, then the causal role of meaning and belief (indeed, of all the other psychological attitudes), being derivative, will fall into place. But these are issues that go beyond the scope of this paper and I will not return to them here.[4]

To put information to work will require understanding how the causal efficacy of a signal is altered by the fact that it carries information. A part of the task, then, is to see how the causal efficacy of S (the signal carrying the information that P) is changed or modified by the fact that, in a certain range of circumstances, it occurs *only when* P is the case. I say that this is *part* (not *all*) of the task since S's occurrence *only when* P is the case does not mean that S carries the information that P. It depends on what *else*, besides co-occurrence (by this I mean the occurrence of S only when P is the case), is required for S to carry the information that P. So showing the causal relevance of co-occurrence will not directly demonstrate the causal relevance of information. Nonetheless, since we are assuming, as a minimal condition on information, that S cannot carry the information that P unless P is the case, unless, that is, S and P *do* co-occur in the relevent conditions, demonstrating the causal relevance of co-occurrence will be an important step in showing that information has a causal job to do.

This isn't as easy as it looks. The job, remember, is to show how the co-occurrence of S with P, the fact that S occurs only when P is the case, makes a difference in S's causal powers. The job is not to show that S *together with* P causes things that S *alone* does not. That latter task is simple enough, but quite irrelevant. It is quite obvious that Tommy and his big brother can do things that Tommy alone cannot. And if Tommy never goes anywhere without his big brother, then Tommy will be a "force" to contend with on the school playground. Strictly speaking, though, the presence of his big brother doesn't enhance *Tommy's* prowess. It merely makes him part of *a team* that is feared by the other boys, a team whose presence is signalled by the appearance of Tommy and, thus, makes (via the beliefs of the other boys) Tommy an intimidating figure on the playground.

Such situations are familiar enough, but they are not what we are after. What we are looking for, instead, is a case where *Tommy's* punches carry increased authority because he (always) has his big brother with him.[5] How can Tommy derive added strength, increased causal powers, from the mere fact (a fact that may even be unknown to Tommy) that his big brother is always nearby? How can the (mere) fact that P is the case when S occurs, whether or not anyone — including S — realizes this fact, change S's causal powers? Until we know how, we won't know how information can make a difference in this world.

INDICATORS AND ARTIFACTS

I think we can make a beginning at understanding how this is possible by thinking about how some elements are *given* a causal job to do because of what they indicate about related conditions. Suppose we want some particular kind of movement or change (call it M) to occur when, and only when, condition P exists. I want an annoying buzzer to go on when, and only when, passengers fail to buckle their seat belts. I want the fan to go on when the engine overheats but not otherwise. I want the light to come on when anyone, or anything, crosses a threshold. The way to get what I want is to make an indicator of P — something that will activate when, and only when, P is the case — into a cause of M. To design such mechanisms is a job for engineers. Find or build something that is selectively sensitive to the occurrence of P and make it into a switch for M. Find (or build) something that is sensitive to passengers with unbuckled seat belts. Make it into a buzzer switch. This device doesn't have to be very fancy — just a little electrical-mechanical gadget that will be activated by weight (on a car seat) and electrical contact (in the seat belt buckle). Joint occurrence of the right set of conditions (P) — the condition in which we want M to occur — is then made into a switch for, a cause of, M, the buzzer. If things work right, we now get M when, and only when, P: the buzzer sounds when, and only when, there are passengers with unfastened seat belts.

Building a gadget like this (and such gadgets are all around us) is an exercise in making a more or less reliable indicator, a structure exhibiting a more or less reliable correlation with P, into a cause of M — the response to be co-ordinated with P. By appropriate design, manufacture, and installation, the causal powers of an indicator, an information-bearing structure, an S which occurs *only when* P is the case, is modified, and, what is most significant, it is modified *because* this indicator (or the appropriate activation of this indicator) occurs when, and only when, a certain other condition (P) occurs. The properties of this internal structure (S) which are relevant to its selection as a cause of M, and hence which explain why it (now) causes M, are not its intrinsic properties — its size, shape, weight, colour, charge, and so on. These might help to explain *how* S is made to cause M, how it can be converted into a cause of M, but not why it is converted into a cause of M. It is, rather, S's relational properties that explain why it was selected (by the engineer designing the device) for this causal job. Anything, no matter what its intrinsic properties (as long as they can be harnessed to do the job), would have done as well. As long as the behaviour of this element exhibits the appropriate degree of correlation with P, it is a candidate for being made into a switch for M, the behaviour we want co-ordinated with P. If, furthermore, an element is selected for its causal role (in the production of M) *because* of its correlation with P, because it does not (normally) occur without P, we have (almost) a case of an element's informational properties explaining its causal properties: it does (or is made to do) this because it carries information about (or co-occurs with) that. It isn't the element's shape, form, or syntax that explains its conversion into a cause of M; it is, instead, its information-carrying, its semantic, properties.

This is all a little too fast, of course. We smuggled into the proceedings an engineer, with purposes and intentions of his own, soldering things here, wiring things there, because of what he knows (or thinks) about the effects to be achieved thereby. I therefore expect to hear the objection that deliberately designed artifacts do not demonstrate the causal efficacy of information. All they illustrate, once again, is the causal efficacy of belief (and purpose). In the case of artifacts, what explains the conversion of an information-bearing element (an indicator of P) into a cause of output (M) is the designer's knowledge (or belief) that it is a reliable indicator and his or her desire to co-ordinate M with P. To make information do some real work, it would be necessary to make the causal powers of S depend on its carrying information, or on its co-occurrence with P, *without* the intercession of cognitive intermediaries with purposes and intentions of their own. The information (correlation) alone, not some agent's recognition of this fact, must carry the explanatory burden.

INDICATORS AND LEARNING

To see how this might be accomplished, simply remove the engineer. Since artifacts do not spontaneously change the way they behave (at least not normally in a desired way) without some help from the outside, replace the seat belt mechanism with a system that *is* capable of such unassisted reconfiguration. That is, replace the artifact with an animal — a rat, say. Put the rat into conditions — a suitably arranged Skinner box will do — in which a certain response is rewarded (with food, say) when, and only when, it occurs in conditions P. The response is punished when it occurs without P. Let P be some condition which the rat can observe — a certain audible tone, say. Let the response be the pressing of a bar. What happens? Given a hungry rat, enough trials, and a tolerance for stray errors, the rat learns to press the bar when, and only when, it hears the tone. A correlation between M (bar pressing) and P (the tone) begins to emerge. The engineer got the seat belt mechanism to behave the way he wanted it to behave, to buzz when a passenger failed to buckle his seat belt, by connecting wires in the right places, by making an internal indicator of P (an unbuckled belt) into a cause of M (buzzer activation). The same thing happens to the rat without the assistance of an engineer or, indeed, *any* intentional agent. An internal indicator of P (in this case a certain tone) becomes a cause of M (in this case bar-pressing movements) not through the intercession of an outside agent, but merely by having the response, M, rewarded *when* it occurs in the right conditions (P).

This kind of learning — discrimination learning — can only occur if there is some internal condition of the learner, call it S, that exhibits some degree of correlation with P (the external condition being discriminated) — unless, that is, there is some internal condition of the learner that under normal conditions carries information about the condition to be discriminated. Unless there is some internal condition that occurs when, and only when, P is the case, it will be impossible to get M, the behaviour, to occur when, and only when P, the discriminated condition, exists. You can't make a system do M when (and only when) P exists if there is nothing in the system to *indicate* when P exists, and having something in the system to indicate when P exists is, among other things, a matter of having something in the system that occurs when, and only when, P exists. So when this type of learning *is* successful, as it often is, there must be, internal to the learner, a condition S that, with some degree of reliability, occurs when (and only when) P exists. There must actually be, inside the rat, something that (under appropriate stimulus conditions) occurs when, and only when, the right tone is sounded.

Furthermore, for this type of learning to occur, there must not only *be* an internal structure, S, carrying information about P, it must, during this type of learning, actually assume control functions it did not formerly have. It must be converted into a switch for M, the behavior that (through this type of learning) becomes co-ordinated with P. Unless S is, through this type of learning, recruited as a cause (or partial cause) of M, there is no way of co-ordinating behaviour with the conditions on which its success depends. For S is, by definition, the internal element that signals *when* the conditions are right (when P exists) for the behavior (M) to achieve success (to be rewarded). So S must be made into a cause of M (at least something on which M depends) if learning is to occur. Otherwise it is sheer magic. Whatever it is in the rat — call it the rat's *perception* of the tone — that signals the occurrence of the tone, it must actually be recruited as a cause of bar-pressing movements in this kind of learning if the rat is to learn to press the bar when the tone occurs.

Not only must an internal indicator be enlisted for control duties in this kind of learning, the properties of the indicator that explain its recruitment (as a cause of movement) are its *semantic* or *relational* properties, the properties that do *not* supervene on its intrinsic neuro-physiological character. What explains why the rat's perception of a tone causes it to press the bar, what explains this internal element's altered causal powers, is not the fact that it has certain neurophysio-logical properties — a certain electrical-chemical-mechanical profile or form. For it presumably had that form *before* learning occurred (the rat could hear the tone before it learned to respond to it in a particular way). Before learning occurred, though, this internal state, this per-ception of the tone, did not cause the same movements (or any move-ments at all). Hence, what explains why the rat's perception of the tone causes movements it did not formerly cause is the fact that it, the rat's perception of the tone, is, specifically, a perception *of the tone*, the fact that it is an internal state exhibiting the requisite correlation with those external conditions on which the success of output depends. What explains the perceptual state's new found causal power is, in other words, its semantic, informational or intentional properties — not what it *is*, but what it is *about*.

If this theory, sketchy as it is, is even approximately right, then we have found a place where information does some honest work: it does real work when living systems are, during learning, reorganizing their control circuits to exploit the correlations (correlations between what is happening inside and what is happening outside) that per-ception puts at their disposal. Whenever there is something inside a system that can, by suitable redeployment, affect output, then there exists an opportunity to put to work whatever information that ele-ment carries. Such information can be exploited if there is a range of behaviours whose benefits (to the animal) depend on their emission in those (external) conditions about which information is carried. If there is such a dependence, then, assuming the animal capable of modifying its behaviour so as to better co-ordinate it with those exter-nal conditions on which its success depends (capable, that is, of learning), the animal can exploit perceptual information by recruit-ing, as a cause of behaviour, the internal vehicles of this information.

I say that this is an honest job for information because, unlike the artifacts discussed earlier, it is information itself, the fact that S does not normally occur unless P, and therefore (other possible conditions being satisfied) the fact that S carries the information that P, that explains the recruitment of internal elements as causes of movement (those movements whose success depends on their coordination with P). At the neuroanatomical level it may be a mystery how such recruitment takes place, how learning actually occurs, but that it *does* occur, in some animals under some circumstances, is perfectly obvious. And it is its occurrence, not details about how it occurs, that demonstrates — indeed, requires — the causal efficacy of information.

There are, it seems to me, profound implications of this fact, the fact that information only begins to find a real causal and hence explanatory use in systems capable of learning. Only here do we find the behaviour of a system explicable in terms of the relational properties of the internal states that produce it. Only here do we begin to see something like *content* or *meaning*, properties (like information) that do not supervene on the intrinsic properties of the internal states that possess it, assuming a significant place in our explanations of animal and human behaviour. It is here, I submit, that psychological explanations of behaviour first get a real, as opposed to merely a metaphorical, purchase. It is only when information begins to do some real explanatory — hence, scientific — work that minds rightfully enter the metaphysical picture.

NOTES

*   I wish to thank the Center for Advanced Study in the Behavioral Sciences, Stanford University, the National Endowment for the Humanities FC-20060-85, and the Andrew Mellon Foundation for their support during 1987-8 when this paper was written.

1   It is better to say that under such conditions they *can be* informationally different. Whether they *are* different will depend, not only on whether P exists in one case but not the other, but on whether there is, in the case where P exists, the required information-carrying dependency between P and the signal.

2   In "common cause" situations, cases where A, though neither the cause nor the effect of B, is correlated with B because they have some common cause C, we may (depending on the details of the case) be able to say that B would not have happened unless A happened and, yet, deny that A in any way *explains* (causally or otherwise) B. An explanatory relation between A and B, a relation that lets us say that B happened *because* A happened, requires *more than* counterfactual-supporting generalizations between A and B.

I disagree, therefore, with Jerry Fodor (1987: 139-40) that (to put it crudely) an adequate story can be told about mental *causation* without making intentional properties (like meaning or information) determine causal roles. It isn't enough to have these intentional properties (like meaning or information) determine causal roles. It isn't enough to have these intentional properties figure in counterfactual-supporting generalizations. That (alone) won't show that people behave the way they do *because* of what they believe and desire.

BIOSEMANTICS

C ausal or informational theories of the semantic content of mental states which have had an eye on the problem of false representations have characteristically begun with something like this intuition. There are some circumstances under which an inner representation has its represented as a necessary and/or sufficient cause or condition of production. That is how the content of the representation is fixed. False representations are to be explained as tokens that are produced under other circumstances. The challenge, then, is to tell what defines certain circumstances as the content–fixing ones.

I.

Note that the answer cannot be just that these circumstances are *statistically* normal conditions. To gather such statistics, one would need to delimit a reference class of occasions, know how to count its members, and specify description categories. It would not do, for example, just to average over conditions-in-the-universe-any-place-any-time. Nor is it given how to carve out relevant description categories for conditions on occasions. Is it "average" in the summer for it to be (precisely) between 80° and 80.5° Fahrenheit with humidity 87%? And are average conditions those which obtain on at least 50% of the occasions, or is it 90%? Depending on how one sets these parameters, radically different conditions are "statistically normal." But the notion of semantic content clearly is not relative, in this manner, to arbitrary parameters. The content-fixing circumstances must be *nonarbitrarily* determined.

A number of recent writers have made an appeal to teleology here, specifically to conditions of normal function or well-functioning of the systems that produce inner representations. Where the represented is R and its representation is "R," under conditions of well-functioning, we might suppose, only Rs can or are likely to produce

0022-362X/89/8606/281–297

"Rs." Or perhaps "R" is a representation of *R* just in case the system was designed to react to *R*s by producing "Rs." But this sort of move yields too many representations. Every state of every functional system has normal causes, things that it is a response to in accordance with design. These causes may be proximate or remote, and many are disjunctive. Thus, a proximate normal cause of dilation of the skin capillaries is certain substances in the blood, more remote causes include muscular effort, sunburn, and being in an overheated environment. To each of these causes the vascular system responds by design, yet the response (a red face), though it may be a natural sign of burn or exertion or overheating, certainly is not a representation of that. If not every state of a system represents its normal causes, which are the states that do?

Jerry Fodor[1] has said that, whereas the content of an inner representation is determined by some sort of causal story, its status *as a representation* is determined by the functional organization of the part of the system which uses it. There is such a thing, it seems, as behaving like a representation without behaving like a representation of anything in particular. What the thing is a representation of is then determined by its cause under content-fixing conditions. It would be interesting to have the character of universal I-am-a-representation behavior spelled out for us. Yet, as Fodor well knows, there would still be the problem of demonstrating that there was only one normal cause per representation type.

A number of writers, including Dennis Stampe,[2] Fred Dretske,[3] and Mohan Matthen,[4] have suggested that what is different about effects that are representations is that their function is, precisely, to represent, "indicate," or "detect." For example, Matthen says of (fullfledged) perceptual states that they are "state[s] that [have] the function of *detecting* the presence of things of a certain type . . ." (*ibid.*, p. 20). It does not help to be told that inner representations are things that have representing (indicating, detecting) as their function, however, unless we are also told what kind of activity repre-

[1] "Banish Discontent," in Jeremy Butterfield, ed., *Language, Mind and Logic* (New York: Cambridge, 1986), pp. 1–23; *Psychosemantics: The Problem of Meaning in the Philosophy of Mind* (Cambridge: MIT, 1987).
[2] "Toward a Causal Theory of Representation," in Peter French, Theodore Uehling Jr., Howard Wettstein, eds., *Contemporary Perspectives in the Philosophy of Language* (Minneapolis: Minnesota UP, 1979), pp. 81–102.
[3] "Misrepresentation," in Radu Bogdan, ed., *Belief: Form, Content, and Function* (New York: Oxford, 1986), pp. 17–36.
[4] "Biological Functions and Perceptual Content," this JOURNAL, LXXXV, 1 (January 1988):5–27.

senting (indicating, detecting) is. Matthen does not tell us how to naturalize the notion "detecting." If "detecting" is a function of a representational state, it must be something that the state effects or produces. For example, it cannot be the function of a state to have been produced in response to something. Or does Matthen mean that it is not the representational states themselves, but the part of the system which produces them, which has the function of detecting? It has the function, say, of producing states that correspond to or covary with something in the outside world? But, unfortunately, not every device whose job description includes producing items that vary with the world is a representation producer. The devices in me that produce calluses are supposed to vary their placement according to where the friction is, but calluses are not representations. The pigment arrangers in the skin of a chameleon, the function of which is to vary the chameleon's color with what it sits on, are not representation producers.

Stampe and Dretske do address the question what representing or (Dretske) "detecting" is. Each brings in his own description of what a natural sign or natural representation is, then assimilates *having the function of representing R* to being a natural sign or representer of R when the system functions normally. Now, the production of natural signs is undoubtedly an accidental side effect of normal operation of many systems. From my red face you can tell that either I have been exerting myself, or I have been in the heat, or I am burned. But the production of an accidental side effect, no matter how regular, is not one of a system's functions; that goes by definition. More damaging, however, it simply is not true that representations must carry natural information. Consider the signals with which various animals signal danger. Nature knows that it is better to err on the side of caution, and it is likely that many of these signs occur more often in the absence than in the presence of any real danger. Certainly there is nothing incoherent in the idea that this might be so, hence that many of these signals do not carry natural information concerning the dangers they signal.

II.

I fully agree, however, that an appeal to teleology, to function, is what is needed to fly a naturalist theory of content. Moreover, what makes a thing into an inner representation is, near enough, that its function is to represent. But, I shall argue, the way to unpack this insight is to focus on representation *consumption*, rather than representation production. It is the devices that *use* representations which determine these to be representations and, at the same time (contra

Fodor), determine their content. If it really is the function of an inner representation to indicate its represented, clearly it is not just a natural sign, a sign that you or I looking on might interpret. It must be one that functions as a sign or representation *for the system itself.* What is it then for a system to use a representation *as* a representation?

The conception of function on which I shall rely was defined in my *Language, Thought, and Other Biological Categories*[5] and defended in "In Defense of Proper Functions"[6] under the label "proper function." Proper functions are determined by the histories of the items possessing them; functions that were "selected for" are paradigm cases.[7] The notions "function" and "design" should not be read, however, as referring only to origin. Natural selection does not slack after the emergence of a structure but actively preserves it by acting against the later emergence of less fit structures. And structures can be preserved due to performance of new functions unrelated to the forces that originally shaped them. Such functions are "proper functions," too, and are "performed in accordance with design."

The notion "design" should not be read—and this is very important—as a reference to innateness. A system may have been designed to be altered by its experience, perhaps to learn from its experience in a prescribed manner. Doing what it has learned to do in this manner is then "behaving in accordance with design" or "functioning properly."[8]

My term 'normal' should be read normatively, historically, and relative to specific function. In the first instance, 'normal' applies to explanations. A "normal explanation" explains the performance of a particular function, telling how it was (typically) historically performed on those (perhaps rare) occasions when it was properly performed. Normal explanations do not tell, say, why it has been common for a function to be performed; they are not statistical explanations. They cover only past times of actual performance, showing how these performances were entailed by natural law, given certain conditions, coupled with the dispositions and structures of the rele-

---

[5] Cambridge: MIT, 1984 (hereafter LTOBC).

[6] *Philosophy of Science*, LVI, 2 (June 1989): 288–302.

[7] An odd custom exists of identifying this sort of view with Larry Wright, who does not hold it. See my "In Defense of Proper Functions." Natural selection is not the only source of proper functions. See LTOBC, chs. 1 and 2.

[8] See LTOBC; and "Truth Rules, Hoverflies, and the Kripke-Wittgenstein Paradox," *The Philosophical Review* (forthcoming).

vant functional devices.[9] In the second instance, 'normal' applies to conditions. A "normal condition for performance of a function" is a condition, the presence of which must be mentioned in giving a full normal explanation for performance of that function. Other functions of the same organism or system may have other normal conditions. For example, normal conditions for discriminating colors are not the same as normal conditions for discriminating tastes, and normal conditions for seeing very large objects are not the same as for seeing very small ones. It follows that 'normal conditions' must not be read as having anything to do with what is typical or average or even, in many cases, at all common. First, many functions are performed only rarely. For example, very few wild seeds land in conditions normal for their growth and development, and the protective colorings of caterpillars seldom actually succeed in preventing them from being eaten. Indeed, normal conditions might almost better be called "historically optimal" conditions. (If normal conditions for proper functioning, hence survival and proliferation, were a statistical norm, imagine how many rabbits there would be in the world.) Second, many proper functions only need to be performed under rare conditions. Consider, for example, the vomiting reflex, the function of which is to prevent (further) toxification of the body. A normal condition for performance of this function is presence, specifically of poison in the stomach, for (I am guessing) it is only under that condition that this reflex has historically had beneficial effects. But poison in the stomach certainly is not an average condition. (Nor, of course, is it a normal condition for other functions of the digestive system.[10])

If it is actually one of a system's functions to produce representations, as we have said, these representations must function as representations for the system itself. Let us view the system, then, as divided into two parts or two aspects, one of which produces representations for the other to consume. What we need to look at is the consumer part, at what it is to use a thing *as* a representation.

[9] This last clarification is offered to aid Fodor ("On There Not Being an Evolutionary Theory of Content" [hereafter NETC], forthcoming), who uses my term 'Normal' (here I am not capitalizing it but the idea has not changed) in a multiply confused way, making a parody of my views on representation. In this connection, see also fns. 13 and 17.

[10] "Normal explanation" and "normal condition for performance of a function," along with "proper function," are defined with considerable detail in LTOBC. The reader may wish, in particular, to consult the discussion of normal explanations for performance of "adapted and derived proper functions" in ch. 2, for these functions cover the functions of states of the nervous system which result in part from learning, such as states of human belief and desire.

Indeed, a good look at the consumer part of the system ought to be all that is needed to determine not only representational status but representational content. We argue this as follows. First, the part of the system which consumes representations must understand the representations proffered to it. Suppose, for example, that there were abundant "natural information" (in Dretske's[11] sense) contained in numerous natural signs all present in a certain state of a system. This information could still not serve the system *as* information, unless the signs were understood by the system, and, furthermore, understood as bearers of whatever specific information they, in fact, do bear. (Contrast Fodor's notion that something could function like a representation without functioning like a representation of anything in particular.) So there must be something about the consumer that *constitutes* its taking the signs to indicate, say, *p*, *q*, and *r* rather than *s*, *t*, and *u*. But, if we know what constitutes the consumer's *taking* a sign to indicate *p*, what *q*, what *r*, etc., then, granted that the consumer's takings are in some way systematically derived from the structures of the signs so taken, we can construct a semantics for the consumer's language. Anything the signs may indicate qua natural signs or natural information carriers then drops out as entirely irrelevant; the representation-producing side of the system had better pay undivided attention to the language of its consumer. The sign producer's function will be to produce signs that are true *as the consumer reads the language.*

The problem for the naturalist bent on describing intentionality, then, does not concern representation production at all. Although a representation always is something that is produced by a system whose proper function is to make that representation correspond by rule to the world, what the rule of correspondence is, what gives definition to this function, is determined entirely by the representation's consumers.

For a system to use an inner item as a representation, I propose, is for the following two conditions to be met. First, unless the representation accords, *so* (by a certain rule), with a represented, the consumer's normal use of, or response to, the representation will not be able to fulfill all of the consumer's proper functions in so responding—not, at least, in accordance with a normal explanation. (Of course, it might still fulfill these functions by freak accident, but not in the historically normal way.) Putting this more formally, that the representation and the represented accord with one another, so, is a

----

[11] *Knowledge and the Flow of Information* (Cambridge: MIT, 1981).

normal condition for proper functioning of the consumer device as it reacts to the representation.[12] Note that the proposal is not that the content of the representation rests on the function of the representation or of the consumer, on what these do. The idea is not that there is such a thing as behaving like a representation of X or as being treated like a representation of X. The content hangs only on there being a certain condition that would be *normal* for performance of the consumer's functions—namely, that a certain correspondence relation hold between sign and world—whatever those functions may happen to be. For example, suppose the semantic rules for my belief representations are determined by the fact that belief tokens in me will aid the devices that use them to perform certain of their tasks in accordance with a normal explanation for success only under the condition that the forms or "shapes" of these belief tokens correspond, in accordance with said rules, to conditions in the world. Just what these user tasks are need not be mentioned.[13]

Second, represented conditions are conditions that vary, depending on the *form* of the representation, in accordance with specifiable correspondence rules that give the semantics for the relevant *system* of representation. More precisely, representations always admit of significant transformations (in the mathematical sense), which accord with transformations of their corresponding representeds, thus displaying significant articulation into variant and invariant aspects. If an item considered as compounded of certain variant and invariant aspects can be said to be "composed" of these, then we can also say that every representation is, as such, a member of a representational system having a "compositional semantics." For it is not that the represented condition is itself a normal condition for proper operation of the representation consumer. A certain correspondence between the representation and the world is what is normal. Coordinately, there is no such thing as a representation consumer

---

[12] Strictly, this normal condition must derive from a "most proximate normal explanation" of the consumer's proper functioning. See LTOBC, ch. 6, where a more precise account of what I am here calling "representations" is given under the heading "intentional icons."

[13] In this particular case, one task is, surely, contributing, in conformity with certain general principles or rules, to practical inference processes, hence to the fulfillment of current desires. So, if you like, all beliefs have the *same* proper function. Or, since the rules or principles that govern practical inference dictate that a belief's "shape" determines what other inner representations it may properly be combined with to form what products, we could say that each belief has a *different* range of proper functions. Take your pick. Cf. Fodor, "Information and Representation," in Philip Hanson, ed., *Information, Language, and Cognition* (Vancouver: British Columbia UP, 1989); and NETC.

that can understand only one representation. There are always other representations, composed other ways, saying other things, which it could have understood as well, in accordance with the same principles of operation. A couple of very elementary examples should make this clear.[14]

First, consider beavers, who splash the water smartly with their tails to signal danger. This instinctive behavior has the function of causing other beavers to take cover. The splash means danger, because only when it corresponds to danger does the instinctive response to the splash on the part of the interpreter beavers, the consumers, serve a purpose. If there is no danger present, the interpreter beavers interrupt their activities uselessly. Hence, that the splash corresponds to danger is a normal condition for proper functioning of the interpreter beavers' instinctive reaction to the splash. (It does not follow, of course, that it is a usual condition. Beavers being skittish, most beaver splashes possibly occur in response to things not in fact endangering the beaver.) In the beaver splash semantic system, the time and place of the splash varies with, "corresponds to," the time and place of danger. The representation is articulate: properly speaking, it is not a splash but a splash-at-a-time-and-a-place. Other representations in the same system, splashes at other times and places, indicate other danger locations.

Second, consider honey bees, which perform "dances" to indicate the location of sources of nectar they have discovered. Variations in the tempo of the dance and in the angle of its long axis vary with the distance and direction of the nectar. The interpreter mechanisms in the watching bees—these are the representation consumers—will not perform their full proper functions of aiding the process of nectar collection in accordance with a normal explanation, unless the location of nectar corresponds correctly to the dance. So, the dances are representations of the location of nectar. The full representation here is a dance-at-a-time-in-a-place-at-a-tempo-with-an-orientation.

Notice that, on this account, it is not necessary to assume that most representations are true. Many biological devices perform their proper functions not on the average, but just often enough. The protective coloring of the juveniles of many animal species, for example, is an adaptation passed on because *occasionally* it prevents a

---

[14] These examples are of representations that are not "inner" but out in the open. As in the case of inner representations, however, they are produced and consumed by mechanisms designed to cooperate with one another; each such representation stands intermediate between two parts of a single biological system.

juvenile from being eaten, though most of the juveniles of these species get eaten anyway. Similarly, it is conceivable that the devices that fix human beliefs fix true ones not on the average, but just often enough. If the true beliefs are functional and the false beliefs are, for the most part, no worse than having an empty mind, then even very fallible belief-fixing devices might be better than no belief–fixing devices at all. These devices might even be, in a sense, "designed to deliver some falsehoods." Perhaps, given the difficulty of designing highly accurate belief-fixing mechanisms, it is actually advantageous to fix too many beliefs, letting some of these be false, rather than fix too few beliefs. Coordinately, perhaps our belief-consuming mechanisms are carefully designed to tolerate a large proportion of false beliefs. It would not follow, of course, that the belief consumers are designed to *use* false beliefs, certainly not that false beliefs can serve all of the functions that true ones can. Indeed, surely if none of the mechanisms that used beliefs ever cared at all how or whether these beliefs corresponded to anything in the world, beliefs would not be functioning as representations, but in some other capacity.

Shifting our focus from producing devices to consuming devices in our search for naturalized semantic content is important. But the shift from the *function* of consumers to *normal conditions* for proper operation is equally important. Matthen, for example, characterizes what he calls a "quasi-perceptual state" as, roughly, one whose job is to cause the system to do what it must do to perform its function, given that it is in certain circumstances, which are what it represents. Matthen is thus looking pretty squarely at the representation consumers, but at what it is the representation's job to get these consumers to do, rather than at normal conditions for their proper operation. As a result, Matthen now retreats. The description he has given of quasi-perceptual states, he says, cannot cover "real perception such as that which we humans experience. Quite simply, there is no such thing as *the* proper response, or even a range of functionally appropriate responses, to what perception tells us" (*op. cit.*, p. 20).[15] On the contrary, representational content rests not on univocity of consumer function but on sameness of normal conditions for those functions. The same percept of the world may be used to guide any of very many and diverse activities, practical or theoretical. What stays the same is that the percept must correspond to environmental configurations in accordance with the same correspondence rules

---

[15] Dretske (in "Misrepresentation," p. 28) and David Papineau [in *Reality and Representation* (New York: Blackwell, 1987), p. 67ff] have similar concerns.

for each of these activities. For example, if the position of the chair in the room does not correspond, so, to my visual representation of its position, that will hinder me equally in my attempts to avoid the chair when passing through the room, to move the chair, to sit in it, to remove the cat from it, to make judgments about it, etc. Similarly, my belief that New York is large may be turned to any of diverse purposes, but those which require it to be a *representation* require also that New York indeed be large if these purposes are to succeed in accordance with a normal explanation for functioning of my cognitive systems.

III.

We have just cleanly bypassed the whole genre of causal/informational accounts of mental content. To illustrate this, we consider an example of Dretske's. Dretske tells of a certain species of northern hemisphere bacteria which orient themselves away from toxic oxygen-rich surface water by attending to their magnetosomes, tiny inner magnets, which pull toward the magnetic north pole, hence pull down (*ibid.*). (Southern hemisphere bacteria have their magnetosomes reversed.) The function of the magnetosome thus appears to be to effect that the bacterium moves into oxygen-free water. Correlatively, intuition tells us that what the pull of the magnetosome represents is the whereabouts of oxygen-free water. The direction of oxygen-free water is not, however, a factor in *causing* the direction of pull of the magnetosome. And the most reliable natural information that the magnetosome carries is surely not about oxygen-free water but about distal and proximal causes of the pull, about the direction of geomagnetic or better, just plain magnetic, north. One can, after all, easily deflect the magnetosome away from the direction of lesser oxygen merely by holding a bar magnet overhead. Moreover, it is surely a function of the magnetosome to respond to that magnetic field, that is part of its normal mechanism of operation, whereas responding to oxygen density is not. None of this makes any sense on a causal or informational approach.

But on the biosemantic theory it does make sense. What the magnetosome represents is only what its *consumers* require that it correspond to in order to perform *their* tasks. Ignore, then, how the representation (a pull-in-a–direction-at-a-time) is normally produced. Concentrate, instead, on how the systems that react to the representation work, on what these systems need in order to do their job. What they need is only that the pull be in the direction of oxygen-free water at the time. For example, they care not at all how it came about that the pull is in that direction; the magnetosome that points toward oxygen-free water quite by accident and not in accordance with any normal explanation will do just as well as one that points that way for the normal reasons. (As Socrates concedes in the *Meno*, true opinion is just as good as knowledge so long as it stays put.) What the magnetosome represents then is univocal; it represents only the direction of oxygen-free water. For that is the only thing that corresponds (by a compositional rule) to it, the absence of which would matter—the absence of which would disrupt the function of those mechanisms which rely on the magnetosome for guidance.

It is worth noting that what is represented by the magnetosome is not proximal but distal; no proximal stimulus is represented at all. Nor, of course, does the bacterium perform an inference from the existence of the proximal stimulus (the magnetic field) to the existence of the represented. These are good results for a theory of content to have, for otherwise one needs to introduce a derivative theory of content for mental representations that do not refer, say, to sensory stimulations, and also a foundationalist account of belief fixation. Note also that, on the present view, representations manufactured in identical ways by different species of animal might have different contents. Thus, a certain kind of small swift image on the toad's retina, manufactured by his eye lens, represents a bug, for that is what it must correspond to if the reflex it (invariably) triggers is to perform its proper functions normally, while exactly the same kind of small swift image on the retina of a male hoverfly, manufactured, let us suppose, by a nearly identical lens, represents a passing female hoverfly, for that is what it must correspond to if the female-chasing reflex it (invariably) triggers is to perform its proper functions normally. Turning the coin over, representations with the same content may be normally manufactured in a diversity of ways, even in the same species. How many different ways do you have, for example, of telling a lemon or your spouse? Nor is it necessary that any of the ways one has of manufacturing a given representation be especially reliable ways in order for the representation to have determinate content. These various results cut the biosemantic approach off from all varieties of verificationism and foundationalism with a clean, sharp knife.

IV.

But perhaps it will be thought that belief fixation and consumption are not biologically proper activities, hence that there are no normal explanations, in our defined sense, for proper performances of human beliefs. Unlike bee dances, which are all variations on the

same simple theme, beliefs in dinosaurs, in quarks, and in the insta-
bility of the dollar are recent, novel, and innumerably diverse, as are
their possible uses. How could there be anything *biologically* normal
or abnormal about the details of the consumption of such beliefs?

But what an organism does in accordance with evolutionary design
can be very novel and surprising, for the more complex of nature's
creatures are designed to learn. Unlike evolutionary adaptation,
learning is not accomplished by *random* generate-and-test procedures. Even when learning involves trial and error (probably the
exception rather than the rule), there are principles in accordance
with which responses are selected by the system to try, and there are
specific principles of generalization and discrimination, etc., which
have been built into the system by natural selection. How these
principles normally work, that is, how they work given normal (i.e.,
historically optimal) environments, to produce changes in the
learner's nervous system which will effect the furthering of ends of
the system has, of course, an explanation—the normal explanation
for proper performance of the learning mechanism and of the states
of the nervous system it produces.

Using a worn-out comparison, there is an infinity of functions
which a modern computer mainframe is capable of performing, depending upon its input and on the program it is running. Each of
these things it can do, so long as it is not damaged or broken, "in
accordance with design," and to each of these capacities there corresponds an explanation of how it would be activated or fulfilled
normally. The human's mainframe takes, roughly, stimulations of the
afferent nerves as input, both to program and to run it.[16] It responds, in part, by developing concepts, by acquiring beliefs and
desires in accordance with these concepts, by engaging in practical
inference leading ultimately to action. Each of these activities may, of
course, involve circumscribed sorts of trial and error learning. When
conditions are optimal, all this aids survival and proliferation in
accordance with an historically normal explanation—one of high
generality, of course. When conditions are not optimal, it may yield,
among other things, empty or confused concepts, biologically useless
desires, and false beliefs. But, even when the desires are biologically
useless (though probably not when the concepts expressed in them
are empty or confused), there are still biologically normal ways for

[16] This is a broad metaphor. I am not advocating computationalism.

them to get fulfilled, the most obvious of which require reliance on true beliefs.[17]

Yet how do we know that our contemporary ways of forming concepts, desires, and beliefs do occur in accordance with evolutionary design? Fodor, for example, is ready with the labels "pop Darwinism" and "naive adaptationism" to abuse anyone who supposes that our cognitive systems were actually selected for their belief and desire using capacities.[18] Clearly, to believe that every structure must have a function would be naive. Nor is it wise uncritically to adopt hypotheses about the functions of structures when these functions are obscure. It does not follow that we should balk at the sort of adaptationist who, having found a highly complex structure that quite evidently is currently and effectively performing a highly complex and obviously indispensable function, then concludes, *ceteris paribus,* that this function has been the most recent historical task stabilizing the structure. To suspect that the brain has not been preserved for thinking with or that the eye has not been preserved for seeing with—to suspect this, moreover, in the absence of any alternative hypotheses about causes of the stability of these structures—would be totally irresponsible. Consider: nearly every human behavior is bound up with intentional action. Are we really to suppose that the degree to which our behaviors help to fulfill intentions, and the degree to which intentions result from logically related desires plus beliefs, is a sheer coincidence—that these patterns are irrelevant to survival and proliferation or, though relevant, have had

[17] A word of caution. The normal conditions for a desire's fulfillment are not necessarily fulfillable conditions. In general, normal conditions for fulfillment of a function are not quite the same as conditions which, when you add them and stir, always effect proper function, because they may well be impossible conditions. For example, Fodor, in "Information and Representation" and NETC, has questioned me about the normal conditions under which his desire that it should rain tomorrow will perform its proper function of *getting* it to rain. Now, the biologically normal way for such a desire to be fulfilled is exactly the same as for any other desire: one has or acquires true beliefs about how to effect the fulfillment of the desire and acts on them. Biologically normal conditions for fulfillment of the desire for rain thus include the condition that one has true beliefs about how to make it rain. Clearly this is an example in which the biological norm fails to accord with the statistical norm: most desires about the weather are fulfilled, if at all, by biological accident. It may even be that the laws of nature, coupled with my situation, prohibit my having any true beliefs about how to make it rain; the needed general condition cannot be realized in the particular case. Similarly, normal conditions for proper function of beliefs in impossible things are, of course, impossible conditions: these beliefs are such that they cannot correspond, in accordance with the rules of mentalese, to conditions in the world.

[18] *Psychosemantics* and NETC.

no stabilizing effect on the gene pool? But the only alternative to biological design, in our sense of 'design', is sheer coincidence, freak accident—unless there is a ghost running the machine!

Indeed, it is reasonable to suppose that the brain structures we have recently been using in developing space technology and elementary particle physics have been operating in accordance with the very same general principles as when prehistoric man used them for more primitive ventures. They are no more performing new and different functions or operating in accordance with new and different principles nowadays than are the eyes when what they see is television screens and space shuttles. Compare: the wheel was invented for the purpose of rolling ox carts, and did not come into its own (pulleys, gears, etc.) for several thousand years thereafter, during the industrial revolution. Similarly, it is reasonable that the cognitive structures with which man is endowed were originally nature's solution to some very simple demands made by man's evolutionary niche. But the solution nature stumbled on was elegant, supremely general, and powerful, indeed; I believe it was a solution that cut to the very bone of the ontological structure of the world. That solution involved the introduction of representations, inner and/or outer, having a subject/predicate structure, and subject to a negation transformation. (Why I believe that that particular development was so radical and so powerful has been explained in depth in LTOBC, chapters 14–19. But see also section v.6 below.)

V.

One last worry about our sort of position is voiced by Daniel Dennett[19] and discussed at length by Fodor.[20] Is it really plausible that bacteria and paramecia, or even birds and bees, have inner representations in the same sense that we do? Am I really prepared to say that these creatures, too, have mental states, that they think? I am not prepared to say that. On the contrary, the representations that they have must differ from human beliefs in at least six very fundamental ways.[21]

(1) *Self-representing Elements.* The representations that the magnetosome produces have three significant variables, each of

[19] *Brainstorms* (Montgomery, VT: Bradford Books, 1978).

[20] "Why Paramecia Don't Have Mental Representations," in P. French, T. Uehling Jr., and H. Wettstein, eds., *Midwest Studies in Philosophy,* x (Minneapolis: Minnesota UP, 1986), pp. 3–23.

[21] Accordingly, in LTOBC I did not call these primitive forms "representations" but "intentional signals" and, for items like bee dances, "intentional icons," reserving the term 'representation' for those icons, the representational values of which must be identified if their consumers are to function properly—see V.5 below.

which refers to itself. The time of the pull refers to the time of the oxygen-free water, the locale of the pull refers to the locale of the oxygen-free water, and the direction of pull refers to the direction of oxygen-free water. The beaver's splash has two self-referring variables: a splash at a certain time and place indicates that there is danger at that same time and place. (There is nothing necessary about this. It might have meant that there would be danger at the nearest beaver dam in five minutes.) Compare the standard color coding on the outsides of colored markers: each color stands for itself. True, it may be that sophisticated indexical representations such as percepts and indexical beliefs also have their time or place or both as significant self-representing elements, but they also have other significant variables that are not self-representing. The magnetosome does not.

(2) *Storing Representations.* Any representation the time or place of which is a significant variable obviously cannot be stored away, carried about with the organism for use on future occasions. Most beliefs are representations that can be stored away. Clearly this is an important difference.

(3) *Indicative and Imperative Representations.* The theory I have sketched here of the content of inner representations applies only to indicative representations, representations which are supposed to be determined by the facts, which tell what is the case. It does not apply to imperative representations, representations which are supposed to determine the facts, which tell the interpreter what to do. Neither do causal-informational theories of content apply to the contents of imperative representations. True, some philosophers seem to have assumed that having defined the content of various mental symbols by reference to what causes them to enter the "belief box," then when one finds these same symbols in, say, the "desire box" or the "intention box," one already knows what they mean. But how do we know that the desire box or the intention box use the same representational system as the belief box? To answer that question we would have to know what constitutes a desire box's or an intention box's using one representational system rather than another which, turned around, is the very question at issue. In LTOBC and "Thoughts Without Laws; Cognitive Science With Content,"[22] I developed a parallel theory of the content of imperative representations. Very roughly, one of the proper functions of the consumer system for an imperative representation is to help *produce* a corre-

---

[22] *The Philosophical Review*, XLV, 1 (1986):47–80.

spondence between the representation and the world. (Of course, this proper function often is not performed.) I also argued that desires and intentions are imperative representations.

Consider, then, the beaver's splash. It tells that there is danger here now. Or why not say, instead, that it tells other nearby beavers what to do now, namely, to seek cover? Consider the magnetosome. It tells which is the direction of oxygen-free water. Or why not say, instead, that it tells the bacterium which way to go? Simple animal signals are invariably both indicative and imperative. Even the dance of the honey bee, which is certainly no simple signal, is both indicative and imperative. It tells the worker bees where the nectar is; equally, it tells them where to go. The step from these primitive representations to human beliefs is an enormous one, for it involves the separation of indicative from imperative functions of the representational system. Representations that are undifferentiated between indicative and imperative connect states of affairs directly to actions, to specific things to be done in the face of those states of affairs. Human beliefs are not tied directly to actions. Unless combined with appropriate desires, human beliefs are impotent. And human desires are equally impotent unless combined with suitable beliefs.[23]

(4) *Inference.* As indicative and imperative functions are separated in the central inner representational systems of humans, they need to be reintegrated. Thus, humans engage in practical inference, combining beliefs and desires in novel ways to yield first intentions and then action. Humans also combine beliefs with beliefs to yield new beliefs. Surely nothing remotely like this takes place inside the bacterium.

(5) *Acts of Identifying.* Mediate inferences always turn on something like a middle term, which must have the same representational value in both premises for the inference to go through. Indeed, the representation consumers in us perform many functions that require them to use two or more overlapping representations together, and in such a manner that, unless the representeds corresponding to these indeed have a common element, these functions will not be properly performed. Put informally, the consumer device *takes* these represented elements to be the same, thus identifying their representational values. Suppose, for example, that you intend to speak to

---

[23] Possibly human intentions are in both indicative and imperative mood, however, functioning simultaneously to represent settled facts about one's future and to direct one's action.

Henry about something. In order to carry out this intention you must, when the time comes, be able to recognize Henry in perception as the person to whom you intend to speak. You must identify Henry as represented in perception with Henry as represented in your intention. Activities that involve the coordinated use of representations from different sensory modalities, as in the case of eye-hand coordination, visual-tactile coordination, also require that certain objects, contours, places, or directions, etc., be identified as the same through the two modalities. Now, the foundation upon which modern representational theories of thought are built depends upon a denial that what is thought of is ever placed before a naked mind. Clearly, we can never know what an inner representation represents by a direct comparison of representation to represented. Rather, acts of identifying are our ways of "knowing what our representations represent." The bacterium is quite incapable of knowing, in this sense, what its representations are about. This might be a reason to say that it does not understand its own representations, not really.

(6) *Negation and Propositional Content.* The representational system to which the magnetosome pull belongs does not contain negation. Indeed, it does not even contain contrary representations, for the magnetosome cannot pull in two directions at once. Similarly, if two beavers splash at different times or places, or if two bees dance different dances at the same time, it may well be that there is indeed beaver danger two times or two places and that there is indeed nectar in two different locations.[24] Without contrariety, no conflict, of course and more specifically, no contradiction. If the law of non-contradiction plays as significant a role in the development of human concepts and knowledge as has traditionally been supposed, this is a large difference between us and the bacterium indeed.[25] In LTOBC, I argued that negation, hence explicit contradiction, is dependent upon subject-predicate, that is, propositional, structure and vice versa. Thus, representations that are simpler also do not have propositional content.

In sum, these six differences between our representations and those of the bacterium, or Fodor's paramecia, ought to be enough amply to secure our superiority, to make us feel comfortably more endowed with mind.

RUTH GARRETT MILLIKAN

University of Connecticut/Storrs

---

[24] On the other hand, the bees cannot go two places at once.

[25] In LTOBC, I defend the position that the law of noncontradiction plays a crucial role in allowing us to develop new methods of mapping the world with representations.

Acknowledgments

Chomsky, Noam. "On the Nature, Use and Acquisition of Language." In *Mind and Cognition: A Reader*, edited by William G. Lycan (Oxford: Basil Blackwell, 1990): 627–46. Reprinted with the permission of Blackwell Publishers.

Clark, Andy. "Magic Words: How Language Augments Human Computation." In *Language and Thought*, edited by Peter Carruthers (New York: Cambridge University Press, 1998: 1–18. Reprinted with the permission of Cambridge University Press.

Pinker, Steven. "Rules of Language." *Science* 253 (Aug. 2, 1991): 530–35. Reprinted with the permission of *Science*. Copyright 1991 American Association for the Advancement of Science.

Dennett, Daniel C. "Can Machines Think?" In *How We Know*, edited by M. Shafto (San Francisco: Harper and Row, 1985): 121–45. Reprinted with the permission of HarperCollins Publishers.

Rapaport, William J. "Understanding Understanding: Syntactic Semantics and Computational Cognition." In *Philosophical Perspectives, 9, AI, Connectionism and Philosophical Psychology, 1995*, edited by James E. Tomberlin (Atascadero, Calif.: Ridgeview Publishing, 1995): 49–88. Reprinted by permission of Ridgeview Publishing Company.

Haugeland, John. "Understanding Natural Language." *Journal of Philosophy* 76 (1979): 619–32. Reprinted with the permission of the Journal of Philosophy, Inc., Columbia University, and the author.

Egan, Frances. "Individualism, Computation, and Perceptual Content." *Mind* 101 (1992): 443–59. Reprinted with the permission of Oxford University Press.

Peacocke, Christopher. "Externalist Explanation." *Proceedings of the Aristotelian Society* 93 (1993): 203–30. Reprinted by courtesy of the Editor of the Aristotelian Society, copyright 1993.

Toribio, Josefa. "Ecological Content." *Pragmatics and Cognition* 5 (1997): 257–85. Reprinted with the permission of John Benjamins Publishing Company.

Block, Ned. "Advertisement for a Semantics for Psychology." In *Midwest Studies in Philosophy*, vol. 10, edited by Peter A. French, Theodore E. Uehling Jr., and Howard K. Wettstein (Minneapolis: University of Minnesota Press, 1986): 615–78. Reprinted with the permission of the University of Minnesota Press. Copyright 1986.

Dretske, Fred. "Putting Information to Work." In *Information, Language, and Cognition*, edited by Philip P. Hanson (Vancouver: University of British Columbia Press, 1990): 112–24. Reprinted with the permission of the University of British Columbia Press.

Millikan, Ruth Garrett. "Biosemantics." *Journal of Philosophy* 86 (1989): 281–97. Reprinted with the permission of the Journal of Philosophy, Inc., Columbia University, and the author.